SO-AIH-585

Retreat into the Mind

Retreat
into the Mind

Victorian Poetry and
the Rise of Psychiatry

BY

EKBERT FAAS

Princeton University Press
Princeton, New Jersey

Published by Princeton University Press, 41 William Street,
Princeton, New Jersey 08540
In the United Kingdom: Princeton University Press, Guildford, Surrey

Library of Congress Cataloging-in-Publication Data

Faas, Ekbert, 1938–
Victorian poetry and the rise of psychiatry / Ekbert Faas.
p. cm.   Bibliography: p.   Includes index.
ISBN 0–691–06748–1 (alk. paper)
1. English poetry—19th century—History and criticism.
2. Psychology in literature. 3. Psychology and literature—History—19th century. 4.
Psychoanalysis and literature—History—19th century. 5. Dramatic monologues—
History and criticism. I. Title.
PR595.P85F34 1988   821'.8'09353—dc19   88-9948   CIP

This book has been composed in Linotron Garamond

Clothbound editions of Princeton University Press books
are printed on acid-free paper, and binding materials are
chosen for strength and durability. Paperbacks, although satisfactory
for personal collections, are not usually suitable for library rebinding

Printed in the United States of America by Princeton University Press,
Princeton, New Jersey

Designed by Laury A. Egan

Work on this book was facilitated by grants from the Social
Sciences and Humanities Research Council of Canada, Associated
Medical Services, Inc., and the Hannah Institute for the History of
Medicine. For these, I should like to express my gratitude to these
institutions. I also want to thank Terri Doughty, Kelly Ryan, and
Jamie Zeppa for helping me with the manuscript, the proofreading,
and the index.

FOR GERDA
AND HORST FAAS

Contents

vii

CONTENTS

Retreat into the Mind

Introduction

Whoever has followed out the history of poetry during the last thirty years must have observed a great change in the subjects selected for treatment, as well as in the manner of treating them. The entity "nature," which before the present era of poetry absorbed so large a proportion of our esthetic energies, has in its turn been absorbed by the real being, man; and the great bulk of poetic force is now brought to bear on the treatment of man, and of man alone—for whatever our poets now find to say about inanimate nature is not of an apostrophic kind, but of an order having reference to nature merely in its bearings on man.[1]

THE WORDS are H. B. Forman's in his 1869 review of *Graffiti d'Italia*, a long-forgotten book of verse by W. W. Story. To the reviewer, this volume, like "many collections of contemporary poems," forms part of a new "Psychological School of Poetry" under the leadership of Robert Browning. The school's prime mode is a new kind of monologue fusing lyrical with dramatic and epic elements. In each such monologue, Forman writes,

> some particular point of interest in the history of a human soul is taken up. The soul, whether historical or fictitious, generally speaks for itself all that is spoken—the artist invariably refraining from any appearance as a spokesman. In the course of the monologue all circumstances in the past development of the soul which are available for illuminating the present point are brought out, and the present and past action of other human beings on the speaker is indicated either by detail on the speaker's part, or by some such artifice as a sudden change in the tone of the monologue, from which we learn that the person addressed has said or done something.[2]

But Forman is less concerned with defining a new genre than he is fascinated by an unprecedented literary obsession: never before had poets been more intent upon exploring the human psyche; nor had they ever evolved subtler techniques for doing so. The "psychological monologue" was, after all, only one of many forms developed in this pursuit. Browning himself, in addition to writing a whole "epic of psychology," composed lyrics and actual plays with similar bias. Tennyson, while writing several psychological monologues like "St. Simeon Stylites," elaborated his peculiar "conception in psychic dynamics" in *Maud*, of all his works perhaps the "greatest in execution."[3]

To Forman, this poetic phenomenon was linked to a scientific one, the rise of mental science. Both, in his view, had evolved during the previous three decades, a time when scientists everywhere, but especially in Britain, laid the groundwork for "a definite and invaluable science of psychology." It would be strange, he concludes, "if there were no corresponding movement in the world of art."[4] For art and science, to him, are far more intimately connected than is suggested by the fact that most scientific disciplines had come into being only quite recently.

Most Victorians seemed to agree with Forman's findings. There were numerous critics who also hailed (or more rarely disparaged) the new tribe of poet-psychologists whom they thought to have been prompted or at least influenced by mental science. If anything, they would have questioned Forman's dates, and for good reason. Perhaps some of them even remembered diverse claims, closely resembling his, but made long before the period that, in Forman's view, witnessed the rise of psychological poetry. While proclaiming "the analysis of particular states of mind" as "the most important department in which metaphysical science has been a pioneer for poetry," W. J. Fox, for instance, hailed the young Tennyson as a poet specializing in precisely that kind of analysis.[5] Wordsworth, even earlier, characterized poetry as a "history or science of feelings" and gave several poems from the *Lyrical Ballads* as instances of both how "to illustrate the manner in which our feelings and ideas are associated in a state of excitement" and how "to follow the fluxes and refluxes of the mind when agitated by the great and simple affections of our nature."[6] No doubt there was a psychological school of poetry whose emergence could be related to the rise of mental science. The problem remains of how to determine the historical circumstances of this relationship.

This, more or less, is the task I have set myself in the following pages. My main subject, at least in principle, is the new psychological poetry in its relationship to contemporary mental science. Yet in practice the main focus rests on two genres in which the psychological school of poetry and the Romantic science of feelings found their modes of expression par excellence. One of these is the "psychological," or what we now call, "dramatic" monologue; the other is the "greater Romantic lyric," so labeled by M. H. Abrams.[7] Wordsworth's "Tintern Abbey" and Coleridge's "Dejection: An Ode" are typical greater Romantic lyrics, which Abrams also calls "fragments of reshaped autobiography."[8] Such poems, he writes,

> present a determinate speaker in a particularized, and usually, a localized, outdoor setting, whom we overhear as he carries on, in a fluent vernacular which rises easily to a more formal speech, a sustained colloquy, sometimes with himself or with the outer scene, but more frequently with a silent human auditor, present or absent. The speaker begins with a description of a landscape; an aspect or change of aspect in the landscape evokes a varied but integral process of memory, thought, anticipation, and feeling which remains closely intervolved with the outer scene. In the course of this meditation the lyric speaker achieves an insight, faces up to a tragic loss, comes to a moral decision, or resolves an emotional problem. Often the poem rounds itself to end where it began, at the outer scene, but with an altered mood and deepened understanding which is the result of the intervening meditation.[9]

To be sure, here again one feels tempted to follow nineteenth-century criticism in putting more emphasis on the genre's psycho-analytic[10] bias and in speaking of "Meditative"[11] or psychological poems rather than greater Romantic lyrics.

But my aim is not to dispense with accepted terms but to reformulate their meaning, wherever necessary, in terms of the existing poetry and its contemporary critical reception. The main sources scrutinized for this purpose were some four hundred Romantic and Victorian poets, the reviews of their works in the nineteenth-century journals available at the British Library, and all relevant critical writings of a more general nature.[12] A major concern here was to obtain a sense of what Wordsworth's and Browning's contemporaries thought of the new psychological poetry and how they defined its diverse forms and techniques. A caveat by J. S. Mill served as a motto in this endeavor: "Let us then attempt, in the way of modest inquiry, not to coerce and confine nature within the bounds of an arbitrary definition, but rather to find the boundaries which she herself has set, and erect a barrier around them."[13]

To adopt Mill's metaphor, such current terms as "greater Romantic lyric" and "dramatic monologue" will serve as my barriers; so also will R. Langbaum's "poetry of experience,"[14] used as an alternative to the "new psychological poetry" comprising both the Romantic and Victorian genres. However, these barriers had to be, so to speak, realigned in light of the new boundaries provided by the historical evidence. As a result, the greater Romantic lyric, in addition to displaying the characteristics pointed out by Abrams, was found, broadly speaking, to delineate the speaker's emotions, psychological makeup, and train of thought; the authors, in composing these "fragments of reshaped autobiography,"[15] were found to accomplish this delineation through the two main techniques of simulated spontaneity and self-dramatization.

Similar insistence on the genre's psycho-analytic bias is called for in talking about the dramatic monologue. Langbaum, among more recent critics, was the first to insist upon the structural kinship between poems like "Tintern Abbey" and "St. Simeon Stylites," correctly locating the main difference between them in the intended reader response to the respective speakers.[16] While the "implied author"[17] of Wordsworth's poem invites us to share or even embrace the speaker's emotions, that of Tennyson's suggests the opposite. Despite our empathic understanding for the persona's character and dilemma, we are supposed to stand back, analyze, even judge the speaker the way an alienist (or psychiatrist) might diagnose his patient. Yet here again, and far more so than in greater Romantic lyrics, one might add that the genre's primary function is to portray the speaker's mind by means of techniques that draw and expand upon those of Romantic poetry. John Wilson no doubt had a point in claiming that Coleridge's "The Nightingale" illustrated the law of association "more philosophically than [either] Hartley or Brown."[18] But surely R. J. Mann, in discussing Tennyson's *Maud*, had even greater reason to wonder where this unprofessional psychologist had "acquired his accurate insight into the phenomena of insanity."[19]

Needless to say, the terms "dramatic monologue" and "greater Romantic lyric" will be used in inclusive rather than exclusive fashion.

Our boundaries here are as fluid as those found in the criticism and poetry of the period. Especially in the transition from Romantic to Victorian, one often finds equally valid reasons for grouping a specific poem (such as Browning's *Pauline*) with either one or the other genre. Similarly, a work like *Maud* juxtaposes dramatic monologues and greater Romantic lyrics with other lyrical forms, which though distinct from the former two genres, share with them a common psychological bias. In the final analysis, it is this general bias that determines a poem's eligibility for discussion in the following pages.

But to what extent was this psychological poetry influenced or perhaps prompted by mental science? To critics like Forman, fascinated by the new discipline, the latter was the prime agent in this relationship. But the facts are more complex. On the one hand, early mental science, particularly in the area of psychological medicine (or our present-day psychiatry), derived many of its impulses from such sources as introspective philosophy, which it shared with the Romantic science of feelings. Moreover, the early alienists freely acknowledged their indebtedness to the psychological insights of poets, and especially to Shakespeare, whose soliloquies also exerted an incalculable influence on how poets from Coleridge to Browning bodied forth the workings of the mind in their greater Romantic lyrics and dramatic monologues. Just as alienist John Charles Bucknill discusses the nature of hallucinations in terms of Macbeth's, so Tennyson's St. Simeon Stylites reaches out for the crown of his imagined heavenly rewards[20] in much the same way that Shakespeare's protagonist tries to clutch the dagger of his mind.[21]

On the other hand, one can hardly exaggerate the impact early mental science, once it established itself as an accredited discipline, exerted on literature and most other cultural domains. We wrongly credit Freud and Jung with being the first to propose psychiatry as a new metaphysics or general framework for most scientific and speculative endeavors. The claim is as old as mental science itself. Probably its most influential advocate among Victorians was Thomas Brown, whose *Lectures on the Philosophy of the Mind* (1820) had gone through a nineteenth edition by 1851. To Brown, Francis Bacon had been the first to suggest that the "science of mind" should be the "common centre" of "every speculation, in every science";[22] now that this science had finally come into its own, there was all the more reason to stress "this central and governing relation, which the philosophy of intellect bears to all other philosophy": "The consideration of mind, as universally present and presiding—at once the medium of all the knowledge which can be acquired, and the subject of all the truths of which that knowledge consists, gives, by its own unity, a sort of unity and additional dignity to the sciences."[23]

Victorian psychiatrists or alienists went furthest in making similar claims. To a contributor of the *American Journal of Insanity*, mental science "is to be regarded as the last and highest term of the scientific series."[24] To F. Lélut, writing for the newly founded *Annales médico-psychologiques*, it should provide the all-encompassing "Cadre de la Philosophie de l'Homme."[25] To Forbes Winslow, editor of the *Journal of Psychological Medicine and Mental Pathology*, the mission of the alienist represents a "holy and sacred office,"[26] which should hold sway over all other professions. "A zealous but indiscreet clergyman," for instance, might, "by the character of his admonitions . . . produce an amount of mental and physical depression, from which the patient may never rally." More generally speaking, the psychologist's task is "holy" in that it studies and treats "diseases affecting the very source, spring, and fountain of that principle which . . . alone can bring us into . . . proximity to DEITY."[27]

In short, mental physicians, after barely beginning to gain recognition for their discipline, already claimed to be the new ideological arbiters regarding all manner of ultimate issues. The psychologist was to step in for the theologian; a new *summa psychologiae* was to take the place of the *summae theologiae* and metaphysical systems of former ages. "Is it possible to exaggerate or over-estimate our character, influence, importance, and dignity," wondered Forbes Winslow in his presidential address to the 1857 annual meeting of the Association of Medical Officers of Asylums and Hospitals for the Insane.[28] Reviewing "recent metaphysics" in the *Journal of Mental Science*, Henry Maudsley makes the same point in more humorous terms. Metaphysicians, he suggests, suffer from the kind of morbidity curable by the "regular discipline of an asylum."[29]

Maudsley's joke barely hides some of the more sinister implications of such universalist claims. To say that most alienists thought of a future, ideal society as an extended asylum under their surveillance is hardly to overstate the case. Even today's most anti-Laingian psychiatrist must be aghast at the wide range of people whom his nineteenth-century predecessors deemed fit for institutionalization. To Amariah

Brigham, characters such as King Lear and Macbeth, or even Hamlet and Jaques, "may now be found in every large Asylum."[30] To Alfred Maury, mystics and stigmatics such as St. Francis and St. Catherine of Sienne differ but little from "some religious monomaniacs" treated in the same institutions.[31] Needless to say, such inquisitorial zeal did not stop short of more recent phenomena such as the "moral epidemic" of the "revolutionary spirit."[32] The difference between maniacs fantasizing about revolutions and those who, in antiquity, raved about Bacchic mysteries or who, during the Middle Ages, went on rampages of dancing mania or demonic possession, was one of mere content rather than general human disposition. "There always exists on the surface of society a large floating mass of individuals, devoted by their organization to mental alienation," warns the *Journal of Psychological Medicine*. Hence, alienists have the solemn task to spot and sequester potential maniacs before it is too late for everyone.

> These people are easily recognised by their manners, their gestures, and conversation; their excessive gaiety without motive; the rapid succession of their ideas; the facility with which they form and as readily abandon a hundred wild projects. . . . In fact, it is possible to foretell by the physiognomy, and we mean by that the whole exterior, that such and such a man will become insane, as we should say of another that the probability is he will die of apoplexy or consumption.[33]

With the same zeal with which alienists thus proposed to watch over public mental health and civic order, they addressed themselves to diverse issues of a judicial, theological, metaphysical, and artistic nature. Some of them argued with judges and prosecutors as to whether certain homicides should be judged in moral or psychiatric terms, executed or institutionalized; others enlightened theologians and metaphysicians as to the hallucinatory nature of genius and prophecy; they told poets and critics that genius is, at least in principle, analogous to idiocy and madness; or that the poetic imagination is essentially characterized by abnormality and "organic flimsiness."[34] In short, there was hardly a domain of human life, be it artistic, religious or social, in which alienists did not presume to have the final word. "Knowledge of mind," claimed one of them, "is the foundation of all improvement, the very basis of our intellectual and moral advancement."[35] The concerns of theology? "Mental science greatly aids the cause of religion." As with theology so

9

with the arts. Without the aid of mental science, no one would ever fathom "the higher order of poetry."[36]

All this raises numerous questions about what psychologists actually had to say about religion and the arts; questions, more specifically, as to how they explained the religious sentiment, biblical prophecy, the nature of mythology, and of transexperience phenomena, or as to how they accounted for the nature of genius, the functioning of the poetic imagination, poetry in general, and its impact on the reader. To what extent did such theorizing affect theologians, philosophers, critics, and poets? Unlike early psychiatric jurisdiction, as surveyed in R. Smith's recent *Trial by Medicine*, none of these issues has yet been studied. It is true that we have books, dealing with nineteenth-century literature, on *The Mysteries of Identity* (R. Langbaum), *The Central Self* (P. Ball), *The Divided Self* (M. Miyoshi), or *The Poet's Sense of Self in Nineteenth-Century Poetry* (F. Kaplan); but all of these approach their subject from a Freudian or otherwise twentieth-century perspective.[37] Even works like W. E. Houghton's *Victorian Frame of Mind* or J. H. Buckley's *Victorian Temper* pay little or no attention to nineteenth-century mental science. Needless to say, such studies as Langbaum's, Ball's, Miyoshi's, and Kaplan's can be of great interest, particularly to readers who happen to share a particular perspective—be it Freudian, Jungian, or other—with the author.

Though sometimes mistaken for a Jungian, I have no such preference for any of the major psychologists of our century. But as a nonspecialist disinclined to parade my skepticism, I should let two world authorities speak instead and explain why mental science, both past and present, seems worthy of study for its contribution to the history of ideas rather than for its cumulative achievement. To Richard Hunter and Ida Macalpine, the history of psychiatry is no "chronicle of feats, facts and discoveries."[38] Instead, it "presents a record of perennial problems, recurrent ideas, disputes and treatments, trailing in the wake of medicine and exhibiting paradoxically—as medicine did of old—a mixture of as many false facts as false theories":

> How far psychiatry is still behind medicine is shown not only by the survival of therapeutic principles long since discarded from the parent science as for instance treatment by shock, but also by the persistence of schools of psychiatry, not to mention psychology or psychotherapy, the like of which vanished from the medical scene

one hundred years ago with the scientific developments of the nineteenth century. . . . Moreover, psychiatric theory and practise have throughout been influenced in much greater measure by social, humanitarian, economic and theological pressures.[39]

There is further reason, even for Freudians or Jungians, why certain areas of nineteenth-century literature and religious thought should be reviewed from the perspective of Victorian, rather than twentieth-century, mental science. Not only did psychologists, from the beginning, have theories about religion and the arts, anticipating those of Freud and Jung; they also, at least broadly speaking, fell into groups presaging either Freud's rationalist skepticism or Jung's endorsement of the irrational and religious. Such disagreement, to give one example, already divided the editors of "the world's first psychiatric journal."[40] Karl Philipp Moritz, friend of Goethe and founder of this *Magazin zur Erfahrungsseelenkunde*, had a strong interest in phenomena like self-fulfilling prophecies, prophetic dreams, or religiomania and dealt with them frequently in his journal. But during his absence in Italy, K. F. Pockels, in assuming Moritz's editorial functions, subjected his predecessor's labors to a systematic review, pouring scorn on all superstitious beliefs and particularly on any credence in premonitions. But matters did not end there. Once returned from abroad, Moritz regained full control of his journal and opened his new reign with a "Review of the Reviews of Herr Pockels,"[41] accusing his substitute editor of moral bigotry, rationalist dogmatism, and, above all, an unscientific attitude. Further instances of similar disagreement run through the extensive literature in which such nineteenth-century alienists as L. F. Lélut, A. Brierre de Boismont, and James Braid applied their psychiatric insights to supernatural and religious issues.

What has been said so far makes it obvious that early mental science's impact on religious, artistic, and general thought can hardly be surveyed in a single volume. The literature waiting to be explored in this area is fascinating and plentiful; but the problems encountered in trying to give an account of it are equal in magnitude. To start with, there is the paucity of previous research in the field. Except for limited forays into this area, early mental science's role in the formation of nineteenth-century thought has not been systematically studied by anyone. This is perhaps because the mass of source materials is just too staggering and diffuse: though surveyable, it is spread throughout hundreds of handbooks, monographs, and pamphlets, as well as thousands of volumes of medical and psychological journals, which are often of difficult access. Another difficulty is inherent in the subject itself. To speak of the impact of early mental science on religious, artistic, and general thought, for instance, is both simplistic and somewhat misleading; for this impact was by no means unilateral. Mental science, in its early phase, absorbed as much from literature and philosophy as it was to contribute to these disciplines later. What is more, all these interdependencies are of so complex and diverse a nature as to confound anyone trying to sum them up in comprehensive fashion. Equally unsatisfactory at this point would be studies focusing on single aspects of the entire field, such as, for instance, the literary and philosophical impulses behind the rise of mental science, the psychologists' actual theories on religion and the arts, or the extent to which writers and literary theorists like E. S. Dallas were affected by the new ideas. Such limited studies could be fruitful if we knew more about the inner dynamics of these diverse interrelationships. Given our present state of ignorance about them, they would no doubt raise more questions than they could answer. What we need, then, is a kind of historical propaedeutic that might allow us to gauge the wider cultural implications behind and due to the rise of mental science.

As it turns out, the dramatic monologue, if studied from a nineteenth-century viewpoint and in light of its origins in the Romantic poetry of experience, provides us with just such a preliminary. The main reasons for this are twofold. First, the dramatic monologue originated, roughly speaking, at about the same time as mental science. Secondly, its prime concerns were of a psychological nature: a fact agreed upon by reviewers, poets, and diverse professional psychologists who discussed some of these poems in their psychiatric journals. Victorian critics, unlike their twentieth-century successors, viewed the dramatic monologue as essentially the poetry of psychology. They spoke of "mental" or "psychological monologues" and of poems of a new "dramatic-psychological kind,"[42] while even tracing the new genre to Romantic poetry. Browning to them was "primarily a psychologist," "the poet of psychology," or a "mighty . . . master of psychology."[43] The poets, in all this, agreed with their critics. Even in *Sordello*, not to speak of his dramatic monologues, Browning's "stress," as he put it, lay on "the incidents in the development of a soul: little else" to him was "worth study."[44] Tennyson, in *Maud*, proposed to dramatize "the history of a morbid, poetic soul";[45] and he was delighted when J. C. Bucknill, editor of the *Asylum Journal of Mental Science*, described the poem as a "true example" of the "theory of the psychopathic origin of insanity" as recently outlined by the Belgian psychiatrist J. Guislain[46] (Chapter I).

Here, then, we have an Ariadne's thread that will guide us safely through some of the labyrinthine complexities outlined above. The first step along the way will be to determine what exactly poets and reviewers meant when they spoke of mental monologues or poets of psychology. Naturally, their terminology in this respect differed from ours. For what we would now call psychiatry, they would use diverse terms such as "medical psychology", "mental science", or simply "psychology." A psychiatrist was called an alienist, medical psychologist, or mental physician. Similarly, the diverse subdisciplines of the whole of mental science or psychology fell into groups that differ from our present ones. Psychology, as now distinguished from psychiatry, was still talked of in close association with introspective philosophy, one of its major roots. A hotly debated area of mental science—which is now extinct but which, through hypnotism, influenced the rise of psychoanalysis—was mesmerism.

Reviewers could learn about such distinctions from numerous articles about mental science featured in the same magazines (such as *Blackwood's* or the *Edinburgh Review*) that published their poetry reviews. Some two thousand volumes surveyed for this purpose reveal a tripartite division: 1) psychological medicine (i.e., psychiatry) as practiced in the asylums; 2) introspective psychology; 3) mesmerism (later hypnotism). The same major categories are found in the period's medical, psychological, and psychiatric journals. Here and elsewhere, of course, mental science is spoken of as comprising further sub-groups such as phrenology.[47] These, however, had no relation to the new psychological poetry and therefore are of little concern to our project (Chapter II).

But to what extent were the authors of dramatic monologues affected by their knowledge of the new science? The question primarily concerns the early writings of Tennyson and Browning at a time when they evolved the new genre. Yet the answer provided by what is known of these two poets' lives and works is contradictory at best. Tennyson, mainly because of the numerous instances of insanity in his family, was clearly familiar with much of contemporary mental science; Browning, though by his own admission interested in little else but the human soul, séems to have made no major efforts to find out what scientists had to say about such matters. However, both Tennyson and Browning, in writing their earliest dramatic monologues, were driven by the same urge to objectify introspection, an impulse also shared by the pioneer alienists as they evolved their new mental science (Chapter III).

Also crucial to the emergence of the dramatic monologue were personal experiences of a psychological and/or pathological nature as reflected in Browning's *Pauline* and numerous early poems by Tennyson. One of these, "Oh! that 'twere possible"—the germ of *Maud*[48] and later made part of that poem—shows how the dramatic monologue served Tennyson, at least originally, as a means of dealing with problems that were better not revealed as his. The same process can be documented in Browning's early career. To look at it from a different angle, the reading public, though eager for news from the hinterland of the human mind, was not about to allow its major poets to talk openly about inhabiting such dubious realms themselves. Insanity, which to the Victorians meant anything from total dementia to moral depravity, was something to be studied in their proliferating and evermore crowded asylums. Similarly, dramatic monologues such as "Porphyria's Lover" and "Johannes Agricola in Meditation"—appropriately named "Madhouse Cells" by Browning[49]—were thought of as objective, case-history-like studies. However gruesome in content, they found the full approval of the Victorians. It mattered little to them that the madman hero of *Maud* bore traits that one might associate with the author himself. Tennyson, after all, had objectified such possibly personal elements, a measure that to most reviewers was an adequate concession to decorum (Chapter IV).

Such findings raise a curious issue. Critics like H. B. Forman who traced the psychological school of poetry to the prior rise and influence of mental science were in obvious error, at least in the case of Browning. Where, then, if not in psychology itself, are the roots of the dramatic-psychological poetry? Rather than the latter owing its existence to the former (or the reverse), both grew simultaneously from common sources in more or less independent fashion. Broadly speaking, these shared origins can be traced to a general reorientation of Western thought, probably starting with Montaigne and Francis Bacon.[50] Before their time, philosophers concerned themselves mainly with speculating about the outer world; since then, their successors have largely been busy questioning the epistemological premises that such essentialist speculation took for granted. In other words, they turned from outer reality to man's inner world. For all its possible derivations, introspective philosophy as a mainstream endeavor is, after all, no older than some three hundred years. The same holds true of what a recent study calls, not inappropriately, "the invention of the self"[51] during the eighteenth century.

For poetry, this meant a gradual shift from imitation of the external world toward expression of the inner world. This development, as we know, led critics and poets to rebel against traditional Aristotelian premises; but while arguing (like eighteenth-century critics Jones and Twining) that someone who spontaneously expresses his feelings cannot be said to imitate them, they never abandoned the mimesis concept completely. In theory they insisted, like Wordsworth, that poetry should be a spontaneous overflow of powerful feelings. But in practice, the demand for such often dogmatically advocated automatism merely prompted poets to evolve elaborate strategies of simulated spontaneity and self-dramatization. Greater Romantic lyrics like Wordsworth's "Tintern Abbey"—the Romantic genre par excellence—were the quintessential products of this complex and contradictory science of feelings. As such, they also form precedents for the dramatic monologue, in turn the most central poetic mode of its age. How the Victorian genre arose from the tensions inherent in the Romantic science of feelings is too complex a process to be summed up in an introduction. It is enough to say here that the poets and critics who brought it about followed a principle that, in similar fashion, guided the pioneers of mental science. Both recognized that introspection, after a certain point, is a futile and dangerous endeavor. Yet whatever had been or still might be achieved in self-analysis could be turned to advantage in the analysis of others (Chapter V).

In tracing the genealogy of Victorian psychological poetry, first to its beginnings and origins in early Tennyson and Browning, and subsequently to its immediate predecessor in the Romantic science of feelings, we have to consider yet another, more remote, but nonetheless influential precedent. This is found in Elizabethan drama and particularly in Shakespeare's soliloquies. Here again, poets and psychologists shared common roots. For all the pride they took in their discipline, alienists were well aware that mental science was no mere specialist's discipline. Introspection and empathy, to most of them, were prime prerequisites for the analysis of others, and who else, they argued, possessed these qualities more thoroughly than Shakespeare. No wonder, then, that mental scientists like Bucknill greeted the playwright as a predecessor, just as they hailed poets like Tennyson as important allies in a common pursuit. In fact, their writings along these lines form a solid body of criticism which helps explain why the psychological school of poetry was, to the Victorians, the true successor of Shakespearean drama (Chapter VI).

Although first evolved during the 1820s and 1830s by Tennyson and Browning, the dramatic monologue did not establish itself as a proper school of psychological poetry until much later. This was after 1855, the publication date of both Tennyson's *Maud* and Browning's *Men and Women*. My chapter on Arnold will focus on the time just previous to that double event: roughly from 1852, the year of E. S. Dallas's *Poetics* as well as Browning's Essay on Shelley, through 1853, when Arnold renounced part of his own poetry in his famous Preface, and 1854, when Aytoun launched his attack on the Spasmodics. These were turbulent years for English poetry; and nothing more clearly than Arnold's career shows why the psychological poetry, which he condemned, offered so many other poets a way out of the Romantic introspective dilemma, which, at the same time, went through its death throes with the decease of the Spasmodic school of poetry (Chapter VII).

Again, it was not until after 1855 that the dramatic monologue received proper critical attention. Only after the emergence of a whole school of psychological poetry, with some thirty major and minor poets writing dramatic monologues largely in imitation of Browning, did reviewers become aware of the structural characteristics and essentially psychological nature of the new genre. But henceforth this almost explosive appearance of the new poetry was accompanied by something equally unprecedented in criticism. Never before in English literature had a specific genre been as intensively defined, circumscribed, praised, and denounced as the dramatic monologue during the later Victorian era. In short, there emerged not only a new school of psychological poetry, but also a tribe of critics (including diverse alienists) who jealously watched over all of that school's activities. Nothing regarding the genre remained undiscussed. Critics commented on its *in medias res* opening, its evocation of a setting or listener, or on the "psychological revivification"[52] of past events from the depth of the speaker's memory. They identified diverse stream-of-consciousness techniques in this kind of "retrospective drama"[53] (Chapter VIII).

More specifically, they located various areas of content that were as suited to the genre's psycho-analytic bias as they were of interest to the psychologists who discussed the same matters in their books and journals. One of these areas was that of reverie, hallucination, insanity, and spectral vision; another, related to what alienists like Lélut pursued under the name of a new "psychology of history,"[54] combined the speaker's self-examination with an exploration of the age he belongs to; a third dealt with moral insanity and homicidal mania, a subject hotly debated between alienists and lawyers (Chapter IX).

The critical activity surrounding the dramatic monologue had somewhat paradoxical results. Encoded as it became in poets' and critics' minds, the genre, once established, showed little development. Even slight variations from the norm were instantly noted as transgressions. What arose so suddenly as a vital tradition, degenerated almost as quickly into a moribund set of formulaic, critically labeled, and widely parodied cliches.[55] The time was ripe for a change, which makes its first appearance in William Morris's *Defense of Guinevere and Other Poems* (1862). While some of Morris's dramatic monologues follow the established patterns, others like "The Wind" engage the reader in psychological processes without allowing him the analytical distance usually provided by the genre. A stream of consciousness engulfs us in its mysterious meanderings rather than being held up for critical analysis. Swinburne, in *Poems and Ballads* (1866), transmogrified the genre in comparable fashion. Where Tennyson and Browning used the dramatic monologue to portray abnormalities the way an alienist might observe and analyze a patient in his madhouse cell, Swinburne made it the mouthpiece of his blasphemous and perverse *poète maudit* predilections. His personae, to quote Thaïs E. Morgan, "are ironic masks, calculated to ambush the publicly prudent but privately prurient Victorian reader."[56]

As with much else regarding nineteenth-century poetry, the critics most alert to such phenomena were the alienists. This is true in the very sense that there emerged, along with mental science as such, a new discipline of psychiatric literary criticism. For instance, there were numerous books and essays by alienists about how Shakespeare and other poets of the past had displayed insight into insanity and related phenomena. Here, as in discussing contemporary poems like *Maud*, the psychologists spoke with the same, often priestly, self-assurance with which they viewed their vocation. They freely took issue with the critics, harangued them for their lack of psychological insight, and corrected their misinterpretations. Outstanding among this general psychiatric criticism are two specific genres that are directly relevant to Swinburne and the *poète maudit* phenomenon. The short psychoanalytic biography, usually based on standard biographies by others, is one of them (Chapter X). Another, equally popular and widely practiced by the psychologists, is the investigation, from concrete examples, of the psychopathological components of artistic creativity in general (Epilogue).

Needless to say, all this criticism written by alienists, along with mental science itself, affected literary criticism in general. Reviewers were quick to pick up on some of the new psychological terminology with the ease (and sometimes glibness) with which some of us now handle concepts like narcissism or archetype. Their often sophisticated jargon, as it came filtering through from the new mental science, shows, more than all else, the extent to which nineteenth-century poets and their reviewers, for reasons whether of mere affinity or direct influence, were the spiritual brethren of the psychologists. The agonies of memory, spectral vision, religious insanity, motiveless malignity, the torments of guilt, and the terrors of conscience—these, among many others, were the obsessions of poets and critics, and these also, of course, were some of the hotly debated issues of the new mental science.

I

Dramatic or Psychological Monologue?

THE DRAMATIC MONOLOGUE, for Robert Langbaum, induces a tension in the reader between "sympathy versus judgment" and dramatizes the mind of a natural person imagined as "other" than the poet.[1] "Now it seems to me," counters a more recent critic, "that the dramatic monologue is built not just as a generalized image of an 'other' person but specifically as an artificial replication of this structure of interpersonal understanding."[2] Other critics, building more directly on Langbaum, stress the "artificial" distance between poet and speaker, arguing that the poet's ironic betrayal of his speaker is crucial to the genre. "Indeed, in the modern view, the peculiar structure of the dramatic monologue depends entirely upon this tension between sympathy and judgment—on the dramatic irony that arises from the contrast between the limited understanding the speaker has of his own words and the larger, encompassing understanding of the poet and reader."[3] Scholars of the dramatic monologue have also emphasized its techniques for portraying character,[4] viewed it as expressive of the "dual claims of the self: objectivity and subjectivity, and the thresholds in between,"[5] or described it as a form that "plays self against context"[6] and creates "conflicts about self-conception."[7] There is good reason for the diversity of these and similar definitions. No doubt a form as complex to the post-Romantic consciousness as the dramatic monologue is open to multiple approaches, and the new light that recent criticism has thrown on it from these various perspectives is considerable. However, as diverse as these perspectives are in one sense, as much do they tend toward uniformity in another. Most of them either downplay or lose sight of an aspect of the genre that Victorian critics considered crucial.[8]

THE DRAMATIC MONOLOGUE AND
VICTORIAN CRITICISM

To Browning's and Tennyson's contemporaries, the dramatic monologue was, above all, the poetry of psychology. Hence, the genre's present denomination was far from the only one. Victorian critics, in fact, preferred to speak of "dramas of mental conflict,"[9] "dramas of the interior,"[10] of "mental monologues,"[11] "psychological monologues,"[12] "portraits in mental photography"[13] and poems of a new "dramatic-psychological kind."[14] To them, Browning, at least since the publication of *Men and Women* (1855), had proven himself to be a "mighty . . . master of psychology."[15] To a hostile critic like Alfred Austin, he was more of an analyst than a poet,[16] but to most others he was simply "the poet of psychology"[17] or "primarily a psychologist."[18]

One of the first to use such terminology was George Eliot who in a review of 1856 coins the phrase of a "dramatic-psychological kind" of poetry found in *Men and Women*. In order to appreciate this new genre, the reader, in George Eliot's view, must shed most of his traditional preconceptions. For in Browning, "he will find out no conventionality, no melodious commonplace, but freshness, originality, sometimes eccentricity of expression; no didactic laying-out of a subject, but dramatic indication, which requires the reader to trace by his own mental activity the underground stream of thought that jets out in elliptical and pithy verse."[19] "Bishop Blougram's Apology" serves George Eliot as an example of such "dramatic-psychological" technique: "The way in which Blougram's motives are dug up from below the roots, and laid bare to the very last fibre, not by a process of hostile exposure, not by invective or sarcasm, but by making himself exhibit them with a self-complacent sense of supreme acuteness, and . . . worldly common sense, has the effect of masterly satire."[20]

Such criticism is by no means blind to the genre's multiple other aspects. Like her fellow reviewers, George Eliot draws attention to the author's irony in betraying his persona to the reader, notes how we are caught in a tension between sympathy and moral judgment, and details other effects as discussed by more recent criticism. But somehow all of these are seen as secondary, if not subservient, to the major concern of psychological exploration. Browning's main purpose in his poems, to the Victorians, was the "acute analysis of supposed states of existence, and the action of the mind therein."[21] In their view, Browning had no peer in analyzing "the minds of men as deftly as a surgeon can dissect their bodies,"[22] or, as John Addington Symonds put it, "of photographing subtle and obscure phases of mental activity and emotion in condensed and artistic pictures."[23]

Even critics who disapproved of the results agreed with Browning's admirers about the poet's main concerns. In describing "what may be called *mind in difficulties*," the poet, in Walter Bagehot's view, produced a second-rate, "grotesque" kind of poetry. Nonetheless, the critic concedes to the poet wonderful powers of intellectual analysis: "Put before him a psychological conundrum, and he will turn you off a dozen solutions in a minute."[24] Even Alfred Austin, Browning's worst opponent in later life, calls him a "subtle, profound, conscious psychologist, who scientifically gets inside souls." What was wrong with his dramatic monologues was that the author, having scrutinized his characters' "thoughts and motives in a prose and methodical fashion, then makes them give the result, as if they had been scrutinising themselves, in verse."[25]

For all his hostility, Austin comes near to ascertaining the peculiar kind of empathy that allowed Browning to enter the inner world of others. Clearly such empathy was not like the "Negative Capability"— "when man is capable of being in uncertainties, Mysteries, doubts, without any irritable reaching after fact and reason"—which Keats had described as the hallmark of Shakespeare's genius.[26] Although the personae of dramatic monologues speak on their own behalf throughout, the author's presence is somehow manifest in all of them. Even Swinburne who otherwise praised Browning's empathetic powers to the utmost, stresses the omnipresent element of subliminal authorial exposition, analysis, and apology in his "mental monologue[s]."[27] Characteristically, he calls it Browning's "gift of moral imagination," observing that this "work of exposition by soliloquy and apology by analysis can only be accomplished or undertaken by the genius of a great special pleader, able to fling himself with all his heart and all his brain, with all the force of his intellect and all the strength of his imagination, into the assumed part of his client; to concentrate on the cause in hand his whole power of illustration and illumination, and bring to bear upon one point at once all the rays of his thought in one focus."[28]

Victorian reviewers also noted more specific aspects of these portraits in mental photography. For instance, they often stressed how the poet managed to convey mental processes below the level of both articulated speech and conscious thought. Browning, at least in his soliloquies, shows us "how people think rather than how they speak."[29] "One of his strongest points," writes another reviewer, "is the faculty of seizing the lower and more bestial currents of thought and feeling, and translating them into human language."[30]

Still, why drag out these dusty Victorian reviews or, worse perhaps, claim that they hold insights neglected by more recent scholarship? After all, Victorian critics clearly exaggerated the psychological perspicacity evident in, say, *Hamlet*, *Macbeth*, or *King Lear*, and might have done the same regarding the new "psychological" monologues. The extremes of crediting Shakespeare with a "deep and accurate science in mental philosophy" (S. T. Coleridge)[31] or with surpassing most other poets in "psychical research" (Victor Hugo)[32] need not be demonstrated in detail. To Charles Lamb, for instance, Shakespeare's plays "are less calculated for performance on a stage, than those of almost any other dramatist whatever." For the playwright was concerned with the inner world of his characters rather than with the outer world of action. Shakespeare, as later reviewers would say of Browning, more often than not shows us how people think rather than how they speak. To Lamb it was obvious "that the form of *speaking*, whether it be in soliloquy or dialogue, is only a medium, and often a highly artificial one, for putting the reader or spectator into possession of that knowledge of the inner structure and workings of mind in a character."[33]

Hence scholars like E. E. Stoll surely had a point when they began to oppose this more than one-hundred-year-old tide of psychological Shakespeare criticism at the beginning of our century.[34] Hamlet's "To be, or not to be," for instance, might well be read as reflecting the silent thoughts of the prince. But to claim that such stream-of-consciousness technique prevailed in the plays or that these were not, in principle, written for stage performance, contradicts everything we know about the Elizabethan dramatist. What could be more natural than to argue that Victorian critics misinterpreted contemporary poetry in similar fashion! However, most evidence seems to suggest the very opposite.

To begin with, most authors of dramatic monologues wholeheartedly agreed with those who called them poet-psychologists. Robert Browning, for instance, did so even as a playwright. *Paracelsus*, his first attempt along these lines, reverses the traditional method of suggesting the inner world of the characters through outward events: "instead of having recourse to an external machinery of incidents," as the author put it, "I have ventured to display minutely the mood itself in its rise and progress."[35] Similar interests prompted his two final plays, written after his ill-fated attempts to produce action dramas for the real stage. One, *Luria*, was composed for a "purely imaginary stage,"[36] the other, conceived in similar spirit, was appropriately entitled "A Soul's Tragedy." Needless to say, Browning made similar comments regarding his narratives and dramatic monologues. His "stress lay on the incidents in the development of a soul: little else is worth study," he said of *Sordello* in 1863. "I, at least, always thought so."[37] Commenting on Tennyson's *The Holy Grail and Other Poems*, he (somewhat erroneously) stressed how much his own main bias differed from the Laureate's. "We look at the object of art in poetry so differently!" he wrote. "Here is an Idyll about a knight being untrue to his friend and yielding to the temptation of that friend's mistress . . . I should judge the conflict in the knight's soul the proper subject to describe: Tennyson thinks he should describe the castle, and effect of the moon on its towers, and anything *but* the soul."[38] Browning even corroborated those who claimed that he showed, at least sometimes, how his characters think rather than how they speak. Hence Arthur Symons can quote *Red Cotton Night-Cap Country* to this effect.[39] Here the poet, by way of introducing one of his characters' soliloquies, wonders whether this persona spoke aloud or merely thought to himself:

> He thought . . . [*sic*]
>   (Suppose I should prefer "He said?"
> Along with every act—and speech is act—
> There go, a multitude impalpable
> To ordinary human faculty,
> The thoughts which give the act significance.
> Who is a poet needs must apprehend
> Alike both speech and thoughts which prompt to speak.)
>   (3276–83)

Comparable evidence can be gathered regarding the dramatic monologues by other poets. Despite Browning's protests to the contrary, Tennyson made no secret of wanting to express the workings of the human mind in some of his poems. *Maud*, he argued, dramatizes "the history of a morbid, poetic soul, under the blighting influence of a recklessly speculative age. . . . The peculiarity of this poem is that different phases of passion in one person take the place of different characters."[40] Robert Buchanan, another, though minor practitioner of the genre, stated that his aim in writing such poems "was, while clearly conveying the caste of the speakers, to afford an artistic insight into their souls."[41]

But does such endorsement by the poets really prove Victorian reviewers right in seeing the dramatic monologue as a basically psychological mode of poetry? After all, the critics might have been as wrong regarding say, Browning, as they may have been, relatively speaking, concerning Shakespeare with his allegedly "deep and accurate science in mental philosophy."[42] But here the Victorians would have been the first to point out the appropriate distinctions. To most of them, the difference between the objective nature of Shakespeare's characters and the more heterogenous, not to say, subjective, cast of Browning's "men and women," for instance, was obvious. When George Bernard Shaw described the Victorian poet's Caliban as "a savage, with the introspective power of a Hamlet, and the theology of an evangelical Churchman,"[43] he only reiterated a critical commonplace. Central to Browning's dramatic monologues, in the words of one critic, was "a rare union of subjective reflectiveness with objective life and vigour, so that [the poet] can make his *personae* speak out his thoughts without prejudice to their own individual being."[44]

Another way of characterizing this subjective objectiveness was to describe it as a fusion of dramatic, epic, and lyric elements. In one contemporary view, Browning's monologues in *The Ring and the Book* "are dramatic, because the speakers are placed in dramatic situations. . . . They are narrative; for they set before us the history, not the actual development, of an event. But they are eminently lyric, because their chief interest is reflective, lying not in the deed or narrative itself, but in the psychological states of the speakers."[45] To use more recent jargon, dramatic monologues offer us the speaker's psychoanalytic confessions plus his implied case history. Although the genre does not allow the poet to comment directly on the words of his persona, the reader feels that this process, as one Victorian critic put it, is "still going on underground."[46]

Shakespeare, by contrast, remains aloof from his characters' soliloquies or, in other words, lets the surrounding plays do the commenting for him. Despite their shared psychological interests, Browning and Shakespeare, then, differ widely in their ways of embodying these concerns. Arthur Symons even ventured to identify the reasons for this difference. Both poets, in his view, have to be seen in the context of their age—Shakespeare in terms of the "vivid and adventurous England of the sixteenth century, full of youth and strength," Browning against the background of "this intensely subjective and analytic nineteenth century, with its . . . ceaseless restless introspection": "How, under these conditions, could the same product ensue? Shakespeare, in his objective drama, summed up into himself the whole character of his age; am I rash in saying that Browning also, in his subjective drama, epitomises our age?"[47]

In sum, it would be wrong to argue that Victorian reviewers, as the victims of some obsession, misinterpreted their dramatic monologues in the same way in which they overemphasized Shakespeare's psychological bias. Where they attributed similar intentions to the writers of dramatic monologues, they not only had these poets' approval, but carefully distinguished between the objective mode of Shakespeare's soliloquies and the subjective objectiveness of Victorian psychological monologues. Given the Shakespeare criticism current at that time, the temptation to trace the genealogy of these portraits in mental photography directly to the model of Shakespeare's soliloquies must have been strong. But the reviewers, for the most part, knew better. What is more, their critical understanding of the new genre gave them insights into its actual origins in Romantic poetry as more recently retraced by Robert Langbaum. Perhaps we have reason to listen to them after all.

THE DRAMATIC MONOLOGUE
AND ITS PRECEDENTS

As early as 1855, reviewers of *Maud* displayed most of these insights into the nature and origins of the genre.[48] Of course, there were critics who, given the speaker's introspective morbidity, simply derided his Spasmodic effusions as those of the author. But others, especially in the trend-setting quarterlies, defended Tennyson against such critical malpractice. Even W. E. Aytoun, while finding *Maud* a "sore disappointment" as a whole, conceded that it was uttered by a "morbid and misanthropical" speaker.[49] Critics were particularly alert to the poem's case-history nature. To one it was "a remarkable sketch of poetic mental psychology,"[50] to a second a subtle and accurate "delineation of the path to madness,"[51] to a third an "exposure of morbid self-investigation."[52] "Where can this unprofessional psychologist have acquired his accurate insight into the phenomena of insanity," wondered a fourth.[53]

Not surprisingly, *Maud* was grouped with "St. Simeon Stylites,"[54] an earlier sketch of poetic mental pathology dramatizing the ravings and actual hallucinations of a religious fanatic. In addition to such immediate antecedents, reviewers also noted the genre's origins in Romantic poetry. Of particular importance here is an essay by George Brimley, which found the express approval of Tennyson. "I wish to assure you," the poet wrote the critic, "that I quite close with your commentary on 'Maud.' I may have agreed with portions of other critiques on the same poem, which have been sent to me; but when I saw your notice I laid my finger upon it and said, 'There, that is my meaning.' Poor little 'Maud' . . . has found a critic."[55]

In search for the source of this enthusiasm, the reader of the essay is disappointed at first. Brimley largely reiterates observations also found elsewhere: the speaker is not to be confused with the author; what he says about nature is meant to reflect his morbid sensibility rather than objective reality; hence the poem is neither lyric, epic, or dramatic, but of an essentially hybrid form. What, then, elicited Tennyson's special praise? For one, Brimley differs from other reviewers in the explicitness with which he characterizes the speaker as a poet-like figure. Of course, we should not, he suggests, simplistically equate persona and author. At the same time, the protagonist may well remind us of Tennyson himself, or at least of a certain type of Romantic poet: "morbid, hysterical, spasmodic," "one in which the sensibilities are keen and delicate, the speculative element strong, the practical judgement unsteady, the will and active energies comparatively feeble." To Brimley, a "Shelley or a Keats may stand for example of his type; not perfect men, certainly, but scarcely so contemptible as not to possess both dramatic interest and some claim to human sympathy. Chatterton, a much lower type than either, has been thought a subject of psychological and moral interest, in spite or in consequence of the vulgar, petulant, weak melodrama of his life and death."[56]

In other words, a poet has every right to dramatize the plight of one of his tribe, even if such character portrayal should point back at the author or perhaps draw upon autobiographical sources. In this way, Brimley is well aware that a crucial section of *Maud*, "O that 'twere possible," was lifted from an earlier publication where it appeared as the poet's lyrical effusion. Such personal elements have their place as long as the speaker's character and development are finally shown to evolve from the interior dynamics of the poem. To Brimley, *Maud* perfectly met this requirement, particularly in the way in which it portrays English society as providing "the unwholesome nutriment for such a character" on his road toward madness;[57] and Tennyson seems to have agreed with the critic. When he called *Maud* "the history of a morbid, poetic soul, under the blighting influence of a recklessly speculative age,"[58] he simply endorsed the main drift of Brimley's argument.

What also must have impressed the poet is how his favorite critic set *Maud* in the context of his poetry in general. Brimley feels no need for expanding on how one passage of the poem ("See what a lovely shell") is "dramatically expressive of a mind on the verge of overthrow," or with how much pathos and realism another ("O that 'twere possible") "presents the incipient stage of madness, springing from the wrecked affections."[59] For what he had said about some of Tennyson's earlier poems also applies to *Maud*. As an example, Brimley quotes from "The Merman" as published in *Poems, Chiefly Lyrical* of 1830:

> There would be neither moon nor star;
> But the wave would make music above us afar—
> Low thunder and light in the magic night—
> Neither moon nor star.

What could such lines have in common with *Maud*? Like much of Romantic poetry, they focus on nature rather than on the speaker. But to Brimley, they are dramatic in a way similar to *Maud*. For their prima facie depictions of natural scenery "are in fact pictures of peculiar character" in which "emotion is presented in connexion with the incidents out of which it rises."[60] What moves such "dramatic landscape-painting" closer to poems like "See what a lovely shell" from *Maud* is its depiction of nature through the medium of a morbid sensibility. This precisely is what Brimley finds in "Mariana." Everything in that poem evokes for him "the morbid sensibility of a woman abandoned to lonely misery":

> If the moss is *blackened*, the flower-pots *thickly crusted*, the nails *rusted*, the sheds *broken*, the latch *clinking*, the thatch *weeded and worn*, not one of these epithets but tells of long neglect, and pro-

longs the key-note of *sad and strange* loneliness. . . . The poplar hard by is never in repose, shaking like a sick man in a fever; for leagues round spreads the "level waste, the rounding grey," with no object, no variety, to interest the attention. What moves, moves always, harassing the nerves,—what is at rest seems dead, striking cold the heart. . . . The effect is felt by the reader with hardly a consciousness . . . of the intense dramatic concentration implied in such employment of language.[61]

At the same time, Brimley is quite aware of what separates a poem like "Mariana" from *Maud*. For whatever dramatic concentration "Mariana" may have is weakened by the fact that the heroine's fate is told in the poet's rather than her own words. In Brimley's idiosyncratic view of Tennyson's development, the poet managed to overcome this deficiency in poems like "The Miller's Daughter." For here the protagonist is allowed to speak *in propria persona*, and, what is more, to tell his story to another person who is part of the fictional realm of the poem. Thus, Brimley, for all the oddities of his judgments, locates another link between the Romantic poem of experience and the full-fledged monologue of the dramatic-psychological kind.[62]

As a poem largely descriptive of nature and lacking the morbid perspective of "Mariana," "The Miller's Daughter," more strongly than the earlier poem, harks back to poems like "Tintern Abbey." At the same time, it has many of the elements—such as an independent speaker telling his story to a listener within a clearly delineated context—that make it a closer ally of the dramatic monologue than "Mariana." No wonder that Brimley, though only half-aware of all these connections, ends up describing "The Miller's Daughter" as an example of the new hybrid genre that Victorian critics generally identified with the dramatic monologue. To him, the poem's "charm of completeness, which is the aim of narrative, is united with the power over the sympathies possessed by the spontaneous outpouring of feeling; and a lyrical flow of emotion is made to hold in solution, as it were, the constituents of a drama."[63] In all of this, the poet, as Brimley elsewhere said of Browning, makes it his business "to enter by sympathy into the lives, characters and conduct of others."[64]

Brimley was probably one of the first to point out some of the links between Romantic poetry and the new genre. However, the categories that allow him to do so derive from previous theorizing not directly concerned with the dramatic monologue. Most notable here is the criticism of Tennyson's early poems and of poetry in general produced by the literary circle surrounding W. J. Fox and his *Monthly Repository*.[65] Fox himself set the trend with his review of Tennyson's *Poems, Chiefly Lyrical* in the *Westminster Review* of 1831. His major emphasis is that poetry, in the hands of this young genius, is about to become a means for "the analysis of particular states of mind."[66] One of Tennyson's techniques along these lines derives from Romantic descriptions of nature. Where Brimley will speak of this new dramatic landscape painting turned character analysis—"in which the objects grouped and the qualities attributed to them are viewed through the medium of the beings associated with the scene"[67]—Fox, more succinctly, points out how Tennyson creates "a scene out of the character, and [makes] the feeling within generate an appropriate assemblage of external objects."[68]

Hence, one is not surprised to find Fox quoting the same lines from "The Merman," which subsequently served Brimley as an example of such landscape painting in the service of psychological exploration.[69] To Fox, they document the peculiar mixture of empathy and analysis that later reviewers describe as the hallmark of the dramatic monologue, i.e., its "rare union of subjective reflectiveness with objective life and vigour."[70] Tennyson, in his view, "has the secret of the transmigration of the soul. He can cast his own spirit into any living thing, real or imaginary. . . . He does not merely assume their external shapes. . . . He takes their senses, feelings, nerves, and brain, along with their names and local habitations; still it is himself in them, modified but not absorbed by their peculiar constitution and mode of being."[71] In a second review of Tennyson, Fox declares the new psychological mode of depicting reality to be modern poetry's characteristic par excellence. "The classic portrayed human character by its exterior demonstrations and influences on the material objects of sense; the modern delineates the whole external world from its reflected imagery in the mirror of human thought and feeling."[72]

Fox's criticism of Tennyson was less appropriate to the young Tennyson than prophetic of things to come, and none of the contributors to his *Monthly Repository* went as far as he in propagating the new poetry of mental analysis. Nonetheless, a concern with some of the issues raised by the editor is evident everywhere. A self-styled *philosophus*, writing "On the Application of the Terms Poetry, Science, and Philosophy" in *The Monthly Repository* of 1834, echoes Fox's distinctions between ancient and modern, claiming that "in the poetry of more refined and cultivated periods, the mind no longer appears as the passive recipient of external influences; it throws itself out upon the visible universe, and clothes it with the hues of its own associations."[73] Another contributor, Henry Crabb Robinson, reiterates Fox's concern with a hybrid kind of empathy in which the poet at once abandons and asserts his individuality. Presaging later definitions of the dramatic monologue, he describes this faculty as a fusion of the three genres—"epic impartiality" and lyric subjectivity ("in which the poet gives mainly objects as they are reflected in the mirror of his own individuality") being united in the dramatic.[74]

The most influential contributor to *The Monthly Repository* was young J. S. Mill whose "What is Poetry?" was written expressly "because [he] wished to write something for Fox."[75] Mill avoids the strongly psychological jargon of his editor but nonetheless declares poetry to be the "delineation of the deeper and more secret workings of human emotion." Its truth, as against that of fiction, which depicts life, "is to paint the human soul truly."[76] Mill's article on Tennyson, published in the *London Review* of July 1835, echoes Fox's comments on the poet's technique of psychological character portrayal through the medium of nature. Mill speaks of "the power of *creating* scenery, in keeping with some state of human feelings."[77]

In sum, Victorian descriptions of the dramatic monologue as an intrinsically psychological genre seem to draw on earlier criticism of Romantic nature poetry. A later chapter will trace this connection to the very core of Romantic poetics. At this point, a different question, implied by almost everything that has been said so far, remains to be answered. Why did Victorian critics stress the psychological nature of the dramatic monologue and poetry generally when their successors in the age of Freud, for the most part, have lost sight of such matters?

PSYCHOLOGICAL POETRY
AND MENTAL SCIENCE

In one sense, the answer is simple. Psychology and psychiatry, as we know them today, emerged during the early nineteenth century and, never more strongly than during that period, struck people as new and exciting in ways entailing changes in every domain of human life. An article on James Mill's *Analysis of the Phenomena of the Human Mind*,

which the *Westminster* published just a few months before Fox's review
of Tennyson, is typical of this excitement. To the reviewer, the new
mental science relates to previous metaphysics in the same way in which
modern chemistry replaced alchemy. Furthermore, this discipline is far
from limited to mere investigations of the human mind. As an all-
encompassing "master science," it will have to answer many issues such
as the nature of good and evil previously dealt with by metaphysics.[78]

We find Fox, in his review of *Poems, Chiefly Lyrical*, extending such
claims into the domain of poetry. The modern poet should be grateful
to the mental scientists. "A new world" has been "discovered for him
to conquer": "The most important department in which metaphysical
science has been a pioneer for poetry is in the analysis of particular states
of mind. . . . The poets of antiquity rarely did more than incidentally
touch this class of topics. . . . Nor let them be blamed; it was for the
philosophers to be the first discoverers and settlers, and for poetry af-
terwards to reap the advantage of their labours. This has only been done
recently, or rather is only beginning to be done at all."[79]

Not surprisingly, Victorian critics of the dramatic monologue made
similar claims. Comments like H. B. Forman's relating the new school
of psychological poetry directly to the rise of mental science abound in
Victorian criticism. Browning's works, to quote one more example,
show "how the scope of human thought has been enlarged by the discoveries of mental science," writes W. B. Worsfold.[80]

The next chapter will show that the new mental science, at least
chronologically speaking, may indeed be said to precede the rise of the
dramatic monologue. But as psychologists were the first to admit, poets
in turn often anticipated the new science. The most frequently invoked
model here was Shakespeare. Alienist A. O. Kellogg, writing in 1866,
still had to concede that he and his colleagues had "little to add to what
Shakespeare appears to have known of these intricate subjects": "At
every step through this wonderful play [*King Lear*] we find evidence
. . . of Shakespeare's great medico-psychological knowledge,—a
knowledge scarcely possessed by any even in our day, except those few
who devote themselves to this special department of medical science."[81]

In fact, whatever psychologists discovered of Browning's and Tennyson's works was greeted with similar enthusiasm. J. H. Balfour-
Browne, reviewing *Red Cotton Night-Cap Country* for the *Journal of Mental Science*, praises Browning as an "anatomist of the very inmost spirit
of humanity" who offers the reader "a careful pathological examination"

and case history of a madman. Generally speaking, the reviewer finds that everything Browning writes "has claims upon the attention of those who study the philosophy of mind."[82] Herbert Spencer felt similarly about a specific poem of Tennyson's. "I happened recently to be re-reading . . . 'The Two Voices,' " he wrote the poet in 1855, "and coming to the verse

> Or if thro' lower lives I came—
> Tho' all experience past became
> Consolidate in mind and frame—

it occurred to me that you might like to glance through a book which applies to the elucidation of mental science, the hypothesis to which you refer. I therefore beg your acceptance of *Psychology* which I send by this post."[83]

Another review in the *Asylum Journal of Mental Science* by its founding member and editor John Charles Bucknill, praises *Maud* as a "remarkable sketch of poetic mental pathology."[84] Bucknill's excitement over the poem was only equaled by the poet's after reading the review. "I seem to have the doctors on my side if no one else," Tennyson wrote to a friend: "I have just received an article by a mad-house doctor giving his testimony as to the truth to nature in the delineation of the hero's madness. Valuable testimony it seems to me."[85] *Maud* struck Bucknill as particularly "true to nature" in depicting the protagonist's insanity in terms of its etiology and premonitory symptoms:

> The hereditary tendency, the early and terrible shock to the emotions, caused by the father's suicide, the recluse mode of life, in which morbid feeling and misanthropic opinions are nourished to an extent productive of hallucination even at that early period of the malady; in which mid-day moans are heard in the wood, and his own sad name is called in corners of the solitary house. All this is most true to the frequent course of events, in that period when insanity is threatening and imminent, but not actually present. Another point touched upon with the singular delicacy of this exquisite poet, is the apprehension which the sufferer evidently entertains, that he will become mad.[86]

Others might have found fault with Tennyson's choice of so disagreeable a hero and so unpleasant a subject. But to Bucknill, Tennyson's scientifically unpitying depiction of this "terrible reality" is the poet's greatest achievement. To him, Tennyson is more than a mere poet. He is a fellow alienist who, in fact, embodied in his poem a "true example" of the "theory of the psychopathic origin of insanity" only recently put forward by Bucknill's colleague Joseph Guislain.[87] Such a claim makes us wonder about the possible relations between the new mental science and the new poetry of dramatic psychological kind. But first a more specific question will claim our attention.

II

The New Mental Science

WHAT DID VICTORIANS, and particularly reviewers of poetry, mean when they talked about the new mental science, psychological medicine, or psychology? As one might expect, their use of such terms differed considerably from ours. For example, Victorians did not use "psychiatry" as a synonym for abnormal psychology, but employed other terms like "mental pathology" or "psychology" instead. Bucknill, for instance, chose the latter option for the title of one of his books, *The Psychology of Shakespeare*. "Psychology," he explained, had formerly stood primarily for what refers "to the soul or mind of man in contradistinction to his material nature"; but more recently its meaning had come to include "all that relates to the department of science which takes cognizance of irregularities and aberrations and diseases of the mind." Bucknill would have preferred "mental pathology" as a more accurate term for his title. But it was simply so much more cumbrous than "psychology."[1]

Nonetheless, the two disciplines were clearly separate to the Victorians. On the one hand, there were the alienists with their asylums, on the other, the actual psychologists busy studying the phenomena of normal consciousness. At least to the early nineteenth century, there was, in fact, yet another new discipline related to these two. Mesmerism or animal magnetism, though largely viewed as the lunatic fringe of mental science, nonetheless aroused scholarly controversies for several decades. Like psychology proper, but unlike mental pathology, it dealt with human consciousness in a state of basic sanity. Like mental pathology, but unlike psychology, it focused primarily on abnormal states of consciousness such as somnambulism, multiple personality, hallucination, and clairvoyance. It was only in the early 1840s, when mesmerism came to be known and practiced as hypnotism, that this semi-occult discipline was absorbed into mainstream psychological medicine.

INTROSPECTIVE PSYCHOLOGY

Of the three disciplines, psychology proper was least of a novelty to the nineteenth century. "Since the time of Hobbes and Locke," wrote T. A. Ribot in his *La psychologie anglaise contemporaine* (1870), "England has been the country which has done most for psychology."[2] Victorians were unlikely to disagree, though most of them would have traced this achievement to the Scottish empiricists in the wake of Thomas Reid rather than, like Ribot, to David Hartley. The history of early introspective psychology is one of amazing coherence and singularity of purpose. Reid is credited with supplanting previous theorizing on the soul by systematic methods of introspective analysis, and if ever there was a coherent tradition of thought, it was that developed by his various followers. Dugald Stewart wrote an account of Reid's life and writings, while Sir William Hamilton edited and copiously annotated his works.[3] Dugald Stewart's *Elements of the Philosophy of the Human Mind*, with "many new and important additions," was edited by Sir William Hamilton.[4] James Mill's *Analysis of the Phenomena of the Human Mind*, was edited and annotated by Alexander Bain and John Stuart Mill, who in turn wrote *An Examination of Sir William Hamilton's Philosophy*.[5]

Reid's main contribution to modern psychology was one of pointing out new directions rather than of making major discoveries. In the introduction to his *Inquiry into the Human Mind*, he claims no further merit "than that of having given great attention to the operation of [his] own mind." To Reid, there was good reason why few had preceded him on this "narrow and rugged" path. For unlike the anatomist of the body, the "anatomist of the mind" has to rely almost exclusively upon himself. "It is his own mind only that he can examine with any degree of accuracy and distinctness. This is the only subject he can look into. He may, from outward signs, collect the operations of other minds; but these signs are for the most part ambiguous, and must be interpreted by what he perceives within himself."[6]

Naturally, Reid would have preferred a more objective account of the human mind like, for instance, "a distinct and full history of all that hath past in the mind of a child, from the beginning of life and sensation, till it grows up to the use of reason." Such an account "would be a treasure of natural history, which would probably give more light into the human faculties, than all the systems of philosophers about them since the beginning of the world."[7] But to Reid, such knowledge was simply out of human reach. The problem with previous analysts of human nature had been precisely that they had tried to accomplish the impossible or simply too much. By contrast, Reid's *Inquiry into the Human Mind* limits itself to an analysis of the five senses.

However, what fascinated Reid's followers was the prospect of exploring the unfathomed mysteries of the mind rather than the limits he had set in this pursuit. To Thomas Brown, physician, poet, and psychologist,[8] the new method of analysis would one day open "a field of discovery in the science of mind as rich . . . as that of the universe without."[9] Within about a century, Reid's principle of analytic introspection was carried into almost every area of mental science. Alexander Crichton applied it to the study of insanity. Anyone involved in this branch of science, he wrote in 1798, should "be capable of abstracting his own mind from himself, and placing it before him, as it were, so as to examine it with the freedom, and with the impartiality of a natural historian."[10] Alfred Maury, in anticipation of Freud, used the same principle in the interpretation of his dreams as well as of those hypnagogic hallucinations experienced between sleeping and waking. His model in this pursuit, like Crichton's, was the Scottish school of self-observation.[11]

Sir William Hamilton, in whom this school reached its culmination, finally used the same methods for analyzing the unconscious. Most consequential here was the observation that we often find one thought rising immediately after another in consciousness without being able to make out the associative link between them. The solution to this riddle was that the missing link B between the two conscious thoughts A and C operates in form of an "unconscious mental modification." Without rising into consciousness, B has the power to make A interconnect with C in ways inscrutable to any but the most self-analytical person. Hamilton uses an example from his own experience to explain this complex process. One day, thinking of Ben Lomond, he writes,

> this thought [A] was immediately followed by the thought [C] of
> the Prussian system of education. Now, conceivable connection
> between these two ideas in themselves, there was none. A little

reflection, however, explained the anomaly. On my last visit to the mountain, I had met upon its summit a German gentleman, and though I had no consciousness of the intermediate and unawakened links between Ben Lomond [A] and the Prussian schools [C], they were undoubtedly these,—the German,—Germany,—Prussia,—[B] and, these media being admitted, the connection between the extremes was manifest.[12]

As others before him, Hamilton notes further unconscious modifications to show that "the infinitely greater part of our spiritual treasures, lies . . . hid in the obscure recesses of the mind."[13] The way in which we may know a language or scientific discipline without actively making use of it and bringing it into consciousness is one of these modifications. Another is evident in the case of the servant girl, discussed in Coleridge's *Biographia Literaria*, who, attacked by a nervous fever, began to talk in Latin, Greek, and Hebrew.[14] Thus "certain abnormal states, as madness, febrile delirium, somnambulism, catalepsy, &c.," may activate treasures of the mind "which were never within the grasp of conscious memory in the normal state."[15] In the case of the servant girl, for instance, the mental resources activated in this way had simply vanished from conscious awareness. It was discovered that as a child, when living with an old pastor, she had often heard the man recite aloud his favorite authors in the original Hebrew, Greek, and Latin.

Though primarily concerned with normal consciousness, introspective psychology, then, was brought to bear on the study of mental disease, dreams, and unconscious cerebration. With Dugald Stewart, it also reached out into the dubious realms of mesmerism. Here the Scottish philosopher was one of the first to point in the right direction. While contemptuous of Mesmer's cosmological theorizing, he noted that animal magnetism drew upon unknown imaginative potentials warranting serious scientific investigation. History, as Hunter-Macalpine write, "proved Stewart more correct than he could have known. The investigation of mesmerism in the middle of the nineteenth century led to Braid's study of what he termed 'hypnotism' which in turn inspired much psychological and clinical research and resulted in the development of the modern schools of dynamic psychology" such as Freud's and Jung's.[16] But to what extent were the early Victorians aware of these precedents to modern depth analysis?

MESMERISM

For several decades, Britain escaped the mesmeromania that had haunted Central Europe since the 1780s. The English took as little notice when Mesmer performed his early magnetic cures as when his disciple Puysegur, to the master's disapproval, discovered that these cures were largely effected through artificially induced somnambulism.[17] They were equally unimpressed by attempts, primarily carried out in Germany, at using the new techniques for exploring extrasensory and supernatural phenomena. Shelley, while in Europe, dabbled in mesmerism and wrote a monologue "The Magnetic Lady to Her Patient."[18] But no major English figure before 1837 shared the enthusiasm of men like Schelling, to whom animal magnetism opened up possibilities for a new experimental metaphysics, or Schopenhauer, to whom it came to constitute "the most momentous discovery ever made" from a philosophical point of view.[19] Even when J. C. Colquhoun, in his 1836 *Isis Revelata: an Inquiry into the Origin, Progress, and Present State of Animal Magnetism*, tried to drum up support for the mysterious discipline,[20] the response was critical rather than enthusiastic.[21] In sum, the mesmeric movement in England from 1800 to 1837, as a recent scholar puts it, "was a pale and scattered shadow of continental activities."[22] But all this was to change radically during 1837–38.

To one witness's dismay, animal magnetism suddenly "became the topic of discussion in every circle—politics and literature were . . . thrown into the shade, so strange were the facts, or so wonderful was the delusion."[23] The immediate cause was a series of public mesmeric demonstrations at University College hospital conducted by the reputable Dr. Elliotson under the guidance of French mesmeriser Dupotet de Sennevoy.[24] Before long, the experiments ended in public scandal, but the excitement lived on for several years. In the wake of publications like S. D. Saunders's *Mesmeric Guide for Family Use* and William Davey's *Illustrated Practical Mesmerist*, neither animals nor plants were safe from the magnetizing fervor of lay enthusiasts. Girls and boys in some educational establishments, as J. H. Bennett reported in 1851, "throw themselves into states of trance and ecstasy, or show their fixed eyeballs and rigid limbs, for the amusement of their companions."[25] The general enthusiasm even took hold among some of the major figures of the century.

One of the first was Charles Dickens who, in the company of his friend Cruikshank, attended the demonstrations at University College hospital. "I have closely watched Dr. Elliotson's experiments from the first," he wrote in 1842, and "after what I have seen with my own eyes, and observed with my own senses, I should be untrue to myself if I shrunk for a moment from saying that I am a believer, and that I became so against all my preconceived opinions and impressions."[26] Before long, the novelist turned ardent magnetiser himself. Another famous "believer, in *spite of papa*,"[27] was Elizabeth Barrett. Other lay mesmerists of note include Alfred Tennyson and Harriet Martineau. Browning wrote a monologue, "Mesmerism," spoken by a magnetiser in the process of exerting his powers over a woman; Richard Monckton Milnes, future editor of Keats's *Life, Letters and Literary Remains*, wrote a poem entitled "Mesmerism in London." Many others like Arnold, Clough, Thackeray, and both Carlyles were interested in mesmerism to varying degrees.[28]

At the same time, Victorian quarterlies and reviews kept their readers up to date on the most recent events in mesmeric research. Several of them ran feature articles surveying the rise and history of the movement. *Fraser's Magazine* in 1830 gave an account of Mesmer's original experiments, of the 1784 inquiry into his practices sponsored by the French government, of Puysegur's reassessment of animal magnetism as artificially induced somnambulism, and of more recent attempts to use mesmerism for anaesthetic purposes in surgery.[29] More extensive surveys of similar kind appeared after Elliotson's demonstrations at the University College hospital and especially subsequent to James Braid's discovery that animal magnetism, far from depending on cosmic "fluids" or "odylic" forces, was "reconcilable with well-known and established physiological and psychological principles."[30] As a result of Braid's experiments, the phenomenon was put into proper perspective. For if artificial somnambulism could be induced by mere auto-suggestion such as by "fixing the eyes, for several minutes consecutively, on some bright object somewhat above and in front of them," then Mesmer's supposed discovery had obvious precedents.[31] As the *Westminster Review* points out, the fakirs of India, for instance, achieved similar effects "by looking at the tips of their noses."[32]

Two articles in *Fraser's Magazine* show the scope such theorizing had reached by 1844–45. The first "convict[s] Mesmer and his followers of having *borrowed* the philosophy and researches of the Hermetic school of Paracelcus, Van Helmont, Kirchner, Goclenius, Dee, and Fludd";[33]

the second, even more ingeniously, relates the new science to subjects as diverse as witchcraft, Hindu religion, and Persian mysticism. Hypnotism, as a result, is found to have been practiced by the ancient Sufis, Hindoos, and other religious groups. "The Eastern devotees, the magi of Persia, and all the other practisers of magic," according to the anonymous author, "were clearly *self*-magnetisers—restraining the breath, and fixing the eyes, and concentrating the attention on an object."[34]

Victorian journals also discussed the mesmeric explorations of extrasensory and supernatural perception. The phenomenon of double consciousness, for instance, had long been familiar to an age as obsessed with the self and its ever-threatening disintegration as the nineteenth century. Now mesmerism offered the possibility of subjecting this split consciousness to systematic analysis. For it was found that "a patient may be taught any thing during the nervous sleep if impressed upon the mind at the proper stage, and that he will be able to repeat his task with verbal accuracy whenever he be thrown into that state again, but shall have no consciousness or knowledge whatever of the act performed when in the ordinary waking condition."[35] Mesmeric research also promised to solve the riddle of how memory and imagination, both in sleep and in certain nervous conditions, accomplish feats that they could never manage in normal consciousness. For was not somnambulism, as inducible through hypnosis, like a dream acted out under the eyes of the operator?[36] And did not the patients, thus entranced, give evidence of a sheer supernatural exaltation of specific senses and of an "extraordinary revivification of memory at a certain stage of mesmeric and hypnotic sleep?"[37]

Coleridge had been intrigued by the servant girl who, in a fever, spoke in Latin, Greek, and Hebrew; Sir Walter Scott by the Scottish gentleman whose dead father told him in a dream of the whereabouts of a legal document needed in a court case;[38] and subsequent writers were as fond of repeating such stories as those of famous men who accomplished amazing feats of problem solving and creativity while asleep.[39] Thanks to mesmerism, such phenomena were now open to systematic exploration. As the *Quarterly Review* assured its readers, somnambulism or "sleep waking" provides instances analogous to all of them. Patients will remember things they never could while awake; a mathematician might work out a difficult problem; "a musician will draw forth most enchanting harmonies from his accustomed instrument; a poet will improvise a torrent of verses."[40]

On the wings of such often credulous enthusiasm, Victorian reviewers also showed remarkable openness toward mesmeric explorations of supernatural phenomena. Most widely discussed here was German poet-physician Justinus Kerner's account of the "Inter-diffusion of a World of Spirits in the One We Inhabit"[41] as experienced by the Seeress of Prevorst, a woman who in magnetic and other states had held communion with ghosts and other emissaries from the beyond.[42] Ghost-seeing as such was nothing new, of course. But never before had a case like this been supervised, manipulated, verified, analyzed, and written about by a group of mesmerists who, like the Professors Eschenmayer and Görres, as much as Kerner himself, were, in the words of the *British Quarterly Review*, "men of high scientific attainments and undoubted veracity."[43] Here then was an account, not just of ordinary apparitions, but of "true scientific ghosts,—physiological ghosts—ghosts that could stand an examination by the theories of the nineteenth century . . . and form as intelligible and consistent a part of one's philosophy as any theory of light, heat, or electricity, which we know of."[44]

While reviewers rejected Kerner's claims, they were sufficiently impressed by his book to try to explain in other ways what the poet-physician attributed to supernatural intervention. Ironically, both parties appealed to mesmerism in this debate. The difference lay in their understanding of this new discipline. Where Kerner and his circle, as did many of their spiritual brethren in England, took mesmerism to be the royal road to the supernatural, Victorian reviewers for the most part thought it to be the means par excellence for demonstrating the essentially psychological nature of spiritualist phenomena. Needless to say, both sides sinned on the side of overloading the mysterious discipline with their grandiose claims. Not till after mesmerism, reinterpreted as hypnotism, was assigned a more strictly functional role in early psychoanalysis did this speculative excitement subside. During the early nineteenth century even the new alienists succumbed to its lure and wrote compendious volumes in which everything from witchcraft to modern spiritualism is explained in terms of its diverse effects.[45]

PSYCHOLOGICAL MEDICINE

Of the three disciplines that made up the bulk of what Victorians summed up under the blanket term "mental science," psychological medicine no doubt had the greatest impact on people's awareness. In

England, in fact, it began with a public scandal.[46] This occurred subsequent to the publication, in 1813, of Samuel Tuke's *Description of the Retreat*. The Retreat, an establishment near York for the treatment of the insane, had been founded by Samuel's grandfather William after a Quaker woman had died under suspicious circumstances in the official York Asylum. Naturally, the officers of that institution took the book as an attack on themselves and a bitter exchange in the local press ensued. This led to public outcry, dramatic revelations, firings and reforms at the York Asylum, to similar investigations at Bethlem in London, and finally to the Parliamentary inquiry into madhouses during 1815–16.

Perhaps because of a drawing made on the spot, the case of one William Norris, found in a cell of the lower gallery at Bethlem, became the *cause célèbre* of the reformers. The picture shows Norris in a dungeon, his emaciated figure shackled around his neck, waist, arms and legs, staring at us with big eyes of unutterable despair and anguish.[47] Equally notorious the world over became the description, by one of the inquiry's official investigators, of the contraption that had held Norris captive for over ten years:

> a stout ring was rivetted round his neck, from which a short chain passed to a ring made to slide upwards or downwards on an upright massive iron bar, more than six feet high, inserted into the wall. Round his body a strong iron bar about two inches wide was rivetted; on each side the bar was a circular projection, which . . . inclosing each of his arms, pinioned them close to his sides. This waist bar was secured by two similar bars which, passing over his shoulders, were rivetted to the waist bar both before and behind. The iron ring round his neck was connected to the bars on his shoulders, by a double link. From each of these bars another chain passed to the ring on the upright iron bar. . . . It was, I conceive . . . out of his power to repose in any other position than on his back.[48]

In sum, public opinion had been alerted to the issue, and men like the Tukes, John Conolly, and John Charles Bucknill kept it astir for the sake of reform. The story of their eventual triumph, of the ever-growing number of mental asylums in Britain, Europe, and North America, of the new professional caste of alienists to whom these institutions served as giant laboratories of the human mind[49]—none of this needs to be detailed in these pages. It has been told again and again, both in the Victorian age and in our own.[50] For good reason, the early alienists, in particular, never tired of recounting the heroic saga of their origins. In this Philippe Pinel, pioneer of French psychiatry, who in the heyday of the French Revolution struck the chains off several lunatics,[51] attained even greater legendary status than William Tuke. Typical of such accounts is the 1853 editorial to the first issue of Bucknill's *Asylum Journal of Mental Science*, which as *The British Journal of Psychiatry* continues publication to this day.

> From the time when Pinel obtained the permission of Couthon to try the humane experiment of releasing from fetters some of the insane citizens chained to the dungeon walls of the Bicêtre . . . a new school of special medicine has been gradually forming. . . . The Physician is now the responsible guardian of the lunatic, and must ever remain so. . . . Since the public in all civilized countries have recognized the fact, that Insanity lies strictly within the domain of medical science, new responsibilities and new duties have devolved upon those who have devoted themselves to its investigation and treatment. Many circumstances have tended, not indeed to isolate cerebro-mental disease from the mainland of general pathology; but to render prominent its characteristics and to stamp it as a specialty.[52]

But such self-advertising accounts were not the only means of keeping this new school of special medicine alive in the mind of the public. Other more sinister aspects of Victorian mental pathology made their impact, particularly on the sensitive and neurotic. To them, the new hospitals of the insane must have loomed threateningly enough; yet what was known about the ever-increasing number of their inmates was even more frightening. Bucknill-Tuke's *Manual of Psychological Medicine* of 1858, for instance, reports almost a tenfold increase for the preceding two decades.[53] Figures revealed by the *North American Review* for Massachusetts were even more alarming.[54] To be sure, Bucknill-Tuke assured their readers that the resultant "belief in the frightful increase of insanity" was unfounded. To them, the disease, due to the virtual nonexistence of psychological medicine in former times, had simply gone unnoticed before.[55] But such an argument simply begged another question. Were there new criteria for certifying as insane people who but a few decades earlier would have continued incognito in their perhaps strange but basically innocuous ways?

The answers proffered by zealous alienists were unlikely to assuage the growing fears of institutionalization. "There is a latent devil in the heart of the best of men," warns Bucknill-Tuke's *Manual*.[56] Alienists should be like detectives able to spot and trap this devil before it unleashes itself on society, adds Forbes Winslow. "How cautiously, zealously, and closely should the physician watch for the incipient dawnings of cerebral mischief," he exclaims:

> An apparently unimportant knitting of the brows,—a trifling sensation of numbness in some part of the body,—a condition of general or local muscular weakness,—a state of *ennui*,—mental peevishness, irritability, and physical restlessness,—an almost inappreciable depression or exaltation of the animal spirits . . . a trivial deviation from the usual mode of talking, such as suddenly pausing in the conversation, as if to regain a lost train of ideas,— a slight defect in the articulation, associated with a transposition of words, and inability to pronounce certain letters, *are all characteristic symptoms, frequently diagnostic of disease having commenced in the brain*.[57]

Not surprisingly, Winslow felt that there was far too much red tape when he or one of his confreres tried to have someone certified and institutionalized for insanity.[58]

Such fervor was partly the outcome of a gradual broadening of the concept of insanity observable throughout the early phase of mental science. A pioneer here was William Battie with his 1758 *Treatise on Madness*. As governor of Bethlem Hospital he not only advocated more humane forms of treatment, but also enlarged the scope of those eligible for such therapy. To traditionalists like his opponent John Monro, madness was an impairment of reason or "vitiated judgment." But to Battie, it was rather a form of "*deluded imagination*." Hence, persons who retained their rational faculties could be diagnosed as "mad" for their "praeternatural state or disorder of Sensation."[59]

To this already widened concept, nineteenth-century alienists added the notion of moral insanity. As a result, even those who showed neither vitiated judgment nor deluded imagination could be declared insane and institutionalized. As Pinel had observed, there were lunatics whose "ideas were clear and connected; they indulged in no extravagances of fancy; they answered with great pertinence and precision the questions that were proposed to them: but they were under the dominion of a most ungovernable fury, and of a thirst equally ungovernable for deeds of blood."[60] In addition to this *manie sans délire*, there was yet another form of insanity without impairment of either reason or imagination. Patients, though suffering from this affliction, were found to "feel, reason, act like everybody else . . . but their emotions, their personality, [were] perverted."[61]

In Britain, where Locke, in a widely quoted phrase, had described lunatics as people who "argue right from wrong Principles,"[62] alienists quickly caught on to these new concepts. Thomas Arnold, in the 1806 edition of his *Observations on . . . Insanity*, was probably the first to use "moral insanity" for what the French called *folie raisonnante*.[63] But it was only after the 1835 publication of J. C. Prichard's *Treatise on Insanity*, the standard text until Bucknill-Tuke's *Manual* of 1858, that the phrase gained general currency. Prichard also gave the concept the strongly moralistic bias, which remained its inquisitorial hallmark throughout the mid-Victorian era. Moral insanity, to him, was a "morbid perversion of the feelings, affections, and active powers, without any illusion or erroneous conviction impressed upon the understanding: it sometimes co-exists with an apparently unimpaired state of the intellectual faculties."[64]

Not surprisingly, Prichard finds many individuals "of a singular, wayward, and eccentric character . . . living at large." Though suffering neither hallucinations nor loss of reason, they might yet be found insane because of "the perverted state of [their] moral feelings."[65] Were the increases of insanity related to this new witch-hunt attitude? Whatever the answer, most Victorian alienists agreed with Prichard. To J. Bower Harrison, writing in 1850, insanity is "far from showing itself merely in hallucinations and illusions, as is commonly supposed. Often the first overt act of insanity is one of moral delinquency or extravagance."[66] For Tuke and Bucknill, mere moral extravagance was often a sufficient sign of imminent mental derangement; for instance, "when the carefully-nurtured and modest female demeans herself in a bold, forward, and indecent manner."[67] How did Victorians react to this new inquisitorial zeal? No doubt many of them were more than just passingly aware of psychological medicine as one of the diverse new sciences. To the neurotic and eccentric, even if unfamiliar with the specifics of the discipline, such awareness must have been a source of genuine apprehension.

These, then, in broad outline, were the main categories Victorian critics would have thought of in hailing Tennyson, Browning, and others as writing an unprecedented poetry of dramatic-psychological kind. Reviewers speaking in such terms could hardly be unaware of introspective psychology, mesmerism, and psychological medicine, particularly since these were repeatedly discussed in the very journals for which they wrote. Victorian criticism in this respect was probably more encyclopedically informative and distinguished than ours. Strictly literary magazines were practically unknown, and in the major quarterlies and reviews a discussion of poetry was likely to find itself next to an article on geology or phrenology rather than beside further literary criticism. In the *London Review* of July 1835, for instance, J. S. Mill's "Tennyson's Poems" was followed by a review of Robert Macnish's *The Philosophy of Sleep*; in August 1814, the *Edinburgh Review* discussed Samuel Tuke's *Description of the Retreat* next to Byron's *Corsair* and *The Bride of Abydos*; in August 1817 the same journal featured a discussion of the reports of Parliamentary inquiry into madhouses during 1815–16 flanked by reviews of Byron's *Manfred* as well as of Hazlitt's *Characters of Shakespeare's Plays* and Coleridge's *Biographia Literaria*.

All this, of course, only raises some further, more complex issues to be explored in the next chapter. Was there a direct relationship between the new mental science and nineteenth-century "psychological" poetry as well as criticism? Did the critics borrow their concepts from the psychologists? Most importantly, there is the question as to whether the emergence of the dramatic monologue was linked directly to the rise of the diverse psychological disciplines.

III

The Psychological School of Poetry: Beginnings

IN STRICTLY chronological terms, mental science may well have influenced the emergence of the dramatic monologue during the 1830s and 1840s. With the possible exception of mesmerism, its major disciplines as practiced in England had begun to evolve long before that time. Most clearly profiled here, as we have seen, was traditional psychology. Dugald Stewart's three-volume *Elements of the Philosophy of the Human Mind* had appeared between 1792 and 1827, Thomas Brown's *Lectures on the Philosophy of the Human Mind* in 1820, and James Mill's *Analysis of the Phenomena of the Human Mind* in 1829. By comparison, British clinical psychiatry was not to produce a major theoretical work until Prichard published his *Treatise on Insanity* in 1835. But Thomas Arnold, in the 1806 reedition of his *Observations on . . . Insanity* (originally 1782–86) had already integrated some of the new concepts of Pinel, while Pinel's own *Traité médico-philosophique sur l'aliénation mentale* (1801) appeared in English translation in 1806. Years before Prichard dedicated his 1835 treatise to the "most distinguished writer of his age on the subjects" of insanity, Monsieur Esquirol, French psychiatry, then clearly the pioneer in the field, had also left its mark on works like G. M. Burrows's *Commentaries on . . . Insanity* (1828).

THE EVOLUTION OF THE NEW GENRE

Hence, mental science was well under way before Tennyson and Browning wrote their earliest dramatic monologues in the 1820s and 1830s. Tennyson here, at least in terms of composition, was the pioneer.[1]

Browning's *Pauline*, a late descendant of the greater Romantic lyric rather than his earliest attempt at a poetry "always dramatic in principle,"[2] was written during 1832–33 and published in 1833; his first two full-fledged dramatic monologues, "Porphyria's Lover" and "Johannes Agricola in Meditation," were probably composed during 1834 and printed in 1836. By contrast, Tennyson's experiments toward a dramatic-psychological kind of poetry go back to about 1825 when the sixteen-year-old poet discovered his penchant for exploring abnormal states of mind. "St. Lawrence," not unlike Browning's "Johannes Agricola," is a study in religious mania. Overconfident of his salvation, the speaker yearns for his martyrdom. Like many dramatic monologues that were to follow, "St. Lawrence" opens with a strong dramatic gesture evoking a clearly delineated setting:

> No portion of my soul misgives.
> Come, strip me: lay me on these bars.
> Too slow—too slow: my spirits yearn
> To float among the cold clear stars.
> I know that my Redeemer lives.
> I cannot argue—I can burn.

Though he never published the poem, Tennyson kept on revising and enlarging it for several years (ca. 1825–33). Meanwhile, he also explored the depressive counterpart to St. Lawrence's suicidal religious enthusiasm. "Remorse," printed in 1827, dramatizes an old man's religious despair in the face of an implacable Calvinistic god.

> And I was cursèd from my birth,
> A reptile made to creep on earth,
> An hopeless outcast, born to die
> A living death eternally!
> (19–22)

Like "Remorse" and "St. Lawrence," other of Tennyson's early experiments along similar lines dramatize diverse forms of religious obsession. "Supposed Confessions of a Second-Rate Sensitive Mind Not in Unity With Itself," for instance, explores another variant of religious despair, later called "folie du doute."[3] St. Simeon Stylites, like St. Lawrence, makes his demented bid for eternal life. In an 1831 version of "St. Lawrence," the speaker already visualizes God as plucking him forth from hell with his own arm. In "St. Simeon Stylites" such vision has turned into genuine hallucination:

> What's here? a shape, a shade,
> A flash of light. Is that the angel there
> That holds a crown? Come, blessèd brother, come.
> I know thy glittering face. I waited long;
> My brows are ready. What! deny it now?
> Nay, draw, draw, draw nigh. So I clutch it. Christ!
> 'Tis gone: 'tis here again; the crown! the crown!
> So now 'tis fitted on and grows to me,
> And from it melt the dews of Paradise
>
> (199–207)

But "St. Simeon Stylites," Tennyson's first full-fledged dramatic monologue, did not appear until 1842 when Browning had already published "Porphyria's Lover" and "Johannes Agricola." Even after 1842, the year of Browning's *Dramatic Lyrics* (with "My Last Duchess," "Count Gismond," "Soliloquy of the Spanish Cloister" et al.) and Tennyson's *Poems* (containing "Ulysses" and "St. Simeon Stylites"), the genre, for obvious reasons, evolved almost exclusively under the aegis of the younger poet.[4] Between then and his death, Browning published several dozen dramatic monologues appearing at regular intervals in collections like *Dramatic Romances and Lyrics* (1845), *Men and Women* (1855), and *Dramatis Personae* (1864). By contrast, Tennyson only brought out isolated specimens of the new genre, let several of them linger in manuscript,[5] and did not publish another group of such poems until *Ballads and Other Poems* of 1880. Even *Maud* (1855), though clearly of the dramatic-psychological kind, was too idiosyncratic in form to exert a major influence on the general evolution of the dramatic monologue proper.

The widespread ramifications of this genre will be surveyed in two later chapters.[6] Let it suffice to say at this point that, starting with the 1840s, it involved most of the major Victorian poets as well as a host of the age's *poetae minores*. Among these, the genre gained general currency shortly after 1855 when reviewers, in response to *Men and Women* and *Maud*, also began to develop the understanding and up-to-date terminology fitting these "portraits in mental photography."[7] Perhaps never before had English literary history witnessed a similar phenomenon: the creation of a radically new genre by the age's two major poets;

its rapid divulgation among at least thirty practitioners and imitators in the field; a reading market glutted with hundreds of such poems, often gathered in collections emulating those of Robert Browning; and a host of reviewers who, though puzzled at first, learned to describe the phenomenon in most of its ramifications and derivations.

CRITICS AND POETS VIS-À-VIS MENTAL SCIENTISTS

This brings us back to our initial question of how much of all this happened under the direct impact of the new science. Such direct indebtedness, though hard to establish in every case, was no doubt the rule among reviewers and critics. H. B. Forman, for instance, mentions his familiarity with the "definite and invaluable science of psychology" recently developed by "an array of really scientific psychologists," and nowhere "more vigorously forwarded than in England."[8] John Addington Symonds, when he spoke of Browning's way "of photographing subtle and obscure phases of mental activity and emotion in condensed and artistic pictures,"[9] was about to edit the miscellaneous writings of his father, physician Dr. Symonds, including a monograph on alienist J. C. Prichard, lectures on sleep and dreams, and an article on apparitions.[10] George Eliot, one of the first to describe Browning's monologues as a "dramatic-psychological" genre,[11] met John Conolly in person, was familiar with Harriet Martineau's experiments in mesmerism, was herself mesmerized by William B. Hodgson, and conducted an extensive correspondence with phrenologist George Combe.[12] W. J. Fox, when demanding a poetry of psychology in the wake of that new science, probably thought of works such as James Mill's *Analysis of the Phenomena of the Human Mind*, which *The Westminster Review* had discussed just a few months before it printed Fox's programmatic statement.[13]

Even general literary theory could be deeply affected in similar ways. Eneas Sweetland Dallas, by no means the greatest or most influential, but probably the most erudite and systematic among Victorian aestheticians, deplored, somewhat unnecessarily, his fellow critics' "ignorance," or "at least disregard of psychology."[14] By contrast, Dallas himself makes no secret of his debt to his teacher William Hamilton, to whom he dedicated his *Poetics: An Essay on Poetry* (1852), or to a physician like John Abercrombie, whose widely read *Inquiries Concerning the*

Intellectual Powers (1830) helped him fathom "Somnambulism and its Wonders" as well as "Memory and its Hidden Work."[15] Such indebtedness determines Dallas's understanding of art in all of its major aspects. Just as poetry, for instance, is created by "unconscious automatic action of the hidden soul," so its appeal, though filtered through consciousness, is to the same "unconscious part of us." The result is what one might call a mesmerist model of art.

> The poet's words, the artist's touches, are electric; and we feel those words, and the shock of those touches, going through us in a way we cannot define, but always giving us a thrill of pleasure, awakening distant associations, and filling us with the sense of a mental possession beyond that of which we are daily and hourly conscious . . . the essential quality of art may be expressed by the pantomime of snapping one's fingers, and by saying, " 'tis that."[16]

In sum, most reviewers and critics, in using psychological terminology regarding the dramatic monologue, seem to have drawn on mental science itself. This leads one to suspect a similar indebtedness on the part of Victorian poets, and in particular Tennyson and Browning. Did "Porphyria's Lover" and "St. Simeon Stylites," or the earliest dramatic monologues generally, owe their existence to the influence of the new science? As we have seen, almost all the pioneer specimens of this genre deal with abnormal mental states of one kind or another. From the perspective of contemporary alienism, St. Lawrence, St. Simeon Stylites, Johannes Agricola, and the speaker of "Remorse" all suffer from some form of total or incipient religious insanity, while Porphyria's murderer is an example par excellence of the morally insane. But did Tennyson and Browning write these poems in awareness of such categories? At least in the case of Tennyson, there is evidence that the poet, from early on, must have been familiar with a good deal of them.

To begin with, there was certainly plenty of psychiatric literature about religious insanity, hallucinations, and spectral apparitions for anyone who cared to read it. Most widely discussed here were spectral apparitions of the kind experienced by St. Simeon Stylites. Such books as John Ferriar's *An Essay Towards a Theory of Apparitions* (1813), Samuel Hibbert's *Sketches of the Philosophy of Apparitions* (1824), and Sir Walter Scott's *Letters on Demonology and Witchcraft* (1830) not only enjoyed wide readership, but were discussed in journals like the *Quarterly* and *Westminster Review*.[17]

Ferriar here was the first to attempt an entirely physio-pathological explanation of supernatural apparitions. "A morbid disposition of the brain," to him, was "capable of producing spectral impressions, without any external prototypes," and "exclusive of actual insanity . . . even while [the patient] is convinced of their fallacy."[18] Sir Humphrey Davy's experiments with nitrous oxide and the widely discussed spectral illusions of Berlin bookseller C. F. Nicolai provided the impetus for further speculations along similar lines. Samuel Hibbert, disciple of Thomas Brown, drew upon these sources in producing "the first comprehensive study of the psychological dynamics of hallucinations and delusions."[19] In his view, apparitions were mere *"waking dreams"* and "nothing more than ideas or the recollected images of the mind, which have been rendered more vivid than actual impressions."[20] John Abercrombie's *Inquiries* added a further dimension to this "physico-pneumatology."[21] Following its lead, this science, according to the *Quarterly Review* of 1831, must enlarge its approach by looking for "new facts and new principles . . . in the phenomena of dreaming, of somnambulism."[22] Artificially induced somnambulism or mesmerism was soon to open another avenue for exploring the supernatural.

Abercrombie also broadened the general understanding of hallucination, which Esquirol, in 1817, had defined in a way that remains valid to date. To the French psychiatrist, a person "is said to labor under a hallucination, or to be a visionary, who has a thorough conviction of the perception of a sensation, when no external object, suited to excite this sensation, has impressed the senses."[23] To Abercrombie, such experiences are traceable to the hallucinant's general propensities, previous associations, and habitual daydreams. Nothing could have been of greater interest to someone like Tennyson, who was to explore similar tracks in "St. Simeon Stylites" and other poems. The poet certainly shared Abercrombie's fascination with "tracing the origin of the particular chain of ideas which arise in individual cases of insanity; and likewise the manner in which similar impressions are modified in different cases, either by circumstances in the natural disposition of the individual, or by the state of his bodily functions at the time."[24]

Another main concern of early mental science shared by the young poet was religious insanity. Long before Amariah Brigham, in 1835, stirred up controversy with his three-volume monograph on the subject,[25] others like Burrows, Pinel, and Crichton had dealt with this subject in their various treatises of insanity. Their case histories, like

Tennyson's religious maniacs, fall into two basic categories. In Alexander Crichton's terms, one is characterized by "a deep melancholy," the other by "a very strong desire of eternal happiness."[26] Crichton also explains the paradox, dramatized in Tennyson's "Remorse" and "St. Lawrence," that both the religious melancholiac and enthusiast have a common propensity for suicide.

> The first is, unfortunately, a very common case in this country, especially among the lower orders of Methodists. The pain which accompanies this melancholy becomes insupportable; a state of despair follows, and the desire of relief which arises as a natural consequence, leads to the completion of the crime. . . . In the other case, there is no despair, the person has an anxious longing for a happiness which he believes he is destined to enjoy as soon as he departs from this world; he cannot brook the delay, and therefore yields to the urgency of the internal impulse.[27]

Moreover, Crichton gives several instances of how such frenzy, particularly of the enthusiastic kind like St. Lawrence's and St. Simeon Stylites's, can give rise to spectral hallucinations.

But there are further reasons for assuming that Tennyson read some of this psychological literature. The most obvious one was concern with his family's and his own mental states. If ever a poet had reason to worry about his sanity it was Tennyson. Epilepsy, then thought of as insanity, afflicted several of his relatives and most notably his father.[28] One of his brothers was institutionalized for most of his life, a second suffered from some form of insanity nearly as incapacitating, a third was an opium addict, a fourth an alcoholic, and the remainder of the family each seems to have gone through at least one major breakdown. Especially during the poet's most formative years preceding and following Arthur Hallam's death in 1833, one disaster of this kind followed another.

Alfred's father, who in 1824 had suffered a serious mental and physical breakdown, died in 1831. By 1832, his brother Edward was complaining, amid tears, that "his mind [was] so unnotched he [was] scarcely able to endure his existence."[29] At the end of that year, Edward was committed to the York asylum where he was to stay until his death. Only some fourteen months later, another of Alfred's brothers, Septimus, seemed about to follow Edward's example. Their grandfather thought it best to keep him at home for two or three months longer, but Alfred protested. Given the family's feuds and psychodramas, Septimus might still be saved precisely by "getting him out into some bustling active line of life *remote from the scene of his early connexions.*" "I have studied the minds of my own family," he wrote his uncle Charles in January 1834:

> I know how delicately they are organized—and how much might be done in this instance by suddenly removing Septimus from all those objects and subjects with which he has been familiar and upon which he has been accustomed to brood, into some situation where he might be enabled to form his own friendships with those of his own age and to feel that there is something to live and to care for—but this, if done should be done immediately, because every hour which he wastes at home tends to increase his malady. At present his symptoms are not unlike those with which poor Edward's unhappy derangement began—he is subject to fits of the most gloomy despondency accompanied with tears—or rather, he spends whole days in this manner, complaining that he is neglected by all his relations, and blindly resigning himself to every morbid influence.[30]

It seems unlikely that Tennyson, in analyzing his family's mental dilemmas, would have ignored the much publicized psychological medicine. His personal neuroses, whether true or imagined, must have further sharpened his interests in that direction. By July 1829, for instance, he was "much distressed by a determination of blood to the Head" affecting his eyes with "muscae volitantes," and had himself cupped by a famous oculist.[31] A year later we find him on his way to London to consult an eminent physician on what he felt might be a matter of life or death.[32] By January 1832, Alfred's "extreme nervous irritation" and "morbidly intense . . . inward contemplation" had Arthur Hallam worried to the point of dispensing the kind of advice Alfred later gave on behalf of his brother Septimus. "Nothing should be left undone that may wean him from overanxious thought. It is most melancholy that he should have so completely cut himself off from those light mental pleasures, which . . . make a man less unhappy, by making him more sociable."[33] Needless to say, these mental crises only became worse following Arthur Hallam's death.

Throughout his life, the poet also displayed considerable expertise in diagnosing his mental symptoms. Among these were the "waking trances," experienced since boyhood, when his individuality, due to the very intensity of his introspective habits, "seemed to dissolve and fade away into boundless being."[34] Also since his youth, there had been "moods of misery unutterable." As he told his son, such misery could prompt semi-hallucinatory vision. "He remembered how, when in London almost for the first time, one of these moods came over him, as he realized that 'in a few years all its inhabitants would be lying horizontal, stark and stiff in their coffins!' "[35] Since all records of the poet's health during his most critical years have disappeared, we do not know the extent to which such symptoms developed in the direction of insanity.[36] All we know is that Tennyson, during the late 1830s, established contact with Dr. M. Allen, pioneer advocate of voluntary seclusion practiced at a nearby lunatic asylum in High Beech.[37] As Spedding wrote in August 1840, Alfred had been "on a visit to a madhouse for the last fortnight . . . and has been delighted with the mad people, whom he reports the most agreeable and the most reasonable persons he has met with."[38] Tennyson, as his friend insists, did not go as a patient; but subsequent visits, as a recent biography suggests,[39] may have been of a different nature.

Be that as it may, contacts with Dr. Allen precipitated perhaps the worst crisis in the poet's life.[40] The doctor's woodcarving scheme, in which Tennyson had invested his entire fortune, went bankrupt, leaving the poet in a state of financial disaster and mental despair. More than ever before, Tennyson needed and actively looked for help. After his break with Dr. Allen, another stay at the High Beech asylum was out of the question, so the poet opted for one of the then fashionable hydropathic establishments instead. Treatment by water cure was thought to be beneficial for a variety of diseases, both physical and mental, and when Dr. Allen's pioneer method of voluntary seclusion for the mentally disturbed was outlawed in 1845, hydropathic establishments naturally attracted the kind of patients who previously would have sought refuge at High Beech. Tennyson is known to have been a patient at various water-cure clinics for a period of several years. "It is a terribly long process," the poet groaned during the late 1840s, "but then what price is too high for health, and health of mind is so involved with health of body."[41]

In sum, we have every reason to assume that Tennyson, then and earlier, must have familiarized himself, however eclectically, with some of the new mental science. Would he not at least glance at studies such as Matthew Allen's *Essay on the Classification of the Insane*? Even when in his teens, such books did not escape his hypochondriac obsessions. As Tennyson admitted later, "I used from having early read in my father's library a great number of medical books to fancy that I had all the diseases in the world, like a medical student."[42]

But what applies to Tennyson does not necessarily apply to Browning. It is true that the younger poet wrote a poem called "Mesmerism," and, in mostly skeptical fashion, discussed the issue with his future wife.[43] But there is little evidence, especially during the 1830s, of his familiarity with any of the major works of introspective psychology and psychological medicine. Naturally, one is tempted to assume that the latter prompted Browning to draw his portrait of moral insanity in "Porphyria's Lover"; however, we have no proof to that effect. Like Tennyson, the young Browning was a voracious reader in his father's library, but he lacked the family background of ubiquitous psychodrama and insanity that channeled the older poet's hypochondriac interests in that direction.

We know that Browning in writing "Porphyria's Lover" made use of two other sources instead. One of these was Bryan Procter's narrative poem "Marcian Colonna," the other—known to be by John Wilson and in turn a source for Procter—was the alleged death-cell confession of a madman condemned for murdering his wife, which *Blackwood's* for August 1818 printed under the title "Extracts from Gosschen's Diary."[44] Neither Procter's nor Wilson's piece directly mentions or discusses "moral insanity," and even Wilson's supposedly homicidal maniac speaks in remarkably poetic, sometimes Byronic terms. But here as in "Porphyria's Lover," a murderer glories in his crime and justifies it with great show of pseudo-logic and persuasiveness.

"Who else loved her so well as to shed her innocent blood? It was I that enjoyed her beauty—a beauty surpassing that of the daughters of men,—it was I that filled her soul with bliss, and with trouble,—it was I alone that was privileged to take her life. . . . Do you think there was no pleasure in murdering her? I grasped her by that radiant, that golden hair,—I bared those snow-white breasts,—I dragged her sweet body towards me, and, as God is my witness, I stabbed, and stabbed her . . . I laid her down upon a bank of flowers,—that were soon stained with her blood. I saw the dim blue eyes beneath the half-closed lids,—that face so changeful in its living beauty was now fixed as ice, and the balmy breath came from her sweet sweet lips no more. My joy, my happiness, was perfect."[45]

Did Browning learn about "moral insanity" from his friend Procter, one of the Metropolitan Commissioners of Lunacy from 1832? A recent critic, after examining these and related questions in detail, concludes that "definite evidence of Browning's contact with current work on lunacy is lacking."[46] In subsequent years the poet repeatedly stressed that his interests were psychological and that little else was worth study.[47] In *Dramatic Lyrics*, he reprinted "Porphyria's Lover" and "Johannes Agricola" under the common title "Madhouse Cells." Critics kept on telling him that he was primarily a psychologist and the founder of an unprecedented psychological school of poetry in the wake of psychology as such. In spite of all this, Browning seems to have paid little or no attention to that science.

THE AGE OF INTROSPECTION

Browning's case, with its apparent lack of direct contact between mental science and the new dramatic-psychological poetry, suggests a common source from which this poetic genre as well as early psychiatry emerged in more or less separate streams. Broadly speaking, this shared source can be described as the "invention of the self" (to use the title of a recent study)[48] preceding Romanticism. It is true that "a form of self-consciousness which implies a simultaneous awareness of experience and the experiencing self" can be traced back as far as to Shakespeare and Montaigne.[49] But at the general level at which it determined modern man's view of himself, this introspective, individualized, and particular sense of the ego did not evolve until the eighteenth century. It is adumbrated in Locke's *Essay Concerning Human Understanding* (1690) and, in the sense of a radical skepticism, finds its first major articulation in David Hume's *Treatise of Human Nature*. Where Descartes, through his *cogito ergo sum*, had salvaged the substantiality of the ego as a guarantor of both God and Reality, Hume, in searching his bosom, could find no coherent principle of this kind. The self was "nothing but a bundle or collection of different perceptions, which succeed each other with an inconceivable rapidity."[50]

British empirical psychology stems largely from such preoccupations; the new discipline could emerge only once the essentialist notions of the ego were replaced by what is truly observable in self-consciousness. Hence, its founding father Thomas Reid claimed no other merit "than that of having given great attention to the operations of his own mind," and, while trying to refute Hume, acknowledged him as his main source of inspiration.[51] The origins of psychiatry are more complex, but even here indebtedness to the same source is manifest at every turn.[52] Pinel, for instance, pays homage to Locke as to few others.[53] Crichton, in applying insights gathered in self-analysis to the study of lunatics, invokes "our British Psychologists, such as Locke, Hartley, Reid, Priestley, Stewart, and Kaims," as his main "fountain head."[54] Even later alienists like Alfred Maury in France, as we have seen, refer back to the same source.[55]

By the time Crichton and Pinel wrote their treatises of insanity, self-analysis, of course, had long ceased to be limited to the thoughtful and sensitive few. Like nothing else, perhaps, it was the all-consuming passion of the age. Poets, therefore, would not have had to consult with psychologists nor psychologists with poets about what their obsession told them so clearly. The whole question of influence, in this way, largely resolves itself in either parallel concerns or complex mutualities. Victorian critics tended to emphasize how much the new psychological poetry was, or ought to be, indebted to the new mental science. But demonstrable instances of the reverse—poets preceding or even influencing the psychologists—are equally numerous.

One example, which also demonstrates how psychiatry, as it evolved into a separate discipline, was indebted to previous philosophy, is found in Alexander Crichton—one of the most influential British alienists before Prichard. Crichton's *Inquiry into the Nature and Origin of Mental Derangement* appeared in 1798, which was three years before the *Traité médico-philosophique sur l'aliénation mentale* by Pinel. Nonetheless, the Frenchman is considered as the founder of clinical psychiatry and Crichton is not. But this is hardly because Crichton drew upon a wide range of philosophical and even poetic sources. Here Pinel, in fact, is as much a borrower as Crichton, and largely from comparable or identical sources. Both of them, as we saw, invoke Locke, and where Pinel draws on Rousseau,[56] Crichton borrows from Rousseau's German counterpart Karl Philipp Moritz.[57] What vitiated Crichton's achievement was not his indebtedness to such sources, but his lack, as pointed out by Pinel himself,[58] of firsthand clinical experience.

Nonetheless, Crichton's basic approach has remained valid right into the age of Freud. Prophetically, he called it "Analysis." Though the concept stems from Reid, its specific techniques of self-objectification and a return to childhood seem to derive from Karl Philipp Moritz, editor of "the world's first psychiatric journal."[59] Anyone practicing analysis of the insane, writes Crichton, ought to "be able to go back to childhood." Furthermore, "he should not only be capable of abstracting his own mind from himself, and placing it before him, as it were, so as to examine it with the freedom, and with the impartiality of a natural historian; but he also should be able to take a calm and clear view of every cause which tends to affect the healthy operations of mind, and to trace their effects."[60] Or as Moritz had stated in his programmatic proposal of a magazine about empirical psychology, it is imperative that anyone engaged in such pursuit, "would have to start with himself; first he ought to map as faithfully as possible the history of his heart from earliest childhood; pay attention to the memories from the earliest years of childhood, and deem nothing unimportant which at any point made a particularly strong impression upon him, with the result that the memory of it still intrudes upon his other thoughts."[61]

Not surprisingly, it was Moritz, neurotic poet turned lay psychologist,[62] who gave final shape to Crichton's treatise, which had been six years in the writing. Like Crichton after him, Moritz stresses that introspection must be taken to the point where the self will become a mere object of observation—"as if I were a stranger whose fortunes and misfortunes I listened to with coldblooded attentiveness."[63] Did Moritz in turn borrow these notions from others? Whether he did or not, his own obsessions and those of his age must have led his anguished soul in the same direction. For good reason, the author of *Werther* saw Moritz as his "younger brother" and as a person of his own kind. The difference was that Goethe had been "favored and advanced" by the same fate that "abandoned and damaged" Moritz.[64]

In sum, much of what informed the new psychological poetry stems from an obsession with self-scrutiny, which in turn was a major impulse behind the rise of mental science. The introspective rage was everywhere, and the results caused increasing anguish. Most people rejected Hume's radical skepticism, but in pursuit of the traditional "true self" encountered precisely what he had said they would, a mere "bundle or collection of different perceptions . . . in perpetual flux and movement."[65] More often than not, their search for an essentialist self turned into a wild goose chase after the ever-elusive "Stranger within" (E. Young),[66] with, on the one hand, the threat of mental disintegration—the dissolving and fading away of self-consciousness "into boundless being" as experienced by Tennyson[67]—and on the other Dr. Jekyll's fear of Mr. Hyde, or what since Bleuler we call the schizophrenic splitting of personality. Two examples may illustrate this growing rift between essentialist claims and actual experience.

If ever a poet had a "self-watching subtilizing mind" and knew the "unfathomable hell within," it was Coleridge.[68] Soon after its early, psychedelic phase had passed, his opium addiction again and again would make him totter "on the verge of madness" in experiencing a "dreadful falling abroad, as it were, of [his] whole frame."[69] Perhaps for these very reasons, Coleridge clung to the belief in an essentialist self with somehow unquestioning desperation. To him, it was "the ground of all our certainty," for in "this, and in this alone, object and subject, being and knowing, are identical."[70] But as "Dejection" suggests, such theoretical insistence barely hides the kind of uncertainty dramatized in the poem. The same paradox is found in Arthur Hallam. To him, as to Coleridge, the substantiality of the ego was "the foundation of all reasoning."[71] At the same time, he admits to moments when he had "felt it miserable to exist, as it were, piece-meal, and in the continual flux of a stream." The splitting of self, which Tennyson's friend observed in the act of memory, was similarly disconcerting. "To know a thing as past," we read in his essay "On Sympathy," "is a source of mingled emotions. There is pleasure, in so far as it is a revelation of self; but there is pain, in so far that it is a divided self, a being at once our own, and not our own."[72]

Most Victorians—both poets and alienists—eventually had to acknowledge that introspection, if taken to its limits, ends in an either farcical or tragic dead end. "When once the mind of man is turned inwards, to the infinite, which he can neither grasp nor comprehend," argued Maury, "he no longer perceives anything except his own sensations; he gazes as if in a magnifying mirror, which returns to him his own image."[73] What is more, introspection might also lead to madness. Such at least was the suspicion of Henry Holland, physician to Queen Victoria and Prince Albert. Generally speaking, "any strong and continuous effort of will to concentrate the mind upon its own workings; to analyse them by consciousness; or even to fix, check, or suddenly change the trains of thought," in his view, "is generally followed by speedy and painful confusion."[74] Hence, it seemed probable to Holland, "that certain cases of madness" depend on a "too frequent and earnest direction of the mind inwards upon itself;—the concentration of the consciousness too long continued upon its own functions."[75] Or as Carlyle put it more simply: "Gazing inward on one's own self,— why, this can drive one mad."[76]

Was there a way out of this impasse? As critic W. L. Courtney put it in 1883, "the only possible corrective to the excessive self-contemplation of the modern poet is the dramatic effort to render objective and concrete human passion and human weakness."[77] To be sure, when Courtney prescribed the remedy, Tennyson, Browning, and others had long since found the cure.[78] And so had the psychologists. To most of them, self-analysis as a stepping stone toward analyzing others, as explicitly demanded by Moritz and Crichton, was the tacit *conditio sine qua non* of the new science. Without it, so Charles Bucknill told the Association of Medical Officers of Asylums and Hospitals for the Insane in his presidential address, the treatment of the insane would be impractical. "No one can understand the insane, or exercise guiding and health-giving moral influence upon them, who cannot and does not, so to say, throw his mind into theirs, and sympathize with their state so far as to make it, at least during brief periods, almost subjectively his own . . . the true mental physician transfers for the moment the mind of his patient into himself in order that, in return, he may give back some portion of his own healthful mode of thought to the sufferer."[79]

In a way, Tennyson and Browning did little else when they threw themselves into the minds of St. Simeon Stylites or Porphyria's lover; as did Shakespeare when, in dramatizing Macbeth's hallucinations, he transferred for the moment the mind of his character into his own. In fact, Bucknill himself explained such feats, as observable in, say, *King Lear* or *Maud* as an "act of mental transmigration . . . combining the knowledge of others with the knowledge of self."[80] W. J. Fox attributed similar powers to the young Tennyson. This poet, so he wrote in 1831, "has the secret of the transmigration of the soul. He can cast his own spirit into any living thing, real or imaginary."[81] Later critics, as already noted, would find similar powers of empathic self-projection in Browning. In Arthur D. Innes's view, the "range of Browning's sympathies—his power of entering into, understanding, accounting for, the most diverse characters—has rarely, if ever, been surpassed."[82] However, neither Browning nor Tennyson was born with such powers of introspection turned empathic impersonation of others. How they acquired them was a process of false starts, errors, and, above all, painful self-exploration. The story of these events, as traceable in Browning's *Pauline* and several of Tennyson's early poems, will illustrate in more detail how the dramatic monologue and Victorian psychological poetry generally arose from processes that might have been reinforced by mental science, as in Tennyson's case, but that, as Browning's case shows, were not dependent on such reinforcement. Although mental science and psychological poetry shared some of the same sources, they largely drew on them in independent fashion.

IV

The Psychological School
of Poetry: Origins

BROADLY SPEAKING, the personal crises that helped bring forth the dramatic monologue were the crises of an age that, partly from the same impulse, created its unprecedented mental science. The major instances of such personal dilemmas are well known.[1] In 1826, J. S. Mill suffered through a crisis "in {his} mental history." His autobiography describes it as one of "dejection" and characteristically quotes Coleridge's famous ode to that effect—"A grief without a pang, void, dark and drear."[2] Meanwhile, Carlyle was traversing his own interior hell. Soon the two men were to meet, but not before they had worked out similar solutions to their problem—Mill in an "anti-self-consciousness" theory of life and in the cultivation of inner feelings,[3] Carlyle in an "Annihilation of Self" and a movement toward a "Spiritual New-birth."[4]

Not surprisingly, Wordsworth served Mill as a Dantean guide through this internal hell. Had not the poet gone through a similar inferno himself? Such at least was Wordsworth's claim in the Preface to *The Excursion* of 1814. Here he revealed the "*Prospectus* of the design and scope" of his never to be completed magnum opus, *The Recluse*, of which *The Excursion* was only a part. A yet unpublished autobiographical "Prelude" to the whole work would review "his own mind, and examine how far Nature and Education had qualified him for" writing this philosophical poem "containing views on Man, Nature, and Society."[5] Wordsworth leaves no doubt as to the arduousness of this task:

> For I must tread on shadowy ground, must sink
> Deep—and, aloft ascending breathe in worlds

63

To which the heaven of heavens is but a veil.
. . . . Not Chaos, not
The darkest pit of lowest Erebus,
Nor aught of blinder vacancy, scooped out
By help of dreams—can breed such fear and awe
As fall upon us often when we look
Into our Minds, into the Mind of Man—
My haunt, and the main region of my song.[6]

ROBERT BROWNING

Browning, whether influenced by Wordsworth or not, pursued similar plans in his first poem. He later explained that *Pauline* was to be the semiautobiographical introduction to a larger work, this first part being spoken by "the *Poet* of the batch, who would have been more legitimately *myself* than most of the others."[7] The speaker himself, in dedicating his "lay" (870) to Pauline, explains his purpose in similarly Wordsworthian terms. Wordsworth's self-appointed task of reviewing his own mind before embarking upon the greater task of writing about life in general is precisely what Pauline enjoined upon him by making him write the poem bearing her name. As she explained to him, "a perfect bard," before he will be able to shadow out "the stages of all life" (883, 884),[8] must first review his own:

> Look on this lay I dedicate to thee,
> Which thro' thee I began, and which I end,
>
> . . . .
>
> Thou know'st, dear friend, I could not think all calm,
> For wild dreams followed me, and bore me off,
> And all was indistinct. Ere one was caught
> Another glanced: so dazzled by my wealth,
> Knowing not which to leave nor which to choose,
> For all my thoughts so floated, nought was fixed—
> And then thou said'st a perfect bard was one
> Who shadowed out the stages of all life,
> And so thou badest me tell this my first stage:—
> 'Tis done: and even now I feel all dim the shift
>   Of thought.
>   (870–71, 877–87)

It is certainly correct to claim that *Pauline*, in this way, is at once Browning's *Sartor Resartus* and his *Prelude*.[9] Yet chronologically speaking it might be truer to say that *Sartor Resartus* and *The Prelude* were their respective author's *Pauline*. The novel, though written during 1830–31,[10] was not published before 1833–34. *The Prelude* did not appear until 1850. Even Mill's account of the crisis "in [his] mental history" was not publicized before 1873. *Pauline*, as published in 1833, then, is the first work of its kind among these others. Though hardly a major poem, it is a pioneer document of the kind of spiritual crisis that pinpoints the turning point between Romantic and Victorian. As such, it also bears witness to the struggle Browning went through in making his naturally introspective bias serve him in analyzing the emotions and problems of others. Like few other works, in other words, it documents the transition from Romantic poetry to the dramatic monologue.

It is in this respect also that *Pauline* differs from *Sartor Resartus, The Prelude*, and Mill's *Autobiography*. In each of these, the crisis is envisaged from the vantage point of one who has lived through it and overcome it; even Coleridge in "Dejection," though unable to arrive at such a solution, looks at this lack as a *fait accompli* from a distance. *Pauline*, by contrast, is not only without resolution, but also mirrors this lack in its form. What T. S. Eliot said of *Hamlet* is truer perhaps of this poem: Browning, in writing it, "tackled a problem which proved too much for him."[11] This problem was still unresolved when, in later years, he tried to camouflage this "ambiguous, feverish" and "altogether foolish"[12] poem by either revising it or making it appear as something it ostensibly was not—his "earliest attempt at 'poetry always dramatic in principle, and so many utterances of so many imaginary persons, not [his]!' "[13]

More recent attempts to read patterns or resolutions into the poem simply continue Browning's Procrustean labors. M. Hancher, in discussing *Pauline* as a dramatic monologue spoken, not by "the young and impassioned Robert Browning, twenty years old, but rather [by] a thoroughly exhausted imaginary gentleman of a certain age," has to admit to considerable evidence to the contrary.[14] Would such a disillusioned old gentleman conclude his "lay" with a final eulogy to Shelley, the "Sun-treader" (1020) and to their shared belief "in God, and truth, / And love" (1020–21)? In turn, how does this conclusion agree with the "pattern of acceptance of reality" that Masao Miyoshi detects in the poem? "Once cured of his colossal egotism," writes Miyoshi, "the poet

is also able to purge himself of what he had once regarded as the 'intens-
est life' (268), that 'most clear idea of consciousness / Of self' " (269–
70). At long last he is able to resolve the poem:

> "I'll look within no more—
> I have too trusted to my own wild wants—
> Too trusted to myself—to intuition"[15]
>
> (937–39)

The speaker, at this point, vows to pursue a cure to his problem,
which, reminiscent of Mill and Carlyle, will reject self-consciousness.[16]
But he returns to self-scrutiny in the end and even manages to reaffirm
some of the concomitant Romantic ideals of beauty, god, truth, and
love in this pursuit. Aided by Pauline, he plans to explore "the un-
shaped images which lie / Within [his] mind's cave"—with the exception of everything relating to his "past doubts" (969–71). Yet despite
this afterthought, he is quite prepared to break his vow to "look within
no more" (937) in trying to reconquer his former "idea of consciousness
/ Of self" (269–70). And once again Shelley becomes his guide:

> Sun-treader, I believe in God, and truth,
> And love; and as one just escaped from death
> Would bind himself in bands of friends to feel
> He lives indeed—so, I would lean on thee.
>
> (1020–23)

In retrospect, this seesaw motion is evident throughout the poem.
Losing its early "mastery of mind" (86), his soul sinks into the "dim
orb" (91) of solipsistic self-worship, "and now / Must stay where it
alone can be adored" (94–95). But Shelley's influence temporarily
transforms solipsism into creativity. The dim orb of self, as if by magic,
turns into "a most clear idea of consciousness / Of self. . . . Existing as
a centre to all things, / Most potent to create, and rule, and call / Upon
all things to minister to it" (269–70, 274–76). Yet soon there is another crisis, with his soul losing itself in self-division (cf. 347–48), only
to be restored again to be able to sing in Shelleyan monologic fashion
(cf. 375ff.). Once again, creativity seems to well from a solipsistic, but
at the same time all-encompassing self: "I first thought on myself—and
here my powers / Burst out" (397–98).

From this and the study of Plato, the speaker suddenly turns to the
opposite extreme, planning "to look on real life, / Which was all new

to me" (441–42), and in the process dismisses most of his previous
Romantic ideals—his "hopes of perfecting mankind," freedom, virtue,
and finally human love (458f.). Hence we are not surprised to find that,
after these and other turnabouts, he should reembrace all these ideals
toward the conclusion. There is no reason why his words, which he had
already contradicted several times, should suddenly convince us just
because they occur here at the end. On the contrary, we trust them as
little as the assertion that all his self-scrutiny taught him "to look
within no more" (937). Again, we have heard him avow and disavow
the same claim before. "Yet I can take a secret pride in calling / The
dark past up—to quell it regally" (289–90), he protests earlier. But
soon thereafter he fears for his sanity in recalling the past (cf. 429).
"Plus ça change, plus c'est la même chose." More than elsewhere, then,
we trust the speaker when he talks about his "struggling aims" (811)
or about versifying his unresolved state of mind as it oscillates between
contradictions.

> I have no confidence,
> So I will sing on—fast as fancies come
> Rudely—the verse being as the mood it paints.
> (257–59)

Such irresolution is one more of the many aspects in which Pauline's
friend can be shown to reflect the concerns of Robert Browning himself.
On the one hand, he is convinced that poetry, as if by magic, will
spring from the self as "centre to all things" (274). On the other, he
denies these idealist claims and decides to "look on real life" (441) instead. It seems that Browning, for several decades, felt unsure as to
which of these two alternatives he should embrace. Was he to be an
"objective poet" of traditional persuasion or a "subjective poet of modern classification?"[17] The one, so he wrote in 1852, reproduces "things
external (whether the phenomena of the scenic universe, or the manifested action of the human heart and brain)"; the other embodies "the
things he perceives, not so much with reference to the many below as
to . . . the supreme Intelligence which apprehends all things in their
absolute truth."[18] At least until the mid-1840s, a long time after writing some of his most famous dramatic monologues, Browning continued to view himself, at least potentially, as a subjective poet. Like Pauline's friend in one of his better moods, he was to "shadow out the
stages of all life" (884), not by dealing "with the combination of hu-

manity in action, but with the primal elements of humanity"; he was
to dig "where he stands,—preferring to seek them in his own soul as
the nearest reflex of that absolute Mind, according to the intuitions of
which he desires to perceive and speak."[19] In other words, he was to
write "what I hope I was born to begin and end—'R. B. a poem' "[20]

Indicative of such hopes was the manner in which he misquotes
J. S. Mill's famous comment that the writer of *Pauline* was "possessed
with a more intense and morbid self-consciousness than [he] ever knew
in any sane human being." What he remembered by 1845 was that Mill
had never known a sane human being with a "deeper" self-consciousness.[21] In this spirit, Browning even seems to have started to work on
his "R. B. a poem." His "faculty of self-consciousness . . . at which
John Mill wondered" had no doubt improved since the writing of *Pauline*, he reported to his future wife—"and, meaning, on the whole, to
be a Poet, if not *the* Poet . . . [*sic*] for I am vain and ambitious some
nights,—I do myself justice, and dare call things by their names to
myself . . . beginning, however tremblingly, in spite of conviction, to
write in this style *for myself*."[22] Elizabeth Barrett fully encouraged
Browning in such endeavors. Aware that for years he had been struggling to become a dramatic poet, she wished him "to take the other
crown besides—and after having made your own creatures speak in clear
human voices, to speak . . . out of that personality which God made,
and with the voice which He tuned into such power and sweetness of
speech."[23]

At the time of *Pauline* there was yet another mentor who encouraged
the poet in the same pursuit. W. J. Fox, whom Browning called his
"literary father,"[24] greeted the poem with the programmatic claim that
the "annals of a poet's mind are poetry." The poem, he wrote, "in which
a great poet should reveal the whole of himself to mankind would be a
study, a delight, and a power, for which there is yet no parallel; and
around which the noblest creations of the noblest writers would range
themselves as subsidiary luminaries."[25] Though hardly the major poem
invoked here, *Pauline* is an attempt in the direction of a poet's exemplary self-analysis as pointed out by Fox. Again and again we hear the
speaker describe his "state as though 'twere none of" his (586); or see
him strip bare his soul in trying to unveil its inner "centre to all things"
(260ff.) from which poetry is to well as if from its own accord. There
are good reasons, however, why Browning came to see *Pauline* as "altogether foolish," "ambiguous," and "feverish."[26] As the poem makes

all too clear, he could hardly be pleased with what self-scrutiny had
revealed to him. For the most part, there is nothing but a "sleepless
brood / Of fancies" (6–7), solipsism (90ff.), "restlessness" (278), "selfishness" (601), sophistry (682f.), fear of madness (429), and, worse, a
semimurderous impulse toward his beloved, as the poet soon was to
analyze more objectively in "Porphyria's Lover." Here is the little fantasy in which the speaker assures himself of Pauline's everlasting affection toward him:

> How the blood lies upon her cheek, all spread
> As thinned by kisses; only in her lips
> It wells and pulses like a living thing,
> And her neck looks, like marble misted o'er
> With love-breath, a dear thing to kiss and love,
> Standing beneath me—looking out to me,
> As I might kill her and be loved for it.
>
> (896–902)

How possibly could the poet have continued to reveal his innermost
impulses in this vein? It was one thing to write an ode on one's "dejection," but quite another to compose a whole *Prelude* in similar mood.
Neither Browning nor the Victorian public was ready for such a verse
epic (à la Sartre's *Nausea*) chronicling a poet's mental disintegration in
the pursuit of the Romantic ideal. The author's misgivings to that effect must have arisen during the very process of writing *Pauline*. The
speaker who only seconds earlier described his lay in solemn Wordsworthian tones suddenly finds that he might come to "despise / This
verse" (991–92). Pauline's note to line 811 about the speaker's "struggling aims" talks in similarly dismissive terms of her "pauvre ami" and
of his sentiments as nothing but "dream and confusion." It suggests
that Browning probably thought of revising the poem—"attempting
better to co-ordinate certain parts"—even while composing it. But
such an attempt, in Pauline's view, would only have detracted from its
main achievement of pointing toward the genre "which has merely been
sketched."

The note only hints at the nature of this genre. In terms of what the
speaker intends it to be, his "lay," in Pauline's view, has neither "conception" nor "execution." In other words, it fails to live up to its self-
proclaimed Wordsworthian goal of surveying the poet's mental growth
before he embarks upon his actual task of shadowing forth all life. What

remains, then, is the delineation of certain psychological phenomena in the absence of any purposive goal-oriented development. In this respect, Browning's self-criticism in Pauline's note is in accord with J. S. Mill's unpublished review, which calls the speaker's "psychological history of himself . . . powerful and truthful."[27] Similarly, Pauline likes "this stirring of the passions which increases at first and then is gradually allayed—these impulses of the soul, this sudden return upon himself, and above all the altogether exceptional cast of mind of my friend." What indeed do we have here other than a description of the new dramatic-psychological genre that *Pauline* points to, however obscurely. But being without proper conception and execution, or lacking, in other words, an objectified persona whose psychological problems are presented in comprehensive, case-history like fashion, it remains a mere foreshadowing of this kind of poetry.

On one level, then, Browning's endeavors to make the poem appear as his first "attempt at 'poetry always dramatic in principle,' "[28] are sheer make-believe. Yet on another they suggest why it was relatively easy for him to proceed from *Pauline* to the writing of poems like "Porphyria's Lover."[29] An even more striking transition of similar kind is obvious in Tennyson's early poetry. Broadly speaking, Browning adapted the strategies of introspection developed in *Pauline* to the analysis of objective personae in his dramatic monologues. With Tennyson, such adaptation is, in at least two cases, mere integration. As evident in *Maud*, poems originally written in a strictly subjective vein are made part of the utterance of a dramatic persona.

To be sure, there are differences as well. Browning, at least in wishful thinking, was a late Romantic. His description of the "subjective poet of modern classification" is one of the most radical statements of its kind in English critical theory. "Not what man sees," he wrote in his essay on Shelley, "but what God sees—the *Ideas* of Plato, seeds of creation lying burningly on the Divine Hand—it is toward these that he struggles."[30] Yet what he calls "modern" in 1852 had long since become obsolete. Even the Spasmodics, who carried such notions into the mid-Victorian era,[31] were soon to succumb to obsolescence and ridicule. Particularly outdated was Browning's sense of the self as "centre of all things" (*Pauline*, 274) and semidivine source of creativity. "The subjective poet, whose study has been himself," we read in the essay, "appeal[s] through himself to the absolute Divine mind, [and hence] prefers to dwell upon those external scenic appearances which strike out most abundantly and uninterruptedly his inner light and power."[32] One could hardly describe the Romantic notion of the poet's self as it unites itself with the divine through nature more succinctly.

By 1852, Browning was about the only major poet or thinker left to believe in such possibilities. A seven-part "Introduction to the Philosophy of Consciousness," which *Blackwood's* printed during 1838–39,[33] pinpoints some of the major changes that area of thought underwent in the transition from the Romantic to the Victorian age. To the anonymous author, known to have been James Frederick Ferrier,[34] the fusion of subject with object has nothing to do with consciousness. Rather, it is a sign of infantile nonconsciousness. "Heaven lies about us in our infancy" (he quotes)[35]—but by no means in the Wordsworthian spirit of wanting to emulate that state.

> Let thyself float back, oh reader! as far as thou canst in obscure memory into thy golden days of infancy. . . . In those days thy light was single and without reflection. Thou wert one with nature, and, blending with her bosom, thou didst drink in inspiration from her thousand breasts. Thy consciousness was faint in the extreme; for as yet thou hadst but slightly awakened *to thyself* . . . Carry thyself back still farther, into days yet more "dark with excess of light," and thou shalt behold, through the visionary mist, an earlier time, when thy consciousness was altogether null—a time when the discrimination of thy sensations into *subject* and *object* . . . had not taken place, but when thyself and nature were enveloped and fused together in a glowing and indiscriminate synthesis. In these days, thy state was indeed blessed, but it was the blessedness of bondage.[36]

Coleridge had written that "We proceed from the self, in order to lose and find all self in GOD."[37] But to Ferrier, the very notion of the human mind as capable of encompassing the Divine Mind is a mere fairy tale invented by metaphysicians, those "blind leaders of the blind." More generally speaking, there is no such thing as an essentialist self. Self-consciousness is what can empirically be known of it, and such knowledge tells us that it evolves during childhood and that it is an "act of negation." It is man's way, not of embracing nature, but of saying "no" to it. "In order to become 'I' it must sunder *itself* from other things by *its own* act," which is its willful declaration of independence from natural bondage. "Our own word 'know' . . . clearly betokens this—it is nothing but 'no,' and knowledge, from lowest to highest, is merely the constant alleging 'no' of things, or, in other words, a continual process of denying them, first of ourselves, and then of one another."[38]

ALFRED TENNYSON

These are radical ideas, which somehow sound more Existentialist than Victorian. Nonetheless, there was little here that might shock a poet like Tennyson. At least one of his later poems echoes the spirit of the "Introduction to the Philosophy of Consciousness" to the point of suggesting direct influence. Young infants, in speaking of themselves in the third person, show "that they have not yet acquired the notion of their own personality," argues the *Blackwood's* author. "But now mark the moment when the child pronounces the word 'I,' and knows what this expression means. . . . Let no one regard this step as insignificant. . . . The origination of this little monosyllable lifts man out of the natural into the moral universe. It places him, indeed, upon a perilous pre-eminence, being the assertion of nothing less than his own absolute independence."[39] Poem 45 of *In Memoriam* develops this notion of the self as a gradually evolving act of negation even further. It points toward Pater's sense of how such negation turns into isolation, with "each mind keeping as a solitary prisoner its own dream of a world."[40]

> The baby new to earth and sky,
>   What time his tender palm is prest
>   Against the circle of the breast,
> Has never thought that "this is I":
> But as he grows he gathers much,
>   And learns the use of "I," and "me,"
>   And finds "I am not what I see,
> And other than the things I touch."
> So rounds he to a separate mind
>   From whence clear memory may begin,
>   As through the frame that binds him in
> His isolation grows defined.
>   (1–12)

But though he may have seen the *Blackwood's* treatise, Tennyson, by 1838, was hardly in need of being taught this new "philosophy of consciousness." The later part of "The Two Voices," which covers most of the same issues, was probably completed just before Ferrier's study appeared in print.[41] Of special interest here is an unpublished notebook passage in which a Cartesian last-ditch stand in defense of "individual unity" becomes the speaker's final argument against suicide after everything else has been called in question. Here as elsewhere, the beliefs of the speaker are easily floored by the Voice or by his own doubts. If "individual unity" were "self-inorbed and perfect," then "it should be always clear":

> Yet step by step it grows, for can
> The retrospection of the man
> Remember when the child began?

The speaker suddenly seems to agree, adding that he ceases to keep his consciousness when he falls asleep or into a swoon. In both cases, "it dips and darkens as the moon / And comes again."[42]

His subsequent advocacy of metempsychosis, through which the self might enjoy a continuity independent of individual memory, simply enumerates further instances of the same phenomenon. One of these is characterized by temporary spells of insanity blotting out the patient's sense of identity (cf. 370–72), which Tennyson may have learned through either studying the minds of his mentally deranged family members or through reading one of the major treatises on insanity. The other is the phenomenon of "double consciousness," which John Abercrombie, among others, describes in his widely read *Inquiries Concerning the Intellectual Powers* (1830) as a form of somnambulism. "It consists," he writes, "in the individual recollecting, during a paroxysm, circumstances which occurred in a former attack, though there was no remembrance of them during the interval."[43] Of the several illustrations Abercrombie gathers from previous studies by Dyce, Combe, and Prichard, here is that of a maid whose "double consciousness" began with "fits of somnolency, which came upon her suddenly during the day":

> She soon began to talk a great deal during the attacks, regarding things which seemed to be passing before her as a dream. . . . In her subsequent paroxysms she began to understand what was said to her, and to answer with a considerable degree of consistency, though the answers were generally to a certain degree influenced by her hallucinations. She also became capable of following her

usual employments during the paroxysm; at one time she laid out the table correctly for breakfast, and repeatedly dressed herself and the children of the family, her eyes remaining shut the whole time. The remarkable circumstance was now discovered, that, during the paroxysm, she had a distinct recollection of what took place in former paroxysms, though she had no remembrance of it during the interval.[44]

Tennyson may have been thinking of a case such as this in making his speaker in "The Two Voices" refer to "trances" in which men

> Forget the dream that happens then,
> Until they fall in trance again.
>
> (353–54)

Or perhaps he drew on personal experience even here. Trance-like states, involving hallucinatory symptoms, though probably not entailing double consciousness in the strict sense of Abercrombie's definition, were a familiar feature of the poet's life. We have already referred to his youthful "moods of misery unutterable" of which we have another account in Tennyson's own words:

I remember once in London the realization coming over me, of the *whole* of its inhabitants lying horizontal a hundred years hence. The smallness & emptiness of life sometimes overwhelmed me. I used to experience sensations of a state almost impossible to describe in words; it was not exactly a trance but the world seemed dead around and myself only alive. It might have been the state described by St. Paul "Whether in the body I cannot tell; or whether out of the body I cannot tell." It sometimes came upon me after repeating my name to myself; through excess of realizing my own personality I seemed to get outside of myself.[45]

Such experiences and his general psychiatric knowledge probably account for Tennyson's impatience, even in early years, with the self-aggrandizement of the subjective poet of modern classification. "The Idealist['s]" presumption of creating everything out of himself becomes an easy target of ridicule in the poem of that title. Even where the matter is treated more seriously, Romantic vision quickly degenerates into hallucination. This happens in his prize-winning "Timbuctoo" of 1829. Charles Wordsworth no doubt had a point in suggesting that this poem, which created a sensation at Cambridge, would have met with a different reception elsewhere. "If such an exercise had been sent up at Oxford," he wrote his brother Christopher, "the author would have had a better chance of being rusticated, with the view of his passing a few months at a Lunatic Asylum, than of obtaining the prize."[46]

Characteristically, "Timbuctoo" strongly tones down the speaker's self-aggrandizement in the earlier "Armageddon" from which it borrows more than half of its 240-odd lines. Changed or dropped altogether here was the speaker's claim to have found in himself a godlike center to all things.

> I felt my soul grow godlike, and my spirit
> With supernatural excitation bound
> Within me, and my mental eye grew large
> With such a vast circumference of thought,
> That, in my vanity, I seemed to stand
> Upon the outward verge and bound alone
> Of God's omniscience. Each failing sense,
> As with a momentary flash of light,
> Grew thrillingly distinct and keen. . . .
>   I wondered with deep wonder at myself:
> My mind seemed winged with knowledge and the strength
> Of holy musings and immense Ideas,
> Even to Infinitude. All sense of Time
> And Being and Place was swallowed up and lost
> Within a victory of boundless thought.
> I was a part of the Unchangeable,
> A scintillation of Eternal Mind,
> Remixed and burning with its parent fire.
> Yea! in that hour I could have fallen down
> Before my own strong soul and worshipped it.

This we read in "Armageddon" (II, 21–29, 40–50). "Timbuctoo" (88–96), while eliminating the entire second passage, retains the psychological detail relating to the speaker's "supernatural excitation"—a concept dear to early mental science—but avoids describing this state in the terms of divine omniscience as found in the earlier work. Even in this most Romantic of Tennyson's poems published during his lifetime, vision is a primarily psychological phenomenon.

In other words, vision as a Romantic dream of ideational absolutes—

"what God sees—the *Ideas* of Plato, seeds of creation lying burningly on the Divine Hand"[47]—has turned into spectral vision as analyzed by contemporary mental science. As such it forms a major focus in Tennyson's early poetry. How the poet learned to deal with it by gradually turning subjective experience into objective analysis is a crucial part of how he evolved his peculiar mode of dramatic-psychological poetry. We have already seen him dramatize the hallucinations of "St. Simeon Stylites." Even more importantly perhaps, spectral vision is central to the two lyrics that, like two powerhouses in miniature, led him to write his two greatest works. "Hark! the dogs howl!" completed in late 1833, contained, according to Hallam Tennyson, "the germ of *In Memoriam*"; "Oh! that 'twere possible," composed during 1833–34, formed, according to the poet himself, the germ of *Maud*.[48]

Other of his later works give evidence of a fascination with the same phenomenon. In 1851, for instance, Tennyson added several lines to the opening of Canto One of *The Princess* (originally published in 1847), allowing the Prince to explain what his court physician diagnoses as fits of catalepsy and himself as hereditary attacks of spectral vision:

> And, truly, waking dreams were, more or less,
> An old and strange affection of the house.
> Myself too had weird seizures, Heaven knows what:
> On a sudden in the midst of men and day,
> And while I walked and talked as heretofore,
> I seemed to move among a world of ghosts,
> And feel myself the shadow of a dream.
> (I, 12–18)[49]

Tennyson, characteristically, objectified the experience in each of these poems dealing with hallucinatory vision; the exception confirming the rule is "Hark! the dogs howl!" which remained unpublished during his lifetime.

Spectral vision thus bearing the probable imprint of personal experience first occurs in *The Lover's Tale*, I–III, as written in the poet's nineteenth year. Its poet-lover protagonist, like his successor in "Oh! that 'twere possible," has several such visions after losing his beloved. In one of these he sees the "lordly Phantasms" (II, 98) of a funeral procession with the bier of his dead love; in a second, prompted by the painting of a ship in midocean, he visualizes a drowning involving both himself and the woman (cf. II, 163ff.); a third, prophetic of things to come, revives his former hallucination of the funeral procession with the dead woman suddenly coming back to life, only to leave him stand "sole beside the vacant bier" (III, 58). Characteristically, the speaker repeatedly tries to explain these visions to himself. Grief and obsession, as he suggests, transmogrify pathetic fallacy or the emotions, which Romantics project upon reality, into its pathological counterpart:

> Always the inaudible invisible thought,
> Artificer and subject, lord and slave,
> Shaped by the audible and visible,
> Moulded the audible and visible;
> All crispèd sounds of wave and leaf and wind,
> Flattered the fancy of my fading brain.
> (II, 101–106)

An instance of such Rorschach test-like spectral vision involving the "cloud-pavilioned element" (II, 107) recurs in the lines that, jotted down shortly after Arthur Hallam's death, became the germ of *In Memoriam*.

> The vapour labours up the sky,
> Uncertain forms are darkly moved,
> Larger than human passes by
> The shadow of the man I loved.
> ("Hark! the dogs howl! " 18–21)

The verses, as we know, were left to linger in manuscript, and where *In Memoriam* deals with comparable experiences, the traces of ghostly vision were carefully eliminated. In the famous line "And mine in his was wound" (XCV, 37)—suggesting how the poet's soul, when in a solitary trance while rereading Hallam's letters, fused with that of the deceased—the word "his" was later changed to "this."[50]

The Lover's Tale, although Parts One and Two had already been type-set for the 1832 volume, almost suffered the fate of "Hark! the dogs howl!" Tennyson, at the last minute, withdrew the poem from the press, arguing that it was "too full of faults."[51] But the deeper reason for this withdrawal was probably that *The Lover's Tale*, as a recent critic points out, was too "intimately related to his inner life."[52] What finally, in 1869, allowed Tennyson to publish the poem, was an approved means of literary camouflage similar to that which Browning, though less successfully, had earlier attempted regarding *Pauline*. A fourth section, *The Golden Supper*, in which a friend concludes the protagonist's tale, was added to the already existing ones. What otherwise might have been read as a largely autobiographical effusion is attributed to a clearly delineated persona described as "crazed, / Though not with such a craziness as needs / A cell and keeper" (IV, 162–64).

To be sure, even such camouflaging did not turn *The Lover's Tale* into a dramatic monologue. In common with this genre, the poem displays a deep concern with "memory's vision" (I, 35) as revitalized in an act of speech addressed to an audience—techniques that were further explored in "The Miller's Daughter" and "The Gardener's Daughter." But like these, *The Lover's Tale* is essentially a first-person narrative. The narrator, instead of describing his hallucinations while they happen to him, tells us what he remembers about them. In contrast, "Oh! that 'twere possible" actually dramatizes such experience.

The history of this poem, before it found its place in *Maud*, is complicated, to say the least.[53] But a few of the major facts that concern us here stand out clearly enough. One is that spectral vision of a deceased beloved is the poem's central focus from the beginning. The speaker sees a shadow flit before him—"Not thou, but like to thee"—and spends half the night yearning for the deceased. Finally, half in dreams, he hears her laugh and sing, only to find, upon awakening, "By the curtains of [his] bed / That dreadful phantom cold." There is no escape from it even by rushing out into "the hubbub of the market":

> It crosseth here, it crosseth there
> Thro all that crowd, confused & loud,
> The shadow, still the same.

This is what we find in the earliest version, an "incomplete fragment" of 1833, written under the immediate impact of Hallam's death.

The second version considerably expands upon the speaker's hallucinatory experiences while adding an important dramatic element. The apparition, a "sunk eye" flitting and fleeting before him, leads the bereaved lover "forth at evening / And lightly winds & steals, / In a cold white robe before" him. But his attitude toward it is no longer passive. Finding that it glares at him when he awakens from his dreams, as in the earliest version, he now, Macbeth-like, bids it depart.

> Get thee hence—nor come again
> Mixing Memory with Doubt

> Pass thou deathlike type of pain
> Pass, & cease to move about
> 'Tis the blot upon the brain
> That will shew itself without

Despite Spedding's praise of these and other additions to the "incomplete fragment," Tennyson felt no inclination to publish the poem. When finally urged to do so, he had "infinite bother" trying to get it into shape by substantially adding to the second version. The half-demented mourner, who originally ends in despair, regains his reason as he visualizes the beneficent counterpart of the "dreadful phantom cold." This is his beloved's "phantom fair and good" who is up in the sky waiting to reunite herself with him.

Apparently this 1837 version was created and published with reluctance, and it was not included in either *Poems* (1842) or *In Memoriam* (1850) as it might have been. Hence one wonders if Tennyson feared that the poem might expose too much of his personal secrets or if, as he claimed in hindsight, it had always been intended as "part of a dramatic poem" that he had never been able to carry out.[54] Whatever the answer, he finally disguised what, as in *The Lover's Tale*, might be read autobiographically as the words of a clearly delineated persona. In the poet's words, Sir John Simeon "begged him to weave a story round" "Oh! that 'twere possible"; in Aubrey De Vere's account, Sir John suggested that in order "to render the poem fully intelligible, a preceding one was necessary. He wrote it; the second poem too required a predecessor: and thus the whole poem was written, as it were, *backwards*."[55]

What is ostensibly wrong in De Vere's account is the phrase "He wrote it." For the poem that was to set "Oh! that 'twere possible" in a dramatic context had already been written. "See what a lovely shell," which also dates back to the 1830s, had never been published before, and it is easy to imagine why. Like its companion piece, it focuses upon the speaker's spectral visions, and in doing so bears an even more obvious imprint of personal experience. Tennyson may well have been reminded of his youthful complaint of *muscae volitantes*, caused by "a determination of blood to the Head,"[56] when he dug up the following lines around 1854.

> Plagued with a flitting to and fro,
> A disease, a hard mechanic ghost
> That never came from on high

> Nor ever arose from below,
> But only moves with the moving eye,
> Flying along the land and the main—
>
> . . . .
>
> Am I to be overawed
> By what I cannot but know
> Is a juggle born of the brain
> (*Maud*, II, 81–86, 88–90)

R. J. Mann, as if to remind the poet of this physical disorder, pointed out in 1856 that the ghost, as described here, "is evidently an internal image—a work of his own mind, for, *musca volitans*-like, '*it moves with the moving eye.*' "[57]

Quite in tune with such autobiographical elements is the form of the poem. Like a belated specimen of the greater Romantic lyric, it starts as a rhetorically dramatized reverie occasioned by a natural object. Only about halfway through the poem are speaker and reader suddenly jolted out of this contemplative mood. While praising the shell as "a work divine" (71) able to withstand cataract seas, which cause shipwreck to mighty vessels on the Breton strand, the protagonist suddenly has more disturbing thoughts invade his consciousness. A double association reminds him of his dark Byronic destiny. He is a shipwrecked exile from his home country ("Breton, not Briton," 78) where he killed another man and left behind his beloved who now haunts him as "a hard mechanic ghost" (82). Unlike a dramatic monologue, the poem makes no attempt to fill out this dimly sketched background. However, it prefigures the genre in delineating a stream-of-consciousness process of unprecedented complexity in English poetry.

One wonders why someone so obviously guilt-ridden and deranged as the speaker should focus on something so seemingly unrelated to his immediate obsessions as a little shell. What explains his fascination with this "objet trouvé"? The question is raised and answered by the speaker in a process of gradual self-realization. What attracted him to the shell was the unconscious memory of a ring on the hand of Maud's brother, which at the time he thought to be the hair of the dying man's mother:

> Strange, that the mind, when fraught
> With a passion so intense
> One would think that it well

Might drown all life in the eye,—
That it should, by being so overwrought,
Suddenly strike on a sharper sense
For a shell, or a flower, little things
Which else would have been past by!
And now I remember, I,
When he lay dying there,
I noticed one of his many rings
(For he had many, poor worm) and
thought
It is his mother's hair.
(*Maud*, II, 106–18)

FROM INTROSPECTION TO
PSYCHO-ANALYSIS

In sum, the genesis of the dramatic monologue involves a basic process common to the rise of both this poetic genre and to much of the new mental science. In this parallel development, poets and psychologists alike made use of the insights gained through introspection for the systematic analysis of others. The difference between Browning's *Pauline* and his first dramatic monologues illustrates this transition. In the earlier poem, he attempted a *Prelude*-type survey of his mind, but with unexpected results. Instead of a creative center of all things, the poet found little else but self-division, solipsism, and confusion. Nonetheless, Browning continued to want to write like a subjective poet in search of the ideational absolutes to be revealed in himself. The result, had he finished his projected "R. B. a poem,"[58] might well have been a versified *La nausée* about the Victorian collapse of the Romantic ideal.

But given Browning's temperament, one such document of self-disgust must have been more than he could stomach. Almost immediately *Pauline* struck him as a painful embarrassment, while the age's major thrust toward analyzing human minds in both health and insanity suggested an obvious way out of this personal dilemma. Why not portray in others some of the problems introspection had revealed in oneself? Always paranoid about his privacy, Browning, in this, insisted that his poems were strictly utterances of so many imaginary persons. But few were convinced by such protests. Even when writing dramatic monologues, some Victorian critics argued, he retained much of the subjective poet. As a result, the new genre, in their view, constituted a "rare union of subjective reflectiveness with objective life and vigour,"[59] quite different, for instance, from Shakespeare's soliloquies.

Tennyson, too, set out by exploring the demiurgical pretensions of the self-enthused Romantic vates, but with immediately negative results. Even in the unpublished "Armageddon" the speaker's claim that his soul grew godlike in visionary ecstasy is called his "vanity" (II, 25). Apparently Tennyson's own experience along these lines quickly led him into the paths explored by contemporary mental science, rather than into questionable regions of Eternal Mind. What was the true, that is to say, empirically verifiable nature of self-consciousness with regard to trance, dreaming, poetic vision, and spectral hallucination? The answers suggested by Tennyson's early poetry are strikingly similar to those proposed by contemporary psychologists. Self-consciousness to Tennyson was not a royal road to the divine, as it was to the subjective poet of Browning's classification. Rather, it isolated the individual from the world it denied. It gradually evolved during childhood and could at any point be disrupted by dreams, trances, double consciousness, and real madness. Vision, both poetic and otherwise, to the young Tennyson, was a state allied to hallucination rather than to the revelation of abstract ideational absolutes.

One wonders why the poet chose to embody such experience in others, rather than speak of it *in propria persona*. T. S. Eliot's afterthought to his claim that poetry is neither a turning loose of emotion nor an expression of personality, but an escape from both, suggests a possible answer. Of course, only those, writes Eliot, "who have personality and emotions know what it means to want to escape from these things."[60] No doubt, there was every motivation for such escape in Tennyson's life. Not only did the poet have "personality and emotions," but he also had ample firsthand experience of how the problems incidental to both can be deepened by mental derangement.

Secondly, there was the Victorian public, avid for news from the borderlands of the mind, but equally anxious that such matters be excluded from its standards of normalcy. Despite the alienists' protests to the contrary, the frightening increase in institutionalization for insanity was to a large extent the result of these rather rigid standards. Given these circumstances, a poet as worried about his mental health as Tennyson had little scope to write poems about his transexperiences. Tennyson nonetheless did, and it accounts for the strength of the impulse that two of the products became the germs of his perhaps two greatest works. But in one case, the poem remained unpublished, in the other, subjective experience, or what could be read as such, was fictionalized as the self-revelation of a dramatis persona. Unquestionably, the poet had reason for such suppression or camouflage. Victorians were far from ready for a poetry of surrealist self-revelation, though they were spellbound by the new science, which subjected such matters to unprecedented methods of analysis. Hence it seems natural that a poet so obviously concerned with his sanity should oblige both himself and his readers by objectifying a personal obsession and thus create a model for the analysis of others. Nor is it surprising to find that alienists, who often came to their new vocation from similar compulsion, eventually discovered Tennyson and Browning as poetic fellow workers in the same endeavor of evolving an unprecedented science of the human mind.

Having traced the Victorian school of psychological poetry to its beginnings and origins in the tension-ridden lives and works of early Tennyson and Browning, our backwards search for its full genealogy will now explore two primary areas of literary precedence. One of these is the Romantic "science of feelings," the school's immediate and often inseparable forebear in both poetry and poetic theorizing. The other is Elizabethan drama and Shakespeare, whose works, as seen through their increasingly psycho-analytic discussions by eighteenth- and nineteenth-century critics, exerted a more indirect, but no less forceful influence on the emergence of the dramatic monologue.

V

Precedents I: The Romantic
"Science of Feelings"

A "SCIENCE OF FEELINGS": what could this notion possibly have to do with Romantic poetry? The very phrase, especially when quoted in full, involves a paradox. "For the Reader," writes Wordsworth, "cannot be too often reminded that Poetry is passion: it is the history or science of feelings."[1] One wonders how poetry can be passion and at the same time a science of such emotion. It is one thing to demand that the poet express himself spontaneously and sincerely; but it is quite another to require that he simultaneously analyze his feelings. The two requests involve a contradiction that is central to Romantic poetry, particularly as it prefigured the dramatic monologue.

The greater Romantic lyric, rightly considered the direct precedent of the new genre, offers an obvious instance. Wordsworth in, say, "Tintern Abbey," may speak *as if* under the direct impression of the scene he describes. But such "spontaneous overflow of powerful feelings" no doubt was tempered by the process of composition. The legend surrounding the poem is that Wordsworth composed it orally during a journey of several days with his sister, Dorothy, who wrote it down for him immediately upon their return from the abbey to Bristol. By Wordsworth's account, it was included at the last moment, virtually unrevised, in the *Lyrical Ballads* (1798), already in Cottle's press.[2] But this does not imply that an extensive process of revision had not taken place in Wordsworth's mind. Whether or not the legend is fact, Wordsworth's practice of composing orally was probably as self-conscious, as painstaking and controlled as that of the poet who, pen in hand, struggles to recapture in solitude an emotionally charged scene or event. It obeyed the rhetorical habits of simulated spontaneity rather than the thought dictation prompted by a specific event. Its spontaneity is a carefully crafted pretense.

SELF-ANALYSIS VERSUS SPONTANEITY

To its earliest advocates, the notion of poetry as a kind of mental science, as it emerged alongside introspective philosophy, presented no particular contradictions. Typical here is Richard Hurd who simply subsumes it under the Aristotelian concept of mimesis. His "Discourse Concerning Poetical Imitation" (1751), in this way, has been rightly said to reflect the "pervasive neoclassical tastes" of the age.[3] But by comparing Hurd's essay with Aristotle's treatise, we notice a major difference. To Aristotle, the main subject matter of mimesis is external. To Hurd, it is primarily psychological. Of course, there is the "material world, or that vast compages of corporeal forms, of which this universe is compounded." But Hurd's real interests lie elsewhere. In addition to the external world, there are two further realms of poetic imitation, both of which are psychological.

> 2. The internal workings and movements of his [i.e., the poet's] own mind, under which I comprehend the manners, sentiments, and passions.
> 3. Those internal operations, that are made objective to sense by the outward signs of gesture, attitude, or action.[4]

For all his neoclassicism, Hurd also reflects the general new psychological concerns of his age. Though no doubt influenced by Hobbes, Locke, and Hume, the critic, in fact, presages the single-mindedly introspective bias of a Thomas Reid whose *Inquiry into the Human Mind* was not published until thirteen years after Hurd's "Discourse." To Hurd, the only access toward a proper portrayal of both the inner world of man in general as well as of the "manners" and "sentiments, which mark and distinguish *characters*," is introspection: "the poet . . . in addressing himself to this province of his art, hath only to consult with his own conscious reflexion. Whatever be the situation of the persons, whom he would make known to us, let him but take counsel of his own heart, and it will very faithfully suggest the fittest and most natural expressions of their character."[5] Hurd's poet, then, anticipates Coleridge's Shakespeare who created his dramatis personae by simply imitating "certain parts of his own character."[6] It is true, Hurd argues, that only the passions actually experienced by the poet, will be truly familiar to him. "But he finds in himself the seeds of all others. . . . Every man, as he can make himself the *subject* of all passions, so he becomes, in a manner, the *aggregate* of all *characters*. . . . In sum, *to catch the manners living, as they rise,* I mean, from our own internal frame and constitution, is the sole way of writing naturally and justly of human life."[7]

Hurd's poet, after a cursory glance at the outside world, approaches these inner realms with the eagerness of a pioneer explorer out to fathom the yet undiscovered other half of the cosmos. He knows that his mission is unique, for only poetry is capable of illumining this essentially invisible world. Painting, for instance, "can express the *material universe*" or, through certain marks and symbols, suggest "the internal movements of the soul." However, "it is poetry alone, which delineates the mind itself, and opens the recesses of the heart to us."[8]

In sum, poetry, to meet the new demands for psychological exploration, simply had to expand its traditional mimetic spectrum. Or so at least it seemed to Richard Hurd and other mid-eighteenth-century critics like Robert Lowth. To the latter, the biblical poetry of the Hebrews was often like a mirror reflecting the turbulent inner life of its poets. "Frequently, instead of disguising the secret feelings of the author, it lays them quite open to public view; and the veil being, as it were, suddenly removed, all the affections and emotions of the soul, its sudden impulses, its hasty sallies and irregularities, are conspicuously displayed."[9]

This notion of poetry as a self-reflective science of feelings became problematic only when it entered its uneasy alliance with the demand that the poet express his inner life in a totally spontaneous manner. On the one hand, the poet was to provide "the effusion of a glowing fancy and an impassioned heart" (W. Duff),[10] or to speak "from the abundance of his heart" and "prompted by his feelings" (H. Blair);[11] on the other hand, he was to make his poetry mimetically scientific. But critics soon realized that one demand excluded the other. At best there was an irreconcilable alternative. If poetry was to be automatic thought dictation, it could never be a science of feelings, though its effusions might well serve as raw materials toward one. If the poet portrayed his inner life in scientifically objective manner, he could never be completely spontaneous.

It is easy to see, at least from our post-surrealist perspective, how eighteenth- and nineteenth-century critics understood only part of this dilemma. Although realizing the incompatibility between spontaneous effusiveness and scientifically mimetic thought portrayal, they never fathomed the full implications of a poetry written as automatic thought dictation, which they tended to advocate. Probably the first to spell out this contradiction was Sir William Jones in his 1772 essay "On the Arts Commonly Called Imitative." Like Richard Hurd, Jones concedes that poetry often imitates "the manners of men and several objects in nature." But this, to him, is only its secondary purpose. Poetry's "greatest effect is not produced by imitation, but by a very different principle, which must be sought for in the deepest recesses of the human mind."[12]

What is this principle? Jones wants the poet not just to explore the mind, but to do so in completely spontaneous fashion. Essentially, then, poetry consists of "a strong and animated expression of the human passions," which is found to be incompatible with the concept of mimesis.[13] Hence Robert Lowth, for one, was wrong in arguing that the Hebrew poets imitated their deepest emotions. "The lamentation of David and his sacred odes or psalms, the song of Solomon, the prophecies of Isaiah, Jeremiah, and the other inspired writers, are truly and strictly poetical; but what did David or Solomon imitate in their divine poems? A man who is really joyful or afflicted cannot be said to imitate joy or affliction."[14]

Ironically, Aristotle's *Poetics* was the main text to disseminate this antimimetic concept during the Romantic and Victorian age. In his 1789 edition of the treatise, which remained the standard one for a century, Thomas Twining resumes some of the issues broached by Jones. Like Jones, he rules that a poetry of genuine self-expression can not be called mimetic. But he also introduces new distinctions, though with only the result of further compounding the issues. Like most of his contemporaries, Twining holds that poetry, even in its mimetic function, should imitate not just external reality but "the emotions, passions, and other internal movements and operations of the mind."[15] While noting different kinds of mimesis—through sounds, description, fiction, and dramatic representation—he even allows for a special kind of "personative" poetry, which, though essentially dramatic, can also be found in other genres. "In dramatic and all personative poetry, then, . . . the conditions of what is properly denominated imitation are fulfilled." When, then, does poetry cease to be mimetic?[16]

For Twining, the issue is one of distinguishing between direct authorial and indirect personative utterance. Or as the critic puts it: "Whenever the poet speaks in his own person and at the same time does not either feign or make 'the sound an echo of the sense' or stay to impress his ideas upon the fancy with some degree of that force and distinctness which we call description, he cannot, in any sense that I am aware of, be said to imitate."[17] But the validity of such a distinction remains questionable. For ontologically speaking, the speaker of a poem, even when voicing the poet's innermost feelings, can never be identified with the author. As a Victorian critic was to say, no one, however hard he may try, "can fully reveal himself without resorting to some oblique, objective, or dramatic mode of expression."[18]

UNCONSCIOUS CREATIVITY AND ITS LIMITS

But the more radical their demands for a complete spontaneity of poetic utterance, the less patience critics showed with pondering such problems. This is most obvious among the advocates of a divinely inspired or, as the new psychological jargon had it, "unconscious" type of creativity. To Edward Young, for instance, the ancient "fable of poetic Inspiration," *aliquo afflatu Divino*, describes how the true poet is overcome by unconscious forces, which use him as a mere medium. "Few authors of distinction," he writes, "but have experienced something of this nature, at the first beamings of their yet unsuspected Genius on their hitherto dark Composition: The writer starts at it . . . is much surprised; can scarce believe it true."[19]

Like other eighteenth-century critics, Young primarily wants to see poetry as a tool for exploring the human mind along the lines he thought to have been initiated by Francis Bacon. Since Bacon, much had been discovered, but more of the wonders of man's inner world, which Young, like later psychologists, compares with those of the outer universe, remains unfathomed. Young echoes Hurd in hailing introspection as the only access to these undiscovered Indies of the human mind, but there is one major difference. In Hurd, the self, once revealed through introspection, is to be subjected to mimetic analysis. In Young it is left to unfold its mysteries according to its autonomous dynamics. "Therefore dive deep into thy bosom," Young writes,

> learn the depth, extent, bias, and full fort of thy mind; . . . excite, and cherish every spark of Intellectual light and heat, how-

ever smothered under former negligence, or scattered through the dull, dark mass of common thoughts; and collecting them into a body, let thy Genius rise (if a Genius thou hast) as the sun from Chaos; and if I should then say, like an *Indian, worship it*, (though too bold) yet should I say little more than my second rule enjoins, (*viz.*) *Reverence thyself.*[20]

Paradoxically, all these discussions suggest, yet fail to consider, the diverse possibilities of how the poet could tap these unconscious powers as well as capture them in his writing. For instance, he might passively await the afflatus of unconscious inspiration, yet always be ready with pen and paper at hand; or he might try to remember the promptings of his inner voice and postpone recording them to some later point. Neither the German Romantics who, like Sulzer, Schelling, and Richter, were the most fervent advocates of unconscious creativity, nor their belated English followers, ever broached these more practical issues. In 1826, William Hazlitt raised the question "Whether Genius is Conscious of Its Powers" concluding that, on the contrary, it acts unconsciously "without premeditation or effort . . . from the natural bent and disposition of the mind."[21] Hardly more specific was Carlyle who, a year later, informed his countrymen of an unprecedented school of German criticism, which, purporting to interpret "between the inspired and the uninspired," showed how true poetry springs "from the general elements of all Thought, and grows up therefrom, into form and expansion by its own growth."[22] Carlyle's own poetics, as further developed in "Characteristics," fuses several notions borrowed from German theoreticians. From Richter, for instance, he took the idea of the unconscious as a "bottomless boundless Deep" stretching "down fearfully to the regions of Death and Night";[23] from Fichte the notion of how poets, in drawing their inspiration from such depths, become "the appointed interpreters" of the "Divine Idea" pervading the visible universe.[24] Like Browning's subjective poet of modern classification, this Carlylean hero-vates, who redefines the Divine for each period, creates from "that mysterious Self-impulse of the whole man, heaven-inspired, and in all senses partaking of the Infinite."[25]

Even E. S. Dallas, who never tires of telling us that unconsciousness is "the last and highest law of poetry,"[26] says next to nothing about the practical aspects of such creativity. Again and again we are reminded that "the automatic or unconscious action of the mind" springs from "the hidden soul," the mind's "double," the "demi-semi-consciousness of a treasure trove which is not in the consciousness proper."[27] Dallas is equally voluble in praising "hidden" thought and in detailing some of its treasures as evident in the "same fables, the same comparisons, the same jests . . . produced and reproduced . . . in successive ages and in different countries."[28] But as much as all this points forward to Carl Jung and the surrealists, as little does it anticipate their investigative practices. Dallas lists the familiar instances of involuntary, somnambulistic, and psychedelic creativity probably gathered from books like John Abercrombie's *Inquiries*: Mozart wrote music because he could not help it; Tartini composed his Devil's Sonata in a dream, and Coleridge his "Kubla Khan" while asleep after taking laudanum.[29] But otherwise there is little, either in Dallas or in his numerous Romantic forebears, to tell us how unconscious creativity is to be practiced. Hence we are not surprised to find how negatively critics responded to genuinely spontaneous or automatic creativity.

His *Milton*, Blake said in 1803, was written "from immediate Dictation, twelve or sometimes twenty or thirty lines at a time, without Premeditation and even against my Will."[30] But to most mid-Victorians, Blake, after all, was the rightly forgotten painter-poet maniac who claimed to write "when commanded by the spirits"[31] as portrayed in Cunningham's *Lives of the Painters*![32] Even Dante Gabriel Rossetti, one of the first to reevaluate Blake, felt that such practices ought to be relegated to the "limbo of the modern 'spiritualist' muse."[33] There was similar reaction when Coleridge, probably apprehensive of hostile criticism, published "Kubla Khan," not "on the ground of any supposed *poetic* merits," but "as a psychological curiosity."[34] Reviewers knowingly commented on the poet's account of how the poem—a mere fragment of a larger one—had been composed during sleep and jotted down automatically upon waking until this process was interrupted by the arrival of the man on business from Porlock. "Allowing every possible accuracy to the statement of Mr. Coleridge," we read in the *Monthly Review*, "we would yet ask him whether ["Kubla Khan"] was not rather the effect of rapid and instant composition after he was awake, than of memory immediately recording that which he dreamt when asleep?"[35] Be that as it may, the reviewer, like most others, dismissed the poem as being "below criticism." William Hazlitt, fervent advocate of his own unconscious genius, found that it showed little else than "that Mr. Coleridge can write better *nonsense* verses than any man in England." Even when critics began to discover the poem's greatness, it was less for its surrealistic qualities than for what John Bowring calls its "perfect music." Ironically, Bowring bestows the praise, which might have been more appropriately given to "Kubla Khan," on the poet's greater Romantic lyrics. Here Coleridge, in the critic's view, "writes . . . more felicitously, from the unforced, and seemingly unguided association of ideas in his own mind, than any man we know of."[36]

In other words, critics, as much as they might favor unconscious creativity in theory, found it hard to stomach its actual products. John Stuart Mill, while defining poetry as "the thoughts and words in which emotion spontaneously embodies itself,"[37] had obvious problems with Browning's early attempt in *Pauline*, to sing "fast as fancies come / Rudely—the verse being as the mood it paints" (258–59). The poet seemed to him to be "possessed with a more intense and morbid self-consciousness" than he had ever known in any sane human being.[38] The madhouse canto in *Maud*, which Tennyson wrote in no more than twenty minutes, came in for similar criticism even though critics realized that it was meant to delineate madness. "The case is bad enough," wrote the *Blackwood's* reviewer, "when young poetasters essay to gain a hearing by dint of maniacal howls; but it is far worse when we find a man of undoubted genius and widespread reputation, demeaning himself by putting his name to such absolute nonsense as this."[39]

In sum, constant pressure was brought to bear on the poet not to write like a "delirious man," who, to quote Tennyson, "mingles all without a plan."[40] Leigh Hunt, commenting on the poet's "The 'How' and the 'Why,' " as published in 1830, hoped that this was not "sick writing."[41] Tennyson did not reprint the poem during his lifetime. Charles Wordsworth's remark that "Timbuctoo," had it been sent up to Oxford, would have earned the author a stay in a lunatic asylum rather than a prize, reflects a similar attitude.[42] Like Victorian alienists watching their unsuspecting fellow citizens for possible signs of incipient madness, reviewers everywhere screened literature for symptoms of morbidity and sickness. To Walter Bagehot, it was the critic's solemn task to spot "the healthiness or unhealthiness of familiar states of feeling" as expressed in literary texts.[43] Readers of nineteenth-century reviews know only too well how few poets escaped his and his colleagues inquisitorial zeal along these lines.

No wonder that poets like Browning and Tennyson had a near paranoid fear of revealing their innermost feelings. When J. A. Froude, in his *Thomas Carlyle: A History of His Life in London, 1836–1881*, described Carlyle's mental instability to the "crowd," the aged Tennyson reacted with predictable ferocity, saying he only wished that, unlike his friend, he would not "be ripped up like a dog" after his death.[44] The young Tennyson, when tempted to pour forth his troubled soul in unpremeditated strains of poetry, no doubt feared similar treatment at the hands of reviewers. It was one thing to advocate such unconscious creativity in theory, but quite another to risk one's reputation and perhaps place in "normal" society by putting such theories into practice. What is more, there was little precedence for doing so. On the contrary, even those who most fervently advocated a spontaneous automatism, used rather more mimetic strategies when writing down their alleged effusions.

EMOTIONS RECOLLECTED
IN TRANQUILLITY

An obvious instance here is Wordsworth's "Tintern Abbey." Granted, the Preface to the *Lyrical Ballads* repeatedly defines poetry as "the spontaneous overflow of powerful feelings."[45] But at the same time, it stresses that this process differs from the kind of experimental immediacy dramatized in the poem. Instead, composition "takes its origin in emotion recollected in tranquillity." Wordsworth, in fact, draws a clear line between actual experience and its imagined counterpart as prompting poetic creativity. The passions that the poet, unlike other persons, can conjure up in himself "are indeed far from being the same as those produced by real events." In this way, "the Poet is chiefly distinguished from other men by a greater promptness to think and feel without immediate external excitement."[46]

In clarifying the distinction between "immediate external excitement" and the feelings inspiring poetic composition, Wordsworth adopts a major principle of traditional mimesis. Aristotle, he had been told, "said, that Poetry is the most philosophic of all writing," and he agreed wholeheartedly with that notion; "it is so; its object is truth, not individual and local, but general, and operative." Although his focus is upon the inner world, the poet will apply to it the same "principle of selection" Aristotle wanted him to use in describing the outer world. Hence the "passions and thoughts and feelings" expressed in his poetry will be "the general passions and thoughts and feelings of men."[47]

All this makes perfect sense as long as the poet, as Wordsworth puts it, "speaks through the mouths of his characters." But how can he apply the same screening process to the overflow of his own feelings? Even though this overflow is to proceed from imaginative and mnemonic self-stimulation rather than from actual experience, it nonetheless ought to take its course spontaneously. The poet, in other words, must act as both master conjurer and analyst of his emotions at once. To Wordsworth, this dual process is not just a possibility, but the poet's very way of life. While cultivating his feelings, he continually reflects upon them. Hence even spontaneously uttered emotions will eventually, from long habits of self-analysis, be filtered through such thoughtfulness. Only in terms of this simultaneous spontaneity and reflectiveness can poetry be an "overflow of powerful feelings":

> Poems to which any value can be attached, were never produced
> . . . but by a man, who being possessed of more than usual organic sensibility, had also thought long and deeply. For our continued influxes of feeling are modified and directed by our thoughts, which are indeed the representatives of all our past feelings; and, as by contemplating the relation of these general representatives to each other we discover what is really important to men, so, by the repetition and continuance of this act, our feelings will be connected with important subjects, till at length, if we be originally possessed of much sensibility, such habits of mind will be produced, that, by obeying blindly and mechanically the impulses of those habits, we shall . . . utter sentiments, of such a nature and in such connection with each other, that the understanding of the being to whom we address ourselves, if he be in a healthful state of association, must necessarily be in some degree enlightened.[48]

What is said here suggests the problems of how a poet in writing, say, "Tintern Abbey," would embody such self-reflective spontaneity in the rhetorical structure of his poem; the problems, in other words, of how to express individual, perhaps highly idiosyncratic, emotions in terms that relate them to the general sentiments of mankind on the one hand, and on the other, how to do so without losing the immediate excitement of the original poetic event while composing the poem. To fulfill the first request, there has to be a speaker who, instead of depicting the poet in his individual traits, presents him in those that will make him appear as standing for mankind in general. To realize the second, this "I" of the poem will have to speak as if prompted by an actual situation. In sum, the poem's speaker will be the product of self-dramatization, and his spontaneous utterance a carefully contrived simulation of spontaneity.

Wordsworth, though he failed to address either issue in his criticism, was clearly aware of both. Commenting on his "Lines Written While Sailing in a Boat at Evening," he frankly admitted to the double mendacity of this title. Naturally, he had not written the poem in a boat, but at home in his study recollecting former emotions in tranquillity. Hence, the "I" of the poem was not the poet himself. It was a "poetic self" of the kind that Burns, in Wordsworth's words, had constructed out of "his own character and situation in society" in order to give "point to his sentiments."[49] The speaker of "Lines Written While Sailing in a Boat at Evening," as he emphatically addresses the river, is mere self-dramatization.

> How richly glows the water's breast
> Before us, tinged with evening hues,
> While, facing thus the crimson west,
> The boat her silent course pursues!
> And see how dark the backward stream!

And even this carefully delineated situation, which prompts the speaker to express himself in such spontaneous fashion, is mere evocation. The title of the poem, Wordsworth commented, "is scarcely correct. It was during a solitary walk on the banks of the Cam that I was first struck with this appearance, and applied it to my own feelings in the manner here expressed, changing the scene to the Thames, near Windsor."[50]

SIMULATED SPONTANEITY AND SELF-DRAMATIZATION

For all of what Wordsworth had to say about it, this poetic science of feelings deserves to be called Romantic rather than Wordsworthian. Its roots reach deep into pre-Romantic poetics, while its ramifications, by no means all derived from Wordsworth, branch out far into Victorian criticism, particularly of the dramatic monologue. There is hardly one of its basic concepts that can not be found before 1800. We have already seen how the general reorientation of poetry, away from the imitation of external reality toward a presentation or expression of man's inner world, had become well established during the previous century. In turn, there were those who, like Jones and Twining, confronted the conflict between the demand for a scientific portrayal of man's feelings and the request that these emotions should be voiced spontaneously. Even Wordsworth's solution to this problem—the evocation of spontaneous experience through a dramatization of the poet's self—is adumbrated in eighteenth-century criticism.

Henry Home's *Elements of Criticism* contains the most comprehensive attempt in that direction. Aware that what we call "fiction" can be rooted in "reality," while accounts of allegedly "real" events may be largely "fictitious," he prefers to replace such ontological with psychological distinctions. First, there is what we truly experience as it occurs to us, or "real presence."[51] Then there is "reflective remembrance" or the more or less vague recollection of some event. Thirdly, there is "ideal presence," which, unlike the former two, provides the stuff of poetry. Compared with reflective remembrance, ideal presence may be simply a more vivid type of recollection. What is remembered becomes clear enough to the mind's eye to replace what real presence is to our five senses. Hence, ideal presence is like *"a waking dream"* or "reverie, where a man, losing sight of himself, is totally occupied with the objects passing in his mind, which he conceives to be really existing in his presence." Even in this strictly experimental sense, it involves a degree of self-projection to the point where we see ourselves as spectators watching some event. Lord Kames gives a personal example: "I saw yesterday a beautiful woman in tears for the loss of an only child, and was greatly moved with her distress. Not satisfied with a slight recollection or bare remembrance, I insist on the melancholy scene. Conceiving myself to be in the place where I was an eye-witness, every circumstance appears to me as at first. I think I see the woman in tears and hear her moans."[52]

Home never spells out how the poet, in translating this mental fiction into a verbal one, treats his own ego as part of the same fiction. Such self-dramatization seems to be simply taken for granted. The power of poetic language to evoke the equivalent of the ideal presence experienced by the author, to him, "depends entirely on the artifice of raising such lively and distinct images as are here described. The reader's passions are never sensibly moved, till he be thrown into a kind of reverie; in which state, losing the consciousness of self, and of reading,

. . . he conceives every incident as passing in his presence, precisely as if he were an eye-witness."[53]

Writing long before Coleridge and others evolved the greater Romantic lyric, Home talks about other genres in this context. In his view, drama in which the poet, by force of his sympathy, embodies the experiences of others, is the most powerful means of suggesting ideal presence. Home's models par excellence for the evoking of the inner life of man are, as already noted, Shakespeare's soliloquies. But at least once in *Elements of Criticism*, the same principle is applied to a lyrical poem. Lines 61–68 of Pope's "Elegy to the Memory of an Unfortunate Lady," in Home's view, contain "Sentiments too artificial for a serious passion." A poem of this kind, which otherwise "expresses delicately the most tender concern and sorrow for the deplorable fate of a person of worth," should reject "all fiction with disdain. We therefore can give no quarter to [this] passage, which is eminently discordant with the subject. It is not the language of the heart, but of the imagination indulging its flights at ease."[54]

Also, there were numerous other critics, both before and after Home, who spoke of the poetic self in terms of similar self-dramatization. The same Edward Young who fervently advocated unconscious creativity, for instance, praised odes such as Pindar's for simulating rather than for deriving from such spontaneity. In Young's words, "the imagination, like a very beautiful mistress, is indulged in the appearance of domineering, though the judgment, like an artful lover, in reality carries the point."[55] Hugh Blair, whose *Lectures on Rhetoric and Belles Lettres* prefigure several concepts of Wordsworth's Preface,[56] approvingly quotes de la Motte to similar effect: "Le beau désordre de l'ode est un effet de l'art."[57]

On the surface this seems to contradict both Blair's definition of poetry as "the language of passion, or of enlivened imagination," and his criticism of certain poems for imitating passion instead of emulating the "rude effusions" of primordial man. Yet even such primitive automatism, he suggests, has intrinsic rhetorical structures, which can teach latter-day poets how to simulate spontaneity: "Two particulars would early distinguish this language of song . . . namely, an unusual arrangement of words, and the employment of bold figures of speech. It would invert words, or change them from that order in which they are commonly placed, to that which most suited the train in which they rose in the Speaker's imagination; or which was most accommodated to the cadence of the passion by which he was moved." One main device of such psychological self-dramatization relates to syntax, the other to imagery and tropes:

> Under the influence too of any strong emotion, objects do not appear to us such as they really are, but such as passion makes us see them. We magnify and exaggerate; we seek to interest all others in what causes our emotion; we compare the least things to the greatest; we call upon the absent as well as the present, and even address ourselves to things inanimate. Hence, in congruity with those various movements of the mind, arise those turns of expression, which we now distinguish by the learned names of Hyperbole, Prosopopoeia, Simile, &c.[58]

In other words, Blair objects, not to rhetorical devices as such, but to their being used, so to speak, in cold blood. In turn, no mere effusion of disordered feelings, which he observes in some recent poems, guarantees their proper usage. On the contrary, one of the major problems with modern odes, to him, is that their authors, in trying to emulate "the original Bards" and their "enthusiastic strains," follow an inappropriate notion of spontaneity. "Full of this idea, the Poet, when he begins to write an Ode, if he has any real warmth of genius, is apt to deliver himself up to it, without controul or restraint; if he has it not, he strains after it, and thinks himself bound to assume the appearance, of being all fervour, and all flame." In either case, Blair concludes, there is great danger of writing "without order, method, or connection." The best models for avoiding such extravagance, to him, are Milton's "L'Allegro" and "Il Penseroso," two poems in which there is "nothing forced or exaggerated," though everything is viewed from "one strong point of view."[59] "In the former of these excellent poems, the author personates a chearful man, and takes notice of those things in external nature that are suitable to chearful thoughts . . . in the latter, every object described is serious and solemn, and productive of calm reflection and tender melancholy," writes James Beattie.[60]

Beattie is known to be another of Wordsworth's most notable precursors.[61] For instance, both men help remind us how much the new sense of poetry as a science of feelings, for all its insistence on self-expression, remained committed to traditional mimetic concepts. The primary endeavor for either is what Beattie calls the poetic "science of human nature."[62] The poet's main task, in Wordsworth's terms, is "to illustrate the manner in which our feelings and ideas are associated in a state of excitement [and] . . . to follow the fluxes and refluxes of the mind when agitated by the great and simple affections of our nature."[63] To both Wordsworth and Beattie, the only access toward these "general passions and thoughts and feelings of men"[64] is introspection. Although the true poet, to quote Beattie, "addresses himself to the passions and sympathies of mankind," he cannot hope to do so with success "till his own be raised."[65] According to Wordsworth, poets explore the mysteries of life "by stripping [their] own hearts naked, and by looking out of [themselves] towards men."[66] Beattie pursues similar mysteries by an "examination of his own heart." "It is in the works of nature," he writes, "particularly in the constitution of the human soul, that we discern the first and most conspicuous traces of the Almighty."[67]

Both poets, then, make man's inner life, and first and foremost their own, the primary subject matter of poetry. More than Beattie, Wordsworth insists that the poet express himself spontaneously. But the way in which such spontaneity is achieved through calculated self-stimulation and embodied in elaborate strategies of self-dramatization and simulated spontaneity, is, in its final results, similar to Beattie's concept of lyrical personation. Characteristically, both theories here draw upon Aristotle's distinction between the poet and the historian. Wordsworth's poet, as he recollects his emotions in tranquillity, filters them selectively through habitually acquired modes of thought until they become the general emotions of mankind. Hence his poetry, in his adaptation of Aristotle's distinction, "is the most philosophic of all writing . . . its object is truth, not individual and local, but general, and operative."[68] More succinctly, Beattie makes the rhetoric of self-dramatization and simulated spontaneity—Wordsworth's way of versifying his "spontaneous overflow of powerful feelings" as recollected in tranquillity—an integral part of his psychological reformulation of Aristotle's distinction. Part of the way in which the poet, in contrast to the historian, exhibits things as they might be rather than as they are, is by making the "sentiments more expressive of the feelings and character, and more suitable to the circumstances of the speaker."[69]

Toward the Dramatic Monologue

At least one of the major nineteenth-century critics completely repudiated these carefully worked out distinctions of the Romantic science of feelings with its strategies of self-projection and simulated spontaneity. To E. S. Dallas, poetry was to originate from the *"unconscious activity of the soul,"*[70] and nothing should intervene between this overflow of feelings and its notation. Hence English poetry, even of the Romantic kind, is mostly found wanting. Especially damaging to it is its extreme self-consciousness. Wordsworth, for instance, "not seldom allows a glimpse behind the scenes, and one cannot sufficiently wonder at the hardihood with which he allows it in the midst of that splendid picture which contains the following lines:

> 'The appearance instantaneously disclosed
> Was of a mighty palace—*boldly say*
> A wilderness of building.' "

Dallas echoes Jones's and Twining's claim that true poetry is incompatible with imitation. What's more, he finds that Romantic poets, in dramatizing their feelings, have perpetuated the old mimetic fallacy. Though "the character of most of our lyrical poetry," to him, was "lyrical in form," it remained "imitative in conception": "the English lyric is dramatic . . . there lies its weakness, and . . . this weakness is fatal."[71]

Other nineteenth-century critics might advocate unconscious creativity with similar single-mindedness when talking about poetry in general, but they made clear their reservations when speaking of the creative process in detail. On the one hand, William Hazlitt argues that genius acts "without premeditation or effort . . . from the natural bent and disposition of the mind."[72] On the other, he criticizes the Romantics, including Byron and Wordsworth, for reducing "poetry to a mere effusion of natural sensibility" and, worse, for surrounding "the meanest objects with the morbid feelings and devouring egotism of the writers' own minds." Poetry may indeed give vent to unconscious or unacknowledged emotions of the writer's mind, but it must embody these "indistinct and importunate cravings of the will" by "turning them to shape."[73]

Similarly, poetry, to John Keble, is the "expression of an overflowing mind, relieving itself . . . of the thoughts and passions which most oppress it."[74] It can thus give "healing relief to secret mental emotions" and act as "a safety-valve, preserving men from actual madness." But such pre-Freudian automatism has its distinct Victorian limits. For all his psychoanalytic effusiveness, the poet must proceed "without detriment to modest reserve," applying "the art which under certain veils and disguises . . . reveals the fervent emotions of the mind."[75] De Quincey further explores the particular methods a poet should use in expressing his most intimate emotions.

In agreement with Hazlitt, he argues that what is unconscious must, in one way or other, be made conscious, and what is subjective turned objective. In "project[ing] his own inner mind," the poet must "bring out consciously what yet lurks by involution in many unanalyzed feelings": "in short, to pass through a prism and radiate into distinct elements what previously had been even to himself but dim and confused ideas intermixed with each other. . . . Detention or conscious arrest is given to the evanescent, external projection to what is internal, outline to what is fluxionary, and body to what is vague."[76] In explaining how the poet should treat his own self while thus objectifying his emotions, De Quincey echoes the well-known formula of mental scientists like Moritz, Crichton, and Bucknill: treat your own self like that of another; or as he puts it, use your "powers of introverting the eye upon the *spectator*, as himself the *spectaculum*."[77] De Quincey's poetic model here is Wordsworth's "meditative poetry," which, he prophesied, would probably "maintain most power amongst the generations which are coming." At the same time he emphasizes that this poetic "science of human passion in all its fluxes and refluxes"[78] was, historically speaking, a recent achievement, responding to the unprecedented circumstances of modern life. In Homer's day, for instance, subjective poetry was simply nonexistent, while medieval romances displayed a "shivering character of starvation, as to the inner life of man":

> Not only the powers for introverting the eye upon the *spectator*, as himself the *spectaculum*, were then undeveloped and inconceivable, but the sympathies did not exist to which such an appeal could have addressed itself. Besides, and partly from the same cause, even as objects, the human feelings and affections were too grossly and imperfectly distinguished; had not reached even the infancy of that stage in which the passions begin their processes of intermodification.[79]

In sum, the notion that poets, in expressing their own feelings, use calculated techniques of self-dramatization and simulated spontaneity was fast becoming a critical commonplace. An anonymous *Blackwood's* critic of 1821, pondering the nature of poetic inspiration, concedes that poetry, "and of the noblest kind, may be written while the *mind* is in a state of violent excitement."[80] But the most natural and pleasing kind of verse to him "is not a direct ebullition of the feelings, but a description of them—it is a history of recollections. It is the language of passion revised by the judgment."[81] For all of Dallas's protests to the contrary, poetic composition, as one of his reviewers concluded, was not an unconscious process: "The poetic process may be set in operation by, and accompanied by, any amount of passion or feeling; but the poetic process itself, so far as such distinctions are of any value, is an *intellectual* process. Farther, as to its kind, it is the intellectual process of producing a new or artificial concrete."[82] Another *Blackwood's* critic, writing a few years later, put the same matter in humorous terms. "That man, clerical or lay," he wrote, "who composes a poem, regularly constructed, and duly proportioned in all its parts, in his brown study, and then gives it to the public as a work written on a green hill, is a liar, if not of the first—certainly of the second magnitude."[83]

The most detailed account of how the poet, in expressing his own feelings, produces such "a new and artificial concrete," is found in two articles of 1834 and 1835. Both of them help remind us of all the paradoxes of the Romantic science of feelings. Poetry, according to the first, is "the expression or uttering forth of feelings";[84] but it is so only insofar as the poem, through various techniques, recreates such spontaneity. Hence composition or "the vivid re-production of feelings and impressions previously experienced" is a complex and highly conscious process of simulating certain psychological facts: "The process seems to be this: a poet has observed by what combination of circumstances a particular effect is produced on the feelings in actual life; he conceives a similar combination; he embodies it in language; and through that ideal representation succeeds in producing a state of mind and feeling accordant with it."[85]

The same paradox is found in the second piece entitled "The Philosophy of Poetry" by a certain A. Smith.[86] Poetry, to Smith, is essentially "the *language of emotion*" or "the language in which that emotion vents itself."[87] At the same time, the critic goes to great lengths in discussing various strategies of simulating such spontaneity in poetry. Typical here is his interpretation of the opening line, "Morven, and morn, and spring, and solitude," from John Wilson's "Unimore." "The words," he writes, "pronounced in a certain rhythm and tone, are those of a person placed in the situation described, and in the state of feeling which that situation would excite."[88]

This was written in 1835, and one wonders to what extent Smith's "Philosophy of Poetry" might have been or did prove of use to Tennyson and Browning in evolving the new dramatic-psychological poetry. Obviously, Smith (or his anonymous precursor of the earlier, 1834 article) is speaking of the subjective poetry of an earlier era, not of the hybrid subjective-objective kind that Tennyson and Browning were about to create for the next age. But his analysis of Wilson's "Unimore" uses concepts equally applicable to, say, Tennyson's "St. Lawrence" or Browning's "Porphyria's Lover." What he emphasizes is the speaker, a specific situation, and the emotions this situation elicits from that speaker.

Or take Smith's reading of the opening line of Gray's "Elegy Written in a Country Churchyard." Here the critic, while showing how the poet-speaker is made to respond to a specific situation, also discusses various stream-of-consciousness techniques. To him, the "vital character of [the] line, as constituting poetry," lies in its concern, not with a mere fact, but with the speaker's emotional response to it:

> and, filled as his mind is with this emotion, his fancy first flies away to the origin of the evening bell, and, as we may imagine, rapidly wanders amid the associations of antiquity and romance, which link themselves to the name of the *curfew*. The sound of the bell, intimating the close of day, he invests, for the moment, with the import of the death knell summoning a soul from life; and the epithet "parting," bespeaks the similitude of his present frame of mind to that excited by the interruption of a cherished intercourse with an animated being—with a companion, a friend, a lover.[89]

It was not until after 1855, the year of *Men and Women* and *Maud*, that dramatic monologues met with comparable critical acumen. But in the meantime, the jargon surrounding the Romantic science of feelings proved sufficient to account for those basic aspects of the new genre it shared with the greater Romantic lyric. Also, of course, there was the new psychological criticism of Shakespeare to prepare readers for a new poetry, which, for instance, might show how people think rather than how they speak. Not surprisingly, Smith, by drawing on a previous article on the playwright, demonstrates how Lorenzo's "How sweet the moonlight sleeps upon this bank!"[90] offers simply another instance of the rhetorical strategies evident in "The Curfew tolls the knell of parting day." Whether the speaker is supposed to be the poet himself as in Gray's poem or a dramatis persona as in Shakespeare's line is of little import to the critic. More important to him is that this speaker, in either case, is presented as spontaneously responding to a specific situation.[91] As we have already seen, this, in turn, was precisely what Victorian critics like W. J. Fox and George Brimley, for good reason, described as one of the hallmarks of the new dramatic-psychological poetry.[92]

In sum, writers of dramatic monologues could draw on two major precedents in evolving the new genre. One was Shakespeare's psychological realism, particularly in his soliloquies; the other the Romantic science of feelings, especially as embodied in the greater Romantic lyric. Moreover, there was a related body of criticism discussing these precedents in precisely some of the aspects in which they prefigured and/or influenced the rise of the dramatic monologue. Critics from Henry Home to Charles Bucknill, from the fields of both literature and mental science, drew attention to Shakespeare's expertise in areas in which he could exert such influence. First and foremost, there was his unrivaled art of adapting both language and prosody to the psychological exigencies of situation and character. Shakespeare, unlike Racine or Corneille, made his characters express their emotions rather than describe them. As part of his complex stream-of-consciousness technique, he sometimes showed how people think rather than how they speak. Equally unparalleled were his portrayals of pathological and transexperience phenomena such as somnambulism and hallucination.

What sharpened critics' eyes for such matters was a gradual, though radical, change of the concept of poetry. In the wake of M. H. Abrams's seminal *The Mirror and the Lamp*, we tend to see this transformation as primarily one from mimesis to expression. Yet this development, however crucial, was only secondary to another, more comprehensive one. This was the shift from the notion of poetry as primarily imitating the outer world toward the demand that it explore the inner world of the mind.[93] Henry Home's interest in the stream-of-consciousness technique of Shakespeare's soliloquies, for instance, was no doubt prompted by an attempt, common to much of eighteenth-century criticism, to redefine poetry and criticism within the new "science of human nature."[94] What is more, he seems to anticipate the way in which lyrical, that is spontaneously self-revelatory, poetry was to play a major role in evolving this general poetic science of feelings.

Of course, critics—from Sir William Jones to E. S. Dallas—noted the obvious contradiction between the demand for spontaneity and for an objective analysis of human emotions. But which Romantic or Victorian poet ever poured forth his heart in totally spontaneous fashion? Automatic thought dictation to the point of a *"dérèglement* de *tous les sens,"* as systematically practiced by Rimbaud[95] and the surrealists, was either unknown or confined to the "justly deserved limbo of the modern 'spiritualist' muse."[96] Furthermore, the mere thought of totally unrestrained self-revelation struck most people as dangerous and off-putting. John Keble, advocate of poetry as "expression of an overflowing mind," warned that such effusiveness must be "without detriment to modest reserve."[97] Wordsworth, the most influential spokesman of the same doctrine, admitted that he often found his first expressions "detestable"—"and it is frequently true of second words as of second thoughts, that they are the best."[98]

Paradoxically, such contradictions played midwife to the birth of what Victorians later called the new psychological school of poetry. For by adapting the demand for spontaneity to the general sense of poetry as a science of feelings, poets and critics, both before and after Wordsworth, evolved the direct precedent to the dramatic monologue. In theory, they argued that the poet, in order to capture what is permanent in human feelings while pouring forth his heart, has to pass his private effusions through the sieve of analytic thoughtfulness. In practice, they evolved modes of simulated spontaneity and self-dramatization in which they could embody such generalized and objectified spontaneity. No wonder that the pioneer authors of dramatic monologues, as they applied what introspection had taught them to the analysis of others, also made use of the Romantic art of self-projection in delineating independent personae.

VI

Precedents II: Shakespeare

TO SUGGEST that the dramatic monologue is only one of several symptoms of the age's transition from introspection to psycho-analysis, raises a number of further questions. Why should such a genre originate in England, but not in non-English-speaking countries? Was not France, long before England, in the forefront of the new mental science? Did not Germany, or even Italy, make advances in this field comparable to Britain's? Were not poets everywhere involved in the same introspective dilemmas crying for similar solutions? Why then did there arise a school of dramatic-psychological poetry in the English language alone? It is true that one can find isolated specimens of similar kind elsewhere. None of these, however, is comparable to Tennyson's and Browning's early dramatic monologues, which prompted the perhaps most vital tradition of post-Romantic poetry in the language.

The answers to all these questions, though complex in detail, converge on Shakespeare and Elizabethan drama. Macbeth, groping for the dagger in his mind, for instance, was no doubt Tennyson's model for showing St. Simeon Stylites clutching the heavenly crown of his hallucinations. More generally speaking, Shakespeare's realistic use of language, his subtleties in suggesting shades of tone and feeling, and general insight into the human mind became models for the Victorian authors of dramatic monologues. At least to contemporary reviewers, such influence, especially on Browning, was largely taken for granted. While insisting on Shakespeare's more genuine objectivity, they again and again described the Victorian poet as the direct heir of the Elizabethan playwright. To R. Buchanan, Browning had "a wealth of nature and of perfection of spiritual insight," which so far had only been seen in Shakespeare.[1] To a second reviewer, he was "the most powerful realist

in the representation of human life who has appeared in England since"
the Elizabethan playwright.[2] "He is the most Shakespearean creature
since Shakespeare," exclaimed Oscar Wilde.[3]

THE LINGUISTIC AND PROSODIC MODEL

To document this indebtedness in detail would require a separate study.
Here we are mainly concerned with the reasons why, for reviewers and
psychologists, Shakespeare was a model to the authors of dramatic monologues. One of these was Shakespeare's skill in reflecting both spoken
voice and silent thought; the other was his metrical virtuosity in enhancing this linguistic and psychological realism. In terms of their effect upon Victorian poets, these two poetic skills were considered,
whether rightly so or not, as part of Shakespeare's main endeavor to
reveal his characters' innermost thoughts. Browning, for instance, was
thought to have had no superior since Shakespeare "for the utterance of
the right physiognomical word and phrase."[4] Others might criticize
him for his grotesque realism,[5] or Tennyson for making a deplorable
"approach to the prosaic style" in *Maud*.[6] But to W. M. Rossetti, advocate of Pre-Raphaelite particularity in *The Germ*, such critics were
wrong to accuse Browning for spoiling "fine thoughts by a vicious,
extravagant, and involved style."[7] For what to superficial readers appeared as such was "the result more truly of a most earnest and single-
minded labor after the utmost rendering of idiomatic conversational
truth."[8] Browning as a dramatic poet, in Arthur Symons's view, had
"to modulate and moderate, sometimes even to vulgarise, his style and
diction for the proper expression of some particular character, in whose
mouth exquisite turns of phrase and delicate felicities of rhythm would
be inappropriate."[9] To Victorian critics, the model here was obvious.
"It is not difficult to see," writes one of them, "that Mr. Browning has
sat at the feet of the Elizabethan poets"[10] and more specifically of Shakespeare.

Reviewers defended Browning's and Tennyson's metrical realism on
similar grounds. Of course, there were those to whom the verse in *Maud*
had degenerated to "the dead level of prose run mad,"[11] who accused
Browning of disguising a speech in a song,[12] or who thought meter was
strictly incompatible with anything but "the expression of universal
ideas."[13] The opposite view, whereby metrical language is a natural
expression of individual emotion, can be traced back to eighteenth-

century critics like John Dennis, Hugh Blair, and William Enfield.[14] A later exponent of this tradition is Leigh Hunt whose *Imagination and Fancy* may have suggested to Victorian reviewers a way of scanning dramatic monologues in analogy to Shakespearian verse. King Lear's "Blow, winds, and crack your cheeks; rage, blow. / You cataracts and hurricanoes, spout" (3. 2. 1–2), serves him as an example to illustrate his general principle of prosody termed "Variety in Uniformity."[15] There is tonal consistency ("Uniformity") but mainly in order to highlight those deviations from the regular pattern ("Variety"), which underscore a particularly poignant or unexpected emotion. Metrical variety in uniformity, then, is a means toward enhancing the same kind of psychological truthfulness aimed at through oral realism. Thus Lear's lines if scanned, or rather read aright, show how unexpected "locations of the accent double this force [i.e., of verse], and render it characteristic of passion and abruptness."[16]

One of the first to apply such principles to the dramatic monologue was R. J. Mann in his *"Maud" Vindicated* (1856). Tennyson, in Mann's view, had skills of "symboliz[ing] in sound mental states and perceptions" to match his general psychological perspicacity and "accurate insight into the phenomena of insanity."[17] *Maud* I, xvi, in which the protagonist hopes that his love for the heroine might save him from suicide, crime, and madness, serves as an example of such metrical stream-of-consciousness notation: "The first lines [i.e., 537–42] which relate to the brother's movement, have an abrupt rhythm. . . . When, however, the song passes on from this rough and disagreeable topic to the more pleasing theme, the verse at once softens into a sweetly flowing stream, that makes one or two little contracted leaps, and then glides on with the most absolute smoothness [i.e., 543–59]."[18] Browning soon was to find similar vindication. One critic had accused him of embodying his dramatic lyrics in "a wholly unsuitable poetic organism."[19] In reply, a *Quarterly* reviewer of 1865, seems to adopt Leigh Hunt's scanning techniques by way of describing the same lyrics as "a kind of *staccato* mental *notation* in words."[20]

Before long, such analyses fostered tendencies "to disregard all the musty rules of metre and prosody, and to seek the poetic form in the underlying harmonies of cadences, rests, and tone-colors."[21] D. G. Brinton, for instance, finds that Browning's "A Woman's Last Words" reflects "the rhythm of broken sobs," while his "Love Among the Ruins," through a slight variation of the earlier poem's verse scheme, echoes a mood "of long and calm inspirations with alternate rests."[22] Arthur Beatty's *Browning's Verse-Form: Its Organic Character* (1897) is the final, most comprehensive attempt by a Victorian critic to show that Browning's prosody is "the incarnation of the thought, emotion and action of the poem."[23] Beatty is particularly perceptive in his reading of Browning's blank verse. Of course, there was the insuperable Shakespeare; but as far as his own age is concerned "Browning's verse is the most dramatic blank verse of the century." This is because its form is "determined from moment to moment, according to the nature of the thought and feeling."[24]

If authors of dramatic monologues looked to Shakespeare for ways of making their language and prosody reflect the emotions of their characters, they did so even more in emulating the playwright's general psychological insights—or so at least argued the reviewers. Robert Buchanan, who in his own dramatic monologues tried to "afford an artistic insight into" his characters' souls,[25] felt that Browning's expertise along similar lines was something "we have been accustomed to find in the pages of Shakespeare, and in those pages only."[26] Even where Browning is thought to outdo nearly everyone else, Shakespeare provides the yardstick. The art of making "his characters betray what they really are," as in "My Last Duchess" and "Andrea del Sarto," for instance, is Browning's unsurpassed achievement to one reviewer. "Nothing in literature is more masterly than the faultless painter's unconscious betrayal of his unknown shame. I know of nothing like this in Shakespeare—nothing so profound in any poet."[27] To another, Browning not only had the "widest range of sympathies" of any poet since Shakespeare, but, due to the recent advances of science, exceeded the playwright along those lines.[28]

In fact, most scientists in the field of psychology probably would have disagreed with the critic. Who could exceed Shakespeare, when their own theoretical efforts were only about to match the playwright's intuitive insights? John Charles Bucknill, who knew Tennyson's *Maud* as well as Shakespeare's plays, reserves his strongest praise for the Elizabethan poet; more importantly, Bucknill understood the links between them. The very nature of this affinity between Shakespeare's dramas and Victorian dramatic-psychological poetry, as viewed by the alienist, is all the more interesting because it also broaches the issue of Shakespeare's possible impact on the rise of mental science.

SHAKESPEARE AND THE ALIENISTS

As we recall, Bucknill praised *Maud* as a "remarkable sketch of poetic mental pathology."[29] "Where can this unprofessional psychologist have acquired his accurate insight into the phenomena of insanity," wondered fellow physician R. J. Mann.[30] Bucknill, in his subsequent *The Psychology of Shakespeare*, addresses that very question. Shakespeare's psychological knowledge, to him, was even more amazing than Tennyson's. For in presenting, in *Maud*, a case bearing out J. Guislain's psychiatric theories,[31] the Victorian poet might have actually read the alienist. Such borrowing, though unlikely even with Tennyson, was totally out of the question with Shakespeare. How then could this unprofessional playwright-psychologist of a former age have anticipated some of the major recent insights of mental pathology?

Bucknill himself took pride in having been one of the first to discover the fact that "morbid emotion [was] an essential part of mental disorder."[32] Previously, insanity had been viewed as "an affection of the intellectual and not of the emotional part of man's nature." Then Guislain pointed out "the immense influence of emotional suffering in the causation of insanity." But it remained to Bucknill himself to explain "the wider and still more important principle, that morbid emotion is an essential part of mental disorder." "How completely," exclaims the alienist, "is this theory supported by the development of insanity, as it is portrayed in Lear!"

> Shakespeare, who painted from vast observation of nature, as he saw it without and felt it within, places this great fact broadly and unmistakably before us. It has, indeed, been long ignored by the exponents of medical and legal science, at the cost of ever futile attempts to define insanity by its accidents and not by its essence; and, following this guidance, the literary critics of Shakespeare have completely overlooked the early symptoms of Lear's insanity; and, according to the custom of the world, have postponed its recognition until he is running about a frantic, raving, madman.[33]

In accounting for insights so obviously ahead of their time, Bucknill indirectly describes the dual process that made him a psychiatrist as it made Tennyson and others writers of dramatic monologues. Shakespeare "painted from vast observation of nature, as he saw it without and felt it within." Bucknill's preface to *The Psychology of Shakespeare* explains the matter in more explicit terms. He grants that the play-wright worked largely from external reality; but such observationally acquired knowledge, he argues, was hardly sufficient when it came to delineating his characters' deepest motives and innermost thoughts. Here observation of external reality had to be enhanced by insights gathered introspectively.

Hence it was wrong to claim, as Coleridge did, that Shakespeare drew his characters "by the simple force of meditation" and that he only had "to imitate certain parts of his own character . . . and they were at once true to nature, and fragments of the divine mind that drew them."[34] Shakespeare, in Bucknill's view, was no semidivine vates cre-ating from a demiurgical center of self. Rather, he seemed to recreate reality in the laboratory of introspection. After exploring the labyrinths of his self, he empathetically assumed the identities of others, scruti-nizing their inner lives with the knowledge gathered in self-analysis. "The peculiarities of a certain character being observed, the great mind which contains all possibilities within itself, imagines the act of mental transmigration, and combining the knowledge of others with the knowledge of self, every variety of character possible in nature would become possible in conception and delineation."[35]

Shakespeare, in other words, was neither a subjective poet of modern classification, recreating the world from the encompassing center of his self, nor a strictly objective poet merely reproducing things external. As a psychologist, he was both—just as Browning and Tennyson were when, in writing their dramatic monologues, they made use of their introspective skills in the analysis of others. Characteristically, Buck-nill, in evolving this post-Romantic theory of Shakespeare the psychol-ogist, uses a phrase—"the act of mental transmigration"—that echoes W. J. Fox's 1831 appraisal of young Tennyson's early experiments to-ward the new dramatic-psychological poetry. The poet, Fox had said, "has the secret of the transmigration of the soul. He can cast his own spirit into any living thing, real or imaginary."[36] In turn, the "act of mental transmigration" from introspection toward psycho-analysis, is, as we have seen, Bucknill's and other psychologists' way of describing their basic endeavor and of accounting for the genesis of their disci-pline. The "true mental physician," according to Bucknill, "transfers for the moment the mind of his patient into himself in order that, in return, he may give back some portion of his own healthful mode of thought to the sufferer."[37]

All this, of course, tells us less about Shakespeare himself than about how he relates to Victorian mental science and poetry. But given these limitations, Bucknill has a far deeper grasp of the links between both than most critics. At worst, these would, say, denounce the linguistic realism of *Maud* as "the dead level of prose run mad";[38] at best they might justify it as dramatically appropriate and invoke Shakespeare as a model. Yet even the most radical advocates of such down-to-carth use of language in the new dramatic-psychological poetry hardly allowed for the full spectrum manifest in Shakespeare. Broadly speaking, critics and poets tended toward the kind of compromise Robert Buchanan observed in writing his monologues "Liz" and "Nell." Buchanan claims to have followed nature as "far as poetic speech can follow ordinary speech": "for to obtrude slips of grammar, mis-spellings, and other meaningless blotches, in short, to lay undue emphasis on the mere language employed, would have been wilfully to destroy the artistic verisimilitude of such poems. . . . Vulgarity obtruded is not truth spiritualized and made clear."[39] Bucknill, characteristically, is far more radical in welcoming the new genre's realism of language and content. Critics of *Maud*, he noted, "have found great fault with Mr. Tennyson for choosing so disagreeable a hero" and for making him speak in such "unpleasant and spasmodic" a poetry. But what they objected to, was "wonderfully true to nature" in the alienist's view.[40]

For this, indeed, was exactly what Bucknill was after himself in analyzing his patients, an endeavor in which all preconceived or, worse, metaphysical notions about human nature were more of a hindrance than a help. All he could go by in examining individual cases was careful observation. Bucknill-Tuke's *Manual of Psychological Medicine* reads like a Scotland Yard handbook for detectives when it discusses various clues that might lead to a diagnosis of insanity: "On entering a house in which the head of the family is insane, the physician will not unfrequently find his attention attracted to many little circumstances, testifying to a want of order and direction in the household affairs. In the room principally occupied by the patient, things are especially found to be out of place; bizarreries often present themselves in the decoration of the walls and the arrangement of the furniture."[41]

After investigating the potential patient's family history, the alienist-detective should scrutinize possible peculiarities of dress, bodily condition, gesture, and facial expression. But above all, he must draw the patient out into talking about everything from his "relation to

God" to his "amusements."[42] Here every detail, however repulsive, every slip of the tongue or idiosyncracy of expression, however insignificant it might appear, every inflection or tone of voice, however muted, might be of crucial importance. In sum, an alienist above all else had to listen, and listen carefully. No wonder that Bucknill was delighted to find Shakespeare and Tennyson giving similarly close attention to the peculiarities of spoken language. No doubt, these poets had listened carefully before they made their characters speak. So who would fault them for staying as close to reality as possible in doing so? While the critics downgraded *Maud* for ignoring Aristotelian standards of how poetry must present things as they ought to be, Bucknill praised it precisely for ignoring such standards in showing how things really are.

In sum, alienists had good reason to greet poets like Shakespeare, Tennyson, and Browning as major allies or even precursors in their war against essentialist theorizing about human nature. "There is more real mental science to be learned from the teaching of [Shakespeare]," argues Bucknill, "than in all the metaphysical rubbish which was ever delivered from professional chairs."[43] Though to a lesser extent, this is true of poetry in general. "The Poet or maker . . . is the best guide and helpmate with whom the psychologist can ally himself. . . . Compared with the assistance which the psychologist derives from the true poet, that which he obtains from the metaphysician is as sketchy and indistinct as the theoretical description of a new country might be, given by one who had never been therein."[44] No wonder that books, articles, and comments by Victorian alienists expounding the psychological insights of poets from Aeschylus to Tennyson count by the dozen. To discuss them all adequately would require a separate study; but a few of the more outstanding samples of this unprecedented psychiatric literary criticism antedating Freud and Jung should be mentioned.

The main poets here were the Greek playwrights, Shakespeare, Cervantes, Dr. Johnson, Sir Walter Scott, and, of course, Tennyson and Browning. J. R. Gasquet's seven-part study of "The Madmen of the Greek Theatre," a subject previously surveyed in Bucknill-Tuke's *Manual of Psychological Medicine*, was serialized in the *Journal of Mental Science* between 1872 and 1874. A translation of Dr. Morejon's detailed analysis of Don Quixote's madness, in terms of its causes, predisposition, symptomatology, and eventual cure, appeared in the *Journal of Psychological Medicine* of 1859. Dr. Johnson's account, in *Rasselas*, of the mad astronomer Imlac, Byron's portrait of the insane Haydee, Sir Walter

Scott's of Madge Wildfire, Norna, and Clara Mowbray, as well as other poetic delineations of insanity, were discussed in various articles.[45]

Most numerous, of course, were similar works on Shakespeare. The first book-length study here was Bucknill's *The Psychology of Shakespeare* (1859), previously serialized in the *Journal of Mental Science* during 1858–59. By October 1859, Canadian alienist A. O. Kellogg started to publish his nine-part series of articles on "William Shakespeare as a Physiologist and Psychologist" in the *American Journal of Insanity*, later collected in *Shakespeare's Delineations of Insanity, Imbecility, and Suicide* of 1866. In 1863, John Conolly published a two-hundred-odd-page *Study of Hamlet*; in 1864, G. Ross "Shakespeare: The Mad Characters in his Works";[46] in 1868–69, the renowned French alienist A. Brierre de Boismont, a two-part study of the playwright's "connaissance en alién-ation mentale" in the *Annales médico-psychologiques*. By now, psychiatric criticism of Shakespeare had developed into a well-established genre with dozens of followers all over Europe and especially in Germany.[47]

Such criticism was no mere specialist's hobbyhorse. The pioneer studies of this kind appeared as separate volumes, in major handbooks and in journals. Bucknill-Tuke's *Manual of Psychological Medicine*, the leading text of its kind for many years, surveys the Greek playwrights' treatment of insanity in its first chapter. W. Sweetser's *Mental Hygiene* of 1850 uses illustrations from Shakespeare and other poets such as Spenser, Young, and Byron throughout its nearly four hundred pages. J. C. Bucknill's *Asylum Journal of Mental Science* printed the editor's articles on Tennyson and Shakespeare in some of its earliest issues. Forbes Winslow's earlier *Journal of Psychological Medicine* featured R. H. Horne's "Madness, as Treated by Shakespere" in its second volume of 1849. The first major psychiatric magazine in the English-speaking world, Amariah Brigham's *American Journal of Insanity*, which like the *Asylum Journal* continues publication to date, printed the editor's "In-sanity—Illustrations by Histories of Distinguished Men, and by the Writings of Poets and Novelists" as article two in the opening issue of 1844. Though largely unacknowledged by later writers,[48] Brigham's piece, along with Isaac Ray's on "Shakespeare's Delineations of Insan-ity," featured in volume three of the same journal, set the general trend for subsequent criticism of its kind.

Naturally there is the praise of "the accuracy and extent of Shake-speare's knowledge of mental pathology."[49] Not only did the play-wright understand the principle of moral insanity, but he also gave a demonstration of moral treatment. Brigham confesses that more recent mental science has "very little to add to [the] method of treating the insane" as practiced by the Abbess on Antipholus of Ephesus in *The Comedy of Errors*: "To produce sleep and to quiet the mind by medical and moral treatment, to avoid all unkindness, and when patients begin to convalesce, to guard . . . against everything likely to disturb their minds, and to cause a relapse—is now considered the best and nearly the only essential treatment."[50]

Shakespeare also understood how lunacy, as in the case of Lear, can have an incubation period before it manifests itself in more obvious symptoms like hallucination and incoherence.[51] How subtly the playwright reflected these gradations from ordinary stream of consciousness to "the filiation of the maniac's thoughts!" Even these had their "method in madness"—"that delicate thread which though broken in numerous points, still forms the connecting link between many groups and patches of thought." How accurately, in turn, did Shakespeare portray phenomena such as somnambulism (in Lady Macbeth) and visual as well as aural hallucination (in her husband) while at the same time implying a "true theory of apparitions"[52] au par with the recent studies of a Ferriar or Hibbert!

In all this Shakespeare was clearly ahead of his time. In fact, he had hardly been surpassed by the new mental science, not to speak of the general public, which was slow in assimilating its discoveries. To Isaac Ray, the records of the criminal courts gave "most ample and painful evidence" of how much better than many contemporaries Shakespeare understood the fact of moral insanity as portrayed in *Hamlet*. Most notably, "Shakespeare's science of human nature [was] more profound than that of his critics."[53] How wrong these were in claiming that Hamlet merely feigned his insanity or that Lear turned insane only around the middle of the play! What critics lacked, of course, was the alienists' asylum experience. Like later writers on the same subject, Brigham and Ray repeatedly invoke such experience in corroboration of their reading of Shakespeare. "The insane he has described," notes Brigham, "are not imaginary characters, but may now be found in every large Asylum":

> Here may be seen Jacques, "wrapt in a most humorous sadness."
> . . . Here, too, is Macbeth, much of the time conversing rationally, and manifesting a most noble nature, and at other times

clutching imaginary daggers, or screaming, terrified by the ghosts of the departed. Here, also, is Hamlet . . . overwhelmed with imaginary troubles. . . . Here, also, is King Lear, in a paroxysm of wrath, at some trivial occurrence, but much of the time venting all his rage upon his relations and friends.[54]

Did Shakespeare gather his astounding knowledge in mental pathology from observation or introspection? Even here, Brigham's and Ray's answers anticipate the complex reasoning of later alienists like Bucknill. Though Shakespeare obviously lacked the multiple experience of a nineteenth-century madhouse doctor, it was "not to be supposed . . . that he was guided solely by intuition" as suggested by Coleridge. No doubt a deep understanding of himself helped him greatly in portraying his men and women. But what was thus refined in the alembic of introspection first had to be gathered by his "unrivalled powers of observation."[55] "One visit to the Bedlam Hospital, would teach him much; for, what on other minds would have made no impression, or been immediately forgotten, was by Shakespeare treasured up, even as to the most minute particulars, and when he wished, every look, word, or action of the patient, and every idea he heard advanced by the attendants, he was able to recall."[56]

For all his introspective and intuitive powers, Shakespeare, claimed the alienists, "unquestionably did observe the insane." The rest was achieved by a singular "kind of sagacity." The playwright, "from a single trait of mental disease that he did observe, was enabled to infer the existence of many others that he did not observe, and from this profound insight into the law of psychological relations, he derived the light that observation had failed to supply." Shakespeare, in all this, never betrayed his absolute "fidelity to nature"[57] even in its most minute particulars. This, above all else, made him the precursor of the nineteenth-century alienists and, as one might add, of the writers of dramatic monologues.

SHAKESPEARE'S PSYCHOLOGY AND
PRE-ROMANTIC CRITICISM

No doubt, then, nineteenth-century alienists were the first to systematically study Shakespeare's portrayals of human consciousness in both sanity and insanity. But the idea of Shakespeare the psychologist was far from new. Physicians who modestly advised themselves as to how much they could learn from the playwright could have taken similar suggestion from Hazlitt's *Characters of Shakespeare's Plays* (1817). In the author's view, Shakespeare "alone pourtrayed the mental diseases,—melancholy, delirium, lunacy,—with such inexpressible, and, in every respect, definite truth, that the physician may enrich his observations from them in the same manner as from real cases."[58] In fact, when Hazlitt, Coleridge, Lamb, and other Romantics praised Shakespeare for scrutinizing "the workings of the passions in their most retired recesses,"[59] the playwright's unrivaled psychological insights had long become a critical commonplace.

As early as 1762, Henry Home, for instance, found that Shakespeare "excels all the ancients and moderns, in knowledge of human nature, and in unfolding even the most obscure and refined emotions."[60] Other eighteenth-century critics praised his "intimate acquaintance with every passion that . . . exalts or debases the human mind." How he "penetrated into the inmost recesses of the human heart!" How "minutely correct" he was in charting "mental operations!"[61] Pre-Romantic critics payed equal attention to his delineations of insanity. Again and again, they debated whether Hamlet's insanity was feigned or genuine: could it be that the prince's disposition was a mere ruse to hide a genuine melancholy "border[ing] on madness, [and] arising from his peculiar situation?"[62] Or they analyzed Shakespeare's portrayal of the more unequivocal madness of a Lear or an Ophelia. Most complex in this respect, to one critic, was *Macbeth*.

> Shakespeare has, in many of his pieces, represented the ravings of a disordered mind with great success; but I think in none so well as in this tragedy. . . . The circumstance of [Lady Macbeth's] constantly rubbing her hand in order to wipe out the stain made by Duncan's murder, is admirably imagined; and her exclamation, "Who would have thought that there was so much blood in the old man's body!" [5.1.37f.] is a most natural representation of the state of a mind racked with the consciousness of having committed murder. The madness of Orestes and Ajax are in comparison but weakly represented by Sophocles, though he surpassed all the other Greek tragedians in the art of moving the passions.[63]

The genius of the century's greatest actor reinforced this new sense of Shakespeare's insight into the dark sides of the human psyche. David

Garrick, according to his 1801 biographer Arthur Murphy, was at his best in acting the madness of Lear and Macbeth. As Victorian alienists liked to remember,[64] he first studied madness in reality before enacting it on the stage. A friend of the actor's had lost his mind after inadvertently letting his baby daughter fall to her death out of a window and spent the rest of his life reliving this fatal event—"playing in fancy with his child . . . dropp[ing] it, and, bursting into a flood of tears, fill[ing] the house with shrieks of grief and bitter anguish."[65] Garrick, as Murphy reports, "was often present at this scene of misery, and was ever after used to say that it gave him the first idea of *King Lear's* madness." In fact, he would often reenact his friend's tragedy in private and conclude his improvisation by pointing out that this is where he "*learned to imitate madness*; I copied nature, and to that owed my success in *King Lear*."[66] Audiences used to the stereotypic image of the lunatic full of sudden starts and violent gesticulation were stunned by Garrick's reinterpretation of the mad king: "his eyes were fixed, or, if they turned to any one near him he made a pause, and fixed his look on the person after much delay; his features at the same time telling what he was going to say before he uttered a word."[67]

Though less concerned with the minutiae of insanity, eighteenth-century Shakespeare critics anticipated their Victorian alienist successors in closely analyzing the playwright's stream-of-consciousness technique and oral realism. Foremost here was Henry Home, whose *Elements of Criticism* (1762) was one of the most popular books of its kind for many decades. At least twenty-five editions and abridgments had appeared by 1883 and several of its chapters were reprinted in the *Encyclopaedia Britannica* from 1771 on.[68] There is reason to assume, then, that *Elements of Criticism*, in what it says about Shakespeare, influenced subsequent criticism of the playwright, and, through that channel, affected discussions of Victorian dramatic-psychological poetry.

Like Victorian alienists after him, Home stresses that Shakespeare "shows more knowledge of human nature than any of our philosophers."[69] This may seem surprising from a critic whose psychological approach relies heavily on the associationist principles of Locke, Hartley, and Hume. But Lord Kames has his reasons. One is the poet's general avoidance of abstract terms and his adherence to detail, principles later to be upheld by Victorian alienist and literary reviewers in defense of both Shakespearean drama and the dramatic monologue. Of course, there were many others who, prior to the nineteenth century and in different contexts, advocated the particular against the general in poetry.[70] Quite new, however, is the specificity with which Home describes Shakespeare as "superior to all other writers in delineating passion":

> It is difficult to say in what part he most excels, whether in mould-
> ing every passion to peculiarity of character, in discovering the
> sentiments that proceed from various tones of passion, or in ex-
> pressing properly every different sentiment. He imposes not upon
> his reader, general declamation and the false coin of unmeaning
> words, which the bulk of writers deal in. His sentiments are ad-
> justed, with the greatest propriety, to the peculiar character and
> circumstances of the speaker; and the propriety is not less perfect
> betwixt his sentiments and his diction.[71]

Yet, most seminal, at least in view of later criticism of Shakespeare and of the dramatic monologue, was how Home, in the same spirit, defends the Shakespearean soliloquy against its neoclassical detractors.

To Smollett, for instance, Hamlet's "To be, or not to be" was "a heap of absurdities" in every sense—"whether we consider the situation, the sentiment, the argumentation, or the poetry."[72] In trying to reduce the speech to a syllogistic inner debate, he finds nothing but inconsistency in the prince's "chain of argumentation." In attempting to translate its imagery into pictorial equivalents, he ends up describing Hamlet's rev-erie as an Horatian *Aegri somnia* or "sick man's dream."[73] Not all neo-classicists, of course, were as insensitive to the stream-of-consciousness dynamics of soliloquies like Hamlet's. Thus, Dr. Johnson, for instance, felt called upon to defend Hamlet's speech by taking a more psycholog-ical approach. "Bursting from a man distracted with contrariety of de-sires and overwhelmed with the magnitude of his own purposes," he wrote, it "is connected rather in the speaker's mind than on his tongue."[74] But "To be, or not to be," along with Posthumus's speech in the last act of *Cymbeline* (5. 1. 1–33), are the exceptions from the rule. In general, Dr. Johnson shared the neoclassical distrust of the Shakespearean soliloquy.

All this changed with Lord Kames, to whom this mode is one of the playwright's greatest achievements. Where Smollett is looking for dis-cursive consistency, Home demands psychological truth to fact. Anti-thetical inner debates à la Racine or Corneille are now found wanting for precisely the reasons that elicited praise from neoclassical critics.

Rather than speak in this fashion after receiving an unexpected pardon from Augustus, Aemilia, in Corneille's *Cinna*, for instance, should have been made to express her emotions in rather more turbulent fashion.

> These passions, raised at once to the utmost pitch, are at first too big for utterance; and Aemilia's feelings must, for some moments, have been expressed by violent gestures only. So soon as there is a vent for words, the first expressions are naturally broken and interrupted. At last we ought to expect a tide of intermingled sentiments, occasioned by the fluctuation of the mind betwixt the two passions. Aemilia is made to behave in a very different manner. With extreme coolness she describes her own situation, as if she were merely a spectator; or rather the poet takes the task off her hands.[75]

How true to psychological fact, by contrast, were Shakespeare's "many incomparable soliloquies!" For Home, it was "not easy to conceive any model more perfect." How well did the playwright reflect the turbulent fluctuations of man's inner life—how a person may be "agitated at once by different passions" with his mind "vibrating like a pendulum," or how people tend to disguise their deepest emotions both to themselves and others. What is more, Shakespeare did not adulterate psychological fact with rhetoric. Instead, his soliloquies reflected how the language of violent passion is "broken and interrupted." Most importantly, his soliloquies often tend to show how people think aloud rather than what they might say. Hamlet's "O, that this too too solid flesh would melt" (1. 3. 129–59) serves Home as an instance of how in "a passionate soliloquy one begins with thinking aloud; and the strongest feelings only, are expressed."[76]

In sum, when alienist Conolly, in studying *Hamlet*, concluded that to "depict action . . . verbally is easier than to convey the workings of meditation,"[77] he hardly introduced a new idea; nor did the reviewers of dramatic monologues in pointing out that their authors often show us "how people think rather than how they speak" and how they delineate "the lower . . . currents of thought and feeling"[78] by translating stream of consciousness into articulated language. John Conolly, in interpreting Hamlet's soliloquies, claims that these currents often run too deep to be understood by anyone except a psychologist like himself.[79] But Home and other eighteenth-century critics show that Conolly and his colleagues were far from the first to have such insights.[80] On the contrary, the alienists, when they "discovered" Shakespeare as their precursor, moved in the footsteps of critics who had long been interpreting the playwright in similar terms.

Of all major Victorian poets, only one rejected and opposed the age's increasing psychological bias in poetry, criticism, and poetic theory. Matthew Arnold, in doing so, was far from denying that this tendency could be traced to Shakespeare via the Romantic science of feelings. In fact, it was *Hamlet* that, in his view, launched "the dialogue of the mind with itself,"[81] which had become the central malaise of his age. Nor was Arnold unaware of the tensions that made older poets like Browning and Tennyson escape from their introspective tribulations into poetic genres that would allow them to indulge in self-analysis without revealing the results *in propria persona*. Ironically, no one else was more deeply enmeshed in these tensions nor more strongly committed to working them out within the ideational and structural framework of the greater Romantic lyric. As we know from his 1853 Preface, the attempt, which categorically opposed the psychological school of poetry, ended in failure just at the point when that school was poised to become the period's major movement in poetry and poetics.

In telling this story in detail, I shall reverse the backward oriented trajectory pursued in the first part of this study. That part explored the beginnings, origins, and main precedents of the dramatic monologue, first in the works of early Tennyson and Browning, then in the Romantic science of feelings, and finally in the models provided by Shakespeare. The second half, now proceeding in forward oriented chronological fashion, will, after looking at the new psychological poetry from the viewpoint of its major Victorian opponent, survey that poetry's primary characteristics of form and content, as they began to be critically encoded during the 1850s. It will conclude with a discussion of Swinburne, whose *Poems and Ballads* mark the beginning disintegration of the dramatic monologue as conceived by Victorian poets and critics.

VII

Dead End: Matthew Arnold

TO BE SURE, the dramatic monologue by no means offered the only escape from the Romantic introspective dilemma. Even Tennyson and Browning, the two main pioneers in evolving the new genre, wrote in many other forms as well. Numerous minor poets, and some of the major ones, produced only isolated specimens of the dramatic-psychological kind, or none at all. More general was the trend toward self-effacement, at least to the point where poets could feel safe from the "biographic appetite" (Carlyle)[1] of psychologically minded reviewers. Long before W. L. Courtney, in 1883, suggested that "the only possible corrective to the excessive self-contemplation of the modern poet is the dramatic effort to render objective and concrete human passion and human weakness,"[2] several Victorian poets had proposed similar remedies.

When Thomas Burbidge had to defend his *Poems, Longer and Shorter* against the charge of confessionalism or "exhibition of private feeling," Arthur Hugh Clough discussed the matter in a letter. Aware of the Romantic science of feelings, he concedes that "all poetry must be the language of Feeling of some kind, I suppose, and the imaginative expression of affection must be poetry." At the same time, it seems to Clough "critically best and morally safest to dramatize your feelings where they are of a private personal character."[3] Tennyson, in similar vein, protested that the speaker of *In Memoriam* was not to be mistaken for the poet. "The different moods of sorrow as in a drama are dramatically given . . . 'I' is not always the author speaking of himself, but the voice of the human race speaking thro' him."[4] No major Victorian poet advocated this new objectivity more fiercely than Matthew Arnold. The poet, as he announced in the 1853 Preface to his *Poems*, is "most fortunate, when he most entirely succeeds in effacing himself."[5]

At the same time, Arnold's example goes to show that the urge for objectivity alone was no guarantee that the poetic results achieved in its pursuit would prove as effective as the dramatic monologue. The success of this genre had obvious and manifold reasons. Primarily, the dramatic monologue offered continuity rather than a radical new alternative. It transformed the Romantic science of feelings by assimilating its techniques while avoiding its metaphysical vagaries and introspective morbidity. To poets obsessed with themselves it offered a safe way to live out their obsession. In this way it could become the successor, not only of greater Romantic lyrics like Coleridge's "Dejection," but also of neo-Romantic drama as derived from works like Goethe's *Faust* and Byron's *Manfred*. Critics were far from wrong in grouping Tennyson's *Maud* with that dramatic tradition as lately revived by poets like Bailey, Smith, and Dobell. Yet *Maud*, as some of them failed to realize, offered more than reverie become pathological fallacy or Romantic "*mental theatre*"[6] turned Spasmodic exhibitionism. Like Browning's *Men and Women*, it had moved beyond these Romantic genres by transforming them into a vital new tradition of dramatic-psychological poetry. What Arnold proposed in his 1853 Preface, by contrast, was a dead end. Or at least such it proved to be in his own career as a poet.

The Search for the Buried Self

As we know, Arnold's demand that the poet efface himself in his poetry was made in response to a review of E. S. Dallas's *Poetics* and A. Smith's *Life Drama*, which argued that a "true allegory of the state of one's own mind in a representative history, whether narrative or dramatic in form, is perhaps the highest thing that one can attempt in the way of fictitious art."[7] To Arnold, the claim was simply preposterous. An allegory of the state of one's own mind, the highest thing to be attempted in poetry! "No assuredly, it is not, it never can be so: no great poetical work has ever been produced with such an aim."[8] In determining the true subject of poetry, Arnold resurrects Aristotle's *Poetics* and, at the same time, rejects the Romantic science of feelings. The poet should imitate actions, and do so "without interruption from the intrusion of his personal peculiarities."[9] Talking about drama, Arnold reverses the Romantic emphasis on character and psychology over action. Rather than

Shakespeare, his model is Greek tragedy, and particularly Sophocles whom he values "not so much [for] his contributions to psychology and the anatomy of sentiment, as [for] the grand moral effects produced by *style*."[10] Arnold even wrote a tragedy by way of illustrating his theory; but *Merope*, more than all else, marks his decline as a major poet. Posterity came to agree with Swinburne who viewed the play as the stillborn child of an essentially academic imagination. "As for Professor Arnold's Merope," Swinburne wrote in 1865, "the clothes are well enough but where has the body gone?"[11]

All this is the more surprising, since Arnold, more than any major Victorian poet, wrote in the vein of the Romantic or "subjective poet of modern classification."[12] Most of his greatest poems are cast in the mode of the greater Romantic lyric.[13] His one major drama, *Empedocles on Etna*, is clearly an allegory of Arnold's own mind in a representative history for which Byron's *Manfred* offers a precedent,[14] and Spasmodic drama the immediate though poetically inferior contemporary context. Even in terms of his major quest, Arnold followed similar precedent. If the Romantic poet "digs where he stands"—searching his soul, to quote Browning, for a "reflex of that absolute Mind, according to the intuitions of which he desires to perceive and speak"[15]—then no poet ever dug more doggedly where he stood than Arnold.

Again and again his poems assert the need for self-knowledge as the key to happiness, wisdom, oneness with nature, and understanding of the world. "Sink, O youth, in thy soul! / Yearn to the greatness of Nature; / Rally the good in the depths of thyself!" " 'Resolve to be thyself; and know that he, / Who finds himself, loses his misery!' " "Once read thy own breast right, / And thou hast done with fears; / . . . Sink in thyself! there ask what ails thee, at that shrine!"[16] Convinced that "the disease of the present age" was a "divorce from oneself,"[17] Arnold suggests a cure for this dilemma to his friend Clough: "You ask me in what I think or have thought you going wrong: in this: that you would never take your assiette as something determined final and unchangeable for you and proceed to work away on the basis of that: but were always poking and patching and cobbling at the assiette itself—could never finally, as it seemed—'resolve to be thyself.' "[18]

No doubt, then, Arnold was committed to the central Romantic notion that an appropriate understanding of the world had to be reached through self-knowledge. The question, which Tennyson and Browning, after raising it in their early works, preferred to dodge in their later ones, remains the primary concern of his poetic endeavors. Can we unearth our true self, so as to truly comprehend the world? About to throw himself into the crater, Empedocles still wonders "if we will now at last be true / To our own only true, deep-buried selves, / Being one with which we are one with the whole world" (II, 370–72). Even in later life, long after turning from poetry to criticism, Arnold reasserted his belief in a true self.

> Below the surface-stream, shallow and light,
> Of what we *say* we feel—below the stream,
> As light, of what we *think* we feel—there flows
> With noiseless current strong, obscure and deep,
> The central stream of what we feel indeed.
>   ("Below the Surface-Stream . . .")

There was reason, then, why Arnold should adopt the greater Romantic lyric as one of his major poetic forms. After all, it was in this mode that Wordsworth and Coleridge had dramatized their attempts at uniting their troubled egos with the surrounding world. To Matthew Arnold, William Wordsworth became the model in this pursuit. As Swinburne was the first to remark, "the good and evil influence of that great poet . . . upon Mr. Arnold's work is so palpable and so strong as to be almost obtrusive in its effects."[19] In retrospect, such discipleship makes the follower appear to be out of step with literary history. However, few of Arnold's contemporaries, particularly at the time when he matured into a poet, would have agreed with such hindsighted criticism.

In 1815 Wordsworth himself had announced that every great and original author has had to create "the taste by which he is to be enjoyed";[20] but it was not until the 1830s that he accomplished this feat for himself. Only then did the poet begin to acquire the fame and influence that won him the laureateship in 1843. Wordsworth's role as an evangelist who helped Victorians such as J. S. Mill, "Mark Rutherford," and William James through their spiritual crises is well known.[21] No less was his impact on minor poets. E.G.E.L. Bulwer-Lytton, in 1833, no doubt echoed a widely held opinion in praising Wordsworth's poems as the strongest spiritual bulwark against the period's materialistic thinking.[22] To Alaric A. Watts, as to many of his contemporaries, Wordsworth was the "High Priest of the Nine! Poet, Prophet, and Sage."[23]

Arnold himself bears witness to this belated rise to fame of a poet who, for most of his life, had largely suffered neglect and ridicule. The poetry-reading public, Arnold remembers, "was very slow to recognise him." But during the 1830s, Wordsworth reached the acme of his life-time recognition. "Wordsworth has never, either before or since, been so accepted and popular, so established in possession of the minds of all who profess to care for poetry, as he was between the years 1830 and 1840."[24]

Ironically, then, Arnold came under the sway of Wordsworth while an older man like Tennyson escaped the same influence. According to Wordsworth himself, Tennyson never showed much sympathy with what he most valued in his own attempts—"viz. the spirituality with which I have endeavoured to invest the material universe."[25] In turn, Arnold remembers how Tennyson, during the 1840s "drew to himself, and away from Wordsworth, the poetry-reading public, and the new generations."[26] One of that new generation, "born and baptized" in the church of Tennyson,[27] was Swinburne, who correctly locates Arnold's poetic origins in the limbo of delayed Wordsworthian influence just preceding the Tennysonian era. Arnold, as Swinburne remarks with uncanny insight, was "the last worth reckoning whom 'The Excursion' is ever likely to misguide."[28]

The Greater Romantic Lyric *in Extremis*

The astounding extent of such influence has been amply documented by twentieth-century scholarship. According to U. C. Knoepflmacher, "the core of Arnold's emotional power is Wordsworthian, and it is so by intent and not by mere coincidence. Arnold's poems avail themselves of situations that are Wordsworthian, images that are Wordsworthian, phrases that are Wordsworthian."[29] It has also been shown that Arnold, unlike some of his minor contemporaries, is no mere imitator in this pursuit. A poem like "Resignation," while closely modeled on "Tintern Abbey," essentially uses its deliberate allusiveness in order to deny the Wordsworthian vision. In this way, "Resignation" marks the next step beyond Coleridge's "Dejection."

"Tintern Abbey" deplores the poet's loss of his oneness with nature but ends on the assurance that a similar bond can be reestablished through mature thoughtfulness. "Dejection" dramatizes the speaker's inability to reenter into such emotional intimacy with his surroundings—"I see, not feel, how beautiful they are!" (38) By contrast, "Resignation" neither celebrates fulfillment and joy nor bemoans failure and dejection. Though it avails itself of its predecessors' two basic strategies of self-dramatization and simulated spontaneity, these merely create the framework for stating the impossibility of the Romantic vision. The lack of joy and feeling, which causes mere dismay to Coleridge, becomes the basis of a programmatic new poetics for Arnold. The "despotism of the eye," so vehemently denounced by the Romantics,[30] marks the new poet's most basic attitude toward the world. Rather than feel, he gazes, sees, and surveys. Instead of being one with nature, he is detached from it. A "sad lucidity of soul" ("Resignation," 198) replaces the feeling of "joy." Nature, which benignly responded to the Romantic poet's longings, has become "mute," "lonely," and "strange-scrawled" (265, 268). Instead of "a sense sublime / Of something far more deeply interfused, / . . . [that] rolls through all things" ("Tintern Abbey," 95–96, 102), the poet merely senses "The something that infects the world" ("Resignation," 278).

Arnold reiterates the same message in poem after poem. Some of these, like "Resignation," "Dover Beach," or "The Youth of Nature," are directly modeled on Wordsworthian poems. Others are cast in the form for which "Tintern Abbey" and "Intimations of Immortality" offered the two most outstanding models. "Self-Dependence" is an example of the latter. The poet, standing at the prow of a vessel crossing the nocturnal sea, implores nature to assuage his wearied state of inner division. Sick of asking himself what he is or ought to be, he yearns to relive his childhood when, gazing upon the stars and waters, he felt his soul become vast as these. But nature, in denying the poet's request, simply advises him to emulate the stars and waters in their self-sufficiency. "The Youth of Nature," with its address to the recently deceased Wordsworth and its opening allusion to his "Remembrance of Collins,"[31] follows a similar pattern. The speaker deplores the loss of a vision that seems to have died with the visionary. He wonders if what Wordsworth saw was merely projected upon or indeed intrinsic to nature. Then Nature denies the speaker's implied anthropomorphic claims by protesting her inscrutable self-sufficiency.

> "Race after race, man after man,
> Have thought that my secret was theirs,

Have dreamed that I lived but for them,
That they were my glory and joy.
—They are dust, they are changed, they are gone!
I remain."

(129–34)

But the poem's overall message is far from consistent. Throughout it runs a contradiction, which, as we shall see, saps Arnold's poetic creativity at its very root. While proclaiming her inscrutability, Nature implies that the problem essentially lies with the poet. How can the poet know nature, when he hardly knows himself?

"Hardly his voice at its best
Gives us a sense of the awe,
The vastness, the grandeur, the gloom
Of the unlit gulph of himself.

. . . .

Yourselves and your fellows ye know not; and me,
The mateless, the one, will ye know?
Will ye scan me, and read me, and tell
Of the thoughts that ferment in my breast,
My longing, my sadness, my joy?
Will ye claim for your great ones the gift
To have rendered the gleam of my skies,
To have echoed the moan of my seas,
Uttered the voice of my hills?
When your great ones depart, will ye say:
All things have suffered a loss,
Nature is hid in their grave?"
(99–102, 117–28)

In other words, a proper understanding of Nature's secrets depends upon proper self-knowledge. However discouraging she sounds, Nature still holds out the old Romantic promise, which equally remains Empedocles' even in the hour of suicide—"To see if we will now at last be true / To our own only true, deep-buried selves, / Being one with which we are one with the whole world" (II, 370–72).

Through a shift of perspective, "The Youth of Man" reinforces the same message. Now the poet sides with Nature, both looking down upon an older couple who, when younger, bragged about possessing the world through sheer anthropomorphic projection. What foolish mystics call Nature's intrinsic beauty and life, the couple used to argue, are merely attributes bestowed upon Nature by the feeling observer:

> for she
> Hath neither beauty, nor warmth,
> Nor life, nor emotion, nor power.
> But man has a thousand gifts,
> And the generous dreamer invests
> The senseless world with them all.
> Nature is nothing; her charm
> Lives in our eyes which can paint,
> Lives in our hearts which can feel.
>
> (29–37)

Erroneously, the couple advocates what Ruskin, a few years after Arnold's poem, attacked as the "pathetic fallacy."[32] For what has come of the "proud boasting of their youth" after time and old age dispelled "the mists of illusion" and made "the scales of habit, / Fall away from their eyes"? Merely the memory of their "faded, ignoble lives" in their "weary, unprofitable length" (103, 105, 106–107, 111, 110). The mystics prating of Nature's genuine life, emotion, and power, then, may have been right after all. But how is man to gain access to this truth of nature beyond "pathetic fallacy" and anthropomorphic projection? Once again, introspection is proposed as the only way:

> Sink, O youth, in thy soul!
> Yearn to the greatness of Nature;
> Rally the good in the depths of thyself!
>
> (116–18)

Arnold nowhere discussed the possibility of such knowledge more thoroughly than in "The Buried Life." Addressing his beloved at a moment of unexpected sadness, which has disrupted their "war of mocking words" (1), the poet deplores his basic inability to express his true emotions. At the same time, he affirms the existence of moments when genuine self-knowledge opens up into a knowledge of life in general. This is when "The eye sinks inward, and the heart lies plain." Then,

A man becomes aware of his life's flow,
And hears its winding murmur; and he sees
The meadows where it glides, the sun, the breeze.

. . . .

And then he thinks he knows
The hills where his life rose,
And the sea where it goes.
      (86, 88–90, 96–98)

Yet despite such final assurances, the poem creates a feeling of ambivalence. The speaker merely asserts what the dramatic structure of his lyric fails to evoke as occurring in the actual situation at hand. Here "the nameless feelings that course through" the speaker's breast remain indeed "unexpressed."

And long we try in vain to speak and act
Our hidden self, and what we say and do
Is eloquent, is well—but 'tis not true!
      (62, 63, 64–66)

While assuring us that nature's true reality *can* be known, Arnold also tells us that the prerequisite for such knowledge—an understanding of one's true self—has become near unattainable. His sense of these "deep recesses of our breast" (38) is a far cry from the pioneering optimism of earlier generations who felt that introspection, like an "Open Sesame," could easily unlock man's inner world. The poem's title as well as the imagery, which Arnold, here and elsewhere, associates with his "genuine self" (36), speak for themselves. No one has ever "mined" (56) deeply enough to unearth the true "mystery of this heart" (52). Man's true "identity" (34) is a stream, "obscure and deep," below the "surface-stream."[33] "The soul's subterranean depth" (73) resembles an "unlit gulph."[34] Whatever it is, man's "hidden self" (65) remains "unplumbed, / Unscaled, untrodden."[35] Most frequently Arnold calls it "buried" or "deep-buried."[36] It is our "buried life" or "buried stream," "Eddying at large in blind uncertainty" (48, 42, 43). All we hear of it are faint sounds reaching our ear from a far distance:

. . . from time to time, vague and forlorn,
From the soul's subterranean depth upborne
As from an infinitely distant land,

Come airs, and floating echoes, and convey
A melancholy into all our day.

(72–76)

When compared with similar concepts held by Clough and George
Eliot, Arnold's notion of "the soul's subterranean depth," so one critic
argues, has more in common with recent notions of the unconscious
and particularly with Jung's collective unconscious.[37] Such comparisons
are tempting. However, Arnold's "hidden self" finds even closer parallels with contemporaries like Sir William Hamilton and his disciple
E. S. Dallas. Dallas's terminology in this respect simply duplicates and
expands on Arnold's. His 1852 *Poetics*, which, along with A. Smith's
Life Drama, caused Arnold to denounce poems that are allegories of the
author's own mind, speaks of our "hidden life" and "unknown depth of
our own soul."[38] Dallas's later *Gay Science* describes this "hidden soul"
or "hidden life of thought" as the "great tide of life" or the "inner
shrine."[39] Equally reminiscent of "The Buried Life" is the critic's sense
of the scrambled messages that reach us from this far distant realm: "In
the dark recesses of memory, in unbidden suggestions, in trains of
thought unwittingly pursued, in multiplied waves and currents all at
once flashing and rushing, in dreams that cannot be laid, in the nightly
rising of the somnambulist, in the clairvoyance of passion, in the force
of instinct, in the obscure, but certain, intuitions of the spiritual life,
we have glimpses of a great tide of life ebbing and flowing, rippling
and rolling and beating about where we cannot see it."[40]

In fact, if Jung had a Victorian predecessor, it was Dallas rather than
Arnold. According to *The Gay Science*, it is due to the marvels of memory's "hidden work" that the "same fables, the same comparisons, the
same jests are produced and reproduced like the tunes of a barrel-organ
in successive ages and in different countries."[41] In similarly Jungian
vein, Dallas compares the "hidden efficacy of our thoughts, their pro-
digious power of working in the dark and helping us underhand" with
"the stories of our folk-lore."[42] It is easy to imagine how Arnold must
have balked at such notions. Equally alien to him was Dallas's conviction that modern psychology, and particularly the wonders of somnambulism, would unriddle the enigmas of the unconscious. Nothing to
Dallas was "so much wanted as a correct Psychology,"[43] and if he felt
that mental science, especially as applied to poetry and criticism, was
still in its infancy,[44] it was only in terms of how much he expected from

its maturity. As far as unconscious creativity—"the last and highest law of poetry"[45]—was concerned, it was best to simply abandon oneself to the "automatic action of the mind."[46] No wonder that Keats, in Dallas's view, had known more about such matters than any man of his century.[47]

MATTHEW ARNOLD AND PSYCHOLOGY

Again, nothing could be more contrary to Arnold's convictions. If Keats had let poetry come to him as the leaves come to a tree, then his poems were only the worse for having been written in this fashion. *Endymion*, to Arnold, was "utterly incoherent," while *Isabella* was "so loosely constructed, that the effect produced by it, in and for itself, is absolutely null."[48] The only notion Arnold shared with Dallas was that of "the soul's subterranean depth" as a secret treasure trove of wisdom. But to Arnold these riches were lost or "buried," and no human discipline, least of all psychology, seemed capable of retrieving them.

> But more than all unplumbed,
> Unscaled, untrodden, is the heart of man.
> More than all secrets hid, the way it keeps.
> Nor any of our organs so obtuse,
> Inaccurate, and frail,
> As those wherewith we try to test
> Feelings and motives there.
> (*Merope*, 629–35)

It was not that Arnold lacked psychological insight. On the contrary, his poems alone bear witness to introspective knowledge equaled only by the most radical thinkers of his age. Just as Walter Pater was to speak of the self in terms of its irremediable solipsism—"each mind keeping as a solitary prisoner its own dream of the world"[49]—Arnold repeatedly emphasizes the essential isolation of each individual.

> Yes! in the sea of life enisled,
> With echoing straits between us thrown,
> . . . .
> We mortal millions live *alone*.
> ("To Marguerite—Continued," 1–2, 4)

Just as Arthur Hallam had been haunted by the occasional sense of existing, "as it were, piecemeal, and in the continual flux of a stream,"[50] Arnold comes to see self-division as a normal everyday experience. "My poems are fragments," he confessed in 1849, "i.e. that I am fragments."[51]

Arnold even went as far as to suggest that what we call our self might be a succession of selves, each alien to the other, an area of psychological speculation James Thomson was to explore in his 1865 essay entitled "Sympathy." So disjointed are these successive selves to Thomson, that a given Mr. Smith at age thirty may sympathize more closely with the present Mr. Brown than with his previous identities at, say, twenty or fifteen. In sum, "we are governed by a succession in mysterious permutation of unlike-minded tyrants, all alike deaf in the hours of their supremacy, all alike dumb in the hours of their subjection."[52] Similarly, Arnold, in "Youth's Agitations," anticipates the time, "some ten years hence," when he will "be divorced" from the "poor present self" experienced as his at the moment of utterance (1, 2).

Clearly, Arnold did not lack psychological insight. If anything, he had more of it than he wished to. Be that as it may, contemporary mental science never attracted his special attention. Arnold's rare comments on psychology are conspicuous mainly for highlighting his dismissive, if not contemptuous, attitude to the discipline as he knew it. Psychology, to Arnold, could only explore the surface of our deep-buried selves. As much as he remained committed to questing for these hidden mysteries, as consistently did he repudiate attempts at their categorization.

> Affections, Instincts, Principles, and Powers,
> Impulse and Reason, Freedom and Control—
> So men, unravelling God's harmonious whole,
> Rend in a thousand shreds this life of ours.

Thus we read in a poem, "Written in Butler's Sermons" (1–4), probably from the year 1844. The same critique of Butler's psychology is reiterated over three decades later in "Bishop Butler and the Zeit-Geist," a lecture delivered at the Edinburgh Philosophical Institution. The "instincts and principles of action," which Butler treats as "separate, fixed, and palpable" entities like "the bodily organs which the dissector has on his table before him," are to Arnold the "most obscure, changing, interdependent of phenomena."[53]

The impact of Arnold's antipathy to psychology on his poetic creativity is incalculable. While obsessed with the "buried life" of his unconscious, he knew as early as 1852 that his poetic quest toward unearthing it would probably prove abortive. "I feel now where my poems
. . . are all wrong," he then wrote to Clough, "which I did not a year
ago: but I doubt whether I shall ever have heat and radiance enough to
pierce the clouds that are massed round me."[54] Six years later, such
defeat has become a *fait accompli*. Overburdened by work as a school
inspector, Arnold remembers what would have been necessary for the
fulfillment of his quest—a "knocking yourself to pieces . . . an actual
tearing of oneself to pieces, which one does not readily consent to . . .
unless one can devote one's whole life to poetry." Wordsworth could,
and so could Byron and Shelley.[55] Arnold could not.

The reason for this, of course, was not just his work as a school inspector and critic. To Arnold the main culprit was

> . . . this strange disease of modern life,
> With its sick hurry, its divided aims,
> Its heads o'ertaxed, its palsied hearts. . . .
> ("The Scholar Gipsy," 203–205)

In a different era the quest for the "buried life" might have been easy.
But in his own "deeply *unpoetical*" age, this pursuit only unearthed the
vicissitudes of its own failure. Where the Romantic poet had searched
his soul for a "reflex of that absolute Mind, according to the intuitions
of which he desires to perceive and speak,"[56] his Victorian successor
could merely perceive and speak of the psychological problems that
blocked his way. "It is only in the best poetical epochs" so totally unlike
his own, Arnold felt, "that you can descend into yourself and produce
the best of your thought and feeling naturally, and without an overwhelming and in some degree morbid effort."[57]

The obvious way out of this problem would have been to turn from
introspective morbidity to the analysis of objective personae. This, after
all, was the route older poets like Tennyson and Browning had taken
before him. But given his aversion to psychology, it was either all or
nothing for Arnold. In turn, he criticized both Browning and Tennyson
for writing without the clear inner focus that he could not locate in
himself: neither poet understood that one "must begin with an Idea of
the world in order not to be prevailed over by the world's multitudinousness."[58] Hence Tennyson, to him, seemed to be solely dawdling

with the universe's "painted shell," while Browning merely projected a "confused multitudinousness."[59] No wonder that he would not follow their lead in writing poems of the new dramatic-psychological kind. To Arnold this would have meant abandoning his quest for the "central stream of what we feel indeed," and instead dabbling in "the surface-stream, shallow and light"[60] of what contemporary mental science and its poetic adherents gave out to be man's inner world. Rather, would he cease to write poetry altogether.

Empedocles on Etna AND SPASMODIC DRAMA

This impulse, as we know, reached its most dramatic climax in the omission of *Empedocles on Etna* from the 1853 edition of *Poems*. The reasons for this rejection, as given in the Preface, parallel the negative comments on his lyrical poems elsewhere. In these, as in the play, the author delineates an essentially modern, or rather Arnoldian, phenomenon—"the dialogue of the mind with itself." Empedocles' quest, like Arnold's own, is for his deep-buried self, but, like the poems, the play only reflects the psychological dilemmas incurred in this ultimately abortive pursuit. Hence his situation, "in which a continuous state of mental distress is prolonged, unrelieved by incident, hope, or resistance," is essentially that of the modern poet in this unpoetical Victorian age. There "is inevitably something morbid"[61] about it, just as a poet in these "damned times"[62] could no longer "descend into [himself] and produce the best of [his] thought and feeling naturally . . . without an overwhelming and in some degree morbid effect."[63]

No doubt, then, *Empedocles on Etna* is a "true allegory of the state of [its author's] mind"[64] as more directly delineated in the poems. Again and again, the protagonist Romantically affirms self-knowledge as the proper access to knowledge of the world. "Well, then, the wiser wight / In his own bosom delves" (I, 2, 129–30), he advises Pausanias.

> Once read thy own breast right,
> And thou hast done with fears;
> Man gets no other light,
> Search he a thousand years.
> Sink in thyself! there ask what ails thee, at that shrine!
>
> (I, 2, 142–46)

For "those who know / Themselves" (I, 2, 387–88) little joy is to be derived from intercourse with the world. For Nature, inscrutable and self-sufficient, simply turns a cold shoulder on our wishful thinking. Like the speaker in "The Youth of Man," Empedocles is the declared enemy of all pathetic fallacy and anthropomorphic projection.

> Scratched by a fall, with moans
> As children of weak age
> Lend life to the dumb stones
> Whereon to vent their rage,
> And bend their little fists, and rate the senseless ground;
> So, loth to suffer mute,
> We, peopling the void air,
> Make Gods to whom to impute
> The ills we ought to bear;
> With God and Fate to rail at, suffering easily.
>
> (I, 2, 272–81)

But the prophet despairs of his own message.[65] If there is real truth to be found behind pathetic fallacy, as his basic belief in his deep-buried self assures him, then Empedocles has never found it. Hence, left to himself, he yearns for the reassuring warmth of a world that previous generations read in the light of their anthropomorphic needs. Rationally, he advises Pausanias to accept "dejection" as a fact of existence; emotionally, he feels no different, or worse, than the speaker of Coleridge's poem of that title:

> Oh, that I could glow like this mountain!
> Oh, that my heart bounded with the swell of the sea!
> Oh, that my soul were full of light as the stars!
>
> (II, 323–25)

But he can no longer feel such emotions. Dead "to life and joy," he instead reads "In all things [his] own deadness" (II, 321, 322). Granted that the urge "To see if we will now at last be true / To our own only true, deep-buried selves, / Being one with which we are one with the whole world" (II, 370–72) follows him even into death. But as far as his life is concerned, this quest has resulted in complete failure. All it has given him and us is insight into phenomena that are of as little interest to Empedocles as they were to Arnold himself. Surely both knew to perfection how to shut their eyes

and muse
How our own minds are made.
What springs of thought they use.
(I, 2, 327–29)

There was little to be hoped for from such introspection unless it went all the way in unearthing our deep-buried selves. If this ultimate goal was unattainable, the quest became a mere "dialogue of the mind with itself," forever ruminating on its futility. There clearly was reason why Arnold decided to omit *Empedocles on Etna* from his 1853 *Poems*; or why, in the Preface, he would attack the critic who, taking his cue from A. Smith's *Life Drama*, argued that a "true allegory of the state of one's own mind in a representative history" was "perhaps the highest thing that one can attempt in the way of poetry."[66]

Though primarily leveled at Spasmodic drama, the attack was at least implicitly self-inflicted. For no one would have been more aware of the affinities between this curious genre and *Empedocles on Etna* than Arnold himself. For one, both have common roots in Romantic "*mental theatre*,"[67] particularly Goethe's *Faust* and Byron's *Manfred*. Like these models, Arnold's play, along with its Spasmodic counterparts, is monodramatically built around a Romantic hero-poet protagonist on his more or less nebulous and troubled quest. Most notably perhaps, *Empedocles* shares with later Spasmodic drama a distinct preoccupation with the hero's psychological tribulations, to the point where the plays read like case histories of the diseased Romantic sensibility.

Even before meeting him, we learn that Empedocles has "a settled trouble in his air," is "always moody" and is "half mad / With exile, and with brooding on his wrongs" (I, 1, 68, 74, 23–24). The protagonist merely adds to this picture by telling us that he looks on life "with eyes / Estranged . . . and sad" or that he is "dead to life and joy" (I, 2, 409–10; II, 321). Whatever else ails his troubled soul is amply documented by his tortured soliloquies. For the most part this mental trouble derives, as M. A. Weinstein has said of Bailey's *Festus*, not from "any external stimulus, but . . . from the action of the mind upon itself."[68] Such introspective malaise, of course, plagues the genre's protagonists from the beginning. Faust's breast harbors two souls of which one wants to separate itself from the other.[69] Manfred, like Empedocles after him, is the victim of restless self-analysis; even his slumbers are not real sleep,

But a continuance of enduring thought,
Which then I can resist not: in my heart
There is a vigil, and these eyes but close
To look within

(I, I, 4–7)

Bailey's *Festus*, the prototype of the Spasmodic poet-protagonist proper, writes "amid the ruins of his heart; / They were his throne and theme."[70]

With J. W. Marston's *Gerald* (1842), Spasmodic drama programmatically joins the tradition of poems in which a poet, as Wordsworth put it in the 1814 preface of *The Excursion*, reviews his own mind, making it and "the Mind of Man—/ [His] haunt, and the main region of [his] song."[71] Marston's play, to quote W. J. Fox's review of *Pauline*, presents the "annals of a poet's mind,"[72] or in the playwright's own words, dramatizes "the struggles and experiences of *Genius*."[73] In thus delineating "a great mind, subject to infirmities," Marston's least concern is with action. Instead, he tries to illuminate *"certain points* in Gerald's mental history—to show the *crises* of his developments," by making the hero voice his prelinguistic reveries. Gerald's words "are intended to represent thoughts which one would scarcely express in language to oneself—far less to another—involuntary thoughts by which the mind is borne along without any conscious effort of its own."[74]

A. Smith, in his *A Life-Drama*, was probably the most extreme delineator of "the over-loaded heart."[75] However, more interesting regarding the genre's final development in the direction of the new school of psychological poetry is Sydney Dobell's *Balder*. For diverse metaphysical and pseudo-humanitarian reasons, the protagonist first kills his daughter, succumbs to and recovers from temporary insanity, witnesses, in the company of a doctor, how his wife Amy falls victim to permanent madness, and as the drama draws to a close, is about to kill her as well. When an outraged reading public accused the author for celebrating this dubious hero, Dobell added a preface to the poem's second edition of 1854. Here he argues that Balder was intended as "a warning," not as a model.[76] If reviewers had described the protagonist as "egoistic, self-contained, and sophistical, imperfect in morality, and destitute of recognised religion," then this was precisely the impression Dobell had set out to create. Nonetheless, the playwright grants that

Balder is a true child of this "great, ambitious, but perplexed and dis-concerted time," and as such an at least partial self-portrait: "That I, in common with many of my critics, am not altogether free from some of the sins of my hero is probable on the general principle that 'Balderism' in one form or another is a predominant intellectual misfortune of our day."[77] If hero and author were insufficiently disassociated, they would be more clearly separated later. For the existing drama was only the first of a projected three-part sequence delineating "the Progress of a Human Being from Doubt to Faith, from Chaos to Order."[78] But for reasons directly linked to Arnold's 1853 Preface, these concluding sections of *Balder* were never written.

This was due to the virtual annihilation of the Spasmodics at the hands of W. E. Aytoun who launched his first major attack against that school in a review of Arnold's *Poems* (1853).[79] While noting that Ar-nold's poetry did not comply with his theories, Aytoun nonetheless greets the Preface as an important ally against "the daily practice of the Guffaws," later rechristened Spasmodics. He also criticizes Arnold's slavish adherence to classical models, but finds that in general it "would be well for the literature of the age if sound criticism of this [kind] were more common. Mr. Arnold is undoubtedly correct in holding that the first duty of the poet, after selecting his subject, is to take pains to fashion it symmetrically."[80]

The remainder of Aytoun's crusade against Spasmody is well known. In May 1854, two months after his article on Arnold, he published a burlesque review of an unpublished tragedy, entitled *Firmilian; or, The Student of Badajoz,* alleged to be by T. Percy Jones, most recent disciple of the Spasmodic tribe. Lovers of the school denounced the review as unfair and demanded that the play be released. Aytoun was quick to oblige them and within weeks produced "a real roaring tragedy." "I wish I could show you some of my lines, written *currente calamo,*" he bragged to a friend. "Damme, sir, if crambo isn't the thing after all! And the advantage is, that you can go on slapdash, without think-ing."[81] *Firmilian,* a 153-page "Spasmodic Tragedy," appeared in July of 1854 and some thousand copies of it sold out overnight.

Firmilian accomplished more than its author could have hoped for in his wildest dreams. Two reviewers mistook it for a genuine Spasmodic tragedy. Others hailed it as a model parody. *Firmilian* retroactively en-hanced Aytoun's critical stance and brought about a literal volte-face in literary opinion. Spasmodic drama had been perhaps the most popular poetic phenomenon of its age.[82] Bailey's *Festus* alone went into more than a hundred editions. Notables like Elizabeth Barrett, the young Swinburne, Browning, and Tennyson counted among the admirers of the Spasmodics. Numerous critics, among them A. H. Clough, who in the *North American Review* praised A. Smith to the detriment of Matthew Arnold, spoke admiringly or at least respectfully of Spasmodic poetry. But after *Firmilian* the reaction was almost unanimous. Spasmody was condemned, ridiculed, and/or reviled by the leading journals; and Arnold who had sparked the first offensive against the school, again became a widely invoked ally in its destruction. "Mr. Arnold's style is simple, almost to baldness, and contrasts strongly with the profuse ornaments of the school of 'Balder,' "[83] observed the *London Quarterly*. "Mr. Arnold seems to have been driven, by the consideration of the faults of those writers, into almost an affection of indifference to minute verbal beauties," commented the *Edinburgh Review*.[84]

The poem especially singled out for such praise, of course, fared little better at the hands of posterity than Spasmodic drama itself. *Sohrab and Rustum*—like *Merope* a product of its author's reaction against "Spasmodic" elements in his own poetry—has shared its declining fortunes with poems like *Festus* and *A Life Drama*. The cure, which the Preface prescribed for the dilemma, to all evidence, proved lethal in Arnold's own case. If the controversy that Arnold ignited had a survivor, it was not *Sohrab and Rustum*, but a poem that, published in 1855, was instantly ridiculed as the post-mortem spasm of an already defunct literary school. *Maud*, wrote *The Guardian*, "is a poem in the 'Spasmodic' school of poetry, hardly superior in that kind to *The Roman*, or *Balder*, or *Festus*."[85] Aytoun, finding *Maud* "so very spasmodic" that it reminded him "of the writhing of a knot of worms,"[86] invoked *Balder* and *A Life Drama* as its literary ancestors.[87] D. G. Rossetti thought that *Maud* was worthy of Smith rather than of Tennyson, while someone else claimed that Smith had done a better job than the Laureate.[88]

Maud, or the Way out of the Impasse

At least in one sense, reviewers had reason to write about *Maud* in this vein. For unlike works like *Aurora Leigh* and *Men and Women*, which came under similar attack,[89] *Maud* was truly in the Spasmodic tradition. Closest is the poem's affinity with *Balder* by Sydney Dobell, a poet whom Tennyson admired.[90] The protagonists of both works are depicted as mental victims of what Dobell calls this "perplexed and disconcerted time" and Tennyson this "recklessly speculative age." Balder is "egoistic, self-contained, and sophistical,"[91] Tennyson's hero "an egoist with the makings of a cynic."[92] Both undergo a spell of insanity and recover. In depicting his protagonist's madness, Tennyson may even have drawn upon a central notion in the self-characterization of Balder's insane wife Amy. Both she and Tennyson's male hero think that they have been buried alive while normal life continues above them. The resemblance between *Maud* II, 239ff. and the following lines from *Balder* is close enough to suggest direct influence.

> The worm crawls o'er me; the snail harbours up
> My limbs. I am as dark and all-forgot
> As any stone that never saw the sun
> And is and was and will be in the earth.
> I hear the sound of life above my head,
> The toads leap with it, and the very rock
> Shakes with the overgoing; but I know
> The fallen ruins lie on heap; my cry
> Can never struggle to the day; no man
> Will ever seek me.
>   Hist! they move the stones![93]

Tennyson, like Dobell, was criticized for identifying with the protagonist. In fact, both poets took part of the blame in response; Dobell did by admitting that he suffered from Balderism himself,[94] Tennyson by describing Maud's lover as a "poetic soul"[95] and by endorsing Brimley's interpretation of *Maud* as dramatizing the typical Romantic poet—"morbid, hysterical, spasmodic"—who, even if he did not speak for Tennyson himself, easily stood for poets like Shelley and Keats.[96] Reviewers had no reason to feel indignant about the depiction of a character like Balder, argued Dobell. If they cared to study the lives of some of their most admired poets, they would find Balderism "in the much-observed and well-recorded characters of men who have been, and have more or less deserved to be, praised, loved, followed and revered." Dobell himself refers to "the Autobiography of Haydon; to memorable passages in the letters of Keats; to many lessons from the life of David Scott; to sundry incidents in the history of Goethe."[97]

But for all these resemblances between *Balder* and *Maud*, there remains a major difference. Dobell may protest that he wanted to make his hero appear precisely in the negative light—"egoistic, self-contained, and sophistical, imperfect in morality, and destitute of recognised religion, mistaken in his estimate of his own powers and productions, and sacrificing to visionary hopes and dreamy distant philanthropies the blessing that lay in his embrace, and 'the duty which was nearest' "—in which he had been perceived by hostile reviewers.[98] The trouble is that the play itself fails to provide such a perspective. Except for what might be pieced together from its content, there is little else to make us see the protagonist in this negative light. Dobell might have adopted Ben Jonson's technique, for instance, of introducing a specific character who expresses the author's point of view. But as a friend pointed out to the poet, *Balder*, like Spasmodic drama generally, lacks "any character in the work to show the *author's* moral status, and so to contrast it with the aberrations of the hero."[99] Although *Balder* introduces several additional dramatis personae, all of these serve to highlight rather than offset the protagonist.

Nor do Balder's utterances give us a critical perspective different from that in which he chooses to present himself as the Romantic Faustian hero. In this Dobell's play differs most sharply from Tennyson's "monodrama." The difference is clear from the beginning. *Balder* predictably opens in the hero's "STUDY, WITH BOOKS, MSS. AND STATUES. A WINDOW LOOKS OVER A COUNTRY VALLEY TO THE NEIGHBOURING MOUNTAINS." In this Romantic setting, Balder instantly indulges in reveries, which in equally predictable fashion imbue the outside world with the gloomy colors of his dark Byronic soul.

> Balder (*musing*). To-morrow I count thirty years, save one.
> Ye grey stones
> Of this old tower gloomy and ruinous,
> Wherein I make mine eyrie as an eagle
>
> . . . .
> Or above which I rise, as a great ghost
> Out of its mortal hull; . . .
>   . . . thou sweet vale
> In which my soul, calm lying like a lake,
> Reflects the stars, or, stirred, upon the shores
> Of mountains maketh music, or more loud,
> Rising in sudden flood, and breaking up
> That firmament to heaped and scattered stars,

Chaotic to and fro from hill to hill
Defies the rounding elements, and rolls
Reverberating thunder. [100]

Balder strikes us as presumptuous but hardly as deranged. He may indulge in "pathetic fallacy," but it is only since 1856, when Ruskin coined the phrase, that we have learned to read this Romantic idiosyncracy as expressive of a "more or less irrational" state of mind resulting in a "morbid, that is to say . . . false, idea" about reality. [101] Most of Dobell's immediate contemporaries continued to argue that poetry, being "emotive," as G. H. Lewes puts it, presents nature "through the passionate medium of the speaker's soul." [102]

By contrast, the opening of *Maud* leaves no doubt as to the speaker's at least potentially deranged state of mind. There is clearly more here than what Ruskin calls a mere "falseness in all our impressions of external things" effected by "violent feelings." [103] Pathetic has turned pathological fallacy:

I hate the dreadful hollow behind the little wood,
Its lips in the field above are dabbled with blood-red heath,
The red-ribbed ledges drip with a silent horror of blood,
And Echo there, whatever is asked her, answers 'Death.'

As much as critics disagreed on *Maud* in general, their response to its beginning was surprisingly unanimous. *The Eclectic Review*, staunch supporter of the Spasmodic cause, was "shocked by the ghastly images and snarling, acrid satire with which it opens." [104] Even W. E. Aytoun admitted that this opening established the speaker as "morbid and misanthropical." [105] To the reviewer in *Fraser's* there was no doubt that "from the first the man has in himself the possibility of madness." Surely there could be no more fitting beginning for a poem which as a whole was "a delineation of the path to madness." [106] The speaker, commented the *Edinburgh Review*,

begins by describing a certain "dreadful hollow" behind a wood, which has been made hateful to him by its having been the scene of his father's death. Were Mr. Tennyson writing in his own person, we should feel disposed to quarrel with the expression "blood-red heath" with which the fields are "dabbled," for even the recollection of a death connected with blood, could hardly endue the deepest-coloured heath with such a colour; but on finding out that the supposed writer is a mad man in embryo, we can only admire the care with which this fact is recollected by Mr. Tennyson in every part, one of the most popularly recognised symptoms of incipient madness being a constant dreaming of, and recurrence to, the idea of blood, and the colour red.[107]

Of course, the difference between *Balder* and *Maud* is not a simplistic alternative of author-protagonist identity in one case and of author-protagonist nonidentity in the other. Critics protesting that the speaker of *Maud* had nothing to do with Tennyson were as wrong as those who claimed the opposite. Or so at least argued the author of a remarkable essay in the *Oxford and Cambridge Magazine*, one of the first to comprehend the "rare union of subjective reflectiveness with objective life and vigour"[108] characteristic of the new dramatic-psychological genre.

Despite the "great outcry" in England "against introspective writing," argues the anonymous reviewer, there is nothing wrong with the fact "that much in 'Maud' may have been *suggested* by old struggles"[109] in the poet's own mind. No matter if the poem, even in this semi-autobiographical sense, be indeed a "dialogue of the mind with itself." There is nothing wrong with introspection as such. "For how can a man speak more directly and forcibly to the hearts of his fellows than by speaking from his own heart? How can he more deeply and surely fathom the minds of others than by searching into his own mind, that inner little world which . . . is the miniature of the great world without him." Thus a poem can well be both subjective and objective in one. While prompted by the author's introspective habits, it simply applied the insights developed in this pursuit to "the dramatic exhibition of passions and feelings, and fancies."[110] Those "who have been accusing the poet of diseased 'subjectivity' and what not," argues another critic, should "attend to this peculiarity of the present poem": "All songs or lyrical pieces are, in their very nature, 'subjective,' being expressions either of the poet's personal feelings or of feelings imagined by him as belonging to such and such circumstances; and the positive peculiarity of *Maud* is, that the poet has there contrived to weave together a poem which, though 'subjective' in its parts, is as 'objective' as any one could desire in its total impression."[111]

Another reviewer of *Maud* takes direct issue with the Arnoldian notion that "Action, action, action" is the only possible cure to the diseased subjectivity of the post-Romantic poet. "It is complained," he writes, "that our poets, from Wordsworth downwards, have been psychologists instead of historians: but to our thinking, it would be a fairer complaint that they have been historians without being psychologists."[112] If to anyone, the comment applies to Arnold, who correctly diagnosed his own disease but only by finding himself a deadly cure. *Merope* was no alternative to *Empedocles on Etna*. The step beyond the Romantic "dialogue of the mind with itself" could be found only where the poet transmuted his introspective obsession into a psycho-analytically extroverted creativity. The genesis of *Maud*, as traced in an earlier chapter, clearly delineates this process in Tennyson's life. We know that despite protests to the contrary, Arnold searched for a similar solution, but that he failed. Would he "ever have heat and radiance enough," he wondered in 1852, "to pierce the clouds that [were] massed round [him]?"[113] A prerequisite for that would have been "an actual tearing of oneself to pieces,"[114] but by 1858, when he said so, Arnold had given up on the pursuit. One reason for that was his involvement in other, nonpoetic activities; another his contempt for psychology as he knew it. Even had he managed to explore the true nature of his "buried life," he would hardly have felt inclined to compose a psycho-analytically objectified follow-up to *Empedocles* similar to *Maud*. To him, Tennyson's poem was "a lamentable production, and like so much of our literature thoroughly and intensely *provincial*, not European."[115]

VIII

The Psychological School of Poetry: Patterns

THE BEGINNINGS of the dramatic monologue, as we recall, go back to the 1820s and 1830s. But it was not until after the publication of *Maud* and *Men and Women* in 1855, that is two years after Arnold's Preface, that the genre became a major tradition. Granted, there are isolated specimens written by poets other than Browning and Tennyson before that. Aytoun's "Blind Old Milton" appeared in 1841,[1] Elizabeth Barrett's "Bertha in the Lane" in 1844,[2] "The Runaway Slave at Pilgrim's Point," her "anti-slavery poem for America"[3] in 1848, Charlotte Brontë's "Pilate's Wife's Dream" in 1846.[4] But if we add a few more samples by minor poets[5] we have covered all there is.

By contrast, the number of dramatic monologues after 1855 increases so suddenly and steeply that a bare list of their authors would require a separate paragraph. Among the major poets, these include Morris, Meredith, Clough, the two Rossettis, Swinburne, Kipling, and Hardy.[6] The names of the thirty-odd minor practitioners of the genre are best relegated to an appendix.[7] Be it enough to mention that, following *Men and Women*, comparable collections of such poems appeared in rapid succession. The first of these, of 1857, is found in George W. Thornbury's *Songs of the Cavaliers* . . . , in a separate section entitled "Dramatic Monologues." Others include Edward H. Plumptre's *Lazarus and Other Poems* (1864) and *Master and Scholar* (1866), Robert Buchanan's *Idylls and Legends of Inverburn* (1865) and *London Poems* (1866), Augusta Webster's *Dramatic Studies* (1866) and *Portraits* (1870), Edward R. Bulwer Lytton's *Chronicles and Characters* (1868) and *Poems* (1869), as well as W. W. Story's *Graffiti d'Italia* (1868), whose second edition of 1875 is the perhaps most comprehensive collection of its kind besides *Men and Women.*

Likewise it was not until after 1855 that the new genre received proper critical attention. Most of these attempts, as already noted, stress its "dramatic-psychological" nature. Hence, the genre's present denomination had to compete for a long time with others such as "drama of the interior," "portrait in mental photography," or simply "psychological monologue."[8] Similarly, early definitions emphasize what one reviewer calls Tennyson's "power of penetrating the mood of another mind . . . *in a special situation,*"[9] or what H. B. Forman, in his extensive definition of the new genre, describes as its concern with "the history of a human soul."[10]

Meanwhile, news of the emergence of an unprecedented dramatic-psychological genre also spread across the Channel. M. Louis Etienne's 1870 essay on Robert Browning in the *Revue des deux mondes*, easily the world's most prestigious journal at the time, announced in its title that English literature had given birth to "Une Nouvelle Forme de Poésie Dramatique."[11] What did this form consist of, particularly when looked at through the eyes of Victorian reviewers?

OPENING, SETTING, AND LISTENER

The sight of a crippled girl walking by, the arrival of a letter, a seemingly insignificant phrase spoken by someone—these examples from Meredith's "Martin's Puzzle" as well as Tennyson's "The Grandmother" and "The First Quarrel" show that dramatic monologues (in Hiram Corson's words) often begin "with a startling abruptness, and the reader must read along some distance before he gathers what the beginning means."[12] Yet however arbitrary they appear, these openings somehow manage to catch our attention or even to cause suspense. Why has Fra Lippo Lippi been arrested? Why is the young woman speaker in Tennyson's "The Flight" in a state of extreme nervous tension? One wonders what might be the story behind the painting of the duchess, which the duke in Browning's famous poem unveils so flamboyantly; or behind the gin bottle pointed out at the beginning of Tennyson's "The Northern Cobbler"; or behind the phrase "Wait a little, [I am] sure it'll all come right," which, spoken by her doctor friend and listener, prompts the woman in "The First Quarrel" to tell the tale of her miserable life. Whatever it be, the curtain, to quote another reviewer, is "skilfully lifted at just the right moment"[13] in each case.

Dramatic monologues, in other words, begin not "at the beginning, but, as it were, in the middle, and [imply] what has gone before."[14] Except for its occasional theatrical effects, this technique is similar to that found in greater Romantic lyrics. In this way, Tintern Abbey, in Wordsworth's poem, and the portrait of the "last duchess," in Browning's, perform the same function: while arousing our curiosity as to their possible significance, they prompt the speaker to reveal what he has to tell about his relationship to nature, as in the greater Romantic lyric, or about himself with regard to others, as in the dramatic monologue. H. B. Forman, in heralding the psychological school of poetry, was well aware of the connection. "The entity 'nature' which before the present era of poetry absorbed so large a proportion of our esthetic energies," he wrote in 1869, "has in its turn been absorbed by the real being, man."[15]

Both genres, in that sense, tend to present us with situations evocative of the speaker's past. As in "Fra Lippo Lippi"—with its torchlit midnight scenario in Florence's red-light district, the painter under arrest, one guard holding him by the throat—this opening scene is usually more "dramatic" in the Victorian genre than in its Romantic predecessor. But to Victorian critics, "dramatic" in the sense of an ongoing action is a misnomer when applied to either. Even Browning's dramas, let alone his monologues and lyrics, "consist rather of dramatic situations, momentary in duration, than of dramatic actions," we read in the *Athenaeum*.[16] To Mr. Browning, as C. Vaughan puts it, "the situation is the essential thing . . . we are not confronted with the characters as acting, with the action as taking place; not even with the characters as about to act, and the action as about to assume its irrevocable shape; but . . . with a resuscitation of a possible past."[17]

By comparison with greater Romantic lyrics, dramatic monologues only give limited scope to this setting and sometimes omit it altogether. At the same time, they tend to have more of it than actual dramas. Plays, after all, are performed on stage, where the set can supply what the speaker in dramatic monologues can only suggest. Hence someone like Browning is denied "the dramatic poet's licence of vagueness as to surroundings." Instead, he "sees them himself with instant and intense clearness, and stamps them as clearly on our brain. The picture calls up the mood."[18] Amy Sharp finds a good example of such suggestiveness in Browning's "Master Hugues of Saxe-Gotha": "How vividly the somewhat eerie details of the time and place are brought out,—the church left to its darkness and silence, the glimmer of light from the burning scrap of candle in the organ-loft, the deep shades among the forest of organ-pipes, where, as the organist plays, the master's face seems to lurk. . . ."[19] Rossetti's evocation of an early morning dawn in London in "Jenny" was equally popular with the reviewers:

> Jenny, wake up . . . Why, there's the dawn!
>   And there's an early waggon drawn
> To market, and some sheep that jog
> Bleating before a barking dog;
> And the old streets come peering through
> Another night that London knew;
> And all as ghostlike as the lamps.
>   (302–308)

Yet even where it is less evocative, the setting, as depicted by the speaker, has important functions. One of these is to authenticate what is spoken of in the monologue. The gin bottle of the ex-alcoholic "Northern Cobbler" (A. Tennyson) or "That cross on yonder brow of Calvary" observed by Pilate's wife (in C. Brontë's "Pilate's Wife's Dream")—in each case, the setting, or part of it, authenticates, so to speak, the events of the respective poem. Another, more rarely used function of the setting is symbolical suggestion. Evening, as mentioned in the opening stanza of "Dîs aliter Visum; or, Le Byron de nos Jours" by Browning, is the appropriate time for a rendezvous between the speaker and her ex-lover who, ten years earlier, announced to her one morning that he would sacrifice their love to his career. Sunrise and sunset play a similarly symbolic function in several monologues.[20] Otherwise, as in "Andrea del Sarto," the setting might simply echo the speaker's mood.

> As if—forgive now—should you let me sit
> Here by the window with your hand in mine
> . . . .
> There's the bell clinking from the chapel-top;
> That length of convent-wall across the way
> Holds the trees safer, huddled more inside;
> The last monk leaves the garden; days decrease,

And autumn grows, autumn is everything.

(13–14, 41–45)

It is no coincidence that the lines should remind us of "Dover Beach," where the setting again suggests the mood of the speaker. But in sharing this characteristic, a greater Romantic lyric like Arnold's also differs markedly from a dramatic monologue like Browning's. The difference is clearly spelt out by the period's poetic theorists. Thus Wordsworth, claiming that the feeling developed in poetry gives "importance to the action and situation, and not the action and situation to the feeling,"[21] wants us to identify with whatever emotions he projects onto nature. The way in which the poet (to quote W. J. Fox) "create[s] a scene out of the character, and [makes] the feeling within generate an appropriate assemblage of external objects"[22] is not to be seen as a "pathetic fallacy," but as the appropriate perception of reality. By contrast, "pathetic fallacy," wherever it appears in dramatic monologues, is to be understood as such.[23] The reader is meant to recognize it as a psychological feature of the persona, rather than to identify with it.

Just such a reader is introduced in *James Lee's Wife*, VI, "Reading a Book, Under the Cliff." Here Browning tells us through his persona what he thinks and what use he makes of such fallacies. The wife is reading a poem by a young man who, listening to the wind, finds it moaning and sighing to the tune of his grief. But to her this merely amounts to a distortion of reality resulting from the young man's pride

Of power to see,—in failure and mistake,
Relinquishment, disgrace, on every side,—
Merely examples for his sake.

(VI, 32–34)

A Romantic poem, in other words, is read as a dramatic monologue. How the speaker's emotions are reflected in nature—the hallmark of the greater Romantic lyric—is taken to be a mere sign of how morbid individuals of his type tend to misread reality through their emotions. Given *Pauline*, we are not surprised to find that this individual may well have been the young Browning himself. The poem read and criticized by James Lee's wife (VI, 1–30) was first published in *The Monthly Repository* for 1836.[24]

As already noted in the opening of *Maud*, "pathetic fallacy" in dramatic monologues often assumes pathological dimensions. An early, though imperfect, instance is found in "Porphyria's Lover," where the speaker, in characteristically violent terms, recalls the stormy evening preceding the murder.

> The rain set early in to-night,
>   The sullen wind was soon awake,
> It tore the elm-tops down for spite,
>   And did its worst to vex the lake.
>
> (1–4)

Here and elsewhere, the wind can be a powerful means of suggestion. To the mother in Tennyson's "Rizpah," who secretly buried her executed son Willy in sanctified ground, it becomes one with her son's spectral voice.[25]

More generally speaking, the setting in dramatic monologues, as in greater Romantic lyrics, may remind the speaker of his past, prompt him to speak about it or rechannel his train of thought in sudden, unexpected ways. Just as the landscape in "Tintern Abbey" makes the poet think of his childhood, so the prostitute's room in Rossetti's "Jenny" stirs up the persona's memories, first of his own room and, subsequently, of his youth and childhood. Just as the speaker in Coleridge's "Dejection" is suddenly roused from his torpor when hearing the wind, which has long been raving unnoticed, so Meredith's Juggling Jerry is distracted from his thoughts of death when noticing the odor of the gorse. And there is Meredith's Old Chartist who, in observing a rat, gradually associates the animal with the philistine bourgeoisie he detests.[26]

Yet however much dramatic monologue and greater Romantic lyric resemble each other in delineating the speaker's setting, they differ in their evocation of a second person or listener.[27] For ideally speaking, it is nature herself who should listen to the Romantic poet as he unites himself with her. As *Pauline* can show, actual listeners tend to infiltrate the genre largely as a result of its disintegration. The poet who no longer feels in unison with nature will naturally want to explain his problems to someone else. Turned "crisis-autobiographies"[28] with listeners, greater Romantic lyrics, in fact, can become almost indistinguishable from dramatic monologues. At least among the minor poets, though less among the major ones, we can observe an actual development along these lines.[29]

Most generally speaking, then, the listener in Romantic "crisis autobiographies" as well as in many dramatic monologues tends to assume the role of the modern psychoanalyst toward his patient. The introduction of this second person, as one reviewer puts it, acts "powerfully upon the speaker throughout, [drawing] the latter forth into a more complete and varied expression of his mind."[30] More specifically, the listener may affect the speaker by his or her provocative or hostile presence. Mr. Gigadibs's contempt prompts Bishop Blougram's apology;[31] the laborer in John Davidson's "Thirty Bob a Week" reacts against the whitewashing rhetoric of Mr. Silvertongue;[32] J. B. Selkirk's "semi-delirious" patient rebels against the piously hypocritical harangues of a bishop who "Exhorteth the Sick in Hospital";[33] there is tension between the self-made millionaire on his deathbed and his snobbish, spendthrift son in Kipling's "The 'Mary Gloster,' " as there is in Tennyson's "Charity" between the woman speaker and the friend of the man who ruined her life. Such antagonism occasionally results in physical violence. Browning's Mr. Sludge is taken by the throat by his American patron, as Fra Lippo Lippi is by one of the guards arresting him. A persecutor appearing toward the end of E. B. Browning's "Runaway Slave at Pilgrim's Point" threatens the speaker with a stone.[34]

Such situational melodrama, pinpointing an equally melodramatic tale, has obvious affinities with Victorian narrative painting. In Windus's "Too Late," for instance, a blatantly moribund lady on crutches is shown vis-à-vis a man who covers his face with his hands.[35] Could she speak, she would probably tell a tale like the woman's in L. Morris's "Love in Death":[36] the false news of her husband's death has brought her near death herself, and his unexpected reappearance has obviously come too late. No wonder that there are monologues directly connected with such paintings. Ford Madox Brown, to accompany his painting "The Last of England,"[37] and Browning, inspired by a picture by Leighton,[38] put such poems into the mouths of figures on their respective canvases. Inversely, painters repeatedly tried to recreate the melodramatic climax of dramatic monologues and kindred poems in their art.[39] The invention of daguerrotyping and photography caused several reviewers to comment on a similar affinity. One of them compares dramatic monologues with "portraits in mental photography,"[40] another describes them as "instantaneous photographs": "the representation of the position of affairs at the moment when the action is photographed is so minute and so exact that the reader can reconstruct for himself the events which have preceded."[41]

SITUATION, ACTION, AND CONCLUSION

All this corroborates Walter Pater and others in finding that the dramatic monologue is "pre-eminently the poetry of situations" and that these situations are of a preeminently psychological nature.[42] In order to realize them, writes Pater, "the artist has to employ the most cunning detail, to complicate and refine upon thought and passion a thousandfold."[43] To C. Vaughan, the "situation, which is the reflection of action into thought, is . . . that which alone 'seems worth study' to Mr. Browning."[44] "Dîs aliter Visum; or, Le Byron de nos Jours" serves the critic as an example. Where lies the interest of this poem, he wonders. With the characters set before the reader? "Clearly not, for of them we learn nothing but the single fact that ten years ago they might have agreed, but did not, to become husband and wife. The interest is purely in the situation, in the way in which the woman believes now that the man supposed her to have judged it then. In this double, or triple, reflection from mind to mind of the two agents to a simple event lies the whole fascination of a most fascinating poem."[45]

Which situations recur most frequently in dramatic monologues? In one sense none do, because each poem of this kind deals, at least ideally speaking, with a specific person's unique concerns. In this the dramatic monologue differs from traditional role lyrics, as surveyed by B. W. Fuson, with their stereotypical speakers (e.g., "the lover") and "stock situations" (e.g., "the betrayed or forsaken woman").[46] But naturally there are situations better suited to the genre's psychological bias than others. Most generally speaking, these would be moments of crisis, which make the speaker want to tell his story or simply to talk to someone else. The expectation of one's imminent death, the most dramatic situation of this kind in man's life, is also the one most frequently dealt with in dramatic monologues. As in Roden B. W. Noel's "A Confession Scene.—A Prison Cell. Prisoner (to clergyman loq.)"[47] or D. G. Rossetti's "A Last Confession," it often goes hand in hand with a confession, to either priest or layman, which by itself is another of the genre's most widely rehearsed scenarios.[48] Someone's death,[49] an imminent duel,[50] and the moment after a quarrel[51] or before a flight,[52] recur with somewhat less frequency.[53]

It is worth reemphasizing, however, that in most of these cases the specificity of each situation clearly tends to outweigh its more stereotypical qualities. In this way, "Too Late," spoken by a man upon the death of someone else's wife whom he loved, and "After," a duelist's words after killing his opponent, differ as much from each other as "A Woman's Last Words" and "Andrea del Sarto." Given their particularity of individual circumstance, we barely notice that each pair of monologues deals with a common situation—"Too Late" and "After" with someone's death, "A Woman's Last Words" and "Andrea del Sarto" with the moment after a quarrel. Unlike role lyrics such as Raleigh's "His Pilgrimage" or Pope's "The Dying Christian,"[54] which emphasize the exemplary nature of death, even so-called deathbed monologues[55] stress how each persona confronts the same experience in a particular manner and under special circumstances. To be sure, an instance like Charles Kingsley's "St. Maura. A.D. 304,"[56] whose crucified heroine delivers her seven-page monologue from the cross, shows that there were limits to such specificity.

There are similar limits to what most deserves to be called "dramatic" in the monologues. As critics were keen to point out, interaction between speaker and listener, for instance, may imply but not lapse into actual dialogue. Thus Bishop Blougram repeatedly articulates Mr. Gigadibs's imagined objections before answering them—in Arthur Symons's view a real but easily pardonable "inconsistency." "There is so much practical advantage in giving to thought the form of actual utterance, that we can easily overlook the trifling inaccuracy."[57] Truly inconsistent with the genre, however, is Browning's "Bad Dreams II," where monologue suddenly changes into dialogue.[58] The same, as reviewers emphasized, is true of too much action. "The action is nothing," determines A. T. Lyttelton, "and the personages are interesting to the poet, not because of what they do, but of what they think and feel."[59]

But Lyttelton probably exaggerates. Put less categorically, the action "implied by the speaker as taking place at the various moments of speech" (H. B. Forman)[60] should primarily serve to enliven the persona's psychological self-portrayal, rather than be introduced for its own sake. While "the actor is left to reveal himself," as the Victorians put it, "dramatic action and accessory are reduced to their barest limits,"[61] "incident is subsidiary to thought."[62] Individually speaking, the limits here are often difficult to establish, as, for instance, in Browning's "A Forgiveness" where the speaker finally stabs his confessor, who happens to be the lover of his wife;[63] or in Thornbury's "The Unjust Steward (Temp. James I)"[64] who, like Lucio in *Measure for Measure*, reviles and unmasks a mysterious stranger who turns out to be the master he believed absent. By contrast with such borderline cases, Browning's "Cristina and Monaldeschi" probably exceeds these limits. Within eight lines, the Swedish Queen first has a priest confess her former lover and then has him murdered by hired assassins. H. N. Howard's *The House by the Sea*[65] carries such action implied by the speaker as taking place at the various moments of speech to even further extremes. The woman speaker stabs her husband (who in turn has murdered her lover), has the body removed by a servant, and finally kills herself.[66]

Even where kept within acceptable boundaries, such action tends to climax toward the end. This conclusion often reinvokes the scenario of the beginning. Other typical patterns involve the reappearance of the person whose initial disappearance prompted the speaker to tell his tale (e.g., W. W. Story's "Aunt Rachel's Story"[67] and A. Webster's "Tired");[68] or the final appearance of the person spoken of by the persona.[69] Most stereotypical here are approaching footsteps as heard and reported by the speaker. "Who are these you have let descend my stair?" cries Guido seconds before he is hauled off to his execution. The occasions may be as diverse as life: a girl hears her approaching lover (A. Webster, "The Happiest Girl in the World"),[70] a woman the pallbearers carrying the man who once seduced her (Philip B. Marston, "A Christmas Vigil"),[71] the dying laborer's wife her approaching husband (R. Buchanan, "Liz").[72] But here and elsewhere we hear the same sounds. "Oh his dear step— / He sees me, he is coming; my own love!" "But now the heavy tread upon the stair / Of men who bear / Some strange thing up." "There's Joe! I hear his foot upon the stairs!" The obvious intention in most of these cases is to create surprise. But after reading these and other monologues, one is more likely to simply raise an eyebrow. "But which is that footstep upon the stair," wonders the dying wife in Lewis Morris's "Life in Death."[73] We know that her husband who was reported dead is just about to step in for yet another melodramatic Victorian "too late."

Next to the sound of approaching footsteps, murder, or the attempt at it, is the second most stereotypical event found in the conclusion of dramatic monologues. The speaker of R. Buchanan's "Fra Giacomo," like his counterpart in Browning's "A Forgiveness," stabs his confessor after identifying him as his wife's lover.[74] An exception from most deathbed monologues in Eugene J. Lee-Hamilton's "The Mandolin. [A.D. 1559]" whose speaker, instead of being left to die quietly, is smothered in his pillows.[75] Poets, even the minor ones, were aware of the clichés they adopted, and in the effort to transcend them, strained the form beyond what it could render. Another instance of this kind is the same poet's "Ipsissimus," which tries to revive an already moribund form by injecting it with one of the age's equally sensationalist obsessions. As he tells his confessor, the speaker, in his repeated attempts to murder his opponent, again and again confronts a masked figure who turns out to be his own, deceased double. Needless to say, the end of the monologue once again enacts this ghostly scenario.

> Stretch out thy hands, thou Priest unseen,
> That sittest there behind the screen,
>   And give me absolution quick!
> O God, O God, his hands are dead!
>   His hands are mine, oh, monstrous spell!
> I feel them clammy on my head:
>   Is he my own dead self as well?
> Those hands are mine,—their scars, their shape:
> O God, O God, there's no escape,
>   And seeking Heaven, I fall on Hell![76]

But such gothic-horror theatricality is the exception even at the end of dramatic monologues. Here, as elsewhere in the genre, action tends to be primarily suggestive. Equipped with a royal ransom, Christina Rossetti's Royal Princess decides to confront her people after watching her father suppress a rebellion; a tear he feels drop on his hand convinces the blind Tiresias that his attempt to persuade his son to sacrifice his life for Thebes has been successful;[77] a final handshake between Fra Lippo Lippi and the guards who were about to arrest him testifies to the painter's skill in talking himself out of a tricky spot. In these and other cases, action mainly serves to highlight an emotionally charged situation. "Drabbing, stabbing, et autres gentillesses," which Browning dealt with in some of his plays,[78] find little room in the dramatic monologue. Even personae facing death or execution[79] as a rule do not die until after concluding their speech. In this, dramatic monologues differ from monodramas, like Southey's *Sappho*,[80] which more easily slip into dramatic action. The last words of W. J. Linton's *Delescluze on the Barricade* thus mark the poem as a late offshoot of this short-lived Romantic genre:

Alas! unhappy France—(A shot strikes him down)
I, also, France! have well deserved of thee.[81]

Dramatic monologues, in other words, do not allow for the intrusion of voices other than the persona's, even though it be merely in the form of an indirect stage direction. Or so at least determined the critics. In their view, no authorial comments by the poet should disrupt the illusion created by the speaker. According to H. B. Forman, Tennyson in this way made a mistake in concluding "Lucretius" with a short narrative telling us that the protagonist stabbed himself. The poet, he argues, could have easily "worked up" the poem "to a vigorous climax" instead. After all, there was nothing new to this technique. "That the narrative given in pure prose, in the narrator's words, could have been placed by implication in the concluding phrases of the monologue, cannot be doubted by any one who has studied the monologue in its best forms," Forman concluded in 1871.[82]

DRAMATIC NARRATIVE AND PSYCHOLOGICAL REVIVIFICATION

According to the Victorian reviewers, the speaker should tell his own story as prompted by a specific occasion. In this way, "the situation" may be "the essential thing" to Browning; but only in the sense of prompting the "resuscitation of a possible past."[83] The monologues, as another Browning reviewer put it in the *North British Review*, "are dramatic, because the speakers are placed in dramatic situations"; but, more essentially they are narrative because "they set before us the history, not the actual development, of an event."[84] Of course, there are exceptions, which instead focus, say, on the speaker's reveries while listening to a piece of music (Browning's "A Toccata of Galuppi's"),[85] on his indignation aroused by fate's injustices (Meredith's "Martin's Puzzle"), on his religious beliefs (Browning's "Johannes Agricola in Meditation") or on his attempts at self-vindication (Browning's "Bishop Blougram's Apology"). But even here, details from the persona's past history can usually be gathered by reading between the lines, so to speak.

In any case, speakers of dramatic monologues, at least of the more accomplished kind, rarely just simply relate their story. Prompted as it is by a specific situation, the narrative usually takes the form of how past events are remembered by the persona, not of how they might be told by a poet. More specifically, it can be shown as arising from the depth of long forgotten or repressed memories. In this, the randomness of memory and stream-of-consciousness are as significant as they are in the babblings of a twentieth-century neurotic talking to his psychoanalyst. Or to put it in the pre-Freudian jargon of Victorian reviewers, the dramatic monologue was essentially "retrospective drama" (A. Symons),[86] an amalgam of "dramatic narrative and psychological revivification" (J. A. Symonds).[87] Its basic strategy, as A. Orr decided, was one of "[recalling], rather than relating."[88]

Hence, the speaker should never articulate more than he or she could possibly know. "I cannot tell, as I could never learn it" (495), remarks the speaker-narrator in Browning's "The Flight of the Duchess." Unfortunately, he missed the start of the conversation between the duchess and her gypsy guru, which he overheard from a balcony; Jacynth, who might have witnessed and told him about it, was fast asleep at the time. He also apologizes for being unable to render what he has heard in the appropriate words.

> Had Jacynth only been by me to clap pen
> To paper and put you down every syllable
>   With those clever clerkly fingers,
>   All I've forgotten as well as what lingers
> In this old brain of mine that's but ill able
> To give you even this poor version
>   Of speech I spoil, as it were, with stammering.
>
>   (692–98)

In all this Browning's narrator resembles Lockwood and Nelly Dean in Emily Brontë's *Wuthering Heights*. Given his common sense naiveté and incomprehension, the mysterious tale he tells us becomes, of course, only the more authentic and compelling. "This man," commented J. Fotheringham, "tells the story so far as he understood it."[89]

The same limited "narrator agent" or "unreliable narrator" (W. C. Booth)[90] perspective, typical of most dramatic monologues, is made equally explicit in Robert Buchanan's "Poet Andrew,"[91] the fictitious name Buchanan gave to his dead young poet friend David Gray. "The world called his darling son a poet," wrote Buchanan of Gray's father," and he hardly knew what a poet was. . . . Mysterious 'poetry,' which he had once scorned as an idle thing, deepened and deepened in its

fascination for him."[92] Poet Andrew's father's attitude toward his dead
son in the actual poem is marked by similar "consciousness of silly ignorance." His poet-listener, in whom Buchanan seems to have portrayed himself, benignly listens to the old man's story of Andrew's life:

> You think
> That folk will love him, for the poetry's sake,
> Many a year to come? We take it kind
> You speak so weel of Andrew!—As for me,
> I can make naething of the printed book;
> I am no scholar, sir, as I have said.[93]

Most characteristic of the narratives in dramatic monologues, however, is how they actualize the process of memory. A traditionally approved strategy to this effect, as found, for instance, in Browning's
"Count Gismond," is a change from past into present tense as the narrator reaches the climax of the story. Another example of this technique
is found in Robert Buchanan's "Nell" whose heroine, as she remembers
the arrest and execution of her working-class husband, pours forth a
stream of fragmentary phrases:

> And all the rest is like a dream—the sound
> Of knocking at the door—
> A rush of men—a struggle on the ground—
> A mist—a tramp—a roar;
> For when I got my senses back again,
> The room was empty—and my head went round![94]

More complex techniques serve to portray obsessive memory, incidental amnesia, or general stream of consciousness. A murderer proves
unable to remember the deed, which he repressed, but suddenly the
victim appears to him in the form of a spectral vision. What led to this
sudden revelation is, as we realize in rereading the monologue, the obsessive concern with a specific kind of incident or memory. In inter-
weaving these and other techniques, D. G. Rossetti, in "A Last Confession," wrote the unsurpassed masterpiece portraying the "simple agony
of memory."[95] H. B. Forman, with customary incisiveness, notes the
monologue's "firm fine thread of laughter incidents whereon the poet
has strung the tale of this dying man, into whose very soul a girl's
heartless laugh has entered as iron."[96] The entire narrative, as the murderer realizes himself, is a series of digressions prompted by this and

other obsessions such as the memory of the victim's long hair and the dagger:

> I think
> I have been speaking to you of some matters
> There was no need to speak of, have I not?
> You do not know how clearly those things stood
> Within my mind, which I have spoken of,
> Nor how they strove for utterance.
>   (103–108)

But what most strives for utterance characteristically remains unrevealed. The speaker seems unable to confront what burdens his soul. As we follow his obsessive memories, we find him (in Forman's words) "always leading up to the dreadful climax of his secret, and always, at a point of high suspense, falling back again without accomplishing the actual confession of the crime."[97] Like Lord Jim in Conrad's novel, the protagonist is able to visualize the moment after the deed, but not the deed itself. To once again quote Forman, "the man rushes through the account of the deed, even as the deed itself had been rushed through, and never actually owns that he *did kill* the woman—only says how he came to know he *had stabbed* her."[98] But what he cannot face consciously, his hallucinating mind makes known to him in a spectral vision, which fuses all his obsessions in one.

>   For she took the knife
> Deep in her heart, even as I bade her then,
> And fell; and her stiff bodice scooped the sand
> Into her bosom.
>   And she keeps it, see,
> Do you not see she keeps it?—there, beneath
> Wet fingers and wet tresses, in her heart.
> . . . .
>   For now she draws it out
> Slowly, and only smiles as yet: look, Father,
> She scarcely smiles: but I shall hear her laugh
> Soon, when she shows the crimson steel to God.

Yet while the speaker is unconscious or just half aware of what drives him from digression to digression, *we* are given sufficient clues as to the workings of his stream of consciousness. In this, "A Last Confession," like other dramatic monologues, unites the persona's confession and his case history in one. The speaker just barely realizes how forcefully certain memories throng into his consciousness, striving for utterance; but as readers we come to recognize a set of monomaniac obsessions, which escalate to the point of providing the irresistible impulse for the murder. Except for feeling rejected by one he loves and who once loved him, the speaker lacks all immediate motivation for his deed. He is not even sure that she left him for someone else (cf. 464–66). The woman is stabbed because her laughter struck the murderer as increasingly frivolous and whorish. What precipitates the deed is the sight of a laughing prostitute whom the speaker associates with his beloved:

> A woman laughed above me. I looked up
> And saw where a brown-shouldered harlot leaned
> Half through a tavern window thick with vine.
> Some man had come behind her in the room
> And caught her by her arms, and she had turned
> With that coarse empty laugh on him, as now
> He munched her neck with kisses, while the vine
> Crawled in her neck.
>
> (501–508)

But where factual motivation is lacking the author traces a chain of mental events, which, like the case history of a psychotic, accounts for an otherwise incomprehensible act. In fact, Rossetti was prompted to explicate his poems to that effect. When Robert Buchanan launched his attack against "The Fleshly School of Poetry," he quoted the lines about the brown-shouldered harlot as an outstanding example of "the common stock of the walking gentlemen of the fleshly school."[99] But such prudery, at least in Rossetti's view, completely misses the point. "Assailants may say what they please," he countered, "but no poet or poetic reader will blame me for making the incident recorded in these seven lines as repulsive to the reader as it was to the hearer and beholder. Without this, the chain of motive and result would remain obviously incomplete."[100]

Again, psychiatrists would hardly have shared Buchanan's misgivings. After testifying on behalf of homicidal maniacs with their atrocities and perversions, they were unlikely to feel squeamish about kisses munched in a brown-shouldered harlot's neck. Monologues like "A Last Confession" or "Porphyria's Lover" no doubt struck them as poetic case histories put together, as it were, from the words of actual murderers. So at least concluded Forbes Winslow in printing a dramatic monologue, "The Wife-Slayer," by a certain Edmund Ollier, in the fourth volume of his *Journal of Psychological Medicine*,[101] where it appears just subsequent to A. Brierre de Boismont's "The Last Sentiments of Suicides"[102] as well as an original twelve-page "Murderer's Confession."[103] The poem, in his view, "accurately . . . delineates that morbid and insane state of mind which so often irresistibly and blindly impels to acts of suicide and homicide."[104] Characteristically, its speaker, much like the one in "A Last Confession," is wrestling with the memory of a deed he cannot confront. Just as Rossetti's persona never actually admits that, or describes how, he stabbed the woman, the speaker here can only conceive of his crime as a dream.

> "No, no! I did not kill her! No!
> I say I will not have it so—
> I will not hear it! 'Twas a dream
> From which I woke with sudden scream,
> And found the sweat upon my brow,
> And that dull pain which even now
> Is heavy on my heart and brain:—
> Oh God! I must have slept again,
> And stumble yet through dusky chasms,
> Flesh-quakings, and tremendous spasms!
>   "I have a wife—a dear one.—Nay,
> Start not! I have one *still*, I say,—
> Or shall, when from this dream I wake.
> We were heart-wedded; we did slake
> Our miseries in each other's tears,
> And grew, through all the strange, and years,
> Quiet in grief's own quietness.
> We could walk straight beneath distress,
> And make no cry. But what extreme
> Seiz'd us; and then—then came this dream![105]

IX

The Psychological School of Poetry: Contents

WINSLOW and his confreres had specific reasons for admiring monologues of this kind printed in *The Journal of Psychological Medicine and
Mental Pathology*. One was that many of these poems, by adopting the
perspective of, say, homicidal maniacs like Porphyria's Lover, seemed
to replace traditional morality with something more empathetic, situational, in short, "psychological." This, in fact, was precisely what
Winslow was after in testifying and arguing (successfully) on behalf of
madman assassin Daniel McNaughton[1] and (often less successfully) in
many subsequent cases of a similar nature. Another reason was that
several dramatic monologues seemed to parallel another, though only
marginal, line of investigation pursued by the alienists. This concerned
itself with trying to reread history, both general and biographical, from
a psychological point of view. No doubt, alienists agreed with Ruskin's
praise of Browning's "The Bishop Orders his Tomb at St. Praxed's
Church" as revealing more "of the Renaissance spirit" than any history
book.[2] For this poem seemed to combine the two goals that mental
scientists pursued under the name of a new "psychology of history."[3] It
not only recreated the psychology of a typical individual of a past age;
in doing so it also evoked the spirit or "mass psyche" of that age.

RELATIVIST VERSUS TRADITIONAL MORALITY

Alienists must have noticed that they shared their basic approach in all
these endeavors with the poets. As already noted, British mental science, unlike its often fiercely quantitative German counterpart, oper-

ated largely from the double premise of applied self-analysis in the empathic observation of others. As late as 1860 John Charles Bucknill, perhaps England's most influential alienist of the time, insisted that identification with the patient, to the very point where it might endanger the doctor's sanity, was the primary prerequisite in the pursuit of his profession.[4] Needless to say, poets and critics favored much the same "transmigration of the soul"[5] in the act of creation. Ideas of this nature form the stock in trade of Romantic poetics and can be traced back as far as eighteenth-century Shakespeare criticism.[6] But at no point were they advocated more fervently than at the time just prior to and during the rise of both mental science and the dramatic monologue. Coleridge, ever since his childhood, as he confessed in later life, could only apprehend external reality by a combination of self-projection and observational deconstruction. He would "*abstract* and as it were unrealize whatever of more than common interest [his] eyes dwelt on; and then by a sort of transfusion and transmission of [his] consciousness to identify [himself] with the Object."[7] Romantics generally tended to stress self-projection over empirical observation. To Hazlitt, the poetic imagination was simply identical with "the power of carrying on a given feeling into other situations."[8] Regarding other people, it contemplates, as Arthur Hallam puts it, "a separate being as a separate state of itself."[9] "In relation to his creations," then, the poet, to quote W. J. Fox, "is the omnific spirit in whom they have their being. . . . He only, in them, displays to us fragments of himself."[10]

Authors of dramatic monologues reversed this Romantic emphasis on self-projection in favor of objective observation but retained a heavy dose of the former. Both Browning and Tennyson, in fact, were repeatedly charged with adopting their personae as mere disguises. Wrote one reviewer: "Even when they speak in borrowed masks, we know the voice, and we listen, not to hear what the fictitious personage says, but what the poet says in the guise of his imaginary personages."[11] More appropriately, another critic speaks, as already noted, of the "rare union of subjective reflectiveness with objective life and vigour" by which Browning "can make his *personae* speak out his thoughts without prejudice to their own individual being."[12] The poet in this resembles the Freudian psychoanalyst who can decode the otherwise rambling confessions of his persona or patient in terms of its psychoanalytic subtext. In the words of another Browning critic, his function is "to bring out the thought of a person who is not sufficiently able to do that for himself.

What the many feel, he only is able to express."[13] But whatever under-lying meaning there is must not be imposed from without. Like early psychiatrists who tried to jettison all preconceptions about the human mind, so the poet, at least in Robert Buchanan's view, "should free himself entirely from all arbitrary systems of ethics and codes of opin-ion" in this endeavor.[14]

To some, the resultant relativism was simply part and parcel of mo-dernity, or what Walter Pater called the "cultivation of the 'relative' spirit in place of the 'absolute.' " To this modern spirit, Pater decided, "nothing is or can be rightly known except relatively under condi-tions."[15] "We suspend our judgment much more than our predeces-sors," protested Henry Sidgwick, "and much more contentedly: we see that there are many sides to many questions: the opinions that we do hold we hold if not more loosely, at least more at arm's length: we can imagine how they appear to others, and can conceive ourselves not hold-ing them."[16] Authors of dramatic monologues were widely seen as em-bodying such empathetic relativism in their poetry. Thus "toleration for all men and things, consideration . . . of all sides in all cases" was said to be "the most obvious characteristic of the manner in which [Browning] mirrors life to himself and us." " 'In the tangle of possible motives,' he seems to say, 'who shall be hasty to give judgment for his brother's praise or blame?' "[17] Hence, Browning and others replaced traditional morality with a new "empirical morality"[18]—analysing ac-tions not so much in their relations to absolute right or wrong as in relation to the position and character of the actor."[19]

But where avant-garde journals and writers heralded a new spirit of tolerance, their more traditional counterparts noted a deplorable con-fusion of values. To the *Christian Remembrancer*, Browning's attitude toward Fra Lippo Lippi offered a typical example: "we are called upon to sympathise with a licentious monk artist . . . apologising with unc-tuous minuteness for his shameless course of life."[20] The writer notes similar confusion in "Bishop Blougram's Apology": "We know not whether to call it an apology for hypocrisy, or an argument for scepti-cism. The author evidently desires to show that he can sympathise with both states."[21] The modern reader is more likely to agree with Robert Buchanan who, toward the end of the nineteenth century, attacked Rudyard Kipling for making himself the mouthpiece or "The Voice of 'The Hooligan.' " "Belts," for instance, apotheosizes "the soldier who uses his belt in drunken fury to assault civilians in the streets," while the poems around Tommy Atkins present nothing but "a drunken, swearing, coarse-minded Hooligan, for whom, nevertheless, our sympathy is eagerly entreated."[22]

THE PSYCHOLOGY OF MURDER AND SUICIDE

Similar arguments erupted with psychiatry's growing participation in judicial affairs. Broadly speaking, prosecutors and judges favored judgments in terms of traditional morality, where testifying alienists might try to engage the jury's sympathy by pleading a murderer's moral insanity, irresistible impulse, or lack of proper motivation. The tendency of psychiatrists, at least from the point of view of the bench, was to view "all crime," as Lord Hale put it, "as partial insanity."[23] The judiciary's bias, in the eyes of the alienists, was to judge the most psychopathologically complex cases of homicide *in foro conscientiae* of antiquated absolutist values. Of course, even alienists disagreed as to how far crimes, in their psychologically enlightened age, should be explained and exculpated in terms of scientifically analyzable, but morally value-free motivation. "Should the ethical judgments of men," as M. B. Sampson suggested in *Criminal Jurisprudence Considered in Relation to Cerebral Organization*, "be guided, not by any fixed and determined standard of right and wrong applied to actions, but by the balance of the motives which have led to the actions in question?"[24] Here even the *Journal of Psychological Medicine* disagreed with Sampson, countering *"that the moral principle does exist in the healthy mind, and that it decides with an 'autocratic' power on what is morally right and wrong."*[25]

The famous Townley case offers an instance of such disagreement not only between representatives of the law and alienists, but also among members of the medical profession themselves.[26] Not unlike the speaker of Rossetti's "A Last Confession," Townley had stabbed to death his fiancée Miss Goodwin when she asked him to release her from their three-year engagement in order to marry someone else. "A Woman's a beast," he said after the murder, "and deserves death, who flirts with any one after she is engaged."[27] There was obvious reason for calling in an alienist who, in the person of Forbes Winslow, concluded, after twice interviewing the criminal in jail, that Townley was morally insane and "palpably unable to distinguish between right and wrong, good and evil."[28] In fact, the murderer's "moral sense" struck Winslow as "more vitiated" than he had ever seen in "any other human being."

To the alienist's dismay, Townley not only "denied the existence of a God and of a future world" or "seemed incapable of reasoning correctly on any moral subject"; he also "said it was a matter of perfect indifference whether he was dead or alive." But neither these sentiments, his persecution complex, nor the evidence of insanity in the family swayed the judge or the jury who, after a deliberation of only five minutes, returned to court with a verdict of "guilty" of willful murder.[29]

But matters didn't stop there. Impressed by medical opinion, though convinced of the justice of Townley's conviction, the judge reported to the Home Secretary, Sir George Grey, that the alienists thought the criminal had been absolutely insane at the time of the trial. The Commissioners in Lunacy appointed to reinvestigate the case only compounded the confusion. According to their findings, Townley was insane but had been justly convicted nonetheless. An additional certificate of Townley's insanity signed by two justices and two medical men finally lead Grey to suspend the condemned man's sentence and have him removed to Bethlem. But in the ensuing public outrage, even a number of alienists opposed this decision. Another commission, whose report was signed by Drs. Hood, Bucknill, Meyer, and Helps, found Townley sane,[30] leading Grey to once again change the criminal's sentence from hospitalization in Bethlem into penal servitude for life. Fellow alienists Maudsley and Robertson claimed that Winslow had been duped by the murderer while endorsing the findings of Dr. J. Hitchman, Superintendent Physician of the Derby County Lunatic Asylum, who as a result of his nearly two-hour-long interview with Townley "could not discover in him any of the recognized forms of mental disease."[31]

Except for its conclusion, Hitchman's report resembles many others, particularly in reminding us of poems like "A Last Confession." Everything is done to make Townley reveal his story and state of mind. Facing him, in carefully choreographed seating order, are Dr. Hitchman himself, the attorney for the defense, the prison surgeon, and the governor of the gaol. Townley's somewhat shy and depressed appearance; his clammy tongue, which makes a clicking sound when he gets excited; his hands firmly grasping the bottom of his trouser pockets—nothing escapes the alienist's watchful eye. Dr. Hitchman notes every change of physiognomy and intonation. His strategies in drawing out the prisoner fuse empathy with duplicity. Townley gets agitated in cursing his victim as "a friend" who deceived him, but Dr. Hitchman "understands."[32] He tells Townley that he could "sympathise with him in the bitter disappointment" of seeing himself replaced by another man and "that in the phrensy of the moment he might have wished her dead." But didn't he actually buy the knife with which he stabbed his fiancée on the way to the murder? What, incidentally, were the exact circumstances of the stabbing? Like the protagonist of "A Last Confession" or of the monologue Winslow printed in the *Journal of Psychological Medicine*, Townley cannot remember. But Dr. Hitchman (like Rossetti) records this fact as faithfully as everything else.

> "When a man is in a rage he cannot remember *all* that he has said, or done in that rage; to me, upon reflecting on all that has transpired, it appears a maze, a dream." "Do you know that you stabbed Miss Goodwin several times?" "Yes, I know, she had sadly fooled me, she had done so for months and months; I was mad with rage."[33]

One wonders how Dr. Hitchman and Dr. Winslow might have adjudicated the mental state of Rossetti's protagonist in "A Last Confession." Was the speaker's obsessive behavior sufficient for certifying him as morally insane or as incapable of distinguishing right from wrong at the time of the deed? As in the Townley case, the learned doctors probably would have disagreed, although we shall never know for certain. To my knowledge, neither "A Last Confession" nor any other dramatic monologue of its kind was ever reviewed in a psychiatric journal.

However, a similar work, Browning's narrative *Red Cotton Night-Cap Country*, received precisely that kind of attention. In reviewing the poem for the *Journal of Mental Science*, J. H. Balfour-Browne, not unlike Winslow testifying on behalf of Townley, disagrees with the poet's own findings. In his view, the protagonist Léonce Miranda was not a mere eccentric, as Browning concludes, but a plain madman.[34] Was Léonce Miranda sane or insane? The case, based on the real one of a certain Antoine Mellerio, had been the subject of an actual trial just previous to the composition of the poem.[35] As does Léonce in *Red Cotton Night-Cap Country*, Antoine put an end to his dissipated and turbulent life by throwing himself from a tower on his estate in Normandy. His relatives, in contesting the will in which he left his entire fortune to the Church, only reserving a life interest for his mistress Anna (alias Clara), could point to two previous acts of self-destructive insanity. Always vacillating between dissipation and guilt, sexual and religious fervor,

Antoine once, when his mother reproached him for his extravagance, had thrown himself into the Seine; in a second fit of contrition, subsequent to his mother's death, he had burnt off both hands after destroying old correspondence in the same fire. But the court upheld his sanity and approved the testament.

In researching this recent court case, Robert Browning proceeded like a testifying alienist himself. After first hearing about it from a friend, he procured himself "the legal documents . . . collected the accounts current among the people of the neighbourhood, inspected the house and grounds." "Indeed the facts," Browning wrote in a letter, "are so exactly put down, that, in order to avoid the possibility of prosecution for Libel—that is, telling the exact truth—I changed all the names of persons and places, as they stood in the original 'Proofs.' "[36] Browning even accepted the court's post-mortem verdict on the protagonist's mental state, though for his own reasons. Antoine-Léonce, as he is analyzed in the poem, was neither insane nor truly suicidal. Instead, his misfortunes were due to religious and sexual reasons or, in Browning's own words, "occasioned by religious considerations as well as passionate woman-love."[37] But the very facts that lead him to this verdict make the reviewer of the *Journal of Mental Science* arrive at the opposite conclusion.

J. H. Balfour-Browne endeavors "to prove this proposition from the poem."[38] Ruling out the possibility of "hereditary psychosis," he yet finds enough in Léonce's life to certify the protagonist as insane. Most of this evidence is cumulative. One symptom is the hero's belief in miracles, "fribble mythology," and "drivelling legendary stories of ridiculous cures and saintly interference." For "what was rational in the middle ages would be insanity now." Then there is the hero's crotomania, manifest in the "animal manhood of the youth" or the suddenness with which he fell in love with Clara. In his frequent changes of character "at a time of life when the equilibrium of disposition ought to have become stable," Léonce showed further symptoms of "the inception of mental disease." He was positively insane, however, when he threw himself into the Seine after being scolded by his mother. Other "really mad act[s]" included burning off his hands in an open fire; throwing himself from a tower in the hope that the Virgin of the Ravissante, by way of bearing out his trust in her miraculous powers, would rescue him in midair; and leaving all his money to the Church "in connection with which all his delusion had existed." Browning, siding with the judges of the original Antoine Mellerio, might put down all such behavior to mere "eccentricity." But Balfour-Browne disagrees: "We think that the whole life of Léonce Miranda indicated the existence of mental disease; that there was a fact which confirmed the belief that he wilfully committed suicide, viz., the burning of his hands; and from all the facts before us we cannot but differ from Mr. Browning, and must regard Léonce Miranda as a madman,—the judgment of the first Chamber of the Civil Court at Vire notwithstanding. . . . 'The case is closed.' "[39]

THE PSYCHOLOGY OF HISTORY

"What was rational in the middle ages would be insanity now."[40] To compare the psychology of individuals with that of entire eras, nations, movements, was a commonplace of nineteenth-century poetry and mental science. F. Lélut, after devoting two entire studies to psychoanalyzing and certifying as insane two famous figures of history—Socrates and Pascal[41]—proceeded to further enlarge the claims of his science in a lead article in the recently founded *Annales médico-psychologiques*. According to its title, psychological medicine was to provide an all-encompassing "Cadre de la philosophie de l'homme."[42] Part of this *summa psychologiae* was the analysis of the various ages of man, or of man's collective psyche, in analogy to the study of an individual's psyche. In surveying cases of "Modern Demonology and Divination," a writer of *The Journal of Psychological Medicine* (probably Forbes Winslow) follows a similar approach. "The association of ideas," he writes, "is manifested in national and social as well as individual habits of thought. There is also from age to age a progressive development of nations and societies which, varying in its successive phases, begins and ends in a like manner in every successive cycle, because it is guided onwards by similar associations of ideas, each linked to its predecessor and developing its successor. It follows, therefore, that the stages of development in the lives of nations as well as of individuals are comparable."[43] In fact, the Townley case prompted Dr. Hitchman to draw similar parallels: Winslow, in Hitchman's view, was wrong in calling Townley insane on the basis of his opinions, for instance, regarding "man's responsibility." For as absurd as some of these might be, they hardly differed from those "entertained by hundreds of persons . . . who describe themselves as 'Necessitarians,' or by other sectarian titles": "moreover, the theory has been eloquently, however fallaciously, advocated by the distinguished poet, Percy B. Shelley. Again, although Mr. Townley refers to a wife as *property*, yet he does so, in the same sense as an American slaveholder describes his slave as a 'chattel;' and in regarding betrothals as equivalent to marriage . . . he is in harmony with our ecclesiastical laws prior to the reign of George the Second, and (as I believe) in accordance with the present laws of Scotland."[44]

At least in the eyes of critics, numerous dramatic monologues were inspired by a similarly psycho-analytic spirit in dealing with historical subject matter. Hence a specific figure, traditionally seen in a certain way, could be presented in a completely new light. Browning's "The Glove" is an example of such a reinterpretation of a subject previously dealt with by Leigh Hunt in "The Glove and the Lions," and by Friedrich Schiller in "Der Handschuh." As one critic puts it, "an action of heartless vanity on the part of the lady in the story, who throws her glove within the lion's cage, to be rescued by her knightly lover, is justified; developed with refined physiologic truth under quite a fresh aspect: as a simple test of idle protestation, a test that was needed, and satisfied to *his* rather than her essential loss."[45] In other words, "The Poet as Historian," to quote from an article of that very title, is primarily a psychologist: "He has the loving insight into human nature and quick communion with the purpose of the ages that can read a character from a gesture, a policy from a stray recorded word."[46]

The number of poems thus dramatizing specific characters and sentiments "as the offspring of a given time and place"[47] is of course legion. But among them is a group dealing with biblical subject matter in which this "historic view" was used with especially powerful effect. For it was one thing to reinterpret history psycho-analytically; it was quite another to apply the same method to matters that were not, strictly speaking, historical. Partly this became possible due to the influence of the Higher Criticism, which in "Saul," "Karshish," "Cleon," "A Death in the Desert," and "Imperante Augusto Natus Est—" seems to ally itself with that of the new "psychology of history." In each of these poems Browning views the events surrounding Jesus Christ through a different personal perspective: through the prophetic David; through an Arab doctor to whom Lazarus's resurrection is a mere revival from a prolonged epileptic trance; through a pagan philosopher-poet despairing of his immortality; through one of the evangelists, St. John;

and through a Roman senator foreseeing how one born in "blind Judaea" will topple Rome's emperor worship.

Browning's attitude toward the Higher Criticism is complex,[48] not to say confused. Thus he criticizes Strauss and Renan, where a more thorough knowledge of *Das Leben Jesu* and *La vie de Jésus* would probably have made him discover more parallels between the Higher Criticism and his poetry than he was aware of. Be that as it may, most of his and other poets' monologues dealing with New Testament subject matter share the basic approach outlined by British Higher Critic J. R. Seeley in *Ecce Homo. A Survey of the Life and Work of Jesus Christ.* In pursuit of a new image of Christ, modern believers, so Seeley proposes, may have to place "themselves in imagination at the time when he whom we call Christ bore no such name, but was simply, as St. Luke describes him, a young man of promise, popular with those who knew him and appearing to enjoy the Divine favour."[49] In attempting to throw new poetic light on early Christianity, Browning and his confreres did little else. In the words of a Browning reviewer, they tried to imagine "the different impressions made on different men occupying different points of view in that great Pagan and Polytheistic world, by this new doctrine which they saw creeping in upon them from Judea, and by the facts reported to them concerning its origin."[50]

One such witness who enjoyed particular popularity with the poets was Pilate's wife who, according to Matthew 27:19, sent her husband the following message regarding Jesus: "Have thou nothing to do with that just man: for I have suffered many things this day in a dream because of him." In Lyall's "Pilate's Wife's Dream" the speaker describes her nightly vision to the messenger.[51] In Charlotte Brontë's poem of the same title the heroine professes hatred of her husband and yearning for the new religion while watching the erection of the cross in the early morning dawn.

> Torches burn in Jerusalem, and cast
>   On yonder stony mount a lurid glow.
> I see men stationed there, and gleaming spears;
> A sound, too, from afar, invades my ears.
> Dull, measured strokes of axe and hammer ring
>   From street to street, not loud, but through the night
> Distinctly heard—and some strange spectral thing
>   Is now upreared—and, fixed against the light

Of the pale lamps, defined upon that sky,
It stands up like a column, straight and high.

. . . .

A cross on Calvary . . .

. . . .

And on that cross the spotless Christ must die.[52]

The speakers in most poems of this kind endorse the Christian message either knowingly or unconsciously. E. H. Plumptre's Bar-Abbas, for instance, is made the unwilling mouthpiece of deep theological insights in talking about the crucifixion:

I would not join
Those mockers in their taunts. "He fills my place;"
So thought I to myself. "He dies for me."[53]

Even the skeptical Cleon, while shrugging off Christ and St. Paul, is drawn toward Christian ideals at a deeper level.

Instances in which the same historical method serves to question the Christian message are far less numerous. A complex case here is Swinburne's in "Hymn to Proserpine" or "Laus Veneris," poems that the author himself defended as utterances of imaginary personae, not his.[54] But, for reasons to be discussed in the next chapter, readers then and now have rightly taken the monologues as more or less Swinburne's own critique of Christianity. More convincing than the author's self-defense, then, is Tom Davidson's article on "Laus Veneris" in a *Monthly Magazine . . . Devoted to Religion*. What other reviewers denounced as blasphemy, Davidson explains, springs from the author's quasireligious worship of beauty. Hence a poem like "Laus Veneris" is put to "a fair test" only if we acknowledge Swinburne "as, what he claims to be, an artist in the Greek sense": "We know that the teachings of Christianity were to the Greek foolishness, why need we wonder that the Hellenic spirit appears as a spirit of blasphemy to the Christian."[55]

Similar tendencies are found in the dramatic monologues of W. W. Story. So convincing are the anti-Christian arguments of his contemporaries that the speaker of "A Primitive Christian in Rome"[56] has to search out the reassuring advice of St. Paul. In turn, Story's "Roman Lawyer in Jerusalem—First Century"[57] makes us see Judas in a completely new light. The lawyer, while sympathizing with Christianity, finds the traditional versions of Judas's alleged treachery unacceptable.

On the contrary, Judas was the only person in Christ's entourage who believed in his master's truly divine nature. Full of such devotion, he misinterpreted Christ's prediction that he would betray him as a secret mission: Jesus, through this means, would be enabled to reveal himself as the almighty divinity and judge. Or such at least was the version of the story the lawyer got from Lysias, captain of the centurions, who arrested Christ at Mount Olive. Who then was right, St. John or Lysias? Either Judas was,

> As John affirms, a villain and a thief,
> A creature lost to shame and base at heart,—
> Or else, which is the view that Lysias takes,
> He was a rash and visionary man
> Whose faith was firm, who had no thought of crime,
> But whom a terrible mistake drove mad.[58]

After following the lawyer's arguments, the reader is inclined to reject the New Testament version. There is no reason why Judas, who had been in charge of the common treasure from which he could have stolen far larger sums, would betray Christ for a few silver coins; or why he should have committed suicide when nearly everyone was on his side. "To me it simply seems absurd," concludes the lawyer. To be sure, the speaker's image of Christ

> Thin, high-art nostrils, quivering constantly;
> Long nose, full lips, hand tapering, full of veins;
> His movements nervous

or of the disciples—"A strange mad set and full of fancies wild"—is as startling as his version of the Judas story. On the other hand, most readers would no doubt sympathize with the lawyer's psychologically informed open-mindedness.

> John, Peter, James—and Judas best of all—
> All seemed to me good men without offence,—
> A little crazed,—but who is wholly sane?[59]

FROM REVERIE TO INSANITY

In sum, psychological poetry no doubt held a strong appeal for the alienists. It reflected their own search for a new morality, jurisprudence, and reinterpretation of history; and it did so with an immediacy often absent from their own endeavors. Stream of consciousness, reverie, dream, hallucination, insanity: needless to say, there were numerous articles, handbooks, even monographs, which discussed and/or defined these and other phenomena. But what such scientific studies described in the abstract, a poem might often render far more plausibly, perhaps even more accurately, in concrete. Hence even medical men wondered where these unprofessional poet-psychologists could have acquired such accurate insights into precisely some of the phenomena they researched in asylums and universities, and wrote about in their psychiatric publications. Even what one could read about such poetry in the reviews showed increasing psychological knowledge.

As early as 1848, Browning's tendency "to parenthesize one thought or metaphor within another" was noted by the *North American Review*.[60] As in George Eliot's 1856 review of *Men and Women*,[61] such comments often sprung from the recognition that "a great part of the alleged difficulty and obscurity" of the new dramatic-psychological poetry" arise from its mere merits."[62] At least to James Fotheringham, Browning's monologues, for instance, can be like direct thought transcripts. "There often seems a vital transference of thought and of its motives and process in the mind supposed. The poetry is the frank and direct expression of the man thinking."[63] Naturally, such verse makes far greater demands on us than its traditionally discursive counterpart. As another American critic put it, the reader must not only try to imagine or "vividly realize" the speaker's situation at each point; he must also "supply for himself the gaps often left vacant by the abrupt transitions."[64] For ever so often the poet "leaves out (or out of sight) a link here and another there";[65] or he might connect the speaker's thoughts (to quote A. T. Lyttelton) "by very subtle trains of reasoning, which are often, however, suppressed altogether."[66]

The speaker in Coleridge's "Dejection" gets so lost in his thought that, once awakened by the wind that long has raved unnoticed, he Hamlet-like looks back on his absent-mindedness like another John-a-dreams. Such reverie is an essential part of the greater Romantic lyric and of the philosophy behind it. Those who are subject to this mental state, wrote Shelley, "feel as if their nature were dissolved into the surrounding universe, or as if the surrounding universe were absorbed into their being. They are conscious of no distinction."[67] Victorian poets inherited the Romantics' obsession with the same mental processes; but to them, reverie and related phenomena ceased to be means to the end of higher metaphysical insights. Stripped of such philosophical pretensions, they are dealt with in more strictly psychological terms. Where a greater Romantic lyric invites us to lose ourselves in the reveries of the speaker, dramatic monologues prompt us to analyze associations, which the speaker is largely unaware of. In other words, we are made to listen to the speaker like an analyst to his patient.

As a result, the portrayal of stream-of-consciousness phenomena naturally gained in scope. Though it would claim a separate study to discuss the extent of this in full detail, a few of the major issues, particularly as they were made explicit by poets and critics, should not be left unmentioned here. Especially with the minor poets, the urge to delve into the unconscious often outstrips the means for portraying it. The techniques can be of the crudest kind. Little stage directions in parenthesis, for instance, tell us that the two monologues of the contrite adulteress and her forgiving husband in Philip B. Marston's *He and She* are to be read as interior monologues.[68] Italics and parentheses, as in George Barlow's "A Southern Vengeance," indicate how irrepressible memories of his beloved emerge in the speaker's mind as he fantasizes about burying her alive with her lover.

> Then, brick by brick and stone by stone,
> I will build her up in the vault, alone
> With the man her eyes found fair.
> *(Darling—"the gnat has stung the white*
> *Of your beautiful arm," so I said in the night:*
> *"Lay your arm in the moon's soft light;*
> *Let me suck the poison out—my right!")*
> I will not pause to remember or think.
> Clink goes the trowel. Clink! clink! clink!
> Clink! clink! clink![69]

Such techniques raise the familiar question, which H. B. Forman answered in the negative and Browning in the positive. Should the poet present not only what his personae say, but also what they might think? Needless to say, the modern reader would side with the poet suggesting that

> Along with every act—and speech is act—
> There go, a multitude impalpable

> To ordinary human faculty,
> The thoughts which give the act significance.

He would agree that the poet, as a result, "needs must apprehend /
Alike both speech and thoughts which prompt to speak." (*Red Cotton
Night-Cap Country*, 3277–82.) No doubt such a reader would also endorse the poet's right to make a persona describe his hallucinations, as
Tennyson does so superbly in "St. Simeon Stylites." But should the poet
allow himself the scope of having the speaker articulate dreams while
actually dreaming? Characteristically, it was a minor poet who in this
way extended the genre's limits furthest. Augusta Webster's *Sister Annunciata*, while keeping her vigil, repeatedly loses herself in memories
of "the sins and follies of [her] vain youth." At one point, she even falls
asleep and has a nightmare:

> On let me weep a while if but for shame
> Because I cannot check the foolish passion,
> Because I weep despite myself. Alas!
> Oh Lord my helper, when shall I find rest?
> * * * * * * * * * * * *
> How sweet those roses smell! Look, Angelo,
> That cluster of red roses pictured back
> From the still water. See! see! Catch that branch,
> By your left hand—the boat will drift away!
> How the boat rocks! how it rocks! Am I ashore?
> I thought I was in the boat with you. How it rocks!
> Oh Angelo!
>   What is it? Where am I?
> Who was it screamed? Was it I?
>   I have been dreaming—[70]

Dream transcripts thus embedded in an otherwise traditionally conceived dramatic monologue incline one to agree with Forman's rule that
"a monologue must clearly be formed entirely of such utterances as
might be spoken."[71]

Superbly fitting the genre, in contrast, was the presentation of abnormal states of mind. After all, there was nothing improbable in having madmen voice their insane fantasies. Plenty of such gabble could
be heard every day both in asylums and outside them. For generations,

people had flocked to the theater to listen to Lear's insane ravings. Ever since Romanticism, poets like Coleridge and Wordsworth had shown an increasing interest in mad monks, mad mothers, and idiot boys, often by letting these subjects voice their own follies.[72] So, in one sense, readers were well prepared for the publication of "Porphyria's Lover," "Johannes Agricola in Meditation," and "St. Simeon Stylites." At the same time, there was something distinctly new about these poems. With the possible exception of Shakespeare, no one before Browning and Tennyson had ever portrayed insane subjects with comparable incisiveness and insistence. How diverse, even in these three poems, were the mental states portrayed and the poetic techniques of portraying them: a homicidal maniac, a religious megalomaniac, and an hallucinating visionary—the first speaking of horrors with a frightening "matter-of-fact simplicity" (S. Orr);[73] the second gloating over the imagined tortures of innocent men, women, and children preordained for damnation; the third—"a powerfully graphic, and in some respects appalling satire on the pseudo-aspirations of egotistical asceticism and superstition" (Leigh Hunt)[74]—oscillating between fits of despair and hallucinatory ecstasy.

To be sure, even St. Simeon's hallucinations are couched in modes of discourse decipherable to readers, especially those who knew their Shakespeare. But what about the following lines from *Maud*, which clearly go beyond such traditional stream-of-consciousness interpretability?

> Dead, long dead,
> Long dead!
> And my heart is a handful of dust,
> And the wheels go over my head,
> And my bones are shaken with pain,
> For into a shallow grave they are thrust,
> Only a yard beneath the street,
> And the hoofs of the horses beat, beat,
> The hoofs of the horses beat,
> Beat into my scalp and my brain
> . . . .
> Not that grey old wolf for he came not back
> From the wilderness, full of wolves, where he used to lie;

He has gathered the bones of his o'ergrown whelp to crack;
Crack them now for yourself, and howl, and die.

(II, 239–48, 291–94)

No wonder that at least one critic denounced such self-professed "idiot gabble" as "absolute nonsense."[75] But there were others who recognized that the hero's ostensibly incoherent ramblings resembled a carefully woven tapestry of nightmare visions. Centered on the notion of being buried alive, all of them relate either to some present fact in the asylum or to some incident, image, figure, or emotion previously dealt with in the poem. The "prevailing phantasy in the madman's mind," to quote the *British Quarterly* reviewer,

> is that he is dead and buried, but that they have not buried him deep enough, and that he has no rest in the grave. Within this fancy as a ghastly circumference are jumbled together, as it were, by the wild and incoherent action of a madman's imagination, all the wrecks and relics of his past memory, as well as the sights and sounds that are passing around him among his fellow-maniacs. The red-ribbed hollow, his father's suicide, the old Hall, the garden, and the music of that festive night, Maud's image, that of her lean, grey father, that of her brother lying with the wound in his side, the Quaker preaching peace, the duel, his own old thoughts about war and social wrong—all are commingled, with the gabble and noise of the other madmen, into one hideous, inextricable phantasmagory. One notes throughout it the still remaining strength of the old vein of misanthropy and scorn; and from the jumble of the maniac's allusions one picks out the fixed ideas and collected observations of the sane man.[76]

As one would expect, Dr. Bucknill and Dr. Mann trace even more hidden links between the madhouse canto and the rest of *Maud*. Both of them find that the speaker shows symptoms of incipient insanity in earlier parts of the poem.[77] Characteristically, the hero has premonitions of his imminent madness. His hypersensitivity, which makes him see a curtain hiding his beloved as "death-white" (I, 522) and Maud herself as "Luminous, gemlike, ghostlike, deathlike" (I, 95) prefigures his later hallucinations. The suicidal impulses of the sane man also inform the maniac's fantasy of being buried alive. The son of a man who committed suicide, the speaker "is introduced to us full of morbid emotion, a constant mental sufferer" and what Bucknill takes to be as "a true example of Guislain's theory of the psychopathic origin of insanity."[78]

From Case History
to Surrealistic Effusion

More than most other Victorian poems, the madhouse canto of *Maud* foreshadows *The Waste Land*, but with a difference. Although it is known to have been written "in twenty minutes,"[79] the canto does not present itself in the surrealistic vein that a similarly automatic writing process gave to parts of Eliot's poem.[80] What otherwise might be read in this vein assumes a clearly case history-like character within the context of the poem as a whole. One wonders if Tennyson, once again, passed off personal effusions as his persona's. Significantly, the madhouse canto is given this aspect of a case history by being made to follow "See what a lovely shell" and "Oh! that 'twere possible." Tennyson, as if to reinforce his point, originally called his poem *Maud or the Madness*;[81] just as Browning had his two earliest dramatic monologues, "Porphyria's Lover" and "Johannes Agricola," reprinted under the common title "Madhouse Cells."[82]

But the subjective impulse, which, thus objectified, gave rise to the dramatic monologue, also led to the genre's gradual disintegration. The beginnings of this process can be traced back to 1862, when William Morris, just seven years after *Maud* and *Men and Women*, brought out *The Defence of Guinevere and Other Poems*; or probably even further back to a poem that, first published in *Men and Women*, strikes one as the model behind much of the verse in Morris's volume. "Childe Roland to the Dark Tower Came," which came to Browning "as a kind of dream,"[83] was Morris's declared favorite. "In my own heart I think I love this poem the best of all,"[84] he wrote in a review. Other reviewers had described "Childe Roland" as either a strict allegory or a mere series of fearful pictures; or they had criticized it for failing to specify what happened to the protagonist in the "round, squat turret"; but Morris likes the poem precisely for leaving us in the dark as to some of this narrative detail and for mediating in a twilight zone between dream and reality, freewheeling nightmare phantasmagory and signification-fraught allegory.[85] As in some of his own poems, the autonomous case history-like framework of the dramatic monologue is overwhelmed by a stream of dream-like imagery submerging all persona- and situation-specific details in a subconscious, or, if you like, collective realm.

> Who were the strugglers, what war did they wage,
>> Whose savage trample thus could pad the dank
>> Soil to a plash? Toads in a poisoned tank,
>>> Or wild cats in a red-hot iron cage—

> XXIII
> The fight must so have seemed in that fell cirque.
>> What penned them there, with all the plain to choose?
>> No foot-print leading to that horrid mews,
> None out of it. Mad brewage set to work
> Their brains, no doubt. . . .

To read such lines as the effusions of a maniac, like those of the mad-house canto in *Maud*, would be as one-sided as to take them as the author's mere "fantasy," the term Browning applied to them himself.[86] Like some of Morris's poems, they somehow oscillate between the two.

Of course, Morris, as his reviewers pointed out, has some more traditional monologues as well. To Richard Garnett, "The Judgment of God," for instance, reads "exactly like Browning's dramatic lyrics" except for being "better than any but the very best of them."[87] Un-Browningesque may be the speaker's brutality in reminiscing on the chopped-off hands and head of the man he murdered, as he plans to use his father's crafty fighting tactics against his superior and nobler opponent just minutes before a duel; but otherwise, most of the poem's structural patterns of occasion, setting, listener, and implied action fit the dramatic monologue's traditional patterns.

Even the speaker in Morris's "Concerning Geffray Teste Noire" merely seems to suggest the familiar maniac of previous dramatic monologues at first. Telling a certain Alleyne how he and his band tried to ambush Teste Noire, he is sidetracked into several digressions:[88] while waiting for the attack, the sight of two skeletons, of a knight and of a lady, reminds him of an incident in his youth when, cutting down the Jacquerie with his father, he fainted from smelling the burnt bones of several "dames' skeletons" in a church set on fire by the rebels; he then switches back to the two skeletons in front of him, fantasizing about how they died. But from here on the speaker's train of thought begins to move in directions uncommon in previous dramatic monologues.

The skeleton lady, resurrected in the speaker's mind, gradually emerges as the focus of his sexual or, as one recent critic puts it, "necrophilic" fantasies.[89] So completely is he caught in them that, oblivious to his actual listener, he addresses the lady as if she were actually present.

> Your long eyes where the lids seem like to drop,
>   Would you not, lady, were they shut fast, feel
> Far merrier? there so high they will not stop,
>   They are most sly to glide forth and to steal
> Into my heart; *I kiss their soft lids there,*
>   *And in green garden scarce can stop my lips*
> *From wandering on your face, but that your hair*
>   *Falls down and tangles me, back my face slips.*
>
>   (156–64)

One wonders if he is hallucinating at this point; but the question seems somehow inappropriate. Unlike, say, "St. Simeon Stylites," "Concerning Geffray Teste Noire" is not a mere case study of a specific individual. Instead, the speaker becomes the mouthpiece for unconscious mental processes, which, rather than putting the reader at a distance, submerge him in their trance-like imagery. "My work," said Morris, "is the embodiment of dreams in one form or another."[90]

A poem such as "The Wind" shows that what Morris embodies in this way is often the process as much as the content of dreaming. Like "Concerning Geffray Teste Noire," this poem has some of the trappings of a dramatic monologue. A medieval knight sits in his heavily ornate armchair reminiscing on his former love, Margaret. But all more specific details concerning Margaret's violent death and the speaker's possible role in it are lost in what reads like the direct transcript of a nightmare. Unconscious fantasies are not analyzed, but allowed to speak for themselves. Victorian critics were far from blind to the difference. However complex, the "meaning" of dramatic monologues, they argued, is to be found in the author's analysis of a certain character; but with Morris's poetry, as one reviewer remarked, "you cannot quite make out what it means, or whether it means anything taken altogether."[91] "The strangest creations of sleep," to quote Walter Pater, "seem here, by some appalling license, to cross the limit of the dawn."[92]

In "The Wind," the speaker is engulfed in a nightmare into which we, too, are drawn. Rigidly sitting in his chair, he is afraid to make the slightest movement, lest the chair might "scream" (16), the dogs start to howl for those who went to the war, and an orange placed on the armchair's folds "roll out far / And the faint yellow juice ooze out like blood from a wizard's jar" (16–17). Escaping from this cataleptic immobility, he loses himself in a dream world, which quickly turns into nightmare. Somehow the memories surrounding Margaret, which in this "grim half-slumber" (24) haunt his "worn old brains" (25), are full of rejection, violence, and rapist sexuality.

I held to her long bare arms, but she shudder'd away from me,
While the flush went out of her face as her head fell back on a tree,
And a spasm caught her mouth, fearful for me to see;
And still I held to her arms till her shoulder touch'd my mail,
Weeping she totter'd forward, so glad that I should prevail,
And her hair went over my robe, like a gold flag over a sail.
. . . .
I kiss'd her hard by the ear, and she kiss'd me on the brow,
And then lay down on the grass, where the mark on the moss is now,
And spread her arms out wide while I went down below.

(40–45, 49–51)

He walks away from her, but returns to cover Margaret's silent body with the daffodils he has collected along the way. Then he suddenly realizes that

> there was blood on the very quiet breast,
> Blood lay in the many folds of the loose ungirded vest,
> Blood lay upon her arm where the flower had been prest.

(76–78)

One wonders whether the speaker is relating actual events or merely articulating homicidal fantasies. Instead of providing us with a clear-cut delineation of either, "The Wind" depicts an unconscious train of thought, which we are made to relive rather than analyze, let alone comprehend.[93] It is true that the poem retains some of the patterns of the dramatic monologue to the end. Awakened by the horrors of his nightmare, the speaker "shriek'd and leapt from [his] chair" (79) causing precisely what he tried most to avoid earlier: "the orange roll'd out far, / The faint yellow juice oozed out like blood from a wizard's jar; / And then in march'd the ghosts of those that had gone to the war" (79–81). But neither this ending nor the poem in general gives us an analytic portrait of a man who, in addition to being a homicidal maniac

CONTENTS

like Porphyria's lover, has spectral visions like St. Simeon Stylites. "The Wind," like other of Morris's poems, somehow embodies unconscious emotions more directly, prompting the reader to assume and reenact them in the process. "A passion of which the outlets are sealed," as Walter Pater put it, "begets a tension of nerve, in which the sensible world comes to one with a reinforced brilliancy and relief."[94] But such effects were lost on the Victorians, who barely took notice of Morris's volume. It was a different story when Swinburne, four years later, unleashed similar techniques on the reading public, causing one of the greatest scandals in English literary history.

X

Swinburne, or the Psychopathology of Poetic Creation

IN ONE SENSE, the Victorian reading public was surprisingly open-minded. While balking at Browning's obscurity, it hardly objected when the poet spoke through the mouth of, say, Johannes Agricola as he gloats over those who, despite their good will or innocence, are pre-destined to eternal damnation—"the broken-hearted nun, / The martyr, the wan acolyte, / The incense-swinging child" (54–56). Nor did it take offense at Porphyria's lover who strangles his mistress with her own hair in order to preserve pure the moment of her abandon to him and then proceeds to lavish upon the corpse the affectionate attention he could not muster for the live woman.

> As a shut bud that holds a bee,
>   I warily oped her lids: again
>   Laughed the blue eyes without a stain.
> And I untightened next the tress
>   About her neck; her cheek once more
> Blushed bright beneath my burning kiss:
>   I propped her head up as before,
> Only, this time my shoulder bore
>   Her head, which droops upon it still
>
>   (43–51)

Rather than criticize the poet for his morbid interests, readers clamored for more of the same, praising him for analyzing "the minds of men as deftly as a surgeon can dissect their bodies."[1]

184

But there were definite limits to this open-mindedness. By and large, reviewers tolerated the portrayal of mental perversion only as long as it was done the way in which an alienist would diagnose a morally insane delinquent so as to have him hospitalized for further observation and treatment. Whether insane morally or otherwise, a madman, after all, was a madman, to be pitied, analyzed, and, if possible, cured, but hardly to be let loose upon "normal" society. Like Victorian asylums, dramatic monologues in this sense are a means of sequestration, particularly of their authors' own morbidities. Wherever they deal with mental aberrations, they are "madhouse cells" like "Porphyria's Lover" and "Johannes Agricola in Meditation."

Tennyson and Browning, in their early years, had come up against these limits, and both made the concessions requested by society. Browning, who in *Pauline* has the speaker wonder how he "might kill" his mistress "and be loved for it" (902), received J. S. Mill's rebuke for dealing with "this morbid state" without suggesting a convincing mode of recovery—"for *he* is hardly convalescent, and 'what should we speak of but that which we know?' "[2] We know how the poet reacted by declaring *Pauline* to be his first dramatic monologue. The young Tennyson, when suspected of indulging in "sick writing," responded in similar fashion.[3] This is most obvious from *The Lover's Tale*, whose protagonist fantasizes about forcing the woman he loves, but who loves another, to drown with him:

> Aloud she shrieked;
> My heart was cloven with pain; I wound my arms
> About her: we whirled giddily; the wind
> Sung; but I clasped her without fear: her weight
> Shrank in my grasp, and over my dim eyes,
> And parted lips which drank her breath, down-hung
> The jaws of Death.
>
> (II, 196–202)

As we know, Tennyson withdrew the already typeset poem from inclusion in his 1832 *Poems*, and, when he finally published it in 1869, provided the autobiographical ramblings of the poet narrator Julian with a case-history-type framework. A friend of Julian's continues the story by describing the protagonist as simply "crazed, / Though not with such a craziness as needs / A cell and keeper" (IV, 162–164).

Within these new safeguards Tennyson even ventured to explore the hero's necrophiliac tendencies. His beloved is thought to be dead and Julian, stirred by his fancy to "kiss her on the lips," "To kiss the dead," duly proceeds to the vault where he finds "His lady with the moonlight on her face; / Her breast as in a shadow-prison":

> He softly put his arm about her neck
> And kissed her more than once, till helpless death
> And silence made him bold—
>   (IV, 48, 50, 56–57, 70–73)

Julian, after all, is a declared maniac. Victorians therefore found no reason to reprove the poet for poetically analyzing his aberration the way alienists scrutinized comparable cases in asylums all across the country.

DRAMATIZATIONS OF THE PERVERSE

From this perspective, one has difficulty understanding the uproar over Swinburne's *Poems and Ballads*, or why Victorians should tolerate, for instance, "Porphyria's Lover" while denouncing "The Leper." Was not Swinburne's poem, just like Browning's, simply another case study in necrophilic erotomania? In one sense "Porphyria's Lover" strikes one as even more horrible than "The Leper" for combining necrophilia with homicide, a tendency the younger poet has his speaker fantasize about but not perpetrate. To take another instance, there is Swinburne's "Les Noyades" whose protagonist rejoices at the prospect of being drowned tied breast to breast to the lady he loves but who despises him: "I shall drown with her, laughing for love; and she / Mix with me, touching me, lips and eyes" (55–56). Long before Swinburne, Tennyson made Julian indulge in similar, or worse, fantasies in *The Lover's Tale*.

But where post-Freudian critics notice parallels, contemporary reviewers only saw contrasts. With the same extravagance with which they had praised Browning and Tennyson for exploring the most aberrant manifestations of the human mind, they denounced Swinburne for being "publicly obscene," "unclean for the sake of uncleanness" and for writing poems that were "utterly revolting," "depressing and misbegotten," ravingly blasphemous, or mere deifications of incontinence.[4] Where most critics had learned to distinguish between, say, Browning and his personae, they quickly shed such practices with Swinburne.

Along with his speakers, the author was counted among the "lecherous priests of Venus"; he was called the "libidinous laureate of a pack of satyrs,"[5] or simply a "Swine-born."[6] Where Tennyson had been praised for giving readers a "remarkable sketch of poetic mental pathology" in *Maud*,[7] the author of "Anactoria" or "Dolores" was declared insane himself. "There are many passages," commented the *Pall Mall Gazette*, "which bring before the mind the image of a mere madman, one who has got maudlin drunk on lewd ideas and lascivious thoughts."[8] The worst of it perhaps was that Swinburne might drive his readers insane as well. To read him long, wrote Henry Morley, would either "make you mad" or moral.[9]

It was to little avail that Swinburne, in response, tried to defend his poems the way Browning had defended *Pauline*. *Poems and Ballads*, he protested in *Notes on Poems and Reviews*, is "dramatic, many-faced, multifarious; and no utterance of enjoyment or despair, belief or unbelief, can properly be assumed as the assertion of [the author's] personal feeling or faith."[10] Reviewers then and now remained unconvinced. According to *Punch*, Swinburne's *Notes* simply added a "prurient poetics" to filthy poetry.[11] If the poems were indeed dramatic, what was the justification for dramatizing such subject matter, wondered the *London Review*.[12] But *were* the poems really dramatic? Even where Swinburne in "Hymn to Proserpine," for instance, adopts the masque of a Roman devotee of the ancient divinity, he hardly makes us assume the critical distance that, in most dramatic monologues, tempers our sympathy for the speaker. For one, the ideas put into the mouth of the Roman, as Robert Buchanan pointed out rightly, imply "precisely the same conditions of thought as we find expressed in the lyrical poems elsewhere."[13] Futhermore, Swinburne's mesmerizing prosody and rhetoric, here and elsewhere, constantly lure the reader into identifying with the persona. It is not surprising to learn that young men at Cambridge, as Edmund Gosse reports, joined hands and marched along chanting "Dolores."

Private comments by Swinburne reinforce the impression that there was, as Clyde K. Hyder puts it, "more logic than candour" in his protests that his poems were essentially dramatic.[14] According to Swinburne's *Notes*, "Dolores," for instance, was meant to express "that transient state of spirit through which a man may be supposed to pass, foiled in love and weary of loving, but not yet in sight of rest; seeking refuge in those 'violent delights' which 'have violent ends.' "[15] But, as far as we know, the genesis of neither the poem nor of *Notes* bears out these pious sentiments. Swinburne clearly had as much fun in writing "Dolores" as his student proselytes at Cambridge had in chanting it. Eight recently added lines (173–80), as he bragged to Charles Augustus Howell, contained "une vérité que ne comprendront jamais les sots idolateurs de la vertu." Another ten lines, which came to him while writing the same letter, struck their author as equally successful—"très infâmes et très bien tournés. 'Oh! monsieur—peut-on prendre du plaisir à telles horreurs?' Tu le vois, Justine, je bande—oh! putain, que tu vas souffrir'—."[16] The defense of this (to quote the *London Review*) "especially horrible"[17] poem was conducted in similar tongue-in-cheek highhandedness. "I have proved Dolores to be little less than a second Sermon on the Mount, and Anactoria than an archdeacon's charge," Swinburne wrote to W. M. Rossetti.[18]

Of course, some poems were more fictitious than others, but the critics, as Swinburne recalled gleefully over three decades later, had failed to identify them. "There are photographs from life in the book," he wrote, "and there are sketches from imagination. Some which keensighted criticism has dismissed with a smile as ideal or imaginary were as real and actual as they well could be: others which have been taken for obvious transcripts from memory were utterly fantastic or dramatic."[19] Swinburne identified at least one of his more autobiographical poems. "Félise," particularly on account of the speaker's "antitheism," he confessed to W. M. Rossetti, represents "a mood of mind and phase of thought not unfamiliar to me."[20]

Somewhat confusingly, Swinburne nonetheless insists on the poem's "dramatic" character. "No reader (*as* a reader)," he argued, "has a right (whatever he may conjecture) to assert that this is *my* faith and that the faith expressed in such things as the 'Litany' or 'Carol' or 'Dorothy' is not. Of course it is a more serious expression of feeling; and of course this is evident; but it is not less formally dramatic than the others."[21] "Félise" suggests the peculiar nature of such formal dramatization, which, though imaginary in terms of concrete detail, simply embodies the poet's own yearnings and beliefs. Félise, who attracted the speaker for being "subtly warm, and half perverse" (102), is given a lecture evincing the speaker's predilection for polymorphous perversity, which, if unsatisfied by reality, can always be supplemented by the poetic imagination:

> For many loves are good to see;
> Mutable loves, and loves perverse;
> But there is nothing, nor shall be,
> So sweet, so wicked, but my verse
> Can dream of worse.
>
> (161–65)

Readers, then, had good reason for identifying Swinburne with his personae. For with a few exceptions like "The Leper," his speakers are dramatic merely in the way in which even deliberately confessional poets cannot fully reveal themselves (to quote E. Johnson) "without resorting to some oblique, objective, or dramatic mode of expression."[22] It is true that Swinburne is not confessional in the sense that Wordsworth is in the *Prelude*. In other words, he does not communicate, but rather withholds, facts from his personal life. But he is confessional in expressing, even dramatizing, his opinions, emotional idiosyncracies, and favorite fantasies. The speaker in "Hymn to Proserpine" may be a Roman, but the anti-Christian sentiments he expresses are the author's.

Swinburne's relation to this and other of his personae is neither critical nor empathic. Or where it is, such distance or closeness is circumscribed by the ways with which one views one's own emotional penchants and convictions. Swinburne wanted to shock and he did. Blasphemy and sensuality had been his aims at least since 1858 when he meant to say so publicly, by reviewing himself.[23] Even his closest friends and admirers like the Rossettis, Meredith, and Ruskin had advised him not to publish or at least to "play savagely with a knife among the proofs for the sake of" his fame.[24] But Swinburne defied both enemies and friends and paid the expected price.

In short, where Browning and Tennyson had opted for the disguise, Swinburne spoke out more directly. This is not to say that what the older poets chose to hide was of the same kind as what their younger successor preferred to reveal. But one wonders what might have happened to literary history if Tennyson, for one, had decided to openly draw upon his trances and hallucinations for poetic inspiration instead of suppressing poems like "Hark! the dogs howl!" and passing off others like "See what a lovely shell" as the musings of a madman in embryo. A poet of his stature, undisguisedly writing about his spectral visions, would no doubt have stirred up an uproar similar to that which Swinburne caused with his sadomasochistic and anti-Christian fantasies.

The different between them, in other words, was not so much one of the respective poet's greater or lesser "morbidity," but of his attitude toward it in relation to the public. Browning and Tennyson had turned against themselves in making their pact with Victorian propriety. Hence, both were predictably aghast at discovering this younger poet of unquestionable genius who refused to make the same concessions. To Browning, Swinburne's poems were "moral mistakes, redeemed by much intellectual ability." Swinburne undoubtedly "had genius," but he "wrote verses in which to [Browning's] mind there was no good at all."[25] Even more negative was Tennyson's attitude, partly no doubt because in "condemning some of Swinburne's proclivities," as Leonard M. Findlay puts it, "he would be reminded of the unflattering circumstances behind his abandoning similar themes."[26] The Laureate hardly had to await the publication of *Poems and Ballads* to make up his mind about this poet. When some of the critics fell foul of the "sensuality and materialism" of *Chastelard*, Tennyson "emphatically shared their views, saying that although he thought the poem very fine, his objections to it were as deep as Heaven and Hell."[27]

Whatever poets and critics read of the writings by psychologists about art and artists must have reinforced them in this damnatory attitude. In fact, the diagnostic eagerness of Victorian alienists increasingly encroached upon the reviewers' task. We have already seen how the early psychiatrists mapped out their proper domain of critical analysis in showing how Shakespeare's, Tennyson's, and other poets' works revealed an understanding of the human mind ignored by the literati but paralleling their recent discoveries. A second new critical genre developed by Victorian alienists was that of short psychoanalytic biographies usually based upon larger works written by the standard biographers. Its typical method of applying the "modern insights" of mental science in this area was, as J. F. Nisbet points out in *The Insanity of Genius*, "not unlike that of the family doctor who is called in to examine a patient": "With the help of the biographer I ask the great man, figuratively speaking, to stand up; I look at his tongue, feel his pulse, and inquire into his family history. By this means a wholly different view of genius is obtained from that generally current. The biographer, unfortunately, is too often as troublesome a person to deal with as the family nurse."[28]

INSANE ARTISTS
AND ALIENIST BIOGRAPHERS

One of the first to write this "sort of microscopic biography" was R. R. Madden whose *Infirmities of Genius* of 1833 purports to solve the psychological mysteries surrounding Burns, Byron, Cowper, Dr. Johnson, Pope, and Scott.[29] As Madden keeps reminding us, previous biographers, with the possible exception of Robert Burns's J. Currie, simply could not account for what really motivated these men.[30] Thus T. Moore, for instance, fails to trace the origin of Byron's "morbid sensibility" to its "true cause; we are simply told that his temperament was a poetic one, and that it was unfavorable to the due performance of his social and domestic duties."[31] By contrast, Madden himself, rather than detailing the poet's eccentricities, peccadilloes, or hysterical affections in the gossipy manner of this biographer, simply traces them to their allegedly common root. To him, the "simple fact is" that Byron "laboured under an epileptic diathesis": "If feelings of delicacy induced his biographers to conceal a truth they were aware of, or deemed it better to withold their motive was unquestionably a good one; but it was nevertheless a mistaken delicacy; for there are no infirmities so humiliating to humanity as those irregularities of conduct in eminent individuals; and the only palliation they admit of is often precluded by our ignorance of the bodily disorders under which they may have laboured."[32]

Madden, then, largely tries to find extenuating psychiatric circumstances for what might otherwise shock the public's sense of normalcy and moral propriety. But such liberal-mindedness often changed into a more judgmental attitude as the notion of moral insanity—according to J. C. Prichard a "morbid perversion of the feelings, affections, habits, without any hallucination or erroneous conviction impressed upon the understanding"—gained widespread currency.[33] Poets and artists who previously might have escaped the charge of insanity altogether, came in for the severest censure. The *Autobiography of Benjamin Robert Haydon*, for instance, gave the anonymous reviewer of the *Journal of Psychological Medicine and Mental Pathology* "ample materials for a psychological study of genius" in terms of the new category.[34] Essentially, this study, like many similar ones, is an indictment of the artist for his moral turpitude and hence self-inflicted psychopathological dilemmas. Haydon is charged with "wondrous folly" and "inextinguishable vanity and self-will"; he is found to be dishonest, unjust, "thoroughly obstinate," "morbidly proud," and "irremediably egotistical." Worst of all, his autobiography revealed, even bragged about, his lack of self-control. Haydon's "undisciplined will" was at the core of most of his problems, and, most notably, vitiated his art.

> He "dashes at his canvas like an inspired devil," he "drives" at it, he "flies" at it. This constantly. He continually "races" into the city for money; and if his earliest, his kindest, his very judicious friend hesitates a moment to minister to his wildly incurred necessities, he "pours forth a dreadful torrent of sarcasm" and shakes the unfortunate man "to death." This activity he called "virtuous industry;" it was more nearly allied to the delirious activity of insanity; it had its source in self-gratification—not self-denial.[35]

What post-Freudian psychiatrists tend to trace to repression, their Victorian predecessors largely attributed to the lack of it, and artists were allowed no exception. The verdict passed on Haydon is only typical of what alienist biographers had to say about many of the painter's peers and superiors. Rousseau, for instance, was found "destitute of the power to repress . . . his carnal nature"[36] and "deplorably subject to the hallucinations of erotic insanity."[37] Another alienist speaks of his "erotomania" as one of several symptoms of this "morally mad" genius.[38] Rousseau, in this view, lacked all notion "of truth, rectitude, honesty, in short of the sense of right and wrong." Who else would have preferred "the foul, brutal, sanguinary wild man of the woods to the finest examples of virtue?"[39] Another favorite target of such diagnostic zeal was Edgar Allen Poe whose moral insanity resulted in a "profligacy in intemperance" as well as in bouts of "distempered fancy and unhealthy poetry."[40] Many others, like George Morland, James Gates Percival, and Richard Savage,[41] were found subject to similar "morbidity of the moral sense." Torquato Tasso was said to suffer from "erotic mania,"[42] Swift from "morbid acrimony of temper" and "evil genius,"[43] Friedrich Schiller from dipsomania, not to mention dozens of other artists who were diagnosed for religious melancholia, mania errabunda, "folie circulaire," paroxysmal and suicidal melancholia, delusions and hallucinations.[44]

Even artists who traditionally had been held in high esteem for their respectability or idealism were retroactively diagnosed as victims of moral insanity. A reviewer of the *Journal of Mental Science*, after reading

Dowden's biography of Shelley,[45] found "evidence of an insane temperament" in the poet's "altogether disproportionate regard for the questions arising out of the relations of the sexes." Although not actually insane, Shelley had "an insane diathesis, a strong disposition to mental aberration."[46] Another alienist writing for the *Journal of Psychological Medicine* claimed to have found the key to an understanding of Turner's bizarre existence, a mystery that he claimed eluded the authors of all six of the then existing memoirs of the famous artist. Friends and foes alike, he writes, "failed to discover the key to the mystery, to apply the true solvent to that compound of crudities and jewels which constituted the nature of the man with whom they were dealing. That key and solvent are to be found in unhealth and unsoundness of mind pervading his whole career, but becoming more prominent and palpable at certain periods and under certain influences."[47] Even Carlyle, the wise man of Chelsea, was subjected to a post-mortem analysis of his "lifelong mental condition."[48] In sum, reviewers denouncing Swinburne as an infectious madman drunk with "lewd ideas and lascivious thoughts,"[49] were in basic agreement with Victorian alienists pronouncing similiar judgment on a large number of poets and artists.

A POETICS OF MADNESS AND REVOLT

One of the few to actively try to stem the tide of such denunciatory tirades was Swinburne himself. In this he began by defending others and, in doing so, hammered out his cause several years before making his debut with *Atalanta in Calydon*. The first occasion arose when R. H. Hutton attacked Meredith's *Modern Love* in the *Spectator*. There "is a deep vein of muddy sentiment in most men," Hutton argued, accusing Meredith of not letting "the mud settle," and for boasting of it to the world instead.[50] *Modern Love*, in Hutton's view, should be renamed *Modern Lust*. While dealing with "a deep and painful subject," Meredith had "no convictions to express" regarding it.[51] Ignoring Hutton's abusive tirades, Swinburne, in a letter to the editor, simply takes issue with the reviewer's didactic understanding of poetry: "There are pulpits enough for all preachers in prose; the business of verse-writing is hardly to express convictions. . . . As to subject, it is too much to expect that all schools of poetry are to be for ever subordinate to the one just now so much in request with us, whose scope of sight is bounded by the nursery walls."[52]

Even more prophetic of his own future was Swinburne's pioneering review of Baudelaire's *Les fleurs du mal* whose first edition had been subjected to the prosecution that *Poems and Ballads* was to be threatened with later. Here the English poet found a subject matter that, while akin to his own poetic interests, was strenuously repressed by the censors of his age—"the weariness of pain and the bitterness of pleasure—the perverse happiness and wayward sorrows of exceptional people."[53] Baudelaire's response to the review must have further strengthened Swinburne's evolving "l'art pour l'art" aesthetic. The English poet had tried to prove that "this poetry of strange disease and sin" and of "hideous violence wrought by a shameless and senseless love" has an implicit "background of morality to it."[54] "Je ne suis pas si *moraliste* que vous feignez obligeamment de le croire," Baudelaire wrote Swinburne in a letter: "Je crois simplement 'comme vous sans doute' que tout poème, tout objet d'art *bien fait* suggère naturellement et forcément une *morale*. C'est l'affaire du lecteur. J'ai même une haine très décidée contre toute *intention* morale exclusive dans un poème."[55]

Swinburne took Baudelaire's advice in his influential *William Blake*, most of which was written during 1863 and 1864, again before he began publishing his major poetry.[56] The book, as finally printed in 1867, opens with a motto from Baudelaire's essay on Richard Wagner. It draws on the French poet once again when Swinburne, in Part Two, presses Blake into the service of his by now more radical "l'art pour l'art" doctrine. Those who would like to appreciate Blake, he argues, have to abandon "the heresy of instruction," so denounced by Baudelaire, this "living critic of incomparably delicate insights."[57] However, if Swinburne (to quote Cecil Y. Lang) "rescued Blake"[58] from previous critical contempt or neglect, it was merely by substituting one "heresy of instruction" with another. Swinburne is deeply concerned with Blake's own kind of didacticism or "philosophy" as suppressed by "the abject and faithless and blasphemous timidity of our wretched English literary society."[59]

This was said at a time when Gilchrist's biography had already managed to persuade most readers and reviewers that, contrary to previous allegations, Blake had not been a lunatic after all. Nonetheless, Swinburne found reason for his own crusade. Gilchrist's defense had mainly focused on Blake's hallucinations or "visitors," which the biographer carefully distinguishes from ghosts and other "gross" phenomena invoked by contemporary spiritists.[60] Rather than having "external, or (in German slang) . . . *objective* existence," these visions were simply projections of his imagination, Gilchrist argued. In short, Blake was "an enthusiast, not an *insane* man."[61] As as result of his biography, Blake, overnight, became one of the most cherished figures of the Victorian imagination. As Deborah Dorfman puts it, people "relinquished mad Blake and took to their hearts the gentle and frugal engraver who chanted hymns on his deathbed and died with his debts paid."[62]

Almost as quickly as it arose, this picture of Blake as the prototype of angelic, though eccentric, innocence and respectability was destroyed by Swinburne's book. Hardly acquitted from the charge of insanity, the Romantic poet reappeared under some new form of madness. "Blake . . . whose life . . . was as pure and blameless as one of the winged messengers," complained one critic, "comes out of Mr. Swinburne's crucible with the attributes and aspects of a satyr."[63] The reason for this was that Swinburne praised precisely those aspects of Blake's person and writing which even Gilchrist, echoing current psychiatric notions of the time, put down to eccentricity, irritableness, or even deliberate perversity.[64] Typical of such deplorable extravagance to the biographer were the Proverbs of Hell, which had left Palmer, another Blake devotee and adviser of the biographer, shuddering "like a child for the first time in Madame Tussaud's 'Chamber of Horrors.' "[65] Palmer advised Mrs. Gilchrist, who finalized Blake's biography upon her husband's death, to eliminate the Proverbs from *The Marriage of Heaven and Hell*, and she duly followed his advice; otherwise the book would revolt "every drawing-room . . . in England."[66]

No one could have disagreed more than Swinburne, who once transcribed *The Marriage of Heaven and Hell* from a copy in Richard Monckton Milnes's private library of rare and forbidden books.[67] To him, *The Marriage* was simply "the greatest work of its century"[68] precisely for being centered on the notorious Proverbs. Like Baudelaire's "Litanies de Satan"—"one of the noblest lyrics ever written" and "the key-note to this whole complicated tune" of *Les fleurs du mal*—Blake's poem,[69] to Swinburne's delight, derived its inspiration from "hell instead of heaven." This predilection for the satanic had recently been sharpened by another treasure trove of infernal inspiration thrown open by Lord Houghton's private library: the works of the "Divine" Marquis de Sade. A long annotation to his *William Blake*, illustrating the poet's rebellion against God, directly echoes various of the Marquis' most basic creeds in a universe ruled by crime and destruction:

Nature averse to crime? I tell you, nature lives and breathes by it; hungers at all her pores for bloodshed, aches in all her nerves for the help of sin, yearns with all her heart for the furtherance of cruelty. . . . Friends, if we would be one with nature, let us continually do evil with all our might . . . for nature would fain have it so, that she might create a world of new things; for she is weary of the ancient life: her eyes are sick of seeing and her ears are heavy with hearing; with the lust of creation she is burnt up, and rent in twain with travail until she bring forth change; she would fain create afresh, and cannot, except it be by destroying: in all her energies she is athirst for mortal food, and with all her forces she labours in desire of death.[70]

Unlike Gilchrist's gentle engraver, Swinburne's Blake, then, was the prophet of infernal wisdom walking arm in arm with the Marquis de Sade. For who else but a man of the most trenchant insights could have written proverbs such as "The lust of the goat is the bounty of God."[71] In turn, the reasons for the suppression of Blake and of the Divine Marquis were analogous. Society ostracized both by declaring them mad, actually institutionalizing the one and ridiculing the other. To Swinburne, the parallel was obvious. Whenever a man like Blake or de Sade devoted himself "to the benefit of humanity and the upsetting of its idols (notamment 'cette chimère méprisable qu'on appelle la Vertu, et cette chimère éxécrable qu'on appelle Dieu') . . . humanity rewards their supreme benefactor with a madhouse or a gaol."[72] In short, Gilchrist had missed the point in acquitting Blake from the charge of insanity by staying too close to the arguments of Blake's denunciators. To do so was like proving the innocence of the accused without releasing him from jail. All the "chatter about 'madness' and such-like . . . even when well-meaning and not offensive,"[73] simply obscured the true issue.

For Swinburne the true issue was to vindicate not Blake, the allegedly insane visionary, but Blake, the supposedly deranged artist, whose works, according to an 1809 reviewer were "the wild effusions of a distempered brain."[74] Even Gilchrist, as we remember, had dismissed Blake's religious and moral opinions by attributing both to a perverted creative impulse.[75] But to Swinburne, the "apparent madness of final absurdity"[76] manifest in, say, the Prophetic Books, had "its root in the deepest and soundest part of Blake's mind and faith." If The Marriage of

Heaven and Hell was "the greatest of all his books" as well as "about the greatest" of its century "in the line of high poetry and spiritual speculation," it was precisely because of its "cool insanity of manner."[77]

No doubt, Blake, as Swinburne confessed in private, was not "always wholly sane, or sound in mind, in the . . . vulgar sense."[78] But such hyperexcitability bordering on a definite *"dérèglement de tous les sens"*[79] was precisely what gave him his uniquely "subtle, trenchant and profound" insights.[80] Without it, the poet might never have been able to perpetrate the complete "transvaluation of values" current at his time. Swinburne does not use Nietzsche's terminology but clearly interprets *The Marriage* and other work along these lines. As Ruskin was to argue later, Blake's poems were "the words of a great and wise mind, disturbed, but not deceived, by its sickness; nay, partly exalted by it";[81] in fact, it may well be that Swinburne, in evolving his image of Blake the revolutionary poet-prophet of near-psychotic hypersensitivity, was influenced by what Ruskin said about *Poems and Ballads*.

Of course, there were other influences as well. Thus *William Blake* is Swinburne's partial self-portrait as the Baudelairian *poète maudit* preaching liberation from the crippling constraints of Christian morality in "sudden cries of melodious revolt."[82] From Baudelaire Swinburne also borrowed the idea of how our instinctual nature is demonized by repression; for instance, Venus, to him, grows "diabolic among ages that would not accept her as divine,"[83] while love turns "perverse passion" and "annihilat[ing] all else, falls at last to feed upon itself, to seek out strange things and barren ways."[84] But Ruskin more clearly even than Baudelaire must have impressed upon Swinburne the conviction that only someone who shares such sickness can become its poetic analyst. "There is assuredly something wrong with you," he wrote the young poet,

> awful in proportion to the great power it affects, and renders (nationally) at present useless. So it was with Turner, so with Byron. It seems to be the peculiar judgment-curse of modern days that all their greatest men shall be plague-struck. But the truth and majesty which is in their greatest, causes the plague which is underneath, in the hearts of meaner people, smooth outwardly, to be in them visible outside while there is purity within. The rest are like graves which appear not—and you are rose graftings set in dung.[85]

Of all the critics of *Poems and Ballads*, Ruskin stood out by reversing the consensus of his day, by accusing the reviewers of precisely the moral perversion they purported to find in the poet. No doubt, Swinburne's work was "diseased";[86] but hardly in the ignoble way that marked the sickness of his detractors. Theirs was a disease they misconstrued as normalcy, while the poet's contained its own cure. "There is hardly a piece of music written now in Europe," Ruskin assured Swinburne's father, "hardly a spectacle on any European stage—which is not more or less guilty and vile in a sense in which no thought of your son's ever could be—and it is the people who indulge in this continued viciousness who will most attack his work. The more I read it—the nobler I think it is. It *is* diseased—no question—but—as the blight is most [?] on the moss-rose—and does not touch—however terrible—the inner nature of the flower."[87] But such pre-Laingian insight, which Swinburne in turn applied to Blake, found itself pitted against the consensus of those whose self-righteous claims in determining what was sick and sound in the arts had recently gained fresh support from the newly developed mental science.

Epilogue: Toward a
Poète Maudit *Aesthetic*

IN A WAY, then, the story ends where it began. For the notes of authorial morbidity audible in *Poems and Ballads* are by no means new sounds in the choir of post-Romantic verse. The main difference is that Swinburne, despite pretending to opt for the dramatic disguise, insists provocatively on what remains a largely involuntary confessionalism in poems like Browning's *Pauline* and Tennyson's *Timbuctoo*. Like other works of this earlier period, these testify to a malaise that the "subjective poet of modern classification"[1] incurred in his introspective quest for the truth. Rather than the "seeds of creation lying burningly on the Divine Hand"[2] promised him by the Romantic aesthetic, he encountered a demonized mirror image of himself.

The problem was, of course, shared by others such as philosophers and psychologists; and so was the urge to objectify what introspection had revealed as one's private dilemmas. This impulse was as strong behind the rise of mental science as behind the emergence of the dramatic monologue. Just as alienists analyzed their patients partly in terms of what self-analysis had taught them about themselves, so poets could body forth in their personae mental and other problems they had recognized as their own. Browning's "Madhouse Cells," the collective title for his two earliest dramatic monologues,[3] point to a striking parallel with the hospitalization of the insane. Just as alienists observed their locked up patients for symptoms shared at least partially by themselves, so poets might use the madhouse cells of their monologues to expose to quasiclinical analysis their own most pressing spiritual dilemmas.

It compounds the paradox to know that most Victorian readers were aware of it. Whereas the poets claimed that they only spoke on the personae's behalf, not their own, the reviewers insisted on the opposite. Browning and others, they argued, largely adopted these masks in order to camouflage private emotions. At the same time, most of them were ready to connive at the pretense. Hence, Tennyson, for instance, might get away with voicing spectral or necrophilic fantasies, as long as these were disguised as poetic case histories. But woe betide the poet who might dare articulate his, say, sadomasochistic yearnings *in propria persona*, or adopt the customary means of camouflage, as offered by the dramatic monologue, in all too casual a fashion.

This is, of course, what happened in 1866, when Swinburne published *Poems and Ballads*. But apart from stirring up moral outrage, the volume predictably created feelings of liberation. Students at Cambridge marched hand in hand chanting "Dolores," that "especially horrible poem" according to the *London Review*.[4] In a sense, this is easy to understand. "Dolores," like other of Swinburne's "psychological monstrosities" (G. Sarrazin),[5] cuts right across the compromises and hypocrisies surrounding the dramatic monologue; and it did so precisely by adopting the genre's basic mode. While Tennyson, Browning, and others had hidden behind their personae, Swinburne used them in order to amplify personal concerns. Poetic case histories of morbidity allowing their authors to quarantine, so to speak, their dilemmas, were turned into hymn-like celebrations of abnormality and perversion. The result was something unprecedented in English literature. For the first time a major poet was heard addressing his scandalized readers in the role of the modern *poète maudit*, who unabashedly draws on irrational, abnormal, even insane impulses as mainsprings of his creativity.

The general public, if not downright hostile, responded with incomprehension. And who would blame them, especially in hindsight? Today we have theories, which they lacked, enabling us to associate creativity with psychopathology without damning either the artist or his creations. Following Freud, for instance, one might assess the creative impulse behind *Poems and Ballads* as a process analogous to the functioning of neurosis;[6] following Jung, one could argue that what prima facie looks like a display of private dilemmas, gives voice to a psychic malaise of the time, with the poet, for better or worse, "conjuring up the forms in which the age is most lacking";[7] in the footsteps of surrealist theorists like Breton, one might claim that, given the modern dilemma as first diagnosed by Baudelaire, artists are driven to share the fate of the madman[8] or should induce such derangement by a deliberate *"dérèglement de tous les sens"* à la Rimbaud.[9] Yet Victorians during the 1860s were for the most part unaware of Baudelaire and damned Poe,

Baudelaire's main model for the artist reconvalescent, as an intemperate profligate. And they either ignored or dismissed Swinburne's own efforts to set up Blake as the modern artist-prophet, whose greatest insights were prompted by what makes him appear a madman in the eyes of the general public.

Such at least was the mainstream attitude. Yet whoever can read between the lines will notice a tendency, especially in the writings by alienists, for broaching issues that seem to prepare the ground for our more recent *poète maudit* theorizing. The same men who condemned the moral insanity of diverse artists on the one hand, argued frequently that artistic creativity can or does derive from semipsychotic affections on the other, though usually without bothering to explore the paradox. Before indicting Haydon for moral insanity and subsequent suicidal monomania, the *Journal of Psychological Medicine*, for instance, published an article on "The Insanity of Men of Genius," explaining that madness is a somehow inescapable part of genius. Who can doubt, wonders the author, that "excessive expansion of nervous matter—great sensibility—acute sensitiveness—quickness of apprehension—and vividness of imagination, &c.," so obvious in artistic creativity, "are all indications of a state of brain bordering closely on the confines of disease?"[10] More specifically, he distinguishes various categories of such semipsychotic hyperexcitation. The simplest of these, in his view, is "the *unconscious* creation of false ideas, and [the] absolute dominion of the representative faculty over the judgment." Akin to these and often accompanied by a "derangement of memory," is "rapt attention," "mere abstraction," or "*passive* eccentricity." Then there is hallucinatory vision of two kinds as experienced by either Blake or Fuseli. What the latter knew to be fantasy, the former took for reality. But more essential to the alienist than this distinction is the fact that hallucinatory experience, whether or not recognized as such, is an intrinsic part of artistic creativity. In that sense Nicolai's spectral visions and the phantom figure that induced Mozart to write his "Requiem" were of the same nature.[11] "Thus the hallucinations of Tasso differed from the conscious creations of Shakespeare—the ideal revelations of Blake, (which were unfolded to us by the late John Varley,) from the wild eccentricities of Fuseli. Yet we doubt not that Shakespeare and Fuseli saw in their mind's eye as perfect an Eidolon as Tasso and Blake."[12]

Both "The Insanity of Men of Genius" and the article on Haydon were probably written by Forbes Winslow, the journal's editor. Hence, it is all the more curious to find that the later piece denounces Haydon's moral insanity in the most uncompromising terms, while the earlier one describes both Burns's and Byron's genius as, in part, dependent upon such allegedly psychotic depravity. Without his "deep and unholy passion," Burns, for instance, "would have been a happier and a better man," but at the same time, "the world would have been shorn of the wild poesy of his sentiments." Though "his life would not have ended amidst the regrets of the libertine and the delirium tremens of the drinker," he also would never have penned the "amorous eulogies of his Marys, Janes, and Nancys."[13]

The same contradiction cuts across Victorian psychiatric writing about genius in general. On the one hand, there is the violent denunciation of diverse artists' moral insanity; on the other, a growing awareness that what is most original about an artist's or poet's vision partly depends upon its moral or other deviancy from normal perception; and that art is a medium through which the artist imparts his abnormal experience to the public, thus gradually or suddenly changing their perceptual framework.

Needless to say, such new ideas are a far cry from Plato's divine frenzy; even Renaissance aestheticians like George Chapman distinguished this "Divine Rapture" (or hyperintellectual pursuit of final, essentialist truth) from common *insania*.[14] In analyzing Byron's and other artists' frenzies, Winslow and his confreres were thinking of genuine mental disease, not of some mystical abstraction incurred by contemplating the absolute. Yet here, as when they discussed Shakespeare and other poets in terms of their psychiatric insights, alienists were not the first to develop a new understanding of art as akin to real insanity. As early as 1825, Macaulay, in his essay on Milton, had concluded that perhaps "no person can be a poet, or can even enjoy poetry, without a certain unsoundness of mind."[15] Alienists, in fact, were well aware that Macaulay had anticipated their ideas along these lines. F. Treves, in "The Physiology of the Poetic Mind," for instance, quotes Macaulay's key phrase;[16] the *American Journal of Insanity* for April 1849 reprints relevant passages from his essay under the title "Poets and Insanity."[17]

However, the critic's approach to the issue differs markedly from the alienists'. Macaulay arrives at his startling conclusion by arguing that poetry is simply out of date in an age of science like his. "In a rude state of society," he claims, "we may expect to find the poetical temperament in its highest perfection. In an enlightened age there will be much intelligence, much science, much philosophy, abundance of just classification and subtle analysis . . . but little poetry." Whoever, in this situation, "aspires to be a great poet must first become a little child, he must take to pieces the whole web of his mind. He must unlearn much of that knowledge which has perhaps constituted hitherto his chief title to superiority." It is in this negative sense, not in that of superior or original insight, that the truth of poetry "is the truth of madness": "The reasonings are just; but the premises are false. After the first suppositions have been made, everything ought to be consistent; but those first suppositions require a degree of credulity, which almost amounts to a partial and temporary derangement of the intellect."[18]

Macaulay, in sum, describes the poet as insane mainly for propounding views out of tune with real, that is scientific, truth. His perspective is historical rather than psychological. No wonder that he resorts to Locke for defining madness as a logical kind of reasoning from false premises.[19] By contrast, alienists from the beginning approached the whole issue from a clinical point of view. What they observed as the behavior patterns of their hospitalized psychotic patients, for instance, showed striking parallels with what biographies revealed about artists and poets. What is more, the verbal effusions of these patients were often astoundingly "poetic" or "artistic." Some of the patients even wrote actual poetry.[20] As the antirestraint movement gained in momentum, such activities were encouraged to the point where inmates could get their writings printed in the respective asylum journal. Now and again, specific specimens also would be published and discussed in the official psychiatric journals.[21] Individual volumes of poetry written by madmen sometimes found an even wider readership.[22]

Typical of the often naive enthusiasm surrounding such documents is Pliny Earle's "The Poetry of Insanity," an article printed in the *American Journal of Insanity* for January 1845. Earle, a physician at the Bloomingdale Asylum in New York City, quotes several poems and texts by patients, arguing that they display crucial attributes of poetry such as invention, wit, and imagination. But his favorite document, of which he gives us a condensed version, is a twenty-page account, composed upon recovery, by a young lady who thought she was the Virgin Mary. "Point to me a poem," exclaims the alienist, "the warp and woof of which are woven of a tissue of imagination more exquisite than this." The modern reader is inclined to agree but wonders what comparable nineteenth-century or earlier poetry Earle had in mind as he reads the following extract from the schizophrenic lady's story:

> She thought herself selected as the Bride of the Saviour. Her body was shaken with spasmodic tremor, and her limbs involuntarily assumed an attitude making the form of the cross. While lying in this position, she felt as if wafted away upon a cloud; but at length a poignard was thrust into her side, withdrawn, and the stroke repeated. Her sleep was refreshing. In the morning, she found the minute-hand of her watch split; and, upon placing the watch in her belt, it stopped.[23]

Earle may well have been thinking of "Kubla Khan," the poem most widely invoked in this context. According to an alienist writing for the *Journal of Psychological Medicine*, Coleridge's lines, although inspired by a dream, were indeed "just what an insane person might have written."[24] But even psychiatrists conceded that "Kubla Khan" was hardly typical of poetry in general. Because of what J. A. Symonds, Sr., calls its "mystical indistinctness,"[25] it clearly represented to them what its author had called it, a "psychological curiosity."[26] In short, Earle's enthusiasm for the poetry of the insane points towards the future rather than to his own time. Usually poetic theories follow the poetic event, but here the order seems to be reversed. Long before the advent of surrealist art, Earle and other Victorian alienists developed what in many ways strikes one as a presurrealist aesthetic.

Other impulses in the same direction came from the exploration of hallucination and unconscious cerebration. John Conolly with his *Indications of Insanity* (1830) was one of the first to redefine artistic creativity from such new perspectives. Anticipating what Jung was to call the automatic complex in visionary or extraverted creativity,[27] Conolly emphasizes the involuntary impulses in composition when a work, as Alfieri reported of his play *Merope*, is "forced upon" the poet "during the time [he is] writing it."[28] "I am inclined to believe," he writes, "that many of the shorter kind of poetical performances, and several of the most unbidden but acknowledged felicities of harmonious composition, have intruded themselves upon their authors' minds in the midst of their more serious occupations; bounding in among their graver thoughts like the dancers in a serious pantomine."[29]

Otherwise, the creative temperament, to Conolly, is largely a question of response to inner and outer stimuli. In this, the artist, as when he abandoning himself to the dictates of his unconscious, clearly resembles the madman. The difference between them is not of kind but of degree. Conolly even points toward later theorists like Treves who, by inverting Macaulay's denunciation of poetry as unscientific "madness," argue that the psychopathological component in artistic creativity often accounts for art's most original insights.[30] We admire, Conolly writes,

> the effect of the superadded and accidental excitement of scenery or of passion, as it is exhibited on the susceptibilities of the poet, or the orator, or the painter, or the writer of romance, or the musician: but is probable that many of these admired persons could tell us, on the evidence of their own agitated feelings, and some *have* indeed told us, that the excitements to which they have owed their fame, were often very nearly allied to morbid excitement, if not absolutely morbid. . . . Mozart's sensibility to music was connected with so susceptible a nervous system, that in his childhood the sound of a trumpet would turn him pale, and almost induce a convulsion. . . . Many a lunatic is only a person whose susceptibility to certain stimuli is in like manner excessive, but produces effects less agreeable, or effects which are inconvenient or dangerous to himself and others.[31]

The nature of hallucination, whether drug-induced or natural, was another widely debated issue concerning the potentially insane components of artistic creativity. The main impulse here came from two studies by F. Lélut, *Du démon de Socrate* and *L'Amulette de Pascal*, which argued that both Socrates and Pascal were insane for having undergone hallucinations like those experienced by madmen. Needless to say, the claim elicited passionate opposition. But it also found numerous adherents among alienists and critics. As Lélut brags in the second edition of his book on Socrates, even Sainte-Beuve, a former opponent of his theories, had more recently become a convert.[32] A direct disciple, J. Moreau (de Tours), who in a previous study had explored the relationship of hashish-induced hallucination as well as dreaming to insanity,[33] went as far as to argue, in *La psychologie morbide* (1859), that all genius shares common roots with insanity; or as Moreau puts it, "les dispositions d'esprit qui font qu'un homme se distingue des autres hommes par l'originalité des ses pensées et de ses conceptions, par son excentricité ou l'énergie de ses facultés affectives, par la transcendance de ses facultés intellectuelles, prennent leur source dans les mêmes conditions organiques que les divers troubles moraux dont la *folie* et l'*idiotie* sont l'expression la plus complète."[34] As Freud was to argue later, creative genius, for Moreau, is essentially a neurosis ("une névrose").[35] *La psychologie morbide*, with its indiscriminate theorizing and haphazard lists of geniuses allegedly afflicted by psychological disorders, was an easy target for attack and ridicule.[36] Nevertheless, it set the trend for later and better known works such as C. Lombroso's *The Man of Genius* and J. F. Nisbet's *The Insanity of Genius*, which proliferated toward the end of the century.

It is easy enough to imagine how reviewers, who called Swinburne a madman drunk on lewd and lascivious ideas, found themselves corroborated by what alienists were saying about similarly afflicted poets such as Poe and Rousseau. However, as for explaining the sadomasochistic content of Swinburne's poetry, not a single contemporary critic (with the possible exception of Ruskin) availed himself of Moreau's and others' suggestion that artistic creativity as such, independent of the sane or insane condition of the individual artist, may have pathological roots.

Perhaps this was so because in 1866 there were yet few specific concepts along these lines which a critic might draw upon for his task of analyzing individual poems. It is true that Moreau had called genius a neurosis and that he and others had repeatedly pointed out that poets, artists, and geniuses generally tend to hallucinate. Hence Gilchrist, in his biography of Blake, could acquit this visionary from the charge of insanity. But if artistic creativity was essentially psychopathological, there was still the question of how such morbidity found expression in the work of art. Conolly might speak of "the superadded and accidental excitement of scenery or of passion, as it is exhibited on the susceptibilities of the poet";[37] or Macaulay of the truth of poetry as a logical reasoning from false premises. But such notions were too vague to be of use in an attempt to come to terms with the Swinburnian phenomenon. Even an admirer like Ruskin had to concede that this poet was undoubtedly diseased or morally insane. As convinced as he was that something good might come of this morbidity, however, the problem remained of how to explain this possibility to the common reader. It had been suggested that a possible link existed, for instance, between Robert Burns' moral depravity and his greatness as a poet; but no one, even among the alienists, had as yet explained such connections in detail. Who then could blame reviewers for not accomplishing this feat in a case like Swinburne's, which was so much more complex?

In other words, Ruskin's description of Swinburne's work as in some ways beneficially diseased remains a singularly pioneering feat of psycho-literary perspicacity within the English context. The same is true of Swinburne's advocacy of Blake for managing to perpetrate a transvaluation of traditional values, thanks precisely to his alleged perversity and madness. So radically new were such ideas that, from a theoretical point of view, the whole Swinburne phenomenon was rendered, as Ruskin augured in 1866, "(nationally) at present useless."[38] Yet what was denounced by the critics had an obvious appeal for the masses, to the point where this "libidinous laureate of a pack of satyrs"[39] succeeded the actual Laureate in popularity. Unlike Browning and Tennyson, Swinburne, in addition to being a great poet, was also a major critic vociferously defending "fellow labourers,"[40] like Baudelaire and Blake, while trying to win acceptance for his poetry and ideas. Psychiatric criticism, which long had been poised in the same direction, was soon to reinforce such efforts with its own theorizing. A single example like F. Treves's "Physiology of the Poetic Mind" can show the extent to which it anticipated twentieth-century notions in this respect.

Prima facie, F. Treves's piece merely seems to follow Macaulay and others in arguing that the poetic mind is essentially abnormal. But unlike his predecessors, he inquires into how such abnormality affects the actual work of art. Using typical nineteenth-century jargon about conscious and unconscious cerebration, Treves first explains the functioning of normal experience. Broadly speaking, such experience, in his view, is simply that of automatically responding to an increasing number of gradually acquired concepts, each of which becomes registered in the brain. Let's take the instance of an irregular piece of stone brought to the notice of an individual, Treves argues.

> The details of its form and peculiarities are carried to his nerve centres by, it may be, the myriad centripetal fibres that are called into activity in the estimation of form. It is either, we will suppose, minutely and attentively examined at once, or is brought before the notice with great and deliberate frequency. In either case, by repetition of the stimulus, and frequent reproduction of its effect, the mental process whereby that piece of stone is recognised as of a certain shape becomes organically represented in the

brain . . . the object becomes "known" or "familiar," its details
are "remembered," and its peculiarities "impressed upon the
mind."[41]

Or take something more poetic like a buttercup or primrose.

Is not the very mention of the name alone sufficient to bring the
figure of the flower instantaneously before the mind? The particle
of mental energy whereby a primrose is "known" has an organic
foundation in the brain, and the stimulus required to revive that
knowledge . . . expends itself with no more call upon consciousness than is evoked by the stimulus required for the display of
some ordinary reflex action in the motor system.[42]

How does the poetic differ from the normal mind? Basically, it dis-
rupts, changes, and adds to "normally" programmed experience. Its
primary power is imagination, which "may be regarded as a power that
can add to any ordinary idea a distinct and new intelligence, and engraft
upon it unusual and original elements." What we believe to be known,
familiar, and distinct is made to appear mysterious, alien, and diffuse.
In the "normal mind" the word "buttercup," for instance, will simply
evoke the image of this "golden" flower—"the ideas of gold and of a
cup will present themselves to the mind with the same exactness and
the same defined isolation, so that separate ideas of the flower, of gold
and of a cup, are unlikely to be confused." But in the poetic or "abnormal" mind the effect will be different. "The separate ideas of the flower,
of gold and of a cup will have each but an uncertain organization; the
aspect of gold may call up the tint of the flower, and the tint of the
flower the aspect of gold, and so in like manner, by a mingling of effects, a buttercup may be spoken of as 'a pale gold cup,' and a distinct
novelty of idea in this manner introduced."[43]

Treves, like a true scientist, does not commit himself. While calling
the poetic imagination a "most excellent faculty," he also diagnoses it
as abnormal and characterizes its functioning in terms of basic deficien-
cies. Its neurological equivalent in the brain, in his view, is an "organic
flimsiness"; its frequent social implications a deviancy from the moral
and emotional norm that directly parallels the poet's work for both its
striking originality and often shocking perversity. In terms of the art-

ist's life this might spell the "grossest immorality and wildness of living in the one case, and a hermit-like love of the most unsocial seclusion in the other."[44] In reading the entire article, we are constantly reminded of the nineteenth-century *poète maudit*—sick of mind, reveling in perversion, but full of startling insights—of which Swinburne was the most prominent English representative.

Appendix: Practitioners of the Dramatic Monologue Among Minor Victorian Poets

THE MAIN NAMES are George Barlow, Charles D. Bell, Henry T. M. Bell, Mathilde Blind, Thomas E. Brown, John Davidson, William J. Dawson, Henry A. Dobson, Digby M. Dolben, Arthur C. Doyle, Sebastian Evans, Adam L. Gordon, Richard H. Horne, Jean Ingelow, Charles Kingsley, Mary M. Lamb, later Singleton, later Lady Currie ("Violet Fane"), Eugene J. Lee-Hamilton, William J. Linton, Alfred C. Lyall, Edward R. Bulwer Lytton, 1st Earl of Lytton ("Owen Meredith"), Charles Mackay, Lewis Morris, Frederic W. H. Myers, Roden B. W. Noel, Francis T. Palgrave, Adelaide A. Procter, Sir Arthur T. Quiller-Couch ("Q"), Agnes M. F. Robinson, James B. Stephens, John A. Symonds, John B. L. Warren, 3rd Baron de Tabley and Henry F. Wilson.

For convenience sake, the bulk of this material may be divided into monologues whose speakers 1) are historically identifiable (e.g., R. Browning's "Fra Lippo Lippi"); 2) fit into a historically and or geographically identifiable context (e.g., E. B. Browning's "The Runaway Slave at Pilgrim's Point"); 3) belong to the realm of religion, myth, legend or poetry (e.g., R. Browning, "Caliban upon Setebos"); or 4) are characterized by their fate (e.g., Tennyson's "The Northern Cobbler"), their opinions (e.g., R. Browning's "Bishop Blougram's Apology"), their psychological disposition (e.g., Swinburne's "The Leper"), or simply their character.

Ad 1 see, e.g., W. E. Aytoun, "Charles Edward at Versailles," *Poems*, pp. 87–92, "Blind Old Milton," ibid., pp. 104–108, *Bothwell*, ibid., pp. 133–226; G. Barlow, "The Story of the Life of Caleb Smith the Methodist Minister (Told by Himself)," *Works*, 8:159–266; S. Evans, "Arnaud de Merveil. [At the Abbey Gate.]," *In the Studio*, pp. 33–46, "Michel Angelo of His Madonna," ibid., pp. 117–124; N. R. Gale, "Hannibal, Sagunto Capto, Loquitur," *Poems*, pp. 120–122; R. H. Horne, "Soliloquium Fratris Rogeri Baconis, Anno Domini 1292: (Being the tenth year of his imprisonment)." (London, 1882), repr. from *Fraser's Magazine*; C. Kingsley, "Saint Maura. A.D. 304," *Poems*, pp. 275–81; M. M. Lamb, "The Last Words of Don Carlos. (Spoken to his Confessor, Fray Juan de Avila, Feb. 23, 1568)," *Poems*, 2:111–122; W. J. Linton, "Harry Marten's Dungeon Thoughts," *Poems*, pp. 95–102; E.R.B. Lytton, "Jacqueline, Countess of Holland and Hainault. (1436)," *Chronicles*, 2:97–104, "Thomas Müntzer to Martin Luther. (From Prison.)," ibid., pp. 134–150, "Elisabetta Sirani. 1665," ibid., pp. 239–45; C. Mackay, "Phidias in His Studio," *Works*, pp. 487–88; F. T. Palgrave, "Milton. 1660," *Idyls*, pp. 92–93; E. H. Plumptre, "An Old Story. I.–A.D. 1117," *Master*, pp. 138–43, "II.—A.D. 1142" (Eloisa as speaker), ibid., pp. 143–47, "Chalfont St. Giles. From Thomas Elwood to William Pennington. A.D. 1665," *Things*, pp. 13–28, "Bedford. From William Pennington to Thomas Elwood. A.D. 1665," ibid., pp. 28–40; Sir Arthur T. Quiller-Couch ("Q"), "Columbus at Seville," *Poems*, pp. 112–29; A.M.F. Robinson, "Jützi Schultheiss. Töss, 1300," *Poems*, pp. 212–17; W. W. Story, "Phidias to Pericles," *Poems*, 1:99–108, "Marcus Aurelius to Lucius Verus," ibid., pp. 109-11, "Girolamo, Detto il Fiorentino, Desponds and Abuses the World," ibid., pp. 112–20, "Cleopatra," ibid., pp. 129–34, "Marcus Antonius," ibid., pp. 135–38, "Padre Bandelli Proses to the Duke Ludovico Sforza about Leonardo da Vinci," ibid., pp. 152–58, "Leonardo da Vinci Poetizes to the Duke in His Own Defence," ibid., pp. 159–64, "A Contemporary Criticism: In which Federigo di Montafeltro, Duke of Urbino, Gives His Views of Raffaelle," ibid., pp. 165–74; G. W. Thornbury, "The Dedication of the Cathedral. Temp. 1401. William of Wykeham (moribundus) loquitur," *Ballads*, pp. 29–30; J.B.L. Warren, "Joan of Arc," *Poems*, pp. 114–20, "Machiavel in Minimis," ibid., pp. 120–26; A. Webster, "Jeanne d'Arc," *Studies*, pp. 29–38; H. F. Wilson "Rienzi. *Avignon*, A.D. 1351. *A tower fronting the palace of Innocent VI. Rienzi alone,*" *A Complete Collection of the English Poems which Have Obtained the Chancellor's Gold Medal*, 2:154–60.

Ad 2 see, e.g., G. Barlow, "A Southern Vengeance," *Works*, 6:59–62; M. Bell, "Francisca to Jaspear: A Madeiran Idyl," *Poems*, pp. 86–89; M. Blind, "A Carnival Episode. Nice, '87" *Works*, pp. 264–69;

R. W. Buchanan, "Fra Giacomo," *Works*, 1:8–9, "Liz," ibid., pp. 119–24, "Nell," ibid., pp. 149–52; J. Davidson, *In a Music-Hall* (6 monologues), *In a Music-Hall*, pp. 1–13, "Thirty Bob a Week," *Ballads*, pp. 91–97; D. M. Dolben, "From the Cloister. Brother Jerome Seated in the Cloister," *Poems*, pp. 4–8; S. Evans, "How the Abbey of Saint Werewulf Juxta Slingsby Came by Brother Fabian's Manuscript. *Scene*—Saint Werewulf's Cloister, A.D. 1497. *Time*—Afternoon. Prior Hugo *speaks*," *Brother Fabian's Manuscript*, pp. 3–36; A. Gurney, "The Convict's Tale," *Songs*, pp. 145–61; E. J. Lee-Hamilton, "The Mandolin. [A.D. 1559.]" *Dramatic Sonnets*, pp. 34–42; A. C. Lyall, "Theology in Extremis: Or a soliloquy that may have been delivered in India, June, 1857 . . . Moriturus Loquitur," *Verses*, pp. 9–17, "A Rajpoot Chief of the Old School. Moribundus Loquitur," ibid., pp. 35–43, "Retrospection. 1857–1882," ibid., pp. 48–55, "Amor in Extremis. A garrison story of a hundred years ago," ibid., pp. 109–14; E.R.B. Lytton, "Trial by Combat," *Chronicles*, 2:60–71, "Vanini Lectures Before the Sorbonne (Paris, Sixteenth Century)," *Poems*, 2:208–26; D. M. Mulock, "Looking Death in the Face," *Thirty*, pp. 19–22; E. Nesbit, "The Sick Journalist," *Ballads*, pp. 30–31; W. W. Story, "A Roman Lawyer in Jerusalem. First Century [*The Case of Judas.*]," *Poems*, 1:21–56, "A Jewish Rabbi in Rome. With a Commentary by Ben Israel. [*Fifteenth Century. Reign of Sixtus IV.*]," ibid., pp. 57–82, "A Primitive Christian in Rome," ibid., pp. 83–98, "In the Antechamber of Monsignore del Fiocco," ibid., pp. 175–82, "The Lesson of Monsignore Galeotto," ibid., pp. 183–90, "The Padre and the Novice," ibid., pp. 191–93, "L'Abbate," ibid., pp. 194–97, "In St. Peter's. The Convert Talks to His Friend," ibid., pp. 206–13, "Roba di Roma. *Julietta appears above at a balcony*," ibid., pp. 229–32, "Ginevra da Siena," ibid., 2:3–63; J. A. Symonds, "Pantarkes, The Temple of Zeus at Olympia," *New*, p. 74, "In the Syracusan Stone-Quarries," *Moods*, pp. 30–32; G. W. Thornbury, "Melting of the Earl's Plate," *Songs of the Cavaliers*, pp. 38–39, "The Witch's Champion," ibid., pp. 141–44, "The Convent Drudge. (*Temp. Alfred.*)," ibid., pp. 145–47, "How the Pasty was Poisoned. (*Temp. Elizabeth.*)," ibid., pp. 150–51, "The Succory Water. (*Louis Quatorze.*)," ibid., pp. 152–53, "Saved! (*Temp. George I.*)," ibid., pp. 154–56, "The Unjust Steward (*Temp. James I.*)," ibid., pp. 157–59, "The Jockey's Song," ibid., pp. 220–26, "The Cathedral Builder," ibid., pp. 277–80, "The Two Musicians after the

Opera," ibid., pp. 284–87, "The Lecture-Theatre at Padua. (*Paracelsus.*)," ibid., pp. 312–14.

Ad 3 see, e.g., G. Barlow, "Song of the Women-spirits," *Works*, 6:6–10, "Mary Magdalene," ibid., pp. 11–12; W. C. Bennett, "Alcaeus to Sappho," *Poems*, p. 350; M. Blind, "The Song of the Willi," *Works*, pp. 279–85; C. Brontë, "Pilate's Wife's Dream," *Complete Poems*, pp. 1–6, "The Fairies' Warning," ibid., pp. 120–21, "The Fairies' Farewell," ibid., pp. 123–26; R. W. Buchanan, *The Undertones*, *Works*, 1:24–76, passim, "The Faery Foster-Mother," ibid., pp. 98–99, "The Green Gnome. A Melody," ibid., pp. 99–100; W. J. Dawson, "Pilate at Vienne," *Poems and Lyrics*, pp. 27–35, "The Wind's Daughter," ibid., pp. 69–71; "Michael Field" [i.e., Katherine H. Bradley and Edith E. Cooper], "Penetration (Syrinx to Pan)," *Selections*, p. 59, "Dionysus Zagreus," *Dedicated*, pp. 11–15, "Memnonides," ibid., pp. 65–67, "Glaucus," ibid., pp. 77–81, "One Sin" (Phoebus as speaker), ibid., pp. 86–89; A. L. Gordon, "Podas Okus" (Achilles as speaker), *Poems*, pp. 1–8; R. S. Hawker, "David's Lament," *Works*, p. 279; L. E. Landon, "Sappho's Song," *Works*, p. 425; A. C. Lyall, "Pilate's Wife's Dream" *Verses*, pp. 87–92; C. Mackay, "The Prayer of Adam, Alone in Paradise," *Works*, pp. 8–9, "Enceladus, or Defiance of Fate," ibid., p. 493, "Orpheus in Thrace," ibid., pp. 493–94; R. F. Murray, "Hymn of Hippolytus to Artemis," *Gown*, pp. 4–5; F.W.H. Myers, "Belisarius," *Collected Poems*, pp. 49–68, "Saint Paul," ibid., pp. 105–44, "Saint John the Baptist," ibid., pp. 154–68; R.B.W. Noel, "The Water-Nymph and the Boy," *Poems*, pp. 126–28; J. N. Paton, "Ulysses in Ogygia," *Spindrift*, pp. 101–106, "Actaeon in Hades," ibid., pp. 130–38; E. H. Plumptre, "Adrastos," *Things*, pp. 41–54; A.M.F. Robinson, "Philumene to Aristides," *Poems*, pp. 225–27; W. B. Scott, "The Witch's Ballad," *Poems*, pp. 29–34; J. Skipsey, "The Fairies' Adieu," *Songs*, p. 82; W. C. Smith, "What Pilate Thought of It," *Poetical Works*, pp. 519–27; W. W. Story, "Pan in Love," *Poems*, 2:123–28, "Cassandra," ibid., pp. 139–42, "Orestes," ibid., pp. 143–45, "Cheosiphron," ibid., pp. 148–49, "Tantalus," ibid., pp. 150–51, "Nemesis," ibid., pp. 269–71; J.B.L. Warren, "Semele," *Poems*, pp. 2–4, "Saul," ibid., pp. 4–6, "Minos," ibid., pp. 6–8, "Philoctetes," ibid., pp. 30–32, "Iphigeneia," ibid., pp. 39–41, "Eucrates," ibid., pp. 41–45, "Anchises," ibid., pp. 94–96, "Ariadne," ibid., pp. 96–98, "The New Ahasuerus," ibid., pp. 98–99, "Daedalus," ibid., pp. 104–106, "Niobe," ibid., pp. 106–108, "The

Lament of Phaeton's Sisters," ibid., pp. 112–13, "The Siren to Ulysses," ibid., pp. 138–40, "Nimrod," ibid., pp. 299–302, "The Nymph's Protest, ibid., pp. 339–40, "Orpheus in Hades . . . thus Addresses Proserpine," ibid., pp. 362–71, "Orpheus in Thrace," ibid., pp. 420–25, "The Lament of Echo," ibid., pp. 433–35; A. Webster, "Medea in Athens," *Portraits*, pp. 1–13, "Circe," ibid., pp. 14–22; M. L. Woods, "Serenade of the Fairy Lover," *Poems*, pp. 189–90.

Ad 4 see, e.g., G. Barlow, *A Poet's Gethsemane, Works*, 6:73–106, "A Man's Vengeance," ibid., 10:151–70; C. D. Bell, "Confession," *Diana's Looking Glass*, pp. 70–82; E. H. Bickersteth, "The Two Brothers," *Poems*, pp. 86–110; M. Blind, "The Russian Student's Tale," *Works*, pp. 224–29, "Renunciation," ibid., pp. 229–34; C. Brontë, "Apostasy," *Complete Poems*, pp. 58–61; T. E. Brown, *In The Coach, Collected Poems*, pp. 17–30, "The Christening," ibid., pp. 32–36; R. W. Buchanan, "Poet Andrew," *Works*, 1:84–90, "Edward Crowhurst; or, 'A New Poet' . . . II. After Ten Years," ibid., pp. 137–47, "Attorney Sneak," ibid., pp. 153–55; H. A. Dobson, "A Virtuoso," *Works*, pp. 85–87, "A Gage D'Amour," ibid., pp. 92–94; A. C. Doyle, "The Dying Whip," *Poems*, pp. 34–39; A. L. Gordon, "The Sick Stockrider," *Poems*, pp. 172–78; H. N. Howard, *The House by the Sea, Collected Poems*, pp. 427–35; J. Ingelow, "The Maid-Martyr," *Works*, pp. 762–83, "Perdita," ibid., pp. 824–31; M. M. Lamb, "The Centenarian," *Poems* 2:3–10, "False or True?" ibid., pp. 89–93, "A Wife's Confession," ibid., pp. 140–53; E.R.B. Lytton, "At Home during the Ball," *Poems*, 1:114–16, "Last Words," ibid., 2:244–54; L. Morris, "Love in Death," *Works*, pp. 43–64; D. M. Mulock, later Craik, "Moon-Struck. A Fantasy," *Thirty*, pp. 34–37; R.B.W. Noel, "A Confession Scene.— A Prison Cell: Prisoner (to Clergyman loq.)," *Poems*, pp. 53–55; J. N. Paton, "The Cousins," *Spindrift*, pp. 126–27; A. A. Procter, "My Journal," *Legends*, pp. 71–73, "Too late," ibid., pp. 159–61, "A Contrast," ibid., pp. 241–48; W. C. Smith, "Rothes," *Poetical Works*, pp. 27–30, "Peden the Prophet," ibid., pp. 30–32, *Olrig Grange*, ibid., pp. 39–86, "Raban," ibid., pp. 217–22, "The Public Meeting," ibid., pp. 257–61, "Wee Curly Pow," ibid., pp. 289–98, "Dr. Linkletter's Scholar," ibid., pp. 298–305, "Dick Dalgleish," ibid., pp. 305–12, "The Mad Earl," ibid., pp. 316–23, "Provost Chivas," ibid., pp. 323–28, *Amory Hill*, III, ibid., pp. 354–56, "Miss Bella Japp to Her Young Minister," ibid., pp. 356–59; J. B. Stephens, "A Lost Chance," *Poetical Works*, pp. 59–64, "The Chamber of Faith," ibid., pp. 70–75,

"Drought and Doctrine," ibid., pp. 140–45; W. W. Story, "The Confessional," *Poems*, 2:128–41, "Giannone," ibid., pp. 78–104, "Baron Fisco at Home," ibid., pp. 214–24; J.B.L. Warren, "The Count of Senlis at His Toilet," *Poems*, pp. 140–43; A. Webster, "A Preacher," *Studies*, pp. 3–14, "A Painter," ibid., pp. 14–26, *Sister Annunciata*, ibid., pp. 39–109, "The Happiest Girl in the World," *Portraits*, pp. 23–34, "A Castaway," ibid., pp. 35–62, "A Soul in Prison," ibid., pp. 63–72, "Tired," ibid., pp. 73–89, "Coming Home," ibid., pp. 90–98, "In an Almshouse," ibid., pp. 99–117, "An Inventor," ibid., pp. 118–26, "A Dilettante," ibid., pp. 127–34.

Notes

IN GENERAL, the poetic works of M. Arnold, R. and E. B. Browning, Byron, J. Clare, A. H. Clough, Coleridge, Goethe, T. Hardy, R. Kipling, G. Meredith, W. Morris, D. G. and C. G. Rossetti, R. Southey, Swinburne, A. Tennyson, and Wordsworth are quoted from the respective editions listed in the bibliography without further reference in the endnotes. Anonymous articles and reviews from pre-twentieth-century journals are only listed in the endnotes and not in the bibliography. All other references in the endnotes are given in abbreviations (author's name plus short title of book or of journal with volume number and year) throughout. For full references, see the Bibliography. Please note that *The Journal of Mental Science* was entitled *The Asylum Journal of Mental Science* during its initial years from 1855 to 1857.

INTRODUCTION

1. H. B. Forman, *Fortnightly Review* 11, n.s. 5 (January–June, 1869) p. 117.
2. Ibid., p. 118.
3. H. B. Forman, *Our Living Poets*, p. 35; idem, *Fortnightly Review* 11, n.s. 5 (January–June 1869), p. 117.
4. H. B. Forman, *Fortnightly Review* 11, n.s. 5 (January–June 1869), p. 117.
5. [W. J. Fox], *Westminister Review* 14 (January–April 1831), pp. 210–24, p. 214.
6. W. Wordsworth, *Literary Criticism*, pp. 97, 72.
7. M. H. Abrams in *From Sensibility to Romanticism*, ed. F. W. Hilles and H. Bloom, pp. 527–60.
8. M. H. Abrams, *Natural Supernaturalism*, p. 123.
9. M. H. Abrams, in *From Sensibility to Romanticism*, ed. F. W. Hillis and H. Bloom, pp. 527–28.

10. Here as in the following pages, "psycho-analytic," in contrast to "psychoanalytic," is used in the way pre-Freudian writers spoke, for instance, of the "analysis of particular states of mind." [W. J. Fox] *Westminster Review* 14 (January–April 1831), pp. 210–24, p. 214.

11. J. Bowring, in *Coleridge: Critical Heritage*, p. 549.

12. Part of this work was completed for other of my publications on the subject; see the Bibliography.

13. J. S. Mill, *Autobiography and Literary Essays*, p. 344.

14. R. Langbaum, *Poetry of Experience*, passim.

15. M. H. Abrams, *Natural Supernaturalism*, p. 123.

16. R. Langbaum, *Poetry of Experience*, pp. 76f.

17. W. C. Booth, *Rhetoric of Fiction*, pp. 73–74.

18. J. Wilson, *Essays*, 3: 307.

19. R. J. Mann, *"Maud" Vindicated*, p. 64.

20. "St. Simeon Stylites," 200ff.

21. *Macbeth*, 2.1.33ff.

22. T. Brown, *Lectures*, pp. 276, 102.

23. Ibid., p. 116.

24. *American Journal of Insanity* 17 (1860–61), pp. 233–49, p. 235.

25. L. F. Lélut, *Annales médico-psychologiques* 3 (1844), pp. 157–67.

26. F. Winslow, *Journal of Psychological Medicine* 10 (1857), p. 615.

27. F. Winslow, ibid. 7 (1854), p. 129; 10 (1857), p. 613.

28. F. Winslow, ibid. 10 (1857), p. 612.

29. H. Maudsley, *Journal of Mental Science* 11 (1865–66), p. 538.

30. A. Brigham, *American Journal of Insanity* 1 (1844–45), p. 40.

31. L.F.A. Maury, *Asylum Journal of Mental Science* 2 (1855–56), p. 107.

32. *Journal of Psychological Medicine* 1 (1848), pp. 406–25, p. 423.

33. Ibid., p. 409.

34. F. Treves, *Journal of Mental Science* 24 (1878–79), p. 241.

35. M. J. Rae, *Journal of Psychological Medicine* 8 (1855), p. 386.

36. Ibid., pp. 385, 383.

37. By contrast, mental science and literature in the eighteenth century have been investigated in at least two recent studies. See M. Byrd, *Visits to Bedlam*, passim; and M. V. DePorte, *Nightmares and Hobby-horses*, passim. A general, though very useful, overview of madness in Victorian literature is found in J. R. Reed, *Victorian Conventions*, pp. 193–215. M. M. Tatar's *Studies on Mesmerism and Literature* focuses largely on continental and American materials.

38. R. Hunter and I. Macalpine, *Psychiatry 1535–1860*, p. viii.

39. Ibid., p. ix.

40. Ibid., p. 559.

41. K. P. Moritz, *Magazin* 7, 3 (1789), pp. 3ff.

42. A. C. Swinburne, in *Browning: Critical Heritage*, p. 396; [H. B. Forman], *London Quarterly Review* 32 (April–July 1869), pp. 325–57, p. 331; G. Eliot, in *Browning: Critical Heritage*, p. 176.

43. *Nation* 8 (1869), p. 136; E. C. Stedman, *Poets*, p. 297; R. Bell, in *Browning: Critical Heritage*, p. 227.

44. "To J. Milsand, of Dijon," London: June 9, 1863.

45. Quoted in A. Tennyson, *Poems*, ed. C. Ricks, p. 1039.

46. [J. C. Bucknill], *Asylum Journal of Mental Science* 2 (1855–56), pp. 95–104, pp. 102, 97.

47. For a comprehensive recent study of phrenology as such, see R. Cooter, *Phrenology*, passim. The influence of Gall's phrenology on Romantic psychology has been studied by J. Y. Hall, *SiR* 16 (1977), pp. 305–17.

48. A. Tennyson, *Poems*, ed. C. Ricks, p. 1037.

49. W. C. DeVane, *Browning Handbook*, p. 125.

50. This is an issue I have dealt with in my recent *Shakespeare's Poetics*, pp. 79ff.

51. The study referred to is by J. O. Lyons.

52. J. A. Symonds, *Letters*, p. 215.

53. A. Symons, *Browning Society's Papers*, 2:5.

54. L. F. Lélut, *Annales médico-psychologiques* 3 (1844), p. 162.

55. See, e.g., the parody of the opening lines of Tennyson's "Locksley Hall"—"Cronies leave me in the bar-room, while as yet I have cash to spend, / Leave me here, and if I'm wanted, mum's the word to every friend"—in *Parodies*, ed. W. Hamilton, 1:15. See also ibid., 5: 169, as well as A. C. Swinburne's *Specimens of Modern Poets: the Heptalogia. Complete Works*, 5: 247–97.

56. Thaïs E. Morgan, *VP* 22, 2 (Summer 1984), p. iv.

CHAPTER I

1. R. Langbaum, *Poetry of Experience*, pp. 75ff.

2. R. W. Rader, *CE* 3 (1976–77), p. 135; idem, *VP* 22 (1984), pp. 103–20.

3. A. D. Culler, *PMLA* 90 (1975), p. 367.

4. See P. Honan, *Browning's Characters*, passim.

5. L. M. Shires, *VP* 22 (1984), p. 99. Also see C. T. Christ, *Victorian and Modern Poetics*, pp. 19f.

6. H. F. Tucker, *VP* 22 (1984), p. 127.

7. E. W. Slinn, *Browning*, p. ix.

8. For an exception see D. Bergman, *ELH* 47 (1980), pp. 772–87.

9. *Quarterly Review* 118 (July–October 1865), pp. 77–105, p. 91.

10. A. Symons, *Introduction*, p. 7.

11. A. C. Swinburne, in *Browning: Critical Heritage*, p. 396.

12. [H. B. Forman], *London Quarterly Review* 32 (April–July 1869), pp. 325–57, p. 331.

13. *Quarterly Review* 118 (July–October 1865), pp. 77–105, p. 102.

14. G. Eliot, in *Browning: Critical Heritage*, p. 176.

15. R. Bell, in ibid., p. 227.

16. A. Austin, in ibid., p. 343.

17. E. C. Stedman, *Poets*, p. 297.

18. *Nation* 8 (1869), p. 136.

19. G. Eliot, in *Browning: Critical Heritage*, p. 174.

20. Ibid., p. 176.

21. *Dublin University Magazine* 47 (January–June 1856), pp. 667–81, p. 673.

22. *Browning: Critical Heritage*, p. 368.

23. J. A. Symonds, in ibid., pp. 308–309.

24. W. Bagehot, in ibid., pp. 275, 303.

25. A. Austin, in ibid., p. 343.

26. J. Keats, *Letters*, 1: 193.

27. A. C. Swinburne, in *Browning: Critical Heritage*, p. 396.

28. Ibid., p. 393.

29. *Contemporary Review* 4 (January–April 1867), pp. 1–15, p. 12.

30. *North British Review* 51 (American Edition) (October 1869–January 1870), pp. 51–67, p. 53.

31. S. T. Coleridge, *Lectures and Notes on Shakspere*, p. 471.

32. V. Hugo, *Shakespeare*, p. 201.

33. *Lamb as Critic*, p. 88.

34. See R. Langbaum, *Poetry of Experience*, pp. 162ff.

35. Quoted in W. C. DeVane, *Browning Handbook*, p. 55.

36. Quoted ibid., p. 186. Regarding Browning's career as playwright, see also M. Mason, in *Browning*, ed. I. Armstrong, pp. 240ff.

37. "To J. Milsand, of Dijon," London: June 9, 1863.

38. R. Browning, *Letters*, ed. T. L. Hood, p. 134.

39. A. Symons, *Browning Society's Papers*, 2: 11.

40. Quoted in A. Tennyson, *Poems*, ed. C. Ricks, p. 1039.

41. R. W. Buchanan, *David Gray*, p. 305. Also see R. W. Buchanan's *Drama*, pp. 469–70.

42. S. T. Coleridge, *Lectures and Notes on Shakspere*, p. 471.

43. G. B. Shaw, *Browning Society's Papers*, 1: 122.

44. *Bentley's Miscellany* 39 (1856), pp. 64–70, p. 64. See also W. David Shaw's more recent contention in *VP* 19 (1981), p. 315, that the Victorian poet "can express more of himself in a dramatic form because the artifice of a scene or a mask provides the safety of a disguise without which reticent poets like Tennyson, Browning, and Christina Rossetti cannot *begin* to be personal." See also idem, *Tennyson's Style*, pp. 99ff.

45. *North British Review* 51 (American Edition) (October 1869–January 1870), pp. 51–67, pp. 59–60.

46. Ibid., p. 58. See also *Browning: Critical Heritage*, pp. 288, 291, and R. W. Buchanan, ibid., p. 294.

47. A. Symons, *Browning Society's Papers*, 2: 3.

48. For the following see E. F. Shannon, Jr., *PMLA* 68 (1953), pp. 397–417; and M. Shaw, in *Tennyson*, ed. D. J. Palmer, pp. 79ff.

49. *Blackwood's Magazine* 78 (July–December 1855), pp. 311–21, pp. 312, 315.

50. [J. C. Bucknill], *Asylum Journal of Mental Science* 2 (1855–56), pp. 95–104, p. 102.

51. *Fraser's Magazine* 52 (July–December 1855), pp. 264–73, p. 268.

52. *Oxford and Cambridge Magazine* (March 1856), pp. 136–45, p. 137.

53. R. J. Mann, *"Maud" Vindicated*, p. 64.

54. *Edinburgh Review* 102 (July–October 1855), pp. 498–519, p. 509.

55. H. Tennyson, *Tennyson. A Memoir*, 1: 408.

56. G. Brimley, T.C.C., in *Tennyson: Critical Heritage*, p. 192.

57. Ibid., p. 193.

58. Quoted in A. Tennyson, *Poems*, ed. C. Ricks, p. 1039.

59. G. Brimley-T.C.C., in *Tennyson: Critical Heritage*, p. 194.

60. G. Brimley, *Essays*, pp. 8, 17.

61. Ibid., pp. 9, 10, 11–12.

62. See ibid., pp. 17ff.

63. Ibid., p. 18.

64. G. Brimley, in *Browning: Critical Heritage*, p. 167.

65. Concerning that circle and the criticism it produced, see F. E. Mineka, *The Monthly Repository, 1806–1838*, pp. 299ff.; W. Irvine and P. Honan, *Robert Browning*, pp. 27ff.

66. [W. J. Fox], *Westminster Review* 14 (January–April 1831), pp. 210–24, p. 214. Concerning W. J. Fox's authorship of the review, see I. Armstrong, *Victorian Scrutinies*, p. 62, n. 31.

67. G. Brimley, *Essays*, p. 8.

68. [W. J. Fox], *Westminster Review* 14 (January–April 1831), pp. 210–24, p. 217.

69. Ibid., p. 216.

70. *Bentley's Miscellany* 39 (1856), pp. 64–70, p. 64.

71. [W. J. Fox], *Westminster Review* 14 (January–April 1831), pp. 210–24, p. 216.

72. [W. J. Fox], *Monthly Repository* n.s. 7 (1833), pp. 30–41, p. 33.

73. ———, *Monthly Repository* n.s. 8 (1834), pp. 323–31, p. 326. See also T. N. Talfourd, *Pamphleteer* 5, 9 (February 1815), p. 466; *Fraser's Magazine* 54 (July–December 1856), pp. 347–58, p. 356.

74. [H. C. Robinson], *Monthly Repository* n.s. 7 (1833) , pp. 271–84, p. 282.

75. J. S. Mill, *Autobiography and Literary Essays*, p. xxxiii.

76. Ibid., pp. 345, 346.

77. [J. S. Mill], *London Review* (July 1835), pp. 402–24, p. 404.

78. *Westminster Review* 13 (April–July 1830), pp. 265–92, p. 267.

79. [W. J. Fox], *Westminster Review* 14 (January–April 1831), pp. 210–24, p. 214.

80. W. B. Worsfold, *Principles of Criticism*, p. 197. See also E. Johnson, *Browning Society's Papers*, 1: 363–64: "Psychology itself is comparatively a new and modern study, as a distinct science; but a psychological poet, who has made it his business to clothe psychic abstractions in 'sights and sounds,' is entirely a novel appearance in literature." J. A. Symonds, *Letters*, p. 215.

81. A. O. Kellogg, *Shakspeare's Delineations of Insanity*, pp. 9, 21.

82. J. H. Balfour-Browne, *Journal of Mental Science* 20 (1874–75), pp. 214, 224, 212.

83. H. Tennyson, *Tennyson. A Memoir*, 1: 411.

84. [J. C. Bucknill], *Asylum Journal of Mental Science* 2 (1855–56), pp. 95–104, p. 102.

85. Quoted by E. F. Shannon, *PMLA* 68 (1953), p. 405.

86. [J. C. Bucknill], *Asylum Journal of Mental Science* 2 (1855–56), pp. 95–104, p. 102.
87. Ibid., pp. 102, 97. See also the anonymous review of Tennyson's "Lucretius" in *Journal of Mental Science* 14 (1868–69), pp. 195–99, which praises the poem as "an admirable study in psychology" (p. 195), but finds that Swinburne probably would have managed to portray the speaker's dream life more realistically: "Mr. Tennyson has scarcely conveyed to his readers an adequately gross representation of its loathsome character, and of the horror which it was calculated to produce. If the picture had been touched with something of the sensuality, without the sympathy, of a Swinburnian imagination, it might have been less acceptable to the critics, but it would have been truer artistically. . . . There is no background of the unconscious; all is conscious elaboration—deliberate, artistic execution" (pp. 196, 199).

CHAPTER II

1. J. C. Bucknill, *Psychology of Shakespeare*, p. viii.
2. T. A. Ribot, *Psychology*, p. 34.
3. See T. Reid, *Philosophical Works*.
4. See D. Stewart, *Collected Works*, Vol. 2–4.
5. See J. Mill, *Analysis*.
6. T. Reid, *Philosophical Works*, pp. 96, 201, 98.
7. Ibid., p. 99.
8. See R. Hunter and I. Macalpine, *Psychiatry 1535–1860*, pp. 752–53.
9. Quoted ibid., p. 753.
10. A. Crichton, *Inquiry*, 1: ix–x.
11. L.F.A. Maury, *Sommeil*, p. iv.
12. W. Hamilton, *Lectures*, 1: 353. See also *Journal of Psychological Medicine* 12 (1859), pp. 313–37, pp. 334ff.
13. W. Hamilton, *Lectures*, 1: 339.
14. Cf. ibid., 1: 344. See also S. T. Coleridge, *Biographia Literaria*, pp. 65–67; *American Journal of Insanity* 4 (1847–48), pp. 222–25, for a discussion of Coleridge's anecdote.
15. W. Hamilton, Lectures, 1: 340. See also J. S. Mill, *Examination*, pp. 272ff.; *Journal of Psychological Medicine* 12 (1859), pp. 313–37, especially pp. 333ff. Concerning W. B. Carpenter's and T. Laycock's

investigations of "unconscious cerebration," see, e.g., S. Bushnan, *Journal of Mental Science* 7 (1860–62), pp. 236–75; T. Laycock, ibid. 21 (1875–76), pp. 477–98.

16. R. Hunter and I. Macalpine, *Psychiatry 1535–1860*, p. 641.

17. Cf. H. F. Ellenberger, *PsR* 52 (1965), pp. 281–97. Roy Porter, *HT* 35 (September 1985), pp. 22–29, discusses a short-lived flurry over mesmerism in late eighteenth-century London.

18. See R. Holmes, *Shelley*, p. 627, for an account of the biographical circumstances surrounding the poem.

19. See H. F. Ellenberger, *Discovery of the Unconscious*, p. 159.

20. See also *Medical Quarterly Review* 2 (1834), pp. 135–37 (on Colquhoun's 1833 *Report . . . on Animal Magnetism*); J. C. Colquhoun, "Theory of Animal Magnetism," *Medical Quarterly Review* 2 (1834), pp. 484–85.

21. See, e.g., *Quarterly Review* 61 (January–April 1838), pp. 273–301.

22. F. Kaplan, *JHI* 35 (1974), p. 695. See also L. Chertok and R. de Saussure, *Therapeutic Revolution*, pp. 36ff. Regarding the fortunes of mesmerism in America, see R. C. Fuller, *Mesmerism*, passim.

23. C. Mackay, *Popular Delusions*, 3: 383.

24. For this and the following, see F. Kaplan, *JHI* 35 (1974), pp. 697ff.; F. Kaplan, *Dickens and Mesmerism*, pp. 3ff.; T. M. Parssinen, *VS* 21 (1977–78), pp. 87ff.; E. M. Thornton, *Hypnotism*, pp. 78ff.

25. Quoted by E. M. Thornton, *Hypnotism*, p. 100.

26. Quoted by F. Kaplan, *Dickens and Mesmerism*, p. 54.

27. See ibid., p. 26.

28. *Fraser's Magazine* 1 (February–July 1830), pp. 673–84.

29. See, e.g., ibid.; *Blackwood's Magazine* 42 (July–December 1837), pp. 384–93.

30. *Fraser's Magazine* 29 (January–June 1844), pp. 681–99, p. 693. See also, e.g., *Blackwood's Magazine* 57 (January–June 1845), pp. 219–41; *North British Review* 15 (May–August 1851), pp. 69–82; and J. Braid, *Magic*, pp. 25ff., for Braid's own discussion of critical reactions to his discovery.

31. Cf. J. Braid, *Neurypnology*, pp. 27ff. and passim; *Magic*, pp. 56ff.

32. *Westminster Review* 55 (April–July 1851), pp. 312–28, p. 326.

33. *Fraser's Magazine* 32 (July–December 1845), pp. 1–19, p. 1 (referring to *Fraser's Magazine* 29 [January–June 1844], pp. 681–99).

34. Ibid., p. 5. See also J. Braid, *Magic*, pp. 20f., 77ff., 108ff.

35. *Fraser's Magazine* 29 (January–June 1844), pp. 681–99, p. 697.

36. Cf. *Quarterly Review* 93 (June–September 1853), pp. 501–57, pp. 520ff.

37. *Fraser's Magazine* 29 (January–June 1844), pp. 681 99, p. 695. See also *British Quarterly Review* 12 (August–November 1850), pp. 382–415, p. 413.

38. See J. Abercrombie, *Inquiries*, pp. 278ff.

39. See, e.g., [R. Gray], *Theory of Dreams*, 1: 76ff.; R. MacNish, *Philosophy of Sleep*, p. 13; M. Macario, *Annales médico-psychologiques* 8 (1846), pp. 184ff. ("rêves psychiques"); idem, *Du Sommeil*, pp. 55ff. ("rêves intellectuels"); J. Sheppard, *On Dreams*, pp. 16ff.; W. B. Carpenter, in *Cyclopaedia of Anatomy and Physiology*, ed. R. B. Todd, 4: 687–88; *Journal of Psychological Medicine* 4 (1851), pp. 461–502; *Fraser's Magazine* 50 (July–December 1854), pp. 371–87, pp. 373ff.; B. C. Brodie, *Psychological Inquiries*, pp. 19ff.; *Journal of Psychological Medicine* n.s. 2 (1862), pp. 193–230; C. Elam, *Physician's Problems*, p. 342. See also A. Hayter, *Opium and the Romantic Imagination*, p. 104, on De Quincey's "theory of the dream-work of the imagination"; and ibid., pp. 70ff.

40. *Quarterly Review* 93 (June–September 1853), pp. 501–57, p. 524.

41. The subtitle of Catherine Crowe's 1845 translation, *The Seeress of Prevorst*.

42. Cf. H. Ellenberger, *Discovery of the Unconscious*, pp. 78–81; H. Straumann, *Kerner und der Okkultismus*, passim.

43. *British Quarterly Review* 2 (August–November 1845), pp. 402–27, p. 404.

44. Ibid., p. 403. For further discussions of the Seeress of Prevorst, see *British and Foreign Medical Review* 7 (October–April 1839), pp. 301–52, especially pp. 339ff.; *North British Review* 9 (May–August 1848), pp. 213–26.

45. See, e.g., T. Laycock, *Hysteria*, p. 170; J. Ennemoser, *Magnetismus im Verhältnisse zur Natur und Religion*, pp. iiiff. and passim; idem, *History of Magic*, pp. iff. et passim; J. C. Colquhoun, *Magic, Witchcraft, and Animal Magnetism*, 1: 32ff. and passim; *Journal of Psychological Medicine* 5 (1852), pp. 292–322; J. Braid, *Magic*, pp. 74ff. and passim; R. R. Madden, *Phantasmata*, 2: 274, 281, 282, 334, 386, 402; L. Figuier, *Histoire du merveilleux*, 1: 2 and passim; L.F.A. Maury, *La Magie*, p. 227. See also *Journal of Psychological Medicine* 13 (1860), pp. 1–24, 534–53; ibid. n.s. 1 (1861), pp. 1–24.

46. For this and the following, see R. Hunter and I. Macalpine, *Psy-*

chiatry 1535–1860, pp. 684ff. The precise origins of the anti-restraint movement are, of course, a controversial and widely debated issue. See, e.g., W.Lı.I. Parry-Jones, *Trade in Lunacy*, pp. 170ff.; R. Porter, *Lychnos*, pp. 12–26. The history of the York Retreat, 1796–1914, has been studied in A. Digby's comprehensive *Madness, Morality and Medicine*.

47. Reproduced by R. Hunter and I. Macalpine, *Psychiatry 1535–1860*, p. 695.

48. Ibid., p. 700. See also *Monthly Review* 81 (September–December 1816), pp. 280–89; *Edinburgh Review* 28 (March–August 1817), pp. 431–72; *North American Review* 3 (1816), pp. 336–37.

49. F. G. Alexander and S. T. Selesnick, *History of Psychiatry*, p. 112, call the transformation of madhouses into hospitals where "the psychotic could be studied and treated effectively . . . the greatest single step in the history of psychiatric treatment."

50. See, e.g., ibid., pp. 108ff.; M. Donnelly, *Managing the Mind*, passim; K. Dörner, *Bürger und Irre*, pp. 69ff.; M. Foucault, *Madness and Civilization*, pp. 241ff. M. R. de Groote, *La Folie*, pp. 213ff.; C. Quetel and P. Morel, *Les Fous*, pp. 235ff.; G. Zilboorg, *History of Medical Psychology*, pp. 319ff. Among the many recent sociocritical assessments of the early alienists, see also A. Scull's study of J. Conolly *VS* 27 (1983–84), pp. 203–35.

51. For an account, see *British and Foreign Medical Review* 1 (January–April 1836), pp. 286–87.

52. *Asylum Journal of Mental Science* 1 (November 15, 1853), p. 1.

53. J. C. Bucknill and D. H. Tuke, *Psychological Medicine*, p. 46.

54. E. Jarvis, *North American Review* 56 (1843), p. 124, reports a ratio of 1 insane person per 421 inhabitants for Massachusetts as against 1 per 793 for England and 1 per 1,000 for France. See also A. Brigham, *Remarks*, pp. 76f.; *British and Foreign Medical Review* 4 (July–October 1837), pp. 55–63.

55. Cf. J. C. Bucknill and D. H. Tuke, *Psychological Medicine*, pp. 44f. The whole question of the increase of insanity during the rise of clinical psychiatry is, of course, complex. See, e.g., M. Donnelly, *Managing the Mind*, pp. 77f.; also see this study's bibliography under W. Farr and W. Hallaran for further nineteenth-century documents regarding the issue. Elaine Showalter, *VS* 23 (1979–80), pp. 160ff., discusses the ratio of female versus male hospitalization for alleged insanity during the Victorian period.

56. J. C. Bucknill and D. H. Tuke, *Psychological Medicine*, p. 273.

57. F. Winslow, *Obscure Diseases of the Brain*, pp. 30, 26.

58. Cf. ibid., pp. 30ff.

59. W. Battie, *Treatise on Madness*, pp. 5–6.

60. P. Pinel, *Treatise on Insanity*, p. 151.

61. Quoted by M. Mason, in *Browning*, ed. I. Armstrong, p. 260. See also E. Esquirol, *Maladies Mentales*, 2: 5ff.

62. R. Hunter and I. Macalpine, *Psychiatry 1535–1860*, p. 237.

63. Cf. M. Mason, in *Browning*, ed. I. Armstrong, p. 261. See also V. Skultans, *Madness and Morals*, pp. 6ff., 135ff.; idem, *English Madness*, pp. 52ff. However, as Roy Porter, *Lychnos* (1981–82), p. 20, has shown, "the moral therapy advocated and employed by the Tukes was in practically all respects a commonplace of certain strands of eighteenth-century psychiatric thought."

64. J. C. Prichard, *Treatise on Insanity*, p. 20.

65. Ibid., pp. 20, 22. For contemporary discussions of Prichard's treatise and the concept of "moral insanity," see, e.g., *Medical Quarterly Review* 4 (1835), pp. 1–32; *North American Review* 44 (1837), pp. 91–121; *British and Foreign Medical Review* 7 (October–April 1839) pp. 1–55. See also J. C. Prichard's article "Insanity" in *Cyclopaedia of Practical Medicine*, ed. J. Forbes et al., 3: 26–76, pp. 50ff.

66. J. B. Harrison, *Journal of Psychological Medicine* 3 (1850), pp. 246–62, p. 258.

67. J. C. Bucknill and D. H. Tuke, *Psychological Medicine*, p. 272.

CHAPTER III

1. Cf. B. W. Fuson, *Studies* XIII, No. III (No. 39) (1967), pp. 1–23; E. Faas, *Anglia* 88 (1970), pp. 222ff.; idem, *Poesie*, pp. 20ff.

2. "Author's Preface to Edition of 1868."

3. See P. J. Kovalewsky, *Journal of Mental Science* 33 (1887–88), pp. 209–18.

4. Of course, there are exceptions showing Tennyson's rather than Browning's influence. See, e.g., J. N. Paton, "Ulysses in Ogygia," *Spindrift*, pp. 101–106; F.B.T. Coutts-Nevill, "Tithonus," *Poems*, pp. 78–81.

5. E.g. "Tithon," "Tiresias," and "The Flight."

6. See below Chapters VIII and IX.

7. *Quarterly Review* 118 (July–October 1865), pp. 77–105, p. 102.

8. H. B. Forman, *Fortnightly Review* 11, n.s. 5 (January–June 1869), p. 117.

9. J. A. Symonds, in *Browning: Critical Heritage*, pp. 308–309.

10. See *Miscellanies by John Addington Symonds, M.D.* Selected and Edited, with an Introductory Memoir, by His Son. 1871.

11. G. Eliot, in *Browning: Critical Heritage*, p. 174.

12. Cf. *George Eliot Letters*, 2: 163–164; 1: 188, 302; 2: 6, 33, 121, 126; 1: 180; 8: xvii.

13. Cf. *Westminster Review* 13 (April–July 1830), pp. 265–92, p. 267, with [W. J. Fox], *Westminster Review* 14 (January–April 1831), pp. 210–24, p. 214.

14. E. S. Dallas, *Gay Science*, 1: 57.

15. Ibid., p. xiv.

16. Ibid., pp. 245, 316, 332–33.

17. *Quarterly Review* 9 (March–July 1813), pp. 304–12; *Westminster Review* 1 (January–April 1824), pp. 471–92. See also J. Alderson's *Essay on Apparitions*, which approvingly quotes Ferriar in the introduction (pp. ix–x).

18. Quoted by R. Hunter and I. Macalpine, *Psychiatry 1535–1860*, p. 542.

19. Ibid., p. 760.

20. S. Hibbert, *Philosophy of Apparitions*, pp. 2, v.

21. *Quarterly Review* 45 (April–July 1831), pp. 341–58, p. 343.

22. Ibid., p. 342. See also *North American Review* 36 (1833), pp. 488–518.

23. Quoted by R. Hunter and I. Macalpine, *Psychiatry 1535–1860*, p. 733.

24. J. Abercrombie, *Inquiries*, p. 316.

25. A. Brigham, *Observations on the Influence of Religion upon the Health . . . of Mankind* (1835). See also P. Pinel, *Treatise on Insanity*, pp. 78–79; G. M. Burrows, *Commentaries*, pp. 24–57; *Quarterly Review* 24 (October 1820–January 1821), pp. 169–94, pp. 184f.; N. Bingham, *Religious Delusions*, passim; *British and Foreign Medical Review* 12 (July–October 1841), pp. 54–60.

26. A. Crichton, *Inquiry*, 1: 57–58.

27. Ibid., p. 58.

28. For this and the following, see R. B. Martin, *Tennyson*, p. 10 and passim; and A. C. Colley, *Tennyson and Madness*, pp. 34ff.

29. A. Tennyson, *Letters*, 1: 81.

30. Ibid., p. 106.

31. Ibid., p. 41.

32. Cf. ibid., p. 45.

33. Ibid., p. 68.

34. H. Tennyson, *Tennyson, A Memoir*, 1: 320.

35. Ibid., p. 40.

36. Cf. R. B. Martin, *Tennyson*, p. 237.

37. See M. Allen, *Classification of the Insane*, pp. 28ff.

38. A. Tennyson, *Letters*, 1: 183.

39. Cf. R. B. Martin, *Tennyson*, pp. 237ff.

40. For this and the following, see H. Tennyson, *Tennyson, A Memoir*, 1: 220ff.

41. Ibid., p. 241.

42. Quoted by R. B. Martin, *Tennyson*, p. 280. See also A. C. Colley, *Tennyson and Madness*, p. 38: "Letters, sketches, and numerous medical texts belonging to the family libraries reveal just how frequently and how vociferously the Tennysons, for generations, defined themselves in terms of their morbidness and mental instability." See also ibid., p. 70. According to *Tennyson in Lincoln*, 1: 26, Tennyson had a copy of M. Allen's *Essay on the Classification of the Insane* in his library.

43. Cf. *Letters of R. Browning and E. Barrett Barrett*, 1: 110, 114, 236, 416, 424 and passim.

44. For this and the following, see M. Mason, in *Browning*, ed. I. Armstrong, pp. 255ff.

45. *Blackwood's Magazine* 3 (April–September 1818), pp. 596–98, p. 597.

46. M. Mason, in *Browning*, ed. I. Armstrong, p. 258.

47. "To J. Milsand, of Dijon," London: June 9, 1863.

48. J. O. Lyons, *The Invention of the Self* (1978). See also K. J. Grau, *Entwicklung des Bewusstseinsbegriffes*, passim.

49. R. Ellrodt, *SS* 28 (1975), p. 42.

50. Quoted by S. D. Cox, *Concepts of the Self*, p. 16.

51. T. Reid, *Philosophical Works*, pp. 96, 91.

52. Cf. D. E. Leary's attempts to trace some of the roots of modern psychology to German idealism, *JHP* 18 (1980), pp. 299–317, and more specifically to the philosophy of Kant, in *The Problematic Science*, ed. W. R. Woodward and M. G. Ash, pp. 17–42. See also W. R.

Woodward's general suggestions about "Stretching the Limits of Psychology's History," ibid., pp. 1–14.

53. Cf. P. Pinel, *Treatise on Insanity*, p. 46.

54. A. Crichton, *Inquiry*, 1: xxvii.

55. Cf. L.F.A. Maury, *Sommeil*, p. iv.

56. Cf. W. Riese, *Legacy of Philippe Pinel*, pp. 121ff.

57. Cf. A. Crichton, *Inquiry*, 1: ivff.

58. Cf. P. Pinel, *Treatise on Insanity*, pp. 50–51.

59. R. Hunter and I. Macalpine, *Psychiatry 1535–1860*, p. 559.

60. A. Crichton, *Inquiry*, 1: x, ix–x.

61. K. P. Moritz, *Magazin*, 1: n.p.

62. See M. Boulby, *Karl Philipp Moritz*, passim.

63. K. P. Moritz, *Magazin*, 1: n.p.

64. See Ibid., n.p.

65. Quoted by S. D. Cox, *Concepts of the Self*, p. 16.

66. E. Young, *Conjectures*, p. 53.

67. H. Tennyson, *Tennyson. A Memoir*, 1: 320.

68. S. T. Coleridge, *Poetical Works*, pp. 241, 390.

69. S. T. Coleridge, *Letters*, 1: 174, 2: 618. See also M. Lefebure, *Coleridge: Bondage of Opium*, p. 56 and passim; A. Hayter, *Opium and the Romantic Imagination*, pp. 191–225.

70. S. T. Coleridge, *Biographia Literaria*, pp. 148, 151–52.

71. A. Hallam, *Remains*, p. 103.

72. Ibid., p. 105.

73. L.F.A. Maury, *Journal of Mental Science* 7 (1860–62), p. 95.

74. H. Holland, *Medical Notes*, p. 252.

75. Ibid. See also *Edinburgh Review* 103 (January–April 1856), pp. 423–52, p. 425.

76. T. Carlyle, *Works*, 29: 109.

77. W. L. Courtney, *Fortnightly Review* 40 n.s. 34 (July–December 1883), p. 715. See also *Chamber's Journal* 46 (July 24, 1869), pp. 473–76, which describes Browning's poetry as a welcome reaction against the "subjective school of poets."

78. As early as 1802, in a letter to John Wilson, Wordsworth invokes a similar combination of introspection and observation of others in trying to capture human nature: "But where are we to find the best measure of this? I answer, from within; by stripping our own hearts naked, and by looking out of ourselves towards men." *Literary Criticism*, p. 105. See also E.G.E.L. Bulwer-Lytton, writing: "The ge-

nius of this time is wholly anti-poetic. When Byron passed away, the feeling he had represented craved utterance no more. With a sigh we turned to the actual and practical career of life: we awoke from the morbid, the passionate, the dreaming." Quoted in *Tennyson*, ed. D. J. Palmer, p. 36.

79. R. Hunter and I. Macalpine, *Psychiatry 1535–1860*, pp. 1067–68. Of course, even in England there were numerous alienists and psychologists who, from early on, opposed the mainstream introspective bias of mental science. See, e.g., ibid., p. 753.

80. J. C. Bucknill, *Psychology of Shakespeare*, p. vii.

81. [W. J. Fox], *Westminster Review* 14 (January–April 1831), pp. 210–24, p. 216.

82. A. D. Innes, *Seers*, p. 65.

CHAPTER IV

1. Cf. M. H. Abrams, *Natural Supernaturalism*, pp. 122ff.

2. J. S. Mill, *Autobiography and Literary Essays*, p. 139.

3. Ibid., pp. 145, 147.

4. T. Carlyle, Works, 1: 146, 135.

5. W. Wordsworth, *Literary Criticism*, pp. 170, 171.

6. Ibid., p. 172.

7. Quoted by W. C. DeVane, *Browning Handbook*, p. 41.

8. Significantly, Browning later changed "Who shadowed out the stages of all life" into "Who chronicled the stages of all life." See *Poetical Works*, ed. I. Jack and M. Smith, 1: 96–97.

9. W. C. DeVane, *Browning Handbook*, p. 44.

10. Cf. M. H. Abrams, *Natural Supernaturalism*, p. 134.

11. T. S. Eliot, *Selected Essays*, p. 146.

12. *Letters of R. Browning and E. Barrett Barrett*, 1: 389.

13. "Author's Preface to Edition of 1868." See also G. R. Elliott, *Anglia* 32, n.s. 20 (1909), p. 114; and more recently W. D. Shaw, *Browning*, pp. 7ff.

14. M. Hancher, *YES* 1 (1971), p. 151, cf. ibid., p. 155. Equally unsatisfactory remains W. S. Swisher's psychoanalytic reading of *Pauline*, *PSR* 7 (1920), pp. 115–33.

15. M. Miyoshi, *Divided Self*, p. 127.

16. This may well have been a cure which Browning had to find for the strong introspective bias he inherited from his evangelical mother.

See J. Maynard, *BIS* 3 (1975), pp. 1–16; idem, *Browning's Youth*, pp. 51ff.

17. R. Browning, *Complete Works*, 5: 138.

18. Ibid., pp. 137, 138.

19. Ibid., p. 139. See also A. H. Warren, Jr., *Poetic Theory 1825–1865*, pp. 111ff.

20. *Letters of R. Browning and E. Barrett Barrett*, 1: 17.

21. J. S. Mill, *Autobiography and Literary Essays*, p. 596.

22. *Letters of R. Browning and E. Barrett Barrett*, 1: 24, 17, 75. See also M. Miyoshi, *VS* 9 (1965), pp. 154–63.

23. *Letters of R. Browning and E. Barrett Barrett*, 2: 182.

24. Quoted by W. C. DeVane, *Browning Handbook*, p. 7.

25. [W. J. Fox], *Monthly Repository* n.s. 7 (1833), pp. 252–62, pp. 253–54. Similar plans were already entertained by Shelley, *Criticism*, pp. 68–69. "If it were possible that a person should give a faithful history of his being, from the earliest epochs of his recollection, a picture would be presented such as the world has never contemplated before. . . . But thought can with difficulty visit the intricate and winding chambers which it inhabits. . . . The caverns of the mind are obscure, and shadowy."

26. *Letters of R. Browning and E. Barrett Barrett*, 1: 402–403.

27. J. S. Mill, *Autobiography and Literary Essays*, p. 596.

28. "Author's Preface to Edition of 1868."

29. H. B. Forman, with his customary perspicacity, notes this fact, arguing that *Pauline* is "the natural ancestor of *The Ring and the Book*," *London Quarterly Review* 32 (April–July 1869), p. 331. See also idem, *Living Poets*, pp. 108–109.

30. R. Browning, *Complete Works*, 5: 138–39.

31. Cf. J. H. Buckley, *Victorian Temper*, pp. 41ff.

32. R. Browning, *Complete Works*, 5: 139.

33. *Blackwood's Magazine* 43 (January–June 1838), pp. 187–201, 437–52, 784–91; 44 (July–December 1838), pp. 234–44, 539–52; 45 (January–June 1839), pp. 201–11, 419–30.

34. Cf. ibid. 101 (January–June 1867), pp. 280–300, p. 281.

35. Ibid. 43 (January–June 1838), p. 785.

36. Ibid. 44 (July–December 1838), p. 242.

37. S. T. Coleridge, *Biographia Literaria*, p. 154.

38. *Blackwood's Magazine* 44 (July–December 1838), pp. 239, 243, 244.

39. Ibid., 43 (January–June 1838), pp. 788, 789. A more general discussion of nineteenth-century concepts of the self is found in my *Poesie*, pp. 30ff.

40. [W. Pater], *Westminster Review* 90, n.s. 34 (July–October 1868), pp. 300–12, p. 311.

41. Cf. A. Tennyson, *Poems*, ed. C. Ricks, p. 522.

42. Ibid., pp. 537, 538.

43. J. Abercrombie, *Inquiries*, p. 298.

44. Ibid., pp. 298–99. For later discussions of the same phenomenon, see, e.g., B. C. Brodie, *Lectures*, p. 14; H. Holland, *Medical Notes*, pp. 161ff.; A. L. Wigan, *Duality of the Mind*, pp. 111ff. and passim; J. C. Prichard, "Somnambulism and Animal Magnetism," *Cyclopaedia of Practical Medicine*, ed. J. Forbes et al., 4: 194–211, p. 201; J. C. Browne, *Journal of Mental Science* 8 (1862–63), pp. 385–95, 535–45; R. Hennig, *ZfP* 49 (1908), pp. 1–55.

45. Quoted by R. B. Martin, *Tennyson*, p. 85.

46. Quoted in A. Tennyson, *Poems*, ed. C. Ricks, p. 171.

47. R. Browning, *Complete Works*, 5: 138.

48. Cf. A. Tennyson, *Poems*, ed. C. Ricks, pp. 555, 1037.

49. See also A. B. Draper, *VP* 17 (1979), pp. 180–91.

50. See R. J. Dunn, *VP* 18 (1980), pp. 135–46; A. Tennyson, *In Memoriam*, pp. 187ff. Nonetheless, Tennyson continued to pursue his interests in the occult in private, attempted to communicate with ghosts, consulted with mediums, became a founding member of the Metaphysical Society in 1877, originally named the Psychological Society, and later was among the founders of the Society for Psychical Research. See A. C. Colley, *Tennyson and Madness*, pp. 71, 123ff., 130.

51. Quoted in A. Tennyson, *Poems*, ed. C. Ricks, p. 299.

52. Clarice Short, *PMLA* 82 (1967), p.83.

53. For the following see G. O. Marshall, Jr., *PMLA* 78 (1963), pp. 225–29, from which I quote the poem's earlier versions.

54. Quoted in A. Tennyson, *Poems*, ed. C. Ricks, p. 1037.

55. Quoted ibid.

56. A. Tennyson, *Letters*, 1: 41.

57. R. J. Mann, *"Maud" Vindicated*, p. 57.

58. *Letters of R. Browning and E. Barrett Barrett*, 1: 17.

59. *Bentley's Miscellany* 39 (1856), pp. 64–70, p. 64. Similarly, *The Dublin Review* n.s. 25 (July–October 1869), pp. 48–62, p. 58,

speaks of the "subjective-objectivity" of Browning's characters in *The Ring and the Book*.

60. T. S. Eliot, *Selected Essays*, p. 21.

CHAPTER V

1. W. Wordsworth, *Literary Criticism*, p. 97.
2. See W. Wordsworth, *Selected Poems and Prefaces*, ed. J. Stillinger, p. 108; M. Moorman, *Wordsworth: Early Years*, pp. 401–402.
3. *Eighteenth-Century Critical Essays*, ed. S. Elledge, 2: 1173.
4. R. Hurd, *Works*, 2: 116. See also A. Gerard, "Concerning the Question, Whether Poetry be Properly an Imitative Art?" *Essay on Taste*, pp. 275–84, especially pp. 277f.
5. R. Hurd, *Works* 2: 133, 130.
6. Quoted by M. H. Abrams, *Mirror*, p. 245.
7. R. Hurd, *Works*, 2: 134, 131.
8. Ibid., p. 130.
9. R. Lowth, *Lectures*, p. 50; cf. ibid., pp. 157, 174. See also J. Trapp, *Lectures on Poetry*, p. 14; J. Warton, *Genius of Pope*, 1: 51.
10. W. Duff, *Essay on Original Genius*, p. 270.
11. H. Blair, *Dissertation on Ossian*, p. 94.
12. W. Jones, *Eighteenth-Century Critical Essays*, ed. S. Elledge, 2: 872–73.
13. Ibid., p. 873.
14. R. Lowth, ibid., p. 878.
15. T. Twining, ibid., p. 989.
16. Ibid., p. 994.
17. Ibid.
18. E. Johnson, *Browning Society's Papers*, 1: 354.
19. E. Young, *Conjectures*, pp. 51, 27, 50.
20. Ibid., p. 53. Cf. I. St. John Bliss, *Edward Young*, p. 147.
21. W. Hazlitt, *Complete Works*, 12: 118.
22. T. Carlyle, *Works*, 26: 52.
23. Ibid., 28: 3, 4.
24. Ibid., 26: 58.
25. Ibid., 28: 9.
26. E. S. Dallas, *Poetics*, p. 61. See also W. Hughes's recent discussion of Dallas's poetics in *VP* 23 (1985), pp. 1–21.
27. E. S. Dallas, *Gay Science*, 1: 200, 194, 199ff., 200, 228, 321.

28. Ibid., pp. 201, 221.

29. See ibid., pp. 233, 229, 232.

30. Quoted by M. H. Abrams, *Mirror*, p. 215.

31. Quoted ibid., p. 216.

32. *Blake: Critical Heritage*, pp. 170–98.

33. Quoted by J. Thomson, *Biographical and Critical Studies*, p. 304.

34. S. T. Coleridge, *Poetical Works*, p. 295.

35. *Coleridge: Critical Heritage*, p. 246.

36. W. Hazlitt, in ibid., p. 208; J. Bowring, in ibid., pp. 550, 549.

37. J. S. Mill, *Autobiography and Literary Essays*, p. 356.

38. Ibid., p. 596.

39. *Blackwood's Magazine* 78 (July–December 1855), pp. 311–321, p. 319.

40. A. Tennyson, *Poems*, ed. C. Ricks, p. 878 (*In Memoriam*, 16: 17, 20).

41. Quoted ibid., p. 186.

42. Quoted ibid., p. 171.

43. W. Bagehot, *Collected Works*, 2: 181. Quoted by B. Haley, *Healthy Body*, p. 46, who discusses further instances of the same trend in Victorian criticism in his third chapter (ibid., pp. 46–68).

44. Cf. C. R. Sanders, *PMLA* 76 (1961), p. 96.

45. See, e.g., W. Wordsworth, *Literary Criticism*, pp. 72, 85.

46. Ibid., pp. 85, 78, 82.

47. Ibid., pp. 79, 78, 82.

48. Ibid., pp. 81, 72.

49. W. Wordsworth, *Prose Works* (1974), 3: 125.

50. W. Wordsworth, *Poems*, ed. J. O. Hayden, 1: 929. See also Wordsworth's comments on "Resolution and Independence," in *Early Letters of W. and D. Wordsworth*, p. 305: "I describe myself as having been exalted to the highest pitch of delight by the joyousness and beauty of Nature and then as depressed. . . . A young Poet in the midst of the happiness of Nature is described as overwhelmed by the thought of the miserable reverses which have befallen the happiest of men, viz Poets."

51. H. Home, *Elements of Criticism*, 1: 107.

52. Ibid., pp. 108, 112, 106.

53. Ibid., p. 112. See also A. E. McGuinness, *Henry Home*, pp. 66ff.

54. H. Home, *Elements of Criticism*, 2: 179, 181–82.

55. E. Young, *Eighteenth-Century Critical Essays*, ed. S. Elledge, 1: 412.

56. Cf. M. H. Abrams, *Mirror*, pp. 95ff.

57. H. Blair, *Lectures*, 2: 357.

58. Ibid., pp. 312, 323, 315.

59. Ibid., pp. 353, 355–56, 356, 376.

60. J. Beattie, *Works*, 1: 386.

61. Cf. E. H. King, *James Beattie*, pp. 142ff.

62. J. Beattie, *Works*, 1: 10.

63. W. Wordsworth, *Literary Criticism*, p. 72.

64. Ibid., p. 82.

65. Quoted by E. H. King, *James Beattie*, p. 144.

66. W. Wordsworth, *Literary Criticism*, p. 105.

67. J. Beattie, Works, 1: 10.

68. W. Wordsworth, *Literary Criticism*, p. 79.

69. J. Beattie, Works, 1: 389.

70. E. S. Dallas, *Poetics*, p. 76.

71. Ibid., pp. 67, 147. Cf. E. Gosse criticizing "Barry Cornwall's" poetry for "dealing dramatically with feelings which the poet does not himself pretend to experience." *English Poets*, ed. T. H. Ward, 4: 489.

72. W. Hazlitt, *Complete Works*, 12: 118.

73. Ibid., 5: 70, 53, 8.

74. J. Keble, quoted by M. H. Abrams, *Mirror*, p. 258. See also *Eclectic Review* 17 (January–June 1845), pp. 22–42, pp. 27, 35, 39 and passim.

75. J. Keble, *Lectures*, 1: 55, 22, 47.

76. T. De Quincey, *Collected Writings*, 10: 226–27.

77. Ibid., 11: 386.

78. Ibid., p. 322,

79. Ibid., pp. 387, 386.

80. *Blackwood's Magazine* (October 1820–March 1821), pp. 362–63, p. 363.

81. Ibid.

82. *North British Review* 19 (May–August 1853), pp. 297–344, p. 310. See also ibid. 9 (May–August 1848), pp. 23–39, pp. 26–27; G. H. Lewes, *Criticism*, p. 63; H. Timrod, *Atlantic Review* 96 (July–December 1905), pp. 313–26, pp. 320–21: "A distinction must be made between the moment when the great thought strikes for the first time . . . and the hour of patient, elaborate execution."

83. *Blackwood's Magazine* 27 (January–June 1830), pp. 279–305, p. 288.

84. *Monthly Repository* n.s. 8 (1834), p. 324.

85. Ibid.

86. Cf. M. H. Abrams, *Mirror*, p. 149.

87. [A. Smith], *Blackwood's Magazine* 38 (July–December 1835), pp. 827–39, p. 828.

88. Ibid., p. 830.

89. Ibid., p. 835. A similar interpretation of the opening line of Gray's elegy is already found in J. Scott's 1785 *Critical Essays* as well as in a later essay, "Descriptive Poetry," in *The Knickerbocker* 23 (1844), pp. 1–10, p. 7.

90. *The Merchant of Venice* V. 1.54.

91. Cf. [A. Smith], *Blackwood's Magazine* 38 (July–December 1835), pp. 827–39, p. 835.

92. Cf. [W. J. Fox], *Westminster Review* 14 (January–April 1831), pp. 210–24, p. 217; G. Brimley, *Essays*, p. 8.

93. To trace this shift in detail and with proper emphasis would be a rewarding task for a separate volume. Concerning the possible origins of the development see my *Shakespeare's Poetics*, pp. 79ff.; C. D. Thorpe, *Aesthetic Theory of Thomas Hobbes*, pp. 20ff. and passim; W. J. Ong, *MP* 49 (1951–52), pp. 16–27; J. Engell, *Creative Imagination*, pp. 33ff.

94. Quoted by A. E. McGuinness, *Henry Home*, p. 62. Concerning G. Campbell's similar goals, see *Eighteenth-Century Critical Essays*, ed. S. Elledge, 2: 937, 1181.

95. A. Rimbaud, *Oeuvres complètes*, p. 251.

96. Quoted by J. Thomson, *Biographical and Critical Studies*, p. 304.

97. J. Keble, quoted by M. H. Abrams, *Mirror*, p. 258; J. Keble, *Lectures*, p. 22.

98. *Letters of W. and D. Wordsworth: The Middle Years*, 2: 614.

Chapter VI

1. R. W. Buchanan, *Browning: Critical Heritage*, p. 318.

2. Ibid., p. 519.

3. O. Wilde, in ibid., p. 525.

4. M. D. Conway, in ibid., p. 312.

5. Cf. W. Bagehot, in ibid., pp. 274ff.; *Fraser's Magazine* 53 (January–June 1856), pp. 105–16, p. 113.

6. *Eclectic Review* n.s. 10 (July–December 1855), pp. 568–75, p. 575. See also *Dublin University Magazine* 46 (July–December 1855), pp. 332–40, p. 334.

7. [W. M. Rossetti], *Germ* (1850), pp. 187–92, p. 191.

8. Ibid.

9. A. Symons, *Introduction*, p. 13.

10. *Browning: Critical Heritage*, p. 311. See also G. R. Elliott, *Anglia* 32, n.s. 20 (1909), pp. 90–162.

11. Cf. R. J. Mann, *"Maud" Vindicated*, p. 7. See also E. F. Shannon, Jr., *PMLA* 68 (1953), p. 404.

12. Cf. [R. H. Hutton], *National Review* 17 (July–October 1863), p. 421. See also A. Austin, *Poetry of the Period*, pp. 52, 53; J. H. Stirling, in *Browning: Critical Heritage*, pp. 280ff.

13. W. J. Courthope, *Nineteenth Century* 41 (January–June 1897), pp. 270–84, p. 281: "though metre can only properly be used for the expression of universal ideas, there is in modern society an eccentric or monastic principle at work, which leads men to pervert metre into a luxurious instrument for the expression of merely private ideas." See also F. W. Williams, *Poet-Lore* 2 (1890), pp. 300–305, p. 305.

14. See M. H. Abrams, *Mirror*, pp. 78f., 95, 96. See also P. Fussell, Jr., *Theory of Prosody*, pp. 111ff.; idem, *Poetic Meter*, pp. 42 and 85ff.

15. L. Hunt, *Imagination and Fancy*, p. 35. See also idem, *Literary Criticism*, pp. 65ff.

16. L. Hunt, *Imagination and Fancy*, pp. 38–39. See also [G. Brimley], *Fraser's Magazine* 51 (January–June 1855), pp. 157–72, p. 162: "the various forms of metre, its recurrent emphasis, its various pauses, its divisions into stanza and verse . . . are all originally expressive of the varieties of kind and degree of emotion. Upon this point all philosophy of metre, all criticism of the form of poetry, is to be based."

17. R. J. Mann, *"Maud" Vindicated*, pp. 9, 64.

18. Ibid., p. 34; cf. ibid., pp. 14, 32, 50. See also [H. B. Forman on Morris's poetry], *London Quarterly Review* 33 (October 1869–January 1870), pp. 330–60, p. 335.

19. [R. H. Hutton], *National Review* 17 (July–October 1863), p. 421.

20. *Quarterly Review* 118 (July–October 1865), pp. 77–105, p. 83. See also *Athenaeum* (June 10, 1871), pp. 714–15.

21. D. G. Brinton, *Poet-Lore* 2 (1890), p. 235.

22. Ibid., p. 243.

23. A. Beatty, *Browning's Verse-Form*, p. 25.

24. Ibid., pp. 61, 58.

25. R. W. Buchanan, *David Gray*, p. 305; cf. idem, *Drama*, pp. 469–70.

26. R. W. Buchanan, in *Browning: Critical Heritage*, p. 318.

27. R. H. Stoddard, in ibid., p. 372.

28. J. Kirkman, in ibid., p. 473.

29. [J. C. Bucknill], *Asylum Journal of Mental Science* 2 (1855–56), pp. 95–104, p. 102.

30. R. J. Mann, *"Maud" Vindicated*, p. 64.

31. Cf. [J. C. Bucknill], *Asylum Journal of Mental Science* 2 (1855–56), pp. 95–104, p. 97.

32. J. C. Bucknill, *Psychology of Shakespeare*, p. 133.

33. Ibid., pp. 133, 134.

34. Quoted by M. H. Abrams, *Mirror*, p. 245.

35. J. C. Bucknill, *Psychology of Shakespeare*, p. vii.

36. [W. J. Fox], *Westminster Review* 14 (January–April 1831), pp. 210–24, p. 216.

37. Quoted in R. Hunter and I. Macalpine, *Psychiatry 1535–1860*, pp. 1067–68.

38. Cf. R. J. Mann, *"Maud" Vindicated*, p. 7.

39. R. W. Buchanan, *David Gray*, pp. 304–305. See also H. B. Forman, *Living Poets*, pp. 181–82. For a more general study of the Victorian debate concerning the particular versus the general in poetry, see my *Poesie*, pp. 91ff.; C. T. Christ, *Finer Optic*, passim.

40. [J. C. Bucknill], *Asylum Journal of Mental Science* 2 (1855–56), pp. 95–104, p. 96.

41. J. C. Bucknill and D. H. Tuke, *Psychological Medicine*, p. 277.

42. Ibid., p. 339. Understandably, photography played an increasing role in the diagnosis for insanity; see *Face of Madness*, ed. Sander L. Gilman, passim. See also C. Bell's section on "Madness" in *Philosophy of Expression*, pp. 161–63; and A. Morison, *Physiognomy of Mental Diseases*, passim.

43. [J. C. Bucknill], *Asylum Journal of Mental Science* 2 (1855–56), pp. 95–104, pp. 95–96.

44. J. C. Bucknill, *Psychology of Shakespeare*, p. 2.

45. See, e.g., *American Journal of Insanity* 1 (1844–45), pp. 9–46; I. Ray, ibid. 4 (1847–48), pp. 97–112. See also O. Delepierre's

"Literary Fools" in the *Journal of Psychological Medicine* 12 (1859), pp. 1–9, 169–86.

46. G. Ross, *Studies: Biographical and Literary*, pp. 7–62.

47. See A. Adnès bibliography in his *Shakespeare et la pathologie mentale*, pp. 235–46.

48. For an exception, see A. O. Kellogg, *Shakspeare's Delineations of Insanity*, pp. 9, 37, 83.

49. I. Ray, *American Journal of Insanity* 3 (1846–47), p. 304. See also G. Farren's "Appendix Containing Illustrations of the Progress of Mania, Melancholia, Craziness, and Demonomania, as Displayed in Shakespeare's Characters of Lear, Hamlet, Ophelia, and Edgar," in *Observations* (1829), pp. 97–132, p. 105; H. Halford, *Essays*, pp. 47–56; R. H. Horne, *Journal of Psychological Medicine* 2 (1849), pp. 589–607.

50. *American Journal of Insanity* 1 (1844–45), pp. 9–46, pp. 36, 36–37. Cf. G. Farren, *Observations*, p. 104.

51. Cf. *American Journal of Insanity* 1 (1844–45), p. 31; ibid. 3 (1846–47), p. 293. See also G. Farren, *Observations*, pp. 99, 116.

52. *American Journal of Insanity* 3 (1846–47), pp. 301, 328.

53. Ibid., pp. 319, 310.

54. Ibid. 1 (1844–45), pp. 40–41.

55. Ibid. 3 (1846–47), pp. 291, 299.

56. Ibid. 1 (1844–45), pp. 40–41.

57. Ibid. 3 (1846–47), pp. 291, 299.

58. W. Hazlitt, *Complete Works*, 4: 173. The actual words here are A. W. Schlegel's, which Hazlitt quotes approvingly.

59. S. T. Coleridge, *Shakespearean Criticism*, 1: 176.

60. H. Home, *Elements of Criticism*, 2: 215.

61. E. Malone et al., *Shakespeare: Critical Heritage*, 6: 286, 287; F. Gentleman, in ibid., p. 100.

62. T. Davies, in ibid., p. 383.

63. T. W., in ibid., 5: 289.

64. See, e.g., *American Journal of Insanity* 1 (1844–45), pp. 97–121, p. 101.

65. A. Murphy, in *Shakespeare: Critical Heritage*, 6: 633–34.

66. Ibid., 6: 634.

67. Ibid., p. 633.

68. Cf. ibid., 4: 471.

69. H. Home, *Elements of Criticism*, 1: 197.

70. See, e.g., Joseph Warton, *Genius of Pope*, pp. 48–49: "A minute and particular enumeration of circumstances judiciously selected is what chiefly discriminates poetry from history, and renders the former, for that reason, a more close and faithful representation of nature than the latter." See also R. A. Aubin, *Topographical Poetry*, pp. 56f.; S. Elledge, *PMLA* 62 (1947), pp. 147–82; E. Faas, *GRM* n.s. 22 (1972), pp. 144–45.

71. H. Home, *Elements of Criticism*, 2: 212. See also A. Gerard, *Eighteenth-Century Critical Essays*, ed. S. Elledge, 2: 895ff.

72. T. Smollett, in *Shakespeare: Critical Heritage*, 4: 498.

73. Ibid., pp. 501, 502.

74. S. Johnson, in *Shakespeare: Critical Heritage*, 5: 31.

75. H. Home, *Elements of Criticism*, 2: 161–62.

76. Ibid., pp. 218, 169, 172, 218, 220–21.

77. J. Conolly, *Hamlet*, p. 90.

78. *Contemporary Review* 4 (January–April 1867), pp. 1–15, p. 12; *North British Review* 51 (American Edition) (October 1869–January 1870), pp. 51–67, p. 53.

79. Cf. J. Conolly, *Hamlet*, p. 90.

80. As early as 1794, Walter Whiter, for instance, proposed to investigate Locke's principle of the association of ideas "as it operates on the writer in the ardor of invention by imposing on his mind some remote and peculiar vein of language or of imagery." The results, as documented in Shakespeare, include unconscious processes of imaginative association, which, to use S. Elledge's paraphrase, are fourfold: "a) The poet may use an unusual metaphor or expression because a subject previously discussed or referred to may be still lingering in his mind and thereby supply him with a term he would not otherwise have thought of. . . . b) Sometimes equivocal expressions or homonyms may introduce a new series of metaphorical variations. . . . c) One phrase or metaphor may suggest to the poet an associated, or similar, expression or subject which, though it does not get into the text, will supply him in turn, by way of a second process of association, with the term he finally uses. d) Imagery may come in constellations all derived from some part of the poet's daily life or important experience." *Eighteenth-Century Critical Essays*, ed. S. Elledge, 2: 1073, 1201.

81. M. Arnold, *Poems*, ed. K. Allott, p. 591.

CHAPTER VII

1. T. Carlyle, *Works*, 28: 47.
2. W. L. Courtney, *Fortnightly Review* n.s. 34 (July–December 1883), p. 715.
3. A. H. Clough, *Correspondence*, 1: 73. See also Clough's advocacy of an "objective poetry" in *Rugby Magazine* 1 (July 1835–April 1836), pp. 123–32, p. 126, as discussed in W. E. Houghton, *Clough*, p. 78.
4. H. Tennyson, *Tennyson, A Memoir*, 1: 304–305. See also *North British Review* 8 (American Edition) (May–August 1850), pp. 287–99, p. 297: "In the poem before us [i.e., *In Memoriam*] we behold the result of many years of self-contemplation and observation of others . . . the 'subjectivity' is complete; and the result is wholly admirable, for the self-consciousness which, in most modern artists, has served only to intensify selfishness . . . has arrived . . . at a full conviction of the insignificance of self." After 1848, when Richard Monckton Milnes published *The Life, Letters and Literary Remains of John Keats*, critics began to discuss the poet's objectivity in terms of "Negative Capability" and related Keatsian concepts. See, e.g., *Eclectic Magazine* 16 (January–April 1849), pp. 145–59, pp. 147ff.; *Edinburgh Review* 90 (July–October 1849), pp. 388–433, pp. 425ff. See also E. P. Morton, *Poet-Lore* 12, n.s. 4 (1900), pp. 58–70.
5. M. Arnold, *Poems*, ed. K. Allott, p. 598. See also E. Dowden, *Contemporary Review* 2 (May–August 1866), p. 554: "when we *read into* the appearances of nature some private allegorical meanings of our own, our poetry is always bad." A. Tilley, *Littell's Living Age* 53 (January–March 1886), p. 229: "Defective imagination in lyrical poems is also due to the poet's vision being dimmed by the shadow of his own personal joys and sorrows. Instead of projecting himself by the force of sympathy into the external world, whether of man or nature, he makes it sympathize with him. Consequently, though he gives us a faithful representation of his own feelings, the image that he presents of the external world is blurred and misty."
6. Byron's term, *Letters and Journals*, ed. R. E. Prothero, 5: 347. See also Coleridge's comments on Wordsworth's *The Borderers* in *Collected Letters*, ed. E. L. Griggs, 1: 325, and on his *Remorse* in *Letters*, ed. E. H. Coleridge, 2: 607.

7. *North British Review* 16 (American Edition) (May–August 1853), pp. 159–84, p. 180. Quoted by M. Arnold, *Poems*, ed. K. Allott, pp. 598–99. Arnold omits the phrase "whether narrative or dramatic in form" and substitutes "poetry" for "fictitious art."

8. M. Arnold, *Poems*, ed. K. Allott, p. 599.

9. Ibid., p. 598.

10. *M. Arnold to A. H. Clough*, p. 101.

11. *Swinburne Letters*, 1: 115.

12. Browning's term from his 1852 essay on Shelley, *Complete Works*, 5: 139.

13. This is a fact noted by A. N. Stitelman, *VP* 15 (1977), pp. 134f.

14. See K. Allott, "Arnold's *Empedocles on Etna* and Byron's *Manfred*," *NQ* 207 (1962), pp. 300–302.

15. R. Browning, *Complete Works*, 5: 139.

16. M. Arnold, *Poems*, ed. K. Allott, pp. 254, 144, 162.

17. Quoted by G. R. Stange, *Arnold*, p. 192. See also P. Honan, *Matthew Arnold: A Life*, p. 127.

18. *M. Arnold to A. H. Clough*, p. 130.

19. A. C. Swinburne, *Complete Works*, 15: 83. Concerning Arnold's personal relationship with Wordsworth, see P. Honan, *Matthew Arnold: A Life*, pp. 195ff.

20. W. Wordsworth, *Literary Criticism*, p. 210.

21. See, e.g., M. H. Abrams, *Natural Supernaturalism*, pp. 134ff.

22. Cf. E.G.E.L. Bulwer-Lytton, *England and the English*, 2: 69.

23. A. A. Watts, *Lyrics*, p. 301. See also H. Ellison, "To Wordsworth," *Poetry*, p. 7; C. Lloyd, *Thoughts*, p. 144; *Poems*, 2: 333.

24. M. Arnold, *Complete Prose Works*, 9: 36.

25. W. Wordsworth, *Prose Works* (1876), 3: 390.

26. M. Arnold, *Complete Prose Works*, 9: 37.

27. *Swinburne Letters*, 1: 97.

28. A. C. Swinburne, *Complete Works*, 15: 83.

29. U. C. Knoepflmacher, *VP* 1 (1963), p. 17. See also L. Gottfried, *Arnold and the Romantics*, pp. 219–23; K. Smidt, *VP* 4 (1976), pp. 256–57; and W. E. Buckler, *Poetry of Matthew Arnold*, who describes Arnold's poetic endeavors as "the failed strategies of a poet-critic of Romanticism who was himself unconsciously enervated by the very Romanticism he was attempting to critique" (p. 17). See also

L. Kramer's attempt to trace a tradition of Victorian, often decon-
structivist, "Intimations" odes, *VP* 18 (1980), pp. 315–35.

30. Cf. M. H. Abrams, *Mirror*, p. 160.

31. Cf. M. Arnold, *Poems*, ed. K. Allott, p. 245.

32. J. Ruskin, *Works*, 5: 205.

33. "Below the Surface-Stream . . . ," 4, 1. For the following see also
G. R. Stange, *Arnold*, pp. 167ff.

34. "The Youth of Nature," l. 102.

35. *Merope*, ll. 629–30.

36. *Empedocles on Etna*, 2: 371.

37. G. R. Stange, *Arnold*, p. 172.

38. E. S. Dallas, *Poetics*, pp. 147, 10.

39. E. S. Dallas, *Gay Science*, 1: 201, 209, 244, 250, 248.

40. Ibid., p. 250.

41. Ibid., pp. xiv, 221.

42. Ibid., p. 201.

43. Ibid., p. viii.

44. Cf. ibid., pp. 55–57.

45. E. S. Dallas, *Poetics*, p. 61.

46. E. S. Dallas, *Gay Science*, 1: 194.

47. Cf. E. S. Dallas, *Poetics*, p. 76.

48. M. Arnold, *Poems*, ed. K. Allott, p. 601.

49. [W. Pater], *Westminster Review* 90, n.s. 34 (July–October 1868),
pp. 300–12, p. 311.

50. A. Hallam, *Remains*, p. 105.

51. M. Arnold, *Unpublished Letters*, p. 18. See also A. Hallam, *Writings*, p. xiii, where the poet speaks of his verse as a mere "record of
several states of mind"; J. Nichol, *Death*, p. ix; G. Barlow, *Works*,
10: 37; and among critical discussions of this phenomenon: W. H.
Hudson, *Studies*, p. 118; M. Miyoshi, *Divided Self*, passim.

52. J. Thomson, *Essays*, p. 239; cf. ibid., pp. 243ff.

53. M. Arnold, *Complete Prose Works*, 8: 41–42. Arnold's general distrust of psychology or "fruitful analysis of character" is discussed by
Dorothy Deering, *VP* 16 (1978), p. 28.

54. *M. Arnold to A. H. Clough*, p. 126.

55. M. Arnold, *Letters*, 1: 72.

56. R. Browning, *Complete Works*, 5: 139.

57. M. Arnold, *Letters*, 1: 73.

58. *M. Arnold to A. H. Clough*, p. 97.

59. Ibid., pp. 63, 97.

60. M. Arnold, *Poems*, ed. K. Allott, p. 543.

61. Ibid., pp. 591, 592.

62. *M. Arnold to A. H. Clough*, p. 111.

63. M. Arnold, Letters, 1: 73.

64. M. Arnold, *Poems*, ed. K. Allott, pp. 598–99. See also P. Honan, *Matthew Arnold: A Life*, pp. 206f.; Paul Zietlow, *VP* 21 (1983), p. 241.

65. Cf. W. E. Houghton, *VS* 1 (1957–58), pp. 322ff.

66. M. Arnold, *Poems*, ed. K. Allott, pp. 598–99. "Matthew Arnold's 1853 Preface: Its Origin and Aftermath" is discussed by S.M.B. Coulling, *VS* 7 (1963–4), pp. 233–63. See also I. Armstrong, *Victorian Scrutinies*, pp. 31ff.

67. Byron's term, *Letters and Journals*, ed. R. E. Prothero, 5: 347.

68. M. A. Weinstein, *Aytoun and the Spasmodic Controversy*, p. 69.

69. J. W. von Goethe, *Faust*, 1: 112–13.

70. Quoted by M. A. Weinstein, *Aytoun and the Spasmodic Controversy*, p. 72.

71. W. Wordsworth, *Literary Criticism*, p. 172.

72. [W. J. Fox], *Monthly Repository* n.s. 7 (1833), pp. 252–62, p. 253.

73. Quoted by M. A. Weinstein, *Aytoun and the Spasmodic Controversy*, p. 77.

74. Quoted ibid., pp. 77–78.

75. Quoted ibid., p. 93.

76. S. Dobell, *Poetical Works*, 2: 5.

77. Ibid., pp. 4, 6, 5.

78. Ibid., pp. 3–4. See also *Life and Letters of Sydney Dobell*, 1: 332, 380; and S. Dobell, *Thoughts*, p. 39, where "a Poem" is defined as *"the manifest metaphor of a human mind."*

79. *Blackwood's Magazine* 75 (January–June 1854), pp. 303–14.

80. Ibid., pp. 305, 306.

81. Quoted by M. A. Weinstein, *Aytoun and the Spasmodic Controversy*, pp. 123, 124.

82. For this and the following see ibid., pp. 74, 75, 152, 183, 173, 153ff.

83. Quoted ibid., p. 156.

84. Quoted ibid., p. 155.

85. Quoted ibid., p. 181.

86. *Blackwood's Magazine* 78 (July–December 1855), pp. 311–21, p. 312.

87. Cf. M. A. Weinstein, *Aytoun and the Spasmodic Controversy*, pp. 179–80.

88. Cf. ibid., p. 181.

89. Cf. ibid., pp. 172ff.; D. J. DeLaura, *SBC* 1, 2 (Spring 1974), pp. 55–60, 113–14.

90. Cf. M. A. Weinstein, *Aytoun and the Spasmodic Controversy*, p. 173.

91. S. Dobell, *Poetical Works*, 2: 4.

92. Quoted in A. Tennyson, *Poems*, ed. C. Ricks, p. 1039.

93. S. Dobell, *Poetical Works*, 2: 264. M. A. Weinstein, *Aytoun and the Spasmodic Controversy*, p. 175, notes the resemblance of these lines with *Maud* 2: 239ff., but misquotes them as the protagonist's rather than Amy's.

94. Cf. S. Dobell, *Poetical Works*, 2: 5.

95. Quoted in A. Tennyson, *Poems*, ed. C. Ricks, p. 1039.

96. G. Brimley, T.C.C., in *Tennyson: Critical Heritage*, p. 192.

97. S. Dobell, *Poetical Works*, 2: 6.

98. Ibid., 2: 4.

99. *Life and Letters of Sydney Dobell*, 1: 327–28.

100. S. Dobell, *Poetical Works*, 2: 9, 10–11.

101. J. Ruskin, *Works*, 5: 205, 206–207.

102. G. H. Lewes, *Criticism*, p. 51.

103. J. Ruskin, *Works*, 5: 205.

104. *Eclectic Review* 38, n.s. 10 (July–December 1855), pp. 568–75, p. 570.

105. *Blackwood's Magazine* 78 (July–December 1855), pp. 311–21, p. 315.

106. *Fraser's Magazine* 52 (July–December 1855), pp. 264–73, pp. 267, 268.

107. *Edinburgh Review* 102 (July–October 1855), pp. 498–519, p. 506.

108. *Bentley's Miscellany* 39 (1856), pp. 64–70, p. 64.

109. *Oxford and Cambridge Magazine* (1856), pp. 136–45, pp. 137, 138.

110. Ibid., pp. 138, 137.

111. *British Quarterly Review* 22 (July–October 1855), pp. 467–98, p. 482.

112. *Edinburgh Review* 102 (July–October 1855), pp. 498–519, p. 514.

113. *M. Arnold to A. H. Clough*, p. 127.

114. M. Arnold, *Letters*, 1: 72.

115. *M. Arnold to A. H. Clough*, p. 147.

CHAPTER VIII

1. [W. E. Aytoun], *Blackwood's Magazine* 50 (July–December 1841), pp. 811–13.

2. E. Barrett Browning, in *Poems*, 2 vols. (1844).

3. E. Barrett Browning, *The Letters*, ed. F. G. Kenyon, 1: 315.

4. C. Brontë, in *Poems by Currer, Ellis and Acton Bell* [1854].

5. See, e.g., E. H. Bickersteth, "The Two Brothers" (an. 1845), *Poems*, pp. 86–110; A. T. Gurney, "The Convict's Tale," *Songs*, pp. 145–61.

6. See, e.g., W. Morris, "Concerning Geffray Teste Noire," "The Judgement of God," "Spell-bound"; G. Meredith, "Juggling Jerry," "The Old Chartist," "Martin's Puzzle"; A. H. Clough, "The Song of Lamech," "Jacob," "Sa Majesté très Chrétienne"; C. Rossetti, "The Convent Threshold," "A Royal Princess," "Maggie a Lady," "The Iniquity of the Fathers upon the Children," "The Lowest Room"; D. G. Rossetti, "A Last Confession," "Jenny"; A. C. Swinburne, "Laus Veneris," "Anactoria," "Hymn to Proserpine," "The Leper"; R. Kipling, "One Viceroy Resigns," "Mulholland's Contract," "McAndrew's Hymn," "The 'Mary Gloster' "; T. Hardy, "The Peasant's Confession," "My Cicely."

7. See Appendix, "Practitioners of the Dramatic Monologue Among Minor Victorian Poets."

8. A. Symons, *Introduction*, p. 7; *Quarterly Review* 118 (July–October 1865), pp. 77–105, p. 102; [H. B. Forman], *London Quarterly Review* 32 (April–July 1869), pp. 315–57, p. 331.

9. *National Review* 1 (July–October 1855), pp. 377–410, p. 394.

10. H. B. Forman, *Fortnightly Review* 11, n.s. 5 (January–June 1869), p. 118. See above, Introduction, n. 2.

11. See M. L. Etienne, *Revue des deux mondes* 85 (January–February 1870), pp. 704–35.

12. H. Corson, *Introduction*, p. 86.

13. H. Walker, *Greater Victorian Poets*, p. 65.

14. R. G. White, *Galaxy* 2 (September–December 1866), p. 667.

15. H. B. Forman, *Fortnightly Review* 11, n.s. 5 (January–June 1869),

p. 117. See also [idem], *London Quarterly Review* 32 (April–July 1869), pp. 325–57, pp. 332–33.

16. *Athenaeum* (June 10, 1871), pp. 713–15, p. 715.

17. C. Vaughan, *British Quarterly Review* 80 (July–October 1884), pp. 6, 8.

18. A. Symons, *Introduction*, p. 24.

19. A. Sharp, *Victorian Poets*, p. 55. See also [W. Morris], *Oxford and Cambridge Magazine* 1 (1856), pp. 162–72, p. 165; H. B. Forman, *Living Poets*, pp. 110–11.

20. See, e.g., C. Brontë, "Pilate's Wife's Dream," *Complete Poems*, p. 6; R. W. Buchanan, "Liz," *Works*, 1: 123. See also Tennyson, "The Miller's Daughter," last stanza.

21. W. Wordsworth, *Literary Criticism*, p. 73. By 1829 Wordsworth's poetic credo to this effect had even won over his old enemy Francis Jeffrey who was led to define the "very essence of poetry" as "the fine perception and vivid expression of that subtle and mysterious Analogy . . . which makes outward things and qualities the natural types and emblems of inward gifts and emotions, or leads us to ascribe life and sentiment to every thing that interests us in the aspects of external nature." *Contributions to the Edinburgh Review*, 3: 284.

22. [W. J. Fox], *Westminster Review* 14 (January–April 1831), pp. 210–24, p. 217.

23. Concerning "Pathetic Fallacy in the Nineteenth Century," see J. Miles's study of this title. See also E. K. Helsinger's discussion of "pathetic fallacy" and of Ruskin's changing attitude toward Wordsworth in *Ruskin*, pp. 41ff.; and Wendell S. Johnson's recent argument, in *VP* 19 (1981), p. 20, that Ruskin's "animadversions on poetry of a certain kind are barely veiled censures of his own verse."

24. Cf. W. C. DeVane, *Browning Handbook*, p. 284.

25. See also, e.g., W. W. Story, "Ginevra da Siena," *Poems*, 3–63, p. 21: "Hark! is that he? Oh, save me from that man! / Save me! No, no, you shall not strike him here! / Stab at him through my heart, then, if you will! / Oh yes I see. 'Twas but the jarring door, / The wind." A. Webster, *Sister Annunciata, Studies*, pp. 66–67.

26. See also H. F. Wilson, "Rienzi," *Complete Collection*, 2: 158–59; and M. Blind's "Renunciation," in which a flower reminds the speaker of a moment when her former lover called her his "flower of flowers." "Ah, give me the flowers!—the last year was all / In tune with the flowers from the spring to the fall, / And with singing of

birds in the bowers; / And once—ah, look not so angry, dear!— / He whispered so softly I scarce could hear, / 'You yourself are my flower of all flowers!' " *Works*, p. 232.

27. For a more recent study of the speaker-listener relationship in Browning's dramatic monologues see D. M. Mermin, *UTQ* 45 (1975–76), pp. 139–57; idem, *Audience in the Poem*, passim.

28. M. H. Abrams's term, *Natural Supernaturalism*, p. 275.

29. The main works here are J. Thelwall's "Thoughts and Remembrances," *Poetical Recreations*, pp. 86–90; J. J. Callanan's "The Recluse of Inchidony," *Recluse*, pp. 1–22; Tennyson's *The Lover's Tale*; R. Browning's *Pauline*; Lady Emmeline Stuart-Wortley's *The Visionary, Visionary*, pp. 1–52; J. Ruskin's "Farewell," *Poems*, 2: 151–65; John Clare's "The Exile"; C.E.S. Norton's "The Poet's Choice," *Dream*, pp. 153–56, and E. H. Bickersteth's "The Two Brothers," *Poems*, pp. 86–110. For a discussion of these poems see my *Poesie*, pp. 53ff.

30. E. Johnson, *Browning Society's Papers*, 1: 279.

31. See also, e.g., R. Browning, "Clive"; W. C. Smith, "Provost Chivas," *Poetical Works*, pp. 323–28; A. Webster, "A Dilettante," who describes the listener as a "grumbler" and "chiding friend." *Portraits*, p. 133.

32. J. Davidson, *Ballads*, p. 93. Cf. A. Tennyson's "Despair."

33. J. B. Selkirk, "The Bishop Exhorteth the Sick in Hospital. (The Semi-Delirious One Replieth.)," *Poems*, pp. 182–86. Cf. R. Browning's "The Confessional." Some monologues of this kind end up being satirical portraits of the listener rather than dramatic monologues. See, e.g., Tennyson, "Lady Clara Vere de Vere"; A. Webster, "The Heiress's Wooer," *A Woman Sold*, pp. 94–95; D. M. Mulock, "To a Beautiful Woman," *Thirty*, pp. 51–52; "A Living Picture," ibid., pp. 56–57; J. Rhoades, "Two Characters," *Collected Poems*, p. 26; "A Portrait," ibid., pp. 27–28; J. B. Selkirk, "A Popular Character," *Poems*, pp. 208–10.

34. Occasionally such tension is dissolved by the speaker's persuasive powers. See, e.g., Tennyson, "Tiresias," "Northern Farmer, Old Style," "Northern Farmer, New Style"; R. Browning, "Before," "Bishop Blougram's Apology."

35. See R. Lister, *Victorian Narrative Paintings*, pp. 80–81; A. G. Reynolds, *Painters of the Victorian Scene*, reproduction 47; concerning nar-

rative painting in general, see also S. Sitwell, *Narrative Pictures*, passim.

36. L. Morris, *Works*, pp. 43–46.

37. See R. Lister, *Victorian Narrative Paintings*, pp. 78–79.

38. R. Browning's "Eurydice to Orpheus. A Picture by Leighton." Cf. J. A. Symonds, "For One of Gian Bellini's Little Angels," *Moods*, p. 16.

39. See, e.g., R.E.A. Willmott, *Poets of the Nineteenth Century*, pp. 319ff. (regarding Tennyson's *The May Queen*); ibid., p. 107 (regarding Amelia Opie's "The Orphan Boy's Tale"); E.R.B. Lytton, *Favorite Poems*, p. 83 (regarding "Good-Night in the Porch"); G. W. Thornbury, *Songs of the Cavaliers*, p. 39 (regarding "Melting of the Earl's Plate"); *Ballads*, p. 163 (regarding "In Clover. June"); Bryan W. Procter ("Barry Cornwall"), *Dramatic Scenes*, p. 319 (regarding "Seeing").

40. *Quarterly Review* 118 (July–October 1865), pp. 77–105, p. 102.

41. *Athenaeum* (June 10, 1871), p. 715.

42. W. Pater, *Studies*, p. 187. See also I. F. Bellows, *Poet-Lore* 6 (1894), p. 136.

43. W. Pater, *Studies*, p. 187. See also A. Symons, *Introduction*, pp. 9–10.

44. C. Vaughan, *British Quarterly Review* 80 (July–October 1884), p. 9.

45. Ibid., p. 7.

46. B. W. Fuson, *Browning*, pp. 31, 33, 37 and passim.

47. R.B.W. Noel, *Poems*, pp. 53–55.

48. Cf. R. Browning, "The Confessional," and A. H. Clough, "Sa Majesté très Chrétienne." See also C. D. Bell, "Confession," *Diana's Looking Glass*, pp. 70–82; J. Ingelow, "The Maid-Martyr," *Works*, pp. 762–783; A. C. Lyall, "Amor in Extremis. A garrison story of a hundred years ago." *Verses*, pp. 109–14; W. W. Story, "The Confessional," *Poems* (1885), 2: 128–41.

49. See, e.g., R. Browning, "After," "Evelyn Hope," "Too Late"; Swinburne, "The Leper"; Tennyson, "Charity"; P. B. Marston, "A Christmas Vigil," *Poems*, pp. 41–49; A. A. Procter, "Too Late," *Legends*, pp. 159–61.

50. See, e.g., W. Morris, "The Judgement of God"; E.R.B. Lytton, "Trial by Combat," *Chronicles*, 2: 60–71; G. W. Thornbury, "The Witch's Champion," *Songs of the Cavaliers*, pp. 141–44.

51. See, e.g., R. Browning, "A Woman's Last Word" and "Andrea del Sarto."

52. See, e.g., A. Tennyson, "The Flight"; E.R.B. Lytton, *The Wife's Tragedy* I. "The Evening Before the Flight," *Poems*, 2: 150–56.

53. Similarly stereotypic is the situation created by the disappearance of a specific person—see, e.g., A. Webster, "Tired," *Portraits*, p. 73; W. C. Smith, "Wee Curly Pow," *Poetical Works*, p. 289; W. W. Story, "Aunt Rachel's Story," *Poems*, 2: 105–16; "Giannone," ibid., pp. 78–104—or by someone else's words as picked up by the speaker; see, e.g., A. Tennyson, "The First Quarrel," "Charity"; R. Browning, "Imperante Augusto Natus Est—."

54. See *Oxford Book of English Verse*, pp. 110, 520; B. W. Fuson, *Browning*, pp. 38–39.

55. Cf. B. W. Fuson, *Browning*, pp. 37f.; R. Browning, "Confessions"; R. W. Buchanan, "Liz," *Works*, 1: 119–24; A. C. Doyle, "The Dying Whip," *Poems*, pp. 34–39; A. L. Gordon, "The Sick Stockrider," *Poems*, pp. 172–78; A. Gurney, "The Mother's Last Words," *Songs*, pp. 231–32; A. C. Lyall, "Theology in Extremis: Or a soliloquy that may have been delivered in India, June 1857 . . . Moriturus Loquitur," *Verses*, pp. 9–17; "A Rajpoot Chief of the Old School. Moribundus Loquitur," ibid., pp. 35–43; E.R.B. Lytton, "Jacqueline, Countess of Holland and Hainault. (1436)," *Chronicles* (1868), 2: 97–103; "Elisabetta Sirani. 1665," ibid., pp. 239–45; "Last Words of a Sensitive Second-Rate Poet," ibid., pp. 294–306; L. Morris, "A Last Will," *Works*, pp. 648–54.

56. C. Kingsley, *Poems*, pp. 275–81.

57. A. Symons, *Browning Society's Papers*, 2: 8–9. See also J. Fotheringham, *Poetry of Robert Browning*, p. 74; *National Review* 17 (July–October 1863), pp. 417–46, p. 422; *Temple Bar* 37 (March 1873), pp. 315–28, p. 315.

58. See also E.R.B. Lytton, *The Wife's Tragedy*. III. "The Last Interview," *Poems*, 2: 150–71, pp. 164f.

59. A. T. Lyttelton, *Church Quarterly Review* 7 (October 1878–January 1879), p. 73. See also A. Orr, *Contemporary Review* 23 (December 1873–May 1874), p. 948: "the increasing tendency of his so-called dramatic poems to exhibit character in the condition of motive, excludes them from any definition of dramatic art which implies the presenting it in the form of act"; and H. S. Morris, *Poet-Lore* 1 (1889), p. 411.

60. H. B. Forman, *Living Poets*, p. 225. See also [idem], *London Quarterly Review* 32 (April–July 1869), pp. 325–57, p. 332.

61. W. S. MacCormick, *Three Lectures*, p. 143.

62. *Eclectic Review* n.s. 26 (July–December 1849), pp. 203–14, p. 213.

63. See also R. W. Buchanan, "Fra Giacomo," *Works*, 1: 9.

64. G. W. Thornbury, *Songs of the Cavaliers*, pp. 158–59.

65. H. N. Howard, *Collected Poems*, pp. 434–35: "Draw near, my lord. Kneel so! Beseech! / We slaves bow down to force, / And worship boldness. / Here I reach / The point of my discourse: / I may forgive—I cannot say. / No, sir! I will not kiss! / I *do* forgive you—dog! this way! / And this—old man—and this!— / John, move that screen. Shut out the light: / . . . all is right! / Drag out my husband's corpse / . . . *That* is the first thing I have slain; / I am not nineteen yet, / I vowed to wake my love, and fly / With him to other lands. . . . [*sic*] John, let me die / Alone. . . . [*sic*] He understands." See also A. Webster, "Coming Home," *Portraits*, pp. 90–98; G. W. Thornbury, "The Jockey's Song," *Songs of the Cavaliers*, pp. 220–26; "The Witch's Champion," ibid., pp. 141–44; E.R.B. Lytton, "At Home During the Ball," *Poems*, 1: 119; P. B. Marston, "Caught in the Nets," *Poems*, p. 237; R. Browning, "A Grammarian's Funeral."

66. Similar limits regard the actual length of dramatic monologues and of the implied duration of the utterance as sometimes implied by the speaker. (See, e.g., R. Browning, "Bishop Blougram's Apology," "Imperante Augusto Natus Est—," "Master Hugues of Saxe-Gotha"; W. W. Story, "Giannone," *Poems*, pp. 78–104, p. 78: "Take a cigar—draw up your chair, / There's at least a good half-hour to spare / Before the Capuchin clock strikes one.") Thus W. E. Aytoun, in writing his two-hundred-odd-page *Bothwell*, admitted to the difficulties "of constructing a poem of this length in the form of a Monologue." *Poems*, p. 133 ("Preface to Third Edition").

67. W. W. Story, *Poems*, 2: 105–16.

68. A. Webster, *Portraits*, pp. 73–89. See also R. Browning, "Count Gismond," "Dîs Aliter Visum"; A. Tennyson, "The Northern Cobbler"; A. Gurney, "The Convict's Tale," *Songs*, p. 161; R.B.W. Noel, "The Grandmother's Story," *Poems*, p. 47.

69. An interesting variant of this pattern is found in W. W. Story's "Padre Bandelli Proses to the Duke Ludovico Sforza about Leonardo da Vinci," in which the person talked about is spied upon by the speaker and his listener: "Ah! there he is now—Would your High-

ness look / Behind that pillar in the furthest nook, / That is his velvet cap and flowing robe. / See how he pulls his beard, as up and down / He seems to count the stones he treads upon!"—The same person reappears at the conclusion: "But he approaches, in his hand the book; / Into its pages should your Highness look, / They would amuse you by their strange devices. / Your gracious presence now he recognizes; / That smile and bow and lifted cap I see / Are for his Prince and Patron, not for me." *Poems*, 2: 156, 158. Sometimes the sudden appearance of another person helps throw new light on the speaker. See, e.g., E. B. Browning, "The Runaway Slave at Pilgrim's Point"; M. Bell, "Francisca to Jaspear: A Madeiran Idyll," *Poems*, pp. 86–89; E.R.B. Lytton, "At Home During the Ball," *Poems*, 1: 114–19.

70. A. Webster, *Portraits*, p. 34.

71. P. B. Marston, *Poems*, p. 49.

72. R. W. Buchanan, *Works*, 1: 124.

73. L. Morris, *Works*, p. 46. See also Guido's words at the end of his second monologue in *The Ring and the Book*: "Who are these you have let descend my stair?" (2412).

74. R. W. Buchanan, *Works*, 1: 9.

75. E. J. Lee-Hamilton, *Dramatic Sonnets*, pp. 34–42. See also J. B. Stephens's "A Lost Chance," *Poetical Works*, pp. 59–64, whose insane speaker is taken away in the end; or W. W. Story's "Cassandra," *Poems*, 2: 155–59, who suffers a fit of insanity at the end of the monologue.

76. E. J. Lee-Hamilton, *Dramatic Sonnets*, p. 85. See also F. Heman's earlier "The Crusader's Return," quoted in B. W. Fuson, *Browning*, p. 19; and C. Swain's "Better Days," *Mind*, pp. 215–22, whose speaker finally recognizes her listener as her long lost son, whom she had been talking about. Swain, however, changes from monologue into dialogue and narrative just at the moment of this anagnorisis: "But nevermore my hope—my pride— / Will here return to bless my gaze!— / 'He *is* returned,'—the Stranger cried— / 'Returned!'— *to bring thee better days*!— / 'Thy soul shall lose its sad alarms— / A haven for thine age is won!' / She caught the Stranger in her arms— / She clasped her loved—her long-lost Son!"

77. In A. Tennyson's "Tiresias," lines 159–60. See also W. J. Linton, "Iphigenia at Aulis," *Poems*, pp. 93–94.

78. Quoted by W. C. DeVane, *Browning Handbook*, p. 137.

79. See, e.g., the end of Guido's final monologue in *The Ring and the Book*; R. Kipling, "The Night Before," *Lyrics*, pp. 5–7; J. Ingelow, "The Maid Martyr," *Works*, pp. 763–83; M. M. Lamb, "The Last Words of Don Carlos," *Poems*, 2: 111–22; A. Webster, "Jeanne d'Arc," *Studies*, pp. 29–38.

80. Cf. B. W. Fuson, *Browning*, pp. 68ff. For a more recent study of "Monodrama and the Dramatic Monologue," see A. D. Culler, *PMLA* 90 (1975), pp. 366–85.

81. W. J. Linton, *Voices of the Dead*, p. 14.

82. H. B. Forman, *Living Poets*, p. 43. See also W. Archer, *Poets*, p. 98.

83. C. Vaughan, *British Quarterly Review* 80 (July–October 1884), pp. 6, 8.

84. *North British Review* 51, n.s. 12 (October 1869–January 1870), p. 112.

85. This, by the way, was a subject often dealt with in the dramatic monologue. See, e.g., Edward H. Bickersteth, "On the Quick Movement of Mozart's Symphony in E Flat," *Poems*, pp. 30–35, "On the Slow Movement of the Same," ibid., pp. 36 40; J. R. Rodd, "A Nocturne of Chopin," *Feda*, pp. 153–54, and "A Mazurka of Chopin," *Madonna*, pp. 42–43; J. A. Symonds, "An Improvisation on the Violin. Sonata quasi una fantasia," *New*, pp. 45–48; J. Todhunter, "In a Gondola. [Suggested by Mendelssohn's Andante in G minor, Book I. Lied 6 of the 'Lieder ohne Worte.']," *Laurella*, pp. 121–24.

86. A. Symons, *Browning Society's Papers*, 2: 5.

87. J. A. Symonds, Letters, p. 215.

88. A. Orr, *Contemporary Review* 35 (April–August 1879), p. 294.

89. J. Fotheringham, *Poetry of Robert Browning*, p. 371.

90. W. C. Booth, *Rhetoric of Fiction*, pp. 153, 158–59, and passim.

91. R. W. Buchanan, *Works*, 1: 84–90; see also "Edward Crowhurst; or, 'A New Poet,' " ibid., pp. 136–47; and W. C. Smith, "Raban," *Poetical Works*, pp. 217–22.

92. H. Jay, *Robert Buchanan*, pp. 82–83.

93. R. W. Buchanan, *Works*, 1: 87, 90. See also G. H. Lewes's review of R. W. Buchanan's *Idylls and Legends of Inverburn*, in *Fortnightly Review* I (May–August 1865), p. 452, as well as W. C. Smith's use of a fictitious editor, "Hermann Künst, Philol. Professor," in *Olrig Grange*, *Poetical Works*, pp. 39–86, p. 78 and passim.

94. R. W. Buchanan, *Works*, 1: 150. See also R. Browning, "The Confessional," XII; W. E. Aytoun, "The Execution of Montrose," *Poems*, pp. 15–22, p. 21; M. Blind, "A Carnival Episode. Nice, '87," *Works*, pp. 264–69, p. 269; and R.B.W. Noel, "A Confession Scene.—A Prison Cell: Prisoner (to Clergyman loq.)," *Poems*, pp. 53–55, p. 55, where a murderer unsuccessfully tries to remember the moment when he killed his adulterous wife: "A sickning fear pressed suddenly upon me! / Why does she lie so quiet that her breath / I cannot hear! I have not killed her—no— / Impossible! She means to frighten me / For my unmanly violence but now."

95. A. C. Swinburne, *Fortnightly Review* 13, n.s. 7 (January–June 1870), p. 559. See also A. Orr, *Contemporary Review* 35 (April–August 1879), p. 291, concerning R. Browning's "Martin Relph": "The man's soul is wrestling, not with the memory of a deed, but with the phantom of a motive."

96. H. B. Forman, *Living Poets*, p. 217.

97. Ibid., p. 216.

98. Ibid., p. 217.

99. [R. W. Buchanan]. Alias Thomas Maitland. *Contemporary Review* 18 (August–November 1871), pp. 342, 343.

100. D. G. Rossetti, *Athenaeum* (December 6, 1871), p. 793.

101. *Journal of Psychological Medicine* 4 (1851), pp. 617–19.

102. Ibid., pp. 606–17.

103. Ibid., pp. 582–94.

104. Ibid., p. 617.

105. Ibid., p. 618.

CHAPTER IX

1. Information gathered from unpublished papers housed at the Wellcome Institute for the History of Medicine in London.

2. See J. Ruskin, *Works*, 6: 449.

3. L. F. Lélut, *Annales médico-psychologiques* 3 (1844), p. 162.

4. See R. Hunter and I. Macalpine, *Psychiatry 1535–1860*, p. 1064.

5. [W. J. Fox], *Westminster Review* 14 (January–April 1831), pp. 210–24, p. 216.

6. See, e.g., E. Montagu (quoted by W. J. Bate, *ELH* 12 [1945], p. 157) who in 1769 described Shakespeare's empathy as a kind of magic: "Shakespear seems to have had the art of the Dervise, in the

Arabian tales, to throw his soul into the body of another man, and be at once possessed of his sentiments, adopt his passions, and rise to all the functions and feelings of his situation." See also W. J. Bate, *From Classic to Romantic*, pp. 129ff.; H. C. Beeching, *Two Lectures*, pp. 11ff.

7. S. T. Coleridge, *Letters*, 4: 974–75.

8. W. Hazlitt, *Complete Works*, 8: 42. See also L. Hunt, *Literary Criticism*, p. 52; E. Dowden, *Contemporary Review* 2 (May–August 1866), pp. 542, 548f.

9. A. Hallam, *Writings*, p. 138.

10. [W. J. Fox], *Monthly Repository* n.s. 7 (1833), p. 253.

11. *Edinburgh Review* 172 (July–October 1890), pp. 301–16, p. 314.

12. *Bentley's Miscellany* 39 (1856), pp. 64–70, p. 64.

13. B. Smith, *Browning Society's Papers*, 1: 122. See also M. Wilkinson, *Poet-Lore* 5 (1893), p. 563; A. Groft, ibid. 1 (1889), p. 477.

14. R. W. Buchanan, *David Gray*, p. 229. See also *North British Review* 19 (May–August 1853), pp. 314f. about "the imagination of *states of feeling*."

15. [W. Pater], "Coleridge's Writings," *Westminster Review* 85, n.s. 29 (January–April 1866), pp. 106–32, p. 107.

16. [H. Sidgwick], *Westminster Review* 92, n.s. 36 (July–October 1869), pp. 363–87, p. 364.

17. C. Vaughan, *British Quarterly Review* 80 (July–October 1884), p. 17.

18. A. Orr, *Contemporary Review* 23 (December 1873–May 1874), p. 941.

19. C. Vaughan, *British Quarterly Review* 80 (July–October 1884), p. 17.

20. *Christian Remembrancer* 31 (January–June 1856), pp. 267–308, p. 282.

21. Ibid., pp. 288–89.

22. R. Buchanan, *Contemporary Review* 76 (July–December 1899), pp. 779–80. See also idem, *Contemporary Review* 77 (January–June 1900), pp. 221–30.

23. Quoted by F. Winslow, *Journal of Psychological Medicine* 11 (1858), p. 239.

24. Quoted in *Journal of Psychological Medicine* 1 (1848), pp. 38–48, pp. 40, 41.

25. Ibid., p. 42.

26. For the following, see R. Smith, *Trial by Medicine*, pp. 131ff.

27. Quoted by J. Hitchman, *Journal of Mental Science* 10 (1864–65), p. 25.

28. Quoted ibid., p. 21.

29. *Journal of Mental Science* 9 (1863–64), pp. 591–601, pp. 594, 595.

30. See R. Smith, *Trial by Medicine*, p. 210, n. 31.

31. J. Hitchman, *Journal of Mental Science* 10 (1864–65), p. 27.

32. Ibid., p. 23.

33. Ibid., p. 24.

34. Ibid. 20 (1874–75), pp. 212–24, p. 215.

35. For this and the following, see W. C. DeVane, *Browning Handbook*, pp. 373f.

36. Ibid., p. 371. Browning, in similar context, spoke of his undue liking for "the study of morbid cases of the soul" and "the physiology of wrong." Quoted by I. Jack, *Browning's Major Poetry*, p. 274.

37. Quoted by W. C. DeVane, *Browning Handbook*, p. 371.

38. J. H. Balfour-Browne, *Journal of Mental Science* 20 (1874–75), p. 215.

39. Ibid., pp. 216, 218, 219, 222, 223.

40. Ibid., p. 216.

41. See L. F. Lélut, *L'Amulette de Pascal* and *Du démon de Socrate*.

42. L. F. Lélut, *Annales médico-psychologiques* 3 (1844), pp. 157–67.

43. *Journal of Psychological Medicine* 7 (1854), pp. 1–23, pp. 1–2. Cf. ibid. 9 (1856), pp. 240–82, which speaks of "the *collective character of mental phenomena*" (p. 242). See also R. Hunter and I. Macalpine, *Psychiatry 1535–1860*, pp. 1039f., concerning the origins of the concept of "mental epidemic."

44. J. Hitchman, *Journal of Mental Science* 10 (1864–65), p. 28.

45. *Eclectic Review* n.s. 26 (July–December 1849), pp. 203–14, p. 209. See also *North British Review* 34 (November 1860–May 1861), pp. 350–74, p. 354.

46. W.P.J., *Macmillan's Magazine* 59 (November 1888–April 1889), pp. 36–40, p. 39.

47. C. Vaughan, *British Quarterly Review* 80 (July–October 1884), p. 24. See also J. H. Buckley, *Triumph of Time*, p. 22.

48. See W. O. Raymond, *Infinite Moment*, pp. 19–51; E. S. Shaffer, *"Kubla Khan,"* pp. 191–224, especially, pp. 192, 224. See also E. H. Plumptre, "Vie de Jésus par Ernest Renan," *Lazarus*, pp. 132–

37; R. W. Buchanan's comments on R. Browning's "A Death in the Desert," *David Gray*, p. 33.

49. J. R. Seeley, *Ecce Homo*, p. v. See also J. Parker, *Ecce Deus*, pp. vii–viii.

50. *British Quarterly Review* 23 (January–April 1856), pp. 151–80, p. 171.

51. A. C. Lyall, *Verses*, pp. 87–92.

52. C. Brontë, *Complete Poems*, p. 2. See also W. J. Dawson, "Pilate at Vienne," *Poems and Lyrics*, pp. 27–35; W. C. Smith, "What Pilate Thought of It," *Poetical Works*, pp. 519–27.

53. E. H. Plumptre, *Lazarus*, p. 75; cf. ibid., p. 89.

54. See *Swinburne Replies*, p. 18.

55. T. Davidson, *The Radical. A Monthly Magazine, Devoted to Religion* 3 (September 1867–June 1868), p. 3.

56. W. W. Story, *Fortnightly Review* 6 (August 15–December 1, 1866), pp. 827–36.

57. W. W. Story, *Blackwood's Magazine* 104 (July–December 1868), pp. 479–90. Regarding both poems see also H. B. Forman, *Living Poets*, pp. 158f.

58. W. W. Story, *Blackwood's Magazine* 104 (July–December 1868), p. 488.

59. Ibid., pp. 489, 481. See also H. P. Kimball, "The Saving of Judas. *After the betrayal*, Judas Iscariot communing *with himself*," *Poet-Lore* 9, n.s. 1 (1897), pp. 161–68.

60. *North American Review* 66 (1848), pp. 357–400, p. 399.

61. G. Eliot, in *Browning: Critical Heritage*, pp. 174ff.

62. J. Fotheringham, *Poetry of Robert Browning*, p. 72.

63. Ibid., p. 73. For a more recent discussion of Browning's obscurity, see P. Drew, *Browning*, pp. 70ff.

64. H. B. Carpenter, *Literary World* 13 (January–December 1882), p. 80.

65. T. McNicoll, *Essays on English Literature*, p. 305.

66. A. T. Lyttelton, *Church Quarterly Review* 7 (October 1878–January 1879), p. 67. Analyses of stream-of-consciousness techniques can, of course, be traced to earlier criticism. Wordsworth's self-professed aim, for instance, was "to illustrate the manner in which our feelings and ideas are associated in a state of excitement . . . to follow the fluxes and refluxes of the mind when agitated by the great and simple affections of our nature." *Literary Criticism*, p. 72. Also interesting

here is Wordsworth's comment on the poem that most of all his creations anticipates the dramatic monologue. "The Thorn," he argued, was to demonstrate how "superstition acts upon the mind" of certain individuals and "to shew the manner in which such men cleave to the same ideas; and to follow the turns of passion, always different, yet not palpably different, by which their conversation is swayed." Ibid., pp. 96–97. See also J. Wilson's contention that the "law of association is illustrated in [Coleridge's] 'Nightingale' more philosophically than by Hartley or Brown," *Essays*, 3: 307; F. Hemans's prefatory note to her monologue "Arabella Stuart," *Works*, 5: 137; J. A. Russell's comment on Charles Wolfe's monologue "Jugurtha Incarceratus, Vitam Ingemit Relictam," C. Wolfe, *Remains*, 1: 8.

67. P. B. Shelley, *Criticism*, p. 69. See also E. R. Wasserman, pp. 331–46 in *Romanticism*, ed. R. F. Gleckner et al.

68. P. B. Marston, *Poems*, pp. 247–49.

69. G. Barlow, *Works*, 6: 61. See also W. Miller, "The Poet's Last Song," *Willie Winkie*, pp. 24–26, p. 26; D. M. Mulock, "Looking Death in the Face," *Thirty*, pp. 19–22, p. 20.

70. A. Webster, *Studies*, pp. 95–96.

71. H. B. Forman, *Living Poets*, pp. 224–25. For a more recent discussion of the matter, see, for instance, D. A. Harris, *VP* 22 (1984), pp. 197–215.

72. See, for instance, W. Wordsworth, "The Mad Mother" and "The Idiot Boy"; S. T. Coleridge, "The Mad Monk"; J. Clare, "The Robber"; W. Motherwell, "The Madman's Love," *Poems*, pp. 45–63; G. Dyer, "The Madman. Collected by the Author from Several Characters, Seen in Different Madhouses," *Poems*, pp. 19–22; "Ode VI. Written in Bedlam: On Seeing a Beautiful Young Female Maniac," ibid., p. 23; C. Lloyd, "Stanzas on Seeing a Maniac," *Poems*, pp. 99–101. See also R. Mayo, *PMLA* 69 (1954), pp. 486–522, pp. 498ff.

73. S. Orr, *Handbook*, p. 231. See also D. Eggenschwiler's more recent interpretation of "Porphyria's Lover" in *VP* 8 (1970), pp. 39–48; as well as E. E. Kelly, *SBC* 3, 2 (Fall 1975), pp. 126–28.

74. L. Hunt, in *Tennyson: Critical Heritage*, p. 133.

75. [W. E. Aytoun], *Blackwood's Magazine* 78 (July–December 1855), pp. 311–21, p. 319.

76. *British Quarterly Review* 22 (July–October 1855), pp. 467–98, pp. 478–79.

77. For this and the following see [J. C. Bucknill], *Asylum Journal of*

Mental Science 2 (1855–56), pp. 95–104, pp. 96ff.; R. J. Mann, *"Maud" Vindicated*, pp. 63ff.

78. [J. C. Bucknill], *Asylum Journal of Mental Science* 2 (1855–56), pp. 95–104, p. 97.

79. Cf. A. Tennyson, *Poems*, ed. C. Ricks, p. 1038.

80. See the discussion of T. S. Eliot's *Waste Land* in my *Offene Formen*, pp. 123–41.

81. Cf. A. Tennyson, *Poems*, ed. C. Ricks, p. 1037.

82. Cf. W. C. DeVane, *Browning Handbook*, p. 125.

83. Quoted ibid., p. 231. R. Preyer, *ELH* 26 (1959), p. 533, relates the writing of the poem to the poet's simultaneous preoccupation, during 1852, with the "subjective poet of modern classification" in his essay on Shelley.

84. W. Morris, *Prose and Poetry*, p. 643.

85. Cf. ibid., pp. 643f.

86. Cf. W. C. DeVane, *Browning Handbook*, p. 231.

87. R. Garnett, in *William Morris: Critical Heritage*, p. 35.

88. See D. F. Sadoff's excellent interpretation of this poem in *VP* 13 (1975), pp. 22ff. See also F. Kirchhoff, *William Morris*, pp. 48–49.

89. D. F. Sadoff, *VP* 13 (1975), p. 23.

90. *William Morris to his Family*, p. 17.

91. *William Morris: Critical Heritage*, p. 46.

92. W. Pater, *Selected Works*, p. 79.

93. See also M. A. Lourie's interesting essay on the same phenomenon in William Morris's "Blue Closet" group of poems, *VP* 15 (1977), pp. 193–206; and Deborah B. Wyrick's Jungian interpretation of Morris's "Rapunzel," *VP* 19 (1981), pp. 367–81.

94. W. Pater, *Selected Works*, p. 79.

CHAPTER X

1. *Browning: Critical Heritage*, p. 368.

2. J. S. Mill, *Autobiography and Literary Essays*, p. 597.

3. See L. Hunt in A. Tennyson, *Poems*, ed. C. Ricks, p. 186.

4. Quoted in *Swinburne: Critical Heritage*, pp. xix, xx.

5. Quoted in *Swinburne Replies*, p. 1.

6. Quoted by C. K. Hyder, *Swinburne's Literary Career*, p.61.

7. [J. C. Bucknill], *Asylum Journal of Mental Science* 2 (1855–56), pp. 95–104, p. 102.

8. Quoted in *Swinburne: Critical Heritage*, p. xx.

9. H. Morley, in ibid., p. xxi.

10. *Swinburne Replies*, p. 18.

11. Quoted ibid., p. 5.

12. Quoted ibid., p. 4.

13. R. W. Buchanan, in *Swinburne: Critical Heritage*, p. 32. For a more recent discussion of the same issue, see D. G. Riede, *Swinburne*, pp. 43f.

14. C. K. Hyder, ed., *Swinburne: Critical Heritage*, p. xxi.

15. *Swinburne Replies*, p. 22.

16. *Swinburne Letters*, 1: 123.

17. *Swinburne: Critical Heritage*, p. xix.

18. *Swinburne Letters*, 1: 186.

19. *Swinburne Replies*, p. 92.

20. *Swinburne Letters*, 1: 193.

21. Ibid.

22. E. Johnson, *Browning Society's Papers*, 1: 354.

23. See *Swinburne: Critical Heritage*, p. xiii.

24. Quoted ibid., p. xviii; see also ibid., p. xix.

25. R. Browning, *Swinburne Letters*, 1: 84.

26. L. M. Findlay, *VP* 9 (1971), p. 222. See also K. McSweeney, *VS* 22 (1978–79), pp. 5–28; and C. B. Stevenson, *VP* 19 (1981), pp. 185–95.

27. A. Tennyson, *Swinburne Letters*, 1: 218. As we know, Tennyson later wrote "Lucretius" as a model of "how an indelicate subject might be treated delicately." (See O. Browning, *Memories*, p. 117.) "Happy: The Leper's Bride" was written in similar competition with Swinburne. "[As] he was reading it to me," reports Oscar Browning, he exclaimed: " 'What a mess little Swinburne would have made of this!' " Ibid.

28. J. F. Nisbet, *Insanity of Genius*, p. xvi. For a more general study of *The Mad Genius Controversy*, see G. Becker's recent study of that title.

29. R. R. Madden, *Infirmities of Genius*, 1: 9.

30. Ibid., 2: 281.

31. Ibid., p. 113.

32. Ibid., pp. 129, 130. See also *Quarterly Review* 50 (October 1833–January 1834), pp. 34–56; W. Newnham, *Essay*, passim; *British and Foreign Medical Review* 3 (January–April 1837), pp. 197–98.

33. J. C. Prichard, in *Cyclopaedia of Practical Medicine*, ed. J. Forbes et al., 3: 28.

34. *Journal of Psychological Medicine* 6 (1853), pp. 501–27, p. 501.

35. Ibid., pp. 516, 502, 513, 519, 513, 524.

36. *Journal of Mental Science* 20 (1874–75), pp. 60–74, p. 63.

37. Ibid., p. 69.

38. *Journal of Psychological Medicine* n.s. 5 (1879), pp. 30–90, pp. 68, 69.

39. Ibid., pp. 68, 69.

40. Ibid., pp. 52, 53. See also H. Maudsley, *Journal of Mental Science* 6 (1859–60), pp. 328–69. Maudsley's Poe is "Angry and envious, malignant and cynical, without sense of honour or love" (p. 367), an individual who barely escaped madness (p. 361) and whose poetry, as a result, lacks real emotion as found in Tennyson's (pp. 356ff.).

41. Cf. *Journal of Psychological Medicine* n.s. 6 (1880), pp. 33–75, pp. 61ff.; ibid. n.s. 5 (1879), pp. 30–90, pp. 47ff., 69ff.

42. Ibid., pp. 85ff.

43. *Journal of Psychological Medicine* 2 (1849), pp. 349–72, pp. 361, 358. See also ibid. n.s. 5 (1879), pp. 30–90, pp. 78ff.; *American Journal of Insanity* 5 (1848–49), pp. 206–14; *Fraser's Magazine* 10 (July–December 1834), pp. 18–32.

44. *Journal of Psychological Medicine* n.s. 5 (1879), pp. 30–90, pp. 73ff., 30ff., 34ff., 36ff., 44ff., 82ff., 85ff.

45. *Journal of Mental Science* 33 (1887–88), pp. 113–26, 303–10, 409–17; ibid. 34 (1888–89), pp. 98–113, 242–56.

46. Ibid. 34 (1888–89), pp. 108, 251.

47. *Journal of Psychological Medicine* n.s. 6 (1880), pp. 33–75, p. 68.

48. Ibid., n.s. 7 (1881), pp. 157–73, p. 157. See also I. Ray, "Illustrations of Insanity by Distinguished English Writers," *American Journal of Insanity* 4 (1847–48), pp. 97–112; "Charlotte Corday," ibid., pp. 359–68; C. Mackay, "Want of Sleep, the Real Cause of Southey's Insanity and Death," ibid., pp. 273–75; "Insanity in . . . Sir Isaac Newton, Charles Lamb, and his sister, Mary Lamb," ibid. 5 (1848–49), pp. 65–78; "Insanity of Dean Swift and His Hospital for the Insane," ibid., pp. 206–14; on J. Swift see also *Journal of Psychological Medicine* 2 (1849), pp. 349–72; "The Wear and Tear of Literary Life; or, The Last Days of Robert Southey," ibid., 5 (1852), pp. 1–41; "The Overworked Mind," ibid., pp. 257–76; "The Insanity of William Cowper," *American Journal of Insanity* 14 (1857–58),

pp. 215–40; "Charlotte Brontë—A Psychological Study," *Journal of Psychological Medicine* 11 (1858), pp. 295–317; "Dante: A Psychological Study," ibid. 12 (1859), pp. 413–28; "The Madness of Rousseau," *Journal of Mental Science* 19 (1873–74), pp. 256–59.

49. *Swinburne: Critical Heritage*, p. xx.

50. R. H. Hutton, in *Meredith: Critical Heritage*, p. 96.

51. Ibid., p. 95.

52. A. C. Swinburne, in ibid., p. 98.

53. *Swinburne as Critic*, pp. 28–29.

54. Ibid., pp. 33, 32.

55. C. Baudelaire, in *Swinburne Letters*, 1: 88.

56. See D. Dorfman, *Blake*, p. 90.

57. A. C. Swinburne, *Complete Works*, 16: 138. See also D. Dorfman, *Blake*, p. 91; and J. J. McGann, *Swinburne*, p. 51.

58. C. Y. Lang, ed., *Swinburne Letters*, 1: xviii.

59. Ibid., pp. 208–209.

60. See D. Dorfman, *Blake*, p. 75.

61. Ibid., p. 75.

62. Ibid., p. 83.

63. Quoted ibid., p. 88. See also M. D. Conway, *Fortnightly Review* n.s. 3 (January–June 1868), pp. 216–20.

64. See D. Dorfman, *Blake*, p. 73.

65. Quoted ibid., p. 71.

66. Quoted ibid., p. 72.

67. Cf. *Swinburne Letters*, 1: lxvi, 206.

68. Ibid., p. 102.

69. *Swinburne as Critic*, p. 34.

70. A. C. Swinburne, *Complete Works*, 16: 202–203. See also G. Lafourcade, *La Jeunesse de Swinburne*, 2: 354ff.

71. W. Blake, *Poetry and Prose*, p. 36.

72. *Swinburne Letters*, 1: 86.

73. A. C. Swinburne, *Complete Works*, 16: 60.

74. *Blake: Critical Heritage*, p. 66.

75. See D. Dorfman, *Blake*, pp. 72, 73.

76. A. C. Swinburne, *Complete Works*, 16: 239.

77. Ibid., pp. 246, 247.

78. *Swinburne Letters*, 2: 348.

79. A. Rimbaud, *Oeuvres complètes*, p.251.

80. A. C. Swinburne, *Complete Works*, 16: 260.

81. J. Ruskin, quoted in D. Dorfman, *Blake*, p. 39.
82. A. C. Swinburne, *Complete Works*, 16: 181.
83. *Swinburne Replies*, p. 26.
84. A. C. Swinburne, *Complete Works*, 16: 222.
85. J. Ruskin, in *Swinburne Letters*, 1: 182.
86. Ibid., p. 185. For a recent neuro- and psychopathological assessment of Swinburne's masochism and general psychological problems, see W. B. Ober, *BMC* 39, 6 (November 1975), pp. 501–55.

EPILOGUE

1. R. Browning, *Complete Works*, 5: 138.
2. Ibid.
3. Cf. W. C. DeVane, *Browning Handbook*, p. 125.
4. Cf. *Swinburne: Critical Heritage*, pp. xxv, xix.
5. G. Sarrazin, *Poètes Modernes*, p. 292.
6. See J. J. Spector, *Aesthetics of Freud*, pp. 77ff.
7. C. G. Jung, *Spirit in Man*, p. 82.
8. See A. Breton, *Manifestoes of Surrealism*, pp. 152, 175.
9. A. Rimbaud, *Oeuvres complètes*, p. 251.
10. *Journal of Psychological Medicine* 2 (1849), pp. 262–91, p. 262. See also J. B. Harrison, ibid. 3 (1850), p. 247.
11. *Journal of Psychological Medicine* 2 (1849), pp. 267, 278, 265, 275.
12. Ibid., p. 267. See also, e.g., E. Hohnbaum, *Zeitschrift für psychische Aerzte* 1 (1818), pp. 311–38; *Monthly Review* 88 (January–April 1819), pp. 192–97; *American Journal of Insanity* 5 (1848–49), pp. 65–78; *Harper's Monthly Magazine* 3 (June–November 1851), pp. 327–29; *Journal of Psychological Medicine* 5 (1852), pp. 257–76.
13. *Journal of Psychological Medicine* 2 (1849), pp. 262–91, p. 281. See also F. Winslow's discussion of the "connexion between genius and insanity" in his *Anatomy of Suicide*, pp. 121ff.
14. See E. Faas, *Shakespeare's Poetics*, pp. 139f.
15. T. B. Macaulay, *Essays*, 1: 154.
16. F. Treves, *Journal of Mental Science* 24 (1878–79), pp. 64–75, 233–43, pp. 69, 340–41.
17. *American Journal of Insanity* 5 (1848–49), pp. 377–78. See also ibid. 1 (1844–45), pp. 355–64, p. 358.
18. T. B. Macaulay, *Essays*, 1: 155, 156, 155.
19. Cf. R. Hunter and I. Macalpine, *Psychiatry 1535–1860*, p. 237.

20. This, of course, is an old tradition. See J. Lindsy, *Bedlamite Verses*, passim.

21. See, e.g., *American Journal of Insanity* 3 (1846–47), pp. 97–106, 190; ibid. 4 (1847–48), pp. 290–303; *Asylum Journal of Mental Science* 3 (1856–57), pp. 43–80. See also the series entitled "Autobiography of the Insane" published by the *Journal of Psychological Medicine* beginning in 1855. Probably the most famous document of this kind is "Perceval's Narrative," as reedited by G. Bateson in 1961.

22. Cf. *British and Foreign Medical Review* 13 (January–April 1842), pp. 412–19; *American Journal of Insanity* 3 (1846–47), pp. 97–106. See also R. Hunter and I. Macalpine, *Psychiatry 1535–1860*, p. 994.

23. P. Earle, *American Journal of Insanity* 1 (1844–45), pp. 193–224, p. 213.

24. *Journal of Psychological Medicine* 4 (1851), pp. 461–502, p. 494.

25. J. A. Symonds, Sr., *Miscellanies*, p. 188.

26. S. T. Coleridge, *Poetical Works*, p. 295.

27. Cf. C. G. Jung, *Spirit in Man*, pp. 75ff., 89ff.

28. J. Conolly, *Indications of Insanity*, p. 196.

29. Ibid., p. 190.

30. See F. Treves, *Journal of Mental Science* 24 (1878–79), pp. 64–75, 233–43.

31. J. Conolly, *Indications of Insanity*, pp. 220, 221. See also, e.g., W. C. Dendy, *Philosophy of Mystery*, pp. 80ff.; cf. L.F.A. Maury, *Annales médico-psychologiques* 11 (1848), pp. 26–40, p. 38: "Ceux qui se représentent le mieux les objets, dont les idées s'approchent le plus d'être des images, ne sont pas les métaphysiciens, les mathématiciens, les penseurs, mais les hommes à imagination vive, puissante, les femmes, les poëtes, les artistes. Chez ces derniers, l'idée revêt une forme sensible, non à la suite d'un travail préparatoire intellectuel, mais spontanément. Les idées prennent, en un mot, une autre apparence, à raison de la nature plus vive de l'imagination, par un effet sans doute de la surexcitation du système nerveux, du cerveau. Chez l'aliéné, chez l'homme en proie à une émotion violente, telle que la peur, l'idée s'offre sous la forme d'un image précisément à raison de cette surexcitation."

32. L. F. Lélut, *Dudémon de Socrate*, pp. 64ff.

33. J. Moreau (de Tours), *Du hachisch et de l'aliénation mentale* (1845).

34. J. Moreau (de Tours), *Psychologie morbide*, "Argument."

35. Ibid., p. 464.

36. See, e.g., *Journal of Psychological Medicine* 9 (1856), pp. 102–106; ibid., n.s. 1 (1861), pp. 132–42; P. Flourens, *Génie*, passim.
37. J. Conolly, *Indications of Insanity*, p. 220.
38. *Swinburne Letters*, 1: 182.
39. Quoted in *Swinburne Replies*, p. 1.
40. *Swinburne Letters*, 1: 164.
41. F. Treves, *Journal of Mental Science* 24 (1878–79), p. 74.
42. Ibid.
43. Ibid., pp. 67, 238.
44. Ibid., pp. 243, 241.

Bibliography

Abercrombie, John. *Inquiries Concerning the Intellectual Powers and the Investigation of Truth*. Edinburgh: Waugh and Innes, 1830.

Abrams, M. H. *The Mirror and the Lamp. Romantic Theory and the Critical Tradition*. New York: Norton, 1958.

―――. *Natural Supernaturalism. Tradition and Revolution in Romantic Literature*. New York: Norton, 1973.

―――. "Structure and Style in the Greater Romantic Lyric." In *From Sensibility to Romanticism*, edited by F. W. Hilles and H. Bloom, pp. 527–60. New York: Oxford University Press, 1965.

Adnès, André. *Shakespeare et la pathologie mentale*. Paris: Maloine, 1935.

Alderson, John. *An Essay on Apparitions. . . .* London: Longman, 1823.

Alexander, Franz G., and Sheldon T. Selesnick. *The History of Psychiatry: An Evaluation of Psychiatric Thought and Practice from Prehistoric Times to the Present*. New York: Harper and Row, 1966.

Allen, M. *Essay on the Classification of the Insane*. London: John Taylor, 1837.

Allott, Kenneth. "Arnold's 'Empedocles on Etna' and Byron's 'Manfred.' " *Notes and Queries* 207 (1962): 300–302.

Archer, William. *Poets of the Younger Generation*. London and New York: J. Lane, 1902.

Armstrong, Isobel. *Victorian Scrutinies: Reviews of Poetry, 1830–1870*. London: Athlone Press, 1972.

Arnold, Matthew. *The Complete Prose Works*. 11 vols. Edited by R. H. Super. Ann Arbor: The University of Michigan Press, 1960–77.

―――. *Letters, 1848–1888*. 2 vols. Collected and arranged by George W. E. Russell. New York and London: Macmillan, 1896.

―――. *The Letters of Matthew Arnold to Arthur Hugh Clough*. Edited with an introduction by Howard Foster Lowry. New York: Russell & Russell, 1968.

————. *The Poems*. Edited by Kenneth Allott. London: Longmans, 1965.

————. *Unpublished Letters*. Edited by A. Whitridge. New Haven: Yale University Press, 1923.

Aubin, R. A. *Topographical Poetry in Eighteenth-Century England*. New York: The Modern Language Association of America, 1936.

Austin, Alfred. *The Poetry of the Period*. London: Richard Bentley, 1870.

Aytoun, W. E. *Bothwell. A Poem*. Third Edition, Revised. Edinburgh and London: W. Blackwood & Sons, 1858.

————. Alias Jones, T. Percy. *Firmilian: A "Spasmodic" Tragedy*. New York: Redfield, 1854.

————. *Poems*. London: Oxford University Press, 1921.

Bagehot, Walter. *The Collected Works*. Edited by Norman St. John-Stevas. London: The Economist, 1965–.

Balfour-Browne, J. H. Review of Browning's *Red Cotton Night-Cap Country, or Turf and Towers*. *The Journal of Mental Science* 20 (1874–75): 212–24.

Ball, Patricia. *The Central Self: A Study in Romantic and Victorian Imagination*. London: Athlone Press, 1968.

Barlow, George. *The Poetical Works of George Barlow*. 10 vols. London: Henry J. Glaisher, 1902–14.

Bate, Walter J. *From Classic to Romantic: Premises of Taste in Eighteenth-Century England*. Cambridge, Mass.: Harvard University Press, 1946.

————. "The Sympathetic Imagination in Eighteenth-Century English Criticism." *English Literary History* 12 (1945): 144–64.

Battie, William. *A Treatise on Madness*. Remarks by John Monro. Introduction and Annotations by Richard Hunter and Ida Macalpine. London: Dawsons of Pall Mall, 1962.

Beattie, James. *The Philosophical and Critical Works of James Beattie*. 4 vols. Facsimile edition prepared by Bernhard Fabian. Hildesheim and New York: Georg Olms Verlag, 1974–.

Beatty, Arthur. *Browning's Verse-Form: Its Organic Character*. New York: Thesis: Columbia University 1897.

Becker, G. *The Mad Genius Controversy*. Beverly Hills, Ca.: Sage Publications, 1978.

Beeching, H. C. *Two Lectures Introductory to the Study of Poetry*. Cambridge: Cambridge University Press, 1901.

Bell, Charles D. *Diana's Looking Glass and Other Poems*. London: Arnold, 1894.

Bell, Sir Charles. *The Anatomy and Philosophy of Expression As Connected With The Fine Arts*. London: George Bell and Sons, 1893.

Bell, Mackenzie. *Collected Poems*. London: Burleigh, 1901.

Bellows, Isabel F. "Pippa Passes." *Poet-Lore* 6 (1894): 133–50.

Bennett, William C. *Poems*. London: Routledge, Warne & Routledge, 1862.

Bentley, G. E., Jr., ed. *William Blake: The Critical Heritage*. London and Boston: Routledge & Kegan Paul, 1975.

Bergman, David. "Browning's Monologues and the Development of the Soul." *English Literary History* 47 (1980): 772–87.

Bickersteth, Edward H. *Poems*. Cambridge: Macmillan, Barclay, & Macmillan, 1849.

——. *The Two Brothers* (anon.). Cambridge: Macmillan, 1845.

Bingham, Nathaniel. *Observations on the Religious Delusions of Insane Persons*. London: J. Hatchard and Son, 1841.

Blair, Hugh. *A Critical Dissertation on the Poems of Ossian*. In *The Poems of Ossian*, translated by James Macpherson, pp. 43–119. Leipzig: Bernhard Tauchnitz, 1847.

——. *Lectures on Rhetoric and Belles Lettres*. 2 vols. Edited by Harold F. Harding. Foreword by David Potter. Carbondale and Edwardsville: Southern Illinois University Press, 1965.

Blake, William. *The Poetry and Prose*. Edited by David V. Erdman. Commentary by H. Bloom. Garden City, N.Y.: Doubleday, 1965.

Blind, Mathilde. *The Poetical Works*. Edited by Arthur Symons. With a Memoir by Richard Garnett. London: T. F. Unwin, 1900.

Bliss, Isabel St. John. *Edward Young*. New York: Twayne Publishers, 1969.

Boismont, A. Brierre de. "Etudes psychologiques sur les hommes célèbres. Shakespeare." *Annales médico-psychologiques* 12 (1868): 329–45 and 1 (1869): 1–19.

Booth, Wayne C. *The Rhetoric of Fiction*. Chicago and London: University of Chicago Press, 1961.

Boulby, Mark. *Karl Philipp Moritz: At the Fringe of Genius*. Toronto: University of Toronto Press, 1979.

Braid, Jones. *Magic, Witchcraft, Animal Magnetism, Hypnotism, and Elec-*

tro-Biology. London and Edinburgh: John Churchill and A. & C. Black, 1852.

―――. *Neurypnology; or, the Rationale of Nervous Sleep, Considered in Relation with Animal Magnetism*. London and Edinburgh: John Churchill and Adam & Charles Black, 1843.

Breton, André. *Manifestoes of Surrealism*. Translated from the French by Richard Seaver and Helen R. Lane. Ann Arbor: University of Michigan Press, 1969.

Brigham, Amariah. "Insanity; Illustrated by the Histories of Distinguished Men, and by the Writings of Poets and Novelists." *American Journal of Insanity* 1 (1844–45): 9–46.

―――. *Observations on the Influence of Religion Upon the Health and Physical Welfare of Mankind*. Boston: Marsh, Capen & Lyon, 1835.

―――. *Remarks on the Influence of Mental Cultivation and Mental Excitement Upon Health*. 2d ed. Boston: Marsh, Capen & Lyon, 1833.

Brimley, George. *Essays*. Edited by William George Clark. London: Macmillan, 1882.

Brinton, Daniel G. "The New Poetic Form as Shown in Browning." *Poet-Lore* 2 (1890): 234–46.

Brodie, Sir Benjamin C. *Lectures Illustrative of Certain Local Nervous Affections*. London: Longman, 1837.

―――. *Psychological Inquiries: . . . The Mutual Relations of the Physical Organization and the Mental Faculties*. London: Longman, 1856.

Brontë, Anne, Charlotte, and Emily J. *Poems by Currer, Ellis and Acton Bell*. London: Smith, Elder,[1854].

Brontë, Charlotte. *The Complete Poems*. Edited by Clement Shorter. Bibliography and Notes by C. W. Hatfield. London: Hodder & Stoughton, [1923].

Brown, Thomas. *Lectures on the Philosophy of the Mind*. 2 vols. With a Memoir of the Author, by David Welsh. 19th ed. Edinburgh: Adam & Charles Black, 1851.

Brown, Thomas E. *The Collected Poems*. Edited by H. F. Brown, H. G. Dakyns, and W. E. Henley. London: Macmillan, 1900.

Browne, J. Crichton. "Personal Identity, and its Morbid Modifications." *The Journal of Mental Science* 8 (1862–63): 385–95, 535–45.

Browning, Elizabeth Barrett. *The Letters*. 2 vols. Edited by Frederic G. Kenyon. London: Macmillan, 1897.

―――. *Poems*. 2 vols. London: E. Moxon, 1844.

Browning, Elizabeth Barrett. *The Poetical Works*. Edited by Frederic G. Kenyon. London: Smith, Elder, 1897.

Browning, Oscar. *Memories of Sixty Years*. London: John Lane, 1910.

Browning, Robert. *The Complete Works*. Edited by Roma A. King, Jr. et al. Athens, Ohio: Ohio University Press, 1969–.

―――. *Letters*. Collected by Thomas J. Wise. Edited by Thurman L. Hood. London: Murray, 1933.

―――. *The Letters of Robert Browning and Elizabeth Barrett Barrett 1845–1846*. 2 vols. Edited by Elvan Kintner. Cambridge, Mass.: Harvard University Press, 1969.

―――. *The Poems*. 2 vols. Edited by John Pettigrew. Supplemented and completed by Thomas J. Collins. New Haven and London: Yale University Press, 1981.

―――. *The Poetical Works*. Edited by Ian Jack and Margaret Smith. Oxford: Clarendon Press, 1983–.

―――. *The Works*. 10 vols. Centenary Edition. With introductions by Sir F. G. Kenyon. London: Smith, Elder, 1912.

The Browning Society's Papers. 3 vols. London: Trübner, 1881–91.

Buchanan, Robert W. *Complete Poetical Works*. 2 vols. London: Chatto and Windus, 1901.

―――. *David Gray, and Other Essays, Chiefly on Poetry*. London: Sampson Low, Son, & Marston, 1868.

―――. *The Drama of Kings*. London: Strahan, 1871.

―――. "The Ethics of Criticism. A Word to Sir Walter Besant." *The Contemporary Review* 77 (January–June 1900): pp. 221–30.

―――― (alias Maitland, Thomas). "The Fleshly School of Poetry: Mr. D. G. Rossetti." *The Contemporary Review* 18 (August–November 1871): 333–50.

―――. "The Voice of 'The Hooligan.' " *The Contemporary Review* 76 (July–December 1899): 774–89.

Buckler, William E. *On the Poetry of Matthew Arnold: Essays in Critical Reconstruction*. New York and London: New York University Press, 1982.

Buckley, Jerome H. *The Triumph of Time: A Study of the Victorian Concepts of Time, History, Progress, and Decadence*. Cambridge, Mass.: Harvard University Press, 1967.

―――. *The Victorian Temper: A Study in Literary Culture*. Cambridge, Mass.: Harvard University Press, 1969.

Bucknill, John Charles. *The Psychology of Shakespeare*. London: Longman, 1859.

————, and Daniel H. Tuke. *A Manual of Psychological Medicine*. Philadelphia: Blanchard and Lea, 1858. Facsimile Reprint. With an introduction by Francis J. Braceland. New York and London: Hafner Publishing, 1968.

Bulwer-Lytton, E.G.E.L., 1st Baron Lytton. *England and the English*. 2 vols. New York: J. & J. Harper, 1833.

Burrows, George Man. *Commentaries on the Causes, Forms, Symptoms, and Treatment, Moral and Medical, of Insanity*. London: Thomas and George Underwood, 1828. Facsimile Reprint. New York: Arno Press, 1976.

Bushnan, J. Stevenson. "Laycock and Winslow on the Brain." *The Journal of Mental Science* 7 (1860–62): 236–75.

Byrd, Max. *Visits to Bedlam: Madness and Literature in the Eighteenth Century*. Columbia, S.C.: University of South Carolina Press, 1974.

Byron, George Gordon. *The Complete Poetical Works*. Edited by Jerome J. McGann. Oxford: At the Clarendon Press, 1980–.

————. *Letters and Journals*. 6 vols. Edited by R. E. Prothero. London: J. Murray, 1898–1901.

Campbell, Nancie, comp. *Tennyson in Lincoln. A Catalogue of the Collections in the Research Centre*. 2 vols. Lincoln: City Library, 1971, 1973.

Callanan, J. J. *The Recluse of Inchidony, and Other Poems*. London: Hurst, Chance & Co., 1830.

Carlyle, Thomas. *The Works*. 30 vols. Centenary Edition. [Edited with introductions by H. D. Traill.] London: Chapman and Hall, 1897–99.

Carpenter, H. Bernard. "Robert Browning." *The Literary World* 13 (January–December 1882): 79–80.

Carpenter, W. B. "Sleep." Vol. 4, Part I, of *Cyclopaedia of Anatomy and Physiology*. Edited by Robert B. Todd. London: Longman, 1836–59.

Chertok, Leon, and Raymond de Saussure. *The Therapeutic Revolution: From Mesmer to Freud*. Translated by Dr. R. H. Ahrenfeldt. New York: Brunner/Mazel, 1979.

Christ, Carol T. *The Finer Optic: The Aesthetic of Particularity in Victorian Poetry*. New Haven and London: Yale University Press, 1975.

Christ, Carol T. *Victorian and Modern Poetics*. Chicago: University of Chicago Press, 1984.

Clare, John. *The Poems*. 2 vols. Edited by J. W. Tibble. London: J. M. Dent & Sons, 1935.

Clough, Arthur Hugh. *The Correspondence*. 2 vols. Edited by Frederick L. Mulhauser. Oxford: Clarendon Press, 1957.

————. *The Poems*. 2d ed. Edited by F. L. Mulhauser. Oxford: Clarendon Press, 1974.

Coleridge, Samuel Taylor. *Biographia Literaria*. Edited by George Watson. London and New York: Everyman's Library, 1956.

————. *Collected Letters*. 6 vols. Edited by E. L. Griggs. Oxford: Clarendon Press, 1956–68.

————. *Lectures and Notes on Shakspere and Other English Poets*. Collected by T. Ashe. London: George Bell, 1884.

————. *Letters*. 2 vols. Edited by Ernest Hartley Coleridge. London: William Heinemann, 1895.

————. *Poetical Works*. Edited by Ernest Hartley Coleridge. London, Oxford, New York: Oxford University Press, 1969.

————. *Shakespearean Criticism*. 2 vols. Edited by Thomas M. Raysor. London and New York: Everyman's Library, 1961.

Colley, Ann C. *Tennyson and Madness*. Athens, Ga.: University of Georgia Press, 1983.

Colquhoun, J. C. *An History of Magic, Witchcraft, and Animal Magnetism*. 2 vols. London: Longman, 1851.

————. "Theory of Animal Magnetism." *Medical Quarterly Review* 2 (1834): 484–85.

A Complete Collection of the English Poems Which Have Obtained the Chancellor's Gold Medal. 2 vols. Vol. 1: Cambridge: Macmillan, 1894. Vol. 2: London: Gibbings, 1894.

Conolly, John. *An Inquiry Concerning the Indications of Insanity*. . . . London: John Taylor, 1830. Reprinted with an Introduction by Richard Hunter and Ida Macalpine. Psychiatric Monograph Series, 4. London: Dawsons of Pall Mall, 1964.

————. *A Study of Hamlet*. London: E. Moxon, 1863.

Conway, Moncure D. "Critical Notices: *William Blake: A Critical Essay*, by Algernon Charles Swinburne." *Fortnightly Review* n.s. 3 (January–June 1868): 216–20.

Cooter, Roger. *The Cultural Meaning of Popular Science: Phrenology and the Organization of Consent in Nineteenth Century Britain*. Cambridge: Cambridge University Press, 1984.

Corson, Hiram. *An Introduction to the Study of Robert Browning's Poetry*. Boston: Heath, 1899.

Coulling, Sidney M. B. "Matthew Arnold's 1853 Preface: Its Origin and Aftermath." *Victorian Studies* 7 (1964): 233–63.

Courthope, W. J. "Life in Poetry: Poetical Expression." *The Nineteenth Century* 41 (January–June 1897): 270–84.

Courtney, W. L. "Poets of To-Day." *The Fortnightly Review* 40, n.s. 34 (July–December 1883): 712–27.

Coutts-Nevill, F.B.T., Baron Latymer. *Poems*. London: John Lane, 1896.

Cox, Stephen D. *"The Stranger Within Thee": Concepts of the Self in Late-Eighteenth-Century Literature*. Pittsburgh: University of Pittsburgh Press, 1980.

Crichton, Alexander. *An Inquiry into the Nature and Origin of Mental Derangement*. 2 vols. London: T. Cadell, Jr., and W. Davies, 1798.

Culler, A. Dwight. "Monodrama and the Dramatic Monologue." *PMLA* 90 (1975): 366–85.

Dallas, Eneas Sweetland. *The Gay Science*. 2 vols. London: Chapman & Hall, 1866.

————. *Poetics: An Essay on Poetry*. London: Smith, Elder, 1852.

Davidson, John. *Ballads and Songs*. London: J. Lane, 1894.

————. *In a Music-Hall, and Other Poems*. London: Ward and Downey, 1891.

Davidson, T. "Las Veneris." *The Radical. A Monthly Magazine, Devoted to Religion* 3 (September 1867–June 1868): 316–23.

Dawson, William J. *Poems and Lyrics*. London and New York: Macmillan, 1893.

Deering, Dorothy. "The Antithetical Poetics of Arnold and Clough." *Victorian Poetry* 16 (1978): 16–31.

DeLaura, David J. "Robert Browning the Spasmodic." *Studies in Browning and His Circle* 1, 2 (Spring 1974): 55–60, 113–14.

Delepierre, Octave. "Literary Fools—Bluet D'Arbères, Guillaume Postel, Christopher Smart, and Others." *The Journal of Psychological Medicine and Mental Pathology* 12 (1859): 1–9, 169–86.

Dendy, Walter Cooper. *The Philosophy of Mystery*. London: Longman, 1841.

DePorte, Michael V. *Nightmares and Hobbyhorses: Swift, Sterne and Augustan Ideas of Madness*. San Marino, Ca.: The Huntington Library, 1974.

De Quincey, Thomas. *The Collected Writings*. New and Enlarged Edition. 14 vols. Edited by David Masson. Edinburgh: Adam and Charles Black, 1889–90. New York: AMS Press, 1968.

DeVane, William C. *A Browning Handbook*. New York: Appleton-Century-Crofts, 1955.

Digby, Anne. *Madness, Morality and Medicine*. Cambridge: Cambridge University Press, 1985.

Dobell, Sydney. *The Life and Letters of Sydney Dobell*. 2 vols. Edited by E. J.[olly]. London: Smith, Elder, 1878.

———. *The Poetical Works*. 2 vols. With Introductory Notice and Memoir by John Nichol. London: Smith, Elder, 1875.

———. *Thoughts On Art, Philosophy, and Religion: Selected From the Unpublished Papers of Sydney Dobell*. Introduction by John Nichol. London: Smith, Elder, 1876.

Dobson, Henry A. *The Complete Poetical Works*.[Edited by Alban Dobson.] London: Humphrey Milford, 1923.

Dolben, Digby M. *The Poems*. With Memoir and Letters. Edited by R. Bridges. London: Oxford University Press, 1911.

Donnelly, Michael. *Managing the Mind: A Study of Medical Psychology in Early Nineteenth-Century Britain*. London and New York: Tavistock, 1983.

Dorfman, Deborah. *Blake in the Nineteenth Century: His Reputation as a Poet from Gilchrist to Yeats*. New Haven and London: Yale University Press, 1969.

Dörner, Klaus. *Bürger und Irre; zur Sozialgeschichte und Wissenschaftssoziologie der Psychiatrie*. Frankfurt a.M.: Fischer, 1975.

Dowden, Edward. "The Poetical Feeling for External Nature." *The Contemporary Review* 2 (May–August 1866): 535–56.

Doyle, Sir Arthur Conan. *The Poems*. Collected Edition. London: John Murray, 1922.

Draper, Anita B. "The Artistic Contribution of the 'Weird Seizures' to *The Princess*." *Victorian Poetry* 17 (1979): 180–91.

Drew, Philip. *The Poetry of Browning: A Critical Introduction*. London: Methuen, 1970.

Duff, William. *An Essay on Original Genius* . . . (1767). A Facsimile Reproduction. Edited with an Introduction by John L. Mahoney. Gainesville, Fla.: Scholars' Facsimiles & Reprints, 1964.

Dunn, Richard J. "Vision and Revision: *In Memoriam* XCV." *Victorian Poetry* 18 (1980): 135–46.

Dyer, George. *Poems*. London: J. Johnson, 1800.

Earle, Pliny. "The Poetry of Insanity." *American Journal of Insanity* 1 (1844–45): 193–224.

Eggenschwiler, David. "Psychological Complexity in 'Porphyria's Lover.' " *Victorian Poetry* 8 (1970): 39–48.

Elam, Charles. *Physician's Problems*. Boston: Fields, Osgood & Co., 1869.

Eliot, George. *The George Eliot Letters*. 9 vols. Edited by Gordon S. Haight. New Haven and London: Yale University Press, 1954–78.

Eliot, T. S. *Selected Essays*. London: Faber and Faber, 1976.

Elledge, Scott. "The Background and Development in English Criticism of the Theories of Generality and Particularity." *Publications of the Modern Language Association* 62 (1947): 147–82.

Elledge, Scott, ed. *Eighteenth-Century Critical Essays*. 2 vols. Ithaca, N.Y.: Cornell University Press, 1961.

Ellenberger, Henri F. *The Discovery of the Unconscious: The History and Evolution of Dynamic Psychiatry*. New York: Basic Books, 1970.

———. "Mesmer and Puysegur: From Magnetism to Hypnotism." *Psychoanalytic Review* 52 (1965): 281–97.

Elliott, G. R. "Shakespeare's Significance for Browning." *Anglia* 32, n.s. 20 (1909): 90–162.

Ellison, Henry. *The Poetry of Real Life*. London: John Lee, 1844.

Ellrodt, Robert. "Self-Consciousness in Montaigne and Shakespeare." *Shakespeare Survey* 28 (1975): 37–50.

Engell, J. *The Creative Imagination: Enlightenment to Romanticism*. Cambridge, Mass.: Harvard University Press, 1981.

Ennemoser, Joseph. *The History of Magic*. 2 vols. Translated by William Howitt. Edited by Mary Howitt. Introduction by Omar V. Garrison. New Hyde Park, N.Y.: University Books, 1970.

———. *Der Magnetismus im Verhältnisse zur Natur und Religion*. Stuttgart und Tübingen: J. G. Cotta'scher Verlag, 1842.

Esquirol, Jean Etienne Dominique. *Des maladies mentales*. . . . 2 vols. Paris: Chez J.-B. Baillière, 1838.

Etienne, M. Louis. "Une nouvelle forme de poésie dramatique: Robert Browning." *Revue des deux mondes* 85 (January–February 1870): 704–35.

Evans, Sebastian. *Brother Fabian's Manuscript; and Other Poems*. London: Macmillan, 1865.

———. *In the Studio: A Decade of Poems*. (Poems by J. Charlier de Gerson. . . . Translated from the Latin.) London: Crystal Palace, 1875.

Faas, Ekbert. "Die deskriptive Dichtung als Wegbereiter der romantischen Naturlyrik in England." *Germanisch-Romanische Monatsschrift* n.s. 22 (1972): 142–61.

———. "Dramatischer Monolog und dramatisch-monologische Versdichtung." *Anglia* 87 (1969): 338–66.

———. "Formen der Bewusstseinsdarstellung in der dramatischen Lyrik Pounds und Eliots. (Eine Interpretation von *The Love Song of J. Alfred Prufrock*)." *Germanisch-Romanische Monatsschrift* n.s. 18 (1968): 172–91.

———. "Notes Towards a History of the Dramatic Monologue." *Anglia* 88 (1970): 222–32.

———. *Offene Formen. Zur Entstehung einer neuen Ästhetik*. Munich: Goldmann Verlag, 1975.

———. *Poesie als Psychogramm. Die dramatisch-monologische Versdichtung im viktorianischen Zeitalter*. Munich: Wilhelm Fink Verlag, 1974.

———. *Shakespeare's Poetics*. Cambridge: Cambridge University Press, 1986.

———. *Tragedy and After: Euripides, Shakespeare, Goethe*. Kingston and Montreal: McGill-Queen's University Press, 1984.

Farren, George. *Observations on the Laws of Mortality and Disease, . . . With an Appendix, Containing Illustrations of the Progress of Mania, Melancholia, Craziness, and Demonomania, as Displayed in Shakespeare's Characters of Lear, Hamlet, Ophelia, and Edgar*. London: Dean and Munday, 1829.

Faulkner, Peter, ed. *William Morris: The Critical Heritage*. London and Boston: Routledge & Kegan Paul, 1973.

Ferriar, John. *An Essay Towards a Theory of Apparitions*. London: Cadell & Davies, 1813.

"Field, Michael" [i.e., Katherine H. Bradley and Edith E. Cooper]. *Dedicated: An Early Work*. London: G. Bell & Sons, 1914.

————. Selections. Compiled by T. Sturge Moore. London: Poetry Bookshop, 1923.

Figuier, Louis. *Histoire du merveilleux dans les temps modernes.* 4 vols. Paris: Librairie de L. Hachette, 1860.

Findlay, Leonard M. "Swinburne and Tennyson." *Victorian Poetry* 9 (1971): 217–36.

Flourens, P. *De la raison du génie et de la folie.* Paris: Garnier Frères, 1861.

Forman, H. Buxton. *Our Living Poets: An Essay in Criticism.* London: Tinsley Brothers, 1871.

————. Review of W. W. Story's *Graffiti D'Italia.* *The Fortnightly Review* 11, n.s. 5 (January–June 1869): 117–20.

Fotheringham, James. *Studies in the Poetry of Robert Browning.* London: Kegan Paul, 1887.

Foucault, Michel. *Madness and Civilization; a History of Insanity in the Age of Reason.* Translated from the French by Richard Howard. New York: Vintage Books, 1973.

Fuller, Robert C. *Mesmerism and the American Cure of Souls.* Philadelphia: University of Pennsylvania Press, 1982.

Fuson, B. W. *Browning and his English Predecessors in the Dramatic Monolog.* Iowa City: State University of Iowa Humanistic Studies, vol. 8, 1948.

————. "Tennyson's Chronological Priority Over Browning in Use of the Dramatic Monolog Before 1836." *Studies,* Kobe College (Nishionomiya, Japan), 8, No. 3 (No. 39, 1967): 1–23.

Fussell, Paul, Jr. *Poetic Meter and Poetic Form.* New York: Random House, 1965.

————. *Theory of Prosody in Eighteenth-Century England.* College Monograph, No. 5. New London: Connecticut College, 1954.

Gale, Norman Rowland. *Collected Poems.* London: Macmillan, 1914.

Gasquet, J. R. "The Madmen of the Greek Theatre." *The Journal of Mental Science* 18 (1872–73): 1–8, 174–78, 355–60, 475–82; 19 (1873–74): 47–53, 217–22, 533–40; ibid. 20 (1874–75): 44–48. 48.

Gerard, Alexander. *An Essay on Taste* (1759). A Facsimile Reproduction of the Third Edition (1780). With an Introduction by Walter J. Hipple, Jr. Gainesville, Fla: Scholars' Facsimiles & Reprints, 1963.

Gilman, Sander L., ed. *The Face of Madness: Hugh W. Diamond and the Origin of Psychiatric Photography*. New York: Brunner/Mazel, 1976.

Goethe, Johann Wolfgang von. *Urfaust. Faust I und II, Paralipomena, Goethe über "Faust."* Herausgegeben von W. Dietze. Berlin: Aufbau Verlag, 1973.

Gordon, Adam L. *The Poems*. London and Edinburgh: T. N. Foulis, 1912.

Gottfried, Leon. *Matthew Arnold and the Romantics*. London: Routledge & Kegan Paul, 1963.

Grau, Kurt J. *Die Entwicklung des Bewusstseinsbegriffes im XVII und XVIII Jahrhundert*. Abhandlungen zur Philosophie und ihrer Geschichte. Edited by B. Erdmann. 39. Heft. Halle a.S., 1916.

[Gray, Robert.] *The Theory of Dreams. . . .* 2 vols. London: F. C. and J. Rivington, 1808.

Groft, Alice. "The True Greatness of Browning." *Poet-Lore* 1 (1889): 470–79.

Groote, Michèle Ristich de. *La folie à travers les siècles*. Paris: Robert Laffont, 1967.

Gurney, Archer. *Songs of the Present*. London, 1854.

Haley, Bruce. *The Healthy Body and Victorian Culture*. Cambridge, Mass.: Harvard University Press, 1978.

Halford, Sir Henry. "Shakespeare's Test of Insanity." In *Essays and Orations. . . .* 2d ed., pp. 42–56. London: John Murray, 1833.

Hall, Jason Y. "Gall's Phrenology: A Romantic Psychology." *Studies in Romanticism* 16 (1977): 305–17.

Hallam, Arthur Henry. *Remains in Verse and Prose*. London: John Murray, 1863.

———. *The Writings of Arthur Henry Hallam*. Now first collected and edited by T. H. Vail Motter. New York: Modern Language Association, and London: Oxford University Press, 1943.

Hamilton, Sir William. *Lectures on Metaphysics*. 4 vols. Edited by H. L. Mansel and John Veitch. 6th ed. Edinburgh and London: William Blackwood and Sons, 1872.

Hamilton, Walter, ed. *Parodies of the Works of English and American Authors*. 6 vols. London: Reeves & Turner, 1884–89.

Hancher, Michael. "The Dramatic Situation in Browning's 'Pauline.' " *Yearbook of English Studies* 1 (1971): 149–59.

Hardy, Thomas. *The Complete Poetical Works*. 3 vols. Edited by Samuel Hynes. Oxford: At the Clarendon Press, 1982–85.

Harris, Daniel A. "D. G. Rossetti's 'Jenny': Sex, Money, and the Interior Monologue." *Victorian Poetry* 22 (1984): 197–215.

Harrison, James Bower. "The Human Mind Considered in Some of its Medical Aspects." *The Journal of Psychological Medicine and Mental Pathology* 3 (1850): 246–62.

Hawker, Robert Stephen. *The Poetical Works*. Edited by A. Wallis. London: J. Lane, 1899.

Hayter, Alethea. *Opium and the Romantic Imagination*. London: Faber & Faber, 1968.

Hazlitt, William. *The Complete Works*. 21 vols. Edited by P. P. Howe, after the edition of A. R. Waller and Arnold Glover. London and Toronto: J. M. Dent and Sons, 1930–34.

Helsinger, Elizabeth K. *Ruskin and the Art of the Beholder*. Cambridge, Mass. and London: Harvard University Press, 1982.

Hemans, Felicia. *The Works*. 7 vols. Memoir by her sister [H. Hughes]. Edinburgh: W. Blackwood & Sons, 1839.

Hennig, Richard. "Beiträge zur Psychologie des Doppel-Ichs." *Zeitschrift für Psychologie* 49 (1908): 1–55.

Hibbert, Samuel. *Sketches of the Philosophy of Apparitions; or, An Attempt to Trace Such Illusions to Their Physical Causes*. Edinburgh: Oliver & Boyd, 1824.

Hitchman, John. "An Interview with Victor Townley, and Reflections thereon." *The Journal of Mental Science* 10 (1864–65): 21–34.

Hohnbaum, E. "Ueber die poetische Ekstase im fieberhaften Irreseyn." *Zeitschrift für psychische Aerzte* 1 (1818): 311–38.

Holland, Henry. *Medical Notes and Reflections*. 2d ed. London: Longman, 1840.

Holmes, Richard. *Shelley: The Pursuit*. London: Weidenfeld and Nicolson, 1974.

Home, Henry, Lord Kames. *Elements of Criticism*. 3 vols. Edinburgh: A. Millar, A. Kincaid, & J. Bell, 1762; Facsimile Reprint. Anglistica & Americana, 53. Selected by B. Fabian et al. Hildesheim and New York: Georg Olms Verlag, 1970.

Honan, Park. *Browning's Characters: A Study in Poetic Technique*. New Haven: Yale University Press, 1961.

———. *Matthew Arnold: A Life*. New York: McGraw-Hill, 1981.

Horne, Richard H. "Madness, As Treated by Shakspere." *The Journal of Psychological Medicine and Mental Pathology* 2 (1849): 589–607.

Horne, Richard H. *Soliloquium Fratris Rogeri Baconis, Anno Domini 1292: (Being the tenth year of his imprisonment)*. London: Privately printed [Dryden Press], 1882. "Reprinted from *Fraser's Magazine*, July, 1882."

Houghton, Walter E. "Arnold's 'Empedocles on Etna.' " *Victorian Studies* 1 (1958): 311–36.

———. *The Poetry of Clough: An Essay in Revaluation*. New Haven and London: Yale University Press, 1963.

———. *The Victorian Frame of Mind, 1830–1870*. New Haven and London: Yale University Press, 1957.

Howard, Henry Newman. *Collected Poems*. London: Macmillan, 1913.

Hudson, W. H. *Studies in Interpretation: Keats, Clough, Matthew Arnold*. New York: G. P. Putnam's Sons, 1896.

Hughes, Winifred. "E. S. Dallas: Victorian Poetics in Transition." *Victorian Poetry* 23 (1985): 1–21.

Hugo, Victor. *William Shakespeare*. Translated by Melville B. Anderson. Chicago: A. C. McClurg & Co., 1887.

Hunt, Leigh. *Imagination and Fancy; with . . . an Essay in Answer to the Question "What is Poetry?"* London: Smith, Elder, 1844.

———. *Literary Criticism*. Edited by L. H. and C. W. Houtchens. With an Essay, "Leigh Hunt as Man of Letters" by C. D. Thorpe. New York: Columbia University Press, 1956.

Hunter, Richard, and Ida Macalpine. *Three Hundred Years of Psychiatry 1535–1860*. London: Oxford University Press, 1963.

Hurd, Richard. *The Works*. 8 vols. London: T. Cadell & W. Davies, 1811. Reprinted New York: AMS Press, 1967.

Hyder, Clyde K., ed. *Swinburne: The Critical Heritage*. London: Routledge & Kegan Paul, 1970.

Hyder, Clyde K. *Swinburne's Literary Career and Fame*. Durham, N.C.: Duke University Press, 1933.

Ingelow, Jean. *The Poetical Works*. London: Longmans, 1898.

Innes, Arthur D. *Seers and Singers: A Study of Five English Poets*. London: A. D. Innes, 1893.

Irvine, William, and Park Honan. *The Book, the Ring & the Poet: A Biography of Robert Browning*. New York: McGraw-Hill, 1974.

Jack, Ian. *Browning's Major Poetry*. Oxford: Clarendon Press, 1973.

Jackson, J. R. de J., ed. *Coleridge: The Critical Heritage*. London: Routledge & Kegan Paul, 1970.

Jarvis, Edward. "What Shall We Do with the Insane?" *The North American Review* 56 (1843): 171–91.

Jay, Harriett. *Robert Buchanan: Some Account of His Life, His Life's Work and His Literary Friendships*. London: T. Fisher Unwin, 1903.

Jeffrey, Francis, Lord Jeffrey. *Contributions to the Edinburgh Review*. 4 vols. London: Longman, Brown, 1844.

Johnson, E. "Conscience and Art in Browning." In *The Browning Society's Papers*. 1: 345–80. London: Trübner, 1881–91.

————. "On 'Bishop Blougram's Apology,' " In *The Browning Society's Papers*. 1: 279–92. London: Trübner, 1881–91.

Johnson, Wendell Stacy. "Memory, Landscape, Love: John Ruskin's Poetry and Poetic Criticism." *Victorian Poetry* 19 (1981): 19–34.

Jump, John D., ed. *Tennyson: The Critical Heritage*. London: Routledge & Kegan Paul, 1967.

Jung, Carl Gustav. *The Spirit in Man, Art, and Literature*. Translated by R.F.C. Hull. Bollingen Series XX. Princeton, N.J.: Princeton University Press, 1971.

Kaplan, Fred. *Dickens and Mesmerism: the Hidden Springs of Fiction*. Princeton, N.J.: Princeton University Press, 1975.

————. " 'The Mesmeric Mania': The Early Victorians and Animal Magnetism." *Journal of the History of Ideas* 35 (1974): 691–702.

————. *Miracles of Rare Device. The Poet's Sense of Self in Nineteenth-Century Poetry*. Detroit: Wayne State University Press, 1972.

Keats, John. *The Letters*. Edited by M. B. Forman. 3rd ed. London: Oxford University Press, 1947.

Keble, John. *Lectures on Poetry, 1832–1841*. 2 vols. Translated by E. K. Francis. Oxford: At the Clarendon Press, 1912.

Kellogg, A. O. *Shakspeare's Delineations of Insanity, Imbecility, and Suicide*. New York: Hurd and Houghton, 1866.

Kelly, Edward E. "Porphyria's Lover: Fantasizer, Not Speaker." *Studies in Browning and His Circle* 3, 2 (Fall 1975): 126–28.

Kerner, Justinus. *The Seeress of Prevorst: Being Revelations Concerning the Inner-Life of Man, and the Interdiffusion of a World of Spirits in the One We Inhabit*. Translated by Catherine Crowe. London: J. C. Moore, 1845.

Kimball, Hannah P. "The Saving of Judas. *After the betrayal*, Judas Iscariot communing *with himself*." *Poet-Lore* 9, n.s. 1 (1897): 161–68.

King, Everard H. *James Beattie*. Boston: Twayne Publishers, 1977.

Kingsley, Charles. *Poems.* [With a preface to "The Saint's Tragedy" by J.F.D. Maurice.] London: Macmillan, 1889.

Kipling, Rudyard. *Rudyard Kipling's Verse: Definitive Edition.* London: Hodder & Stoughton, 1966.

———. *Schoolboy Lyrics.* Lahore: "Civil and Military Gazette" Press, 1881.

Kirchhoff, Frederick. *William Morris.* Boston: Twayne Publishers, 1979.

Knoepflmacher, U. C. "Dover Revisited: The Wordsworthian Matrix in the Poetry of Matthew Arnold." *Victorian Poetry* 1 (1963): 17–26.

Kovalewsky, P. J. "*Folie du doute.*" *The Journal of Mental Science* 33 (1887–88): 209–18.

Kramer, Lawrence. "The 'Intimations' Ode and Victorian Romanticism." *Victorian Poetry* 18 (1980): 315–35.

Lafourcade, G. *La jeunesse de Swinburne, 1837–1867.* 2 vols. Paris: Publications de la Faculté des Lettres de l'Université de Strasbourg. Fasc. 44, 45, 1928.

Lamb, Charles. *Lamb as Critic.* Edited by Roy Park. Lincoln and London: University of Nebraska Press, 1980.

Lamb, Mary M. (later Singleton, later Lady Currie) ("Violet Fane"). *Poems.* 2 vols. London: J. C. Nimmo, 1892.

Landon, Laetitia E. *The Poetical Works.* Edited by W. B. Scott. London, [1873].

Langbaum, Robert. *The Mysteries of Identity: A Theme in Modern Literature.* New York: Oxford University Press, 1977.

———. *The Poetry of Experience. The Dramatic Monologue in Modern Literary Tradition.* New York: Norton, 1963.

Laycock, Thomas. *An Essay on Hysteria.* . . . Philadelphia: Haswell, Barrington, and Haswell, 1840.

———. "Reflex, Automatic, and Unconscious Cerebration: A History and a Criticism." *Journal of Mental Science* 21 (1875–76): 477–98.

Leary, David E. "German Idealism and the Development of Psychology in the Nineteenth Century." *Journal of the History of Philosophy* 18 (1980): 299–317.

———. "Immanuel Kant and the Development of Modern Psychology." In *The Problematic Science: Psychology in Nineteenth-Century Thought.* Edited by William R. Woodward and Mitchell G. Ash. New York: Praeger, 1982, 17–41.

Lee-Hamilton, Eugene J. *Dramatic Sonnets, Poems, and Ballads: Selections from the Poems of E. Lee-Hamilton*. With an Introduction by William Sharp. London: The Canterbury Poets, 1903.

Lefebure, Molly. *Samuel Taylor Coleridge: A Bondage of Opium*. London: Victor Gollancz, 1974.

Lélut, L. F. *L'Amulette de Pascal: Pour servir à l'histoire des hallucinations*. Paris: J. B. Baillière, 1846.

———. "Cadre de la philosophie de l'homme." *Annales médico-psychologiques* 3 (1844): 157–67.

———. *Du démon de Socrate: Spécimen d'une application de la science psychologique à celle de l'histoire*. Paris: J. B. Baillière, 1856.

Lewes, George Henry. *Literary Criticism*. Edited by A. R. Kaminsky. Lincoln: University of Nebraska Press, [1964].

———. Review of R. W. Buchanan's *Idylls*. . . . *The Fortnightly Review* 1 (May–August 1865): 443–58.

Lindsy, J., ed. *Loving Mad Tom: Bedlamite Verses of the XVI and XVII Centuries*. Foreword by Robert Graves. Welwyn Garden City: Seven Dials Press, 1969.

Linton, William J. *Poems and Translations*. London: J. C. Nimmo, 1889.

———. *Voices of the Dead*. . . . [New Haven: 1879.]

Lister, Raymond. *Victorian Narrative Paintings*. London: Museum Press, 1966.

Litzinger, B. and D. Smalley, eds. *Browning: The Critical Heritage*. London: Routledge & Kegan Paul, 1970.

Lloyd, Charles. *Desultory Thoughts in London: Titus and Gisippus; with Other Poems*. London: C. and H. Baldwyn, 1821.

———. *Poems on Various Subjects*. Carlisle: Penrith, 1795.

Lombroso, Cesare. *The Man of Genius*. London: Walter Scott, 1891.

Lourie, Margaret A. "The Embodiment of Dreams: William Morris' 'Blue Closet' Group." *Victorian Poetry* 15 (1977): 193–206.

Lowth, Robert. *Lectures on the Sacred Poetry of the Hebrews*. 2 vols. Translated from the Latin by G. Gregory. London, 1787.

Lyall, Sir Alfred C. *Verses Written in India*. 4th ed. London: Kegan Paul, 1896.

Lyons, John O. *The Invention of the Self: The Hinge of Consciousness in the Eighteenth Century*. Carbondale: Southern Illinois University Press, 1978.

Lyttelton, A. T. "Mr. Browning's Poems." *The Church Quarterly Review* 7 (October 1878–January 1879): 65–92.

Lytton, E. R. Bulwer, 1st Earl of Lytton ("Owen Meredith"). *Chronicles and Characters*. 2 vols. London: Chapman & Hall, 1868.

———. *Favorite Poems*. Boston: Osgood, 1877.

———. *Poems*. 2 vols. Boston: Fields, Osgood, 1869.

Macario, M. "Des rêves considérés sous le rapport physiologique et pathologique." *Annales médico-psychologiques* 8 (1846): 170–218.

———. *Du sommeil des rêves et du somnambulisme dans l'état de santé et de maladie*. Lyon and Paris: Perisse Frères, 1857.

Macaulay, Thomas Babington, 1st Baron Macaulay. *Critical and Historical Essays*. 2 vols. Arranged by A. J. Grieve. London and New York: Everyman's Library, 1907.

MacCormick, William S. *Three Lectures on English Literature*. Paisley and London: Alexander Gardner, 1889.

McGann, Jerome J. *Swinburne: An Experiment in Criticism*. Chicago and London: University of Chicago Press, 1972.

McGuinness, Arthur Edward. *Henry Home, Lord Kames*. New York: Twayne, 1970.

Mackay, Charles. *Memoirs of Extraordinary Popular Delusions*. 3 vols. London: Richard Bentley, 1841.

———. *The Poetical Works*. London: F. Warne, 1876.

———. "Want of Sleep, the Real Cause of Southey's Insanity and Death." *American Journal of Insanity* 4 (1847–48): 273–75.

McNicoll, Thomas. *Essays on English Literature*. London: B. M. Pickering, 1861.

MacNish, Robert. *The Philosophy of Sleep*. Hartford: Silas Andrus & Son, 1854.

McSweeney, Kerry. "Swinburne's Tennyson." *Victorian Studies* 22 (1978–79): 5–28.

Madden, R. R. *The Infirmities of Genius*. 2 vols. London: Saunders & Otley, 1833.

———. *Phantasmata or Illusions and Fanaticisms of Protean Forms Productive of Great Evils*. 2 vols. London: T. C. Newby, 1857.

Mann, R. J. *Tennyson's "Maud" Vindicated: An Explanatory Essay*. London: Jarrold & Sons, 1856.

Marshall, George O., Jr. "Tennyson's 'Oh! That 'Twere Possible': A Link between *In Memoriam* and *Maud*." *PMLA* 78 (1963): 225–29.

Marston, Philip B. *The Collected Poems*. With Biographical Sketch by L. C. Moulton. London: Ward & Lock, 1892.

Martin, Robert Bernard. *Tennyson: The Unquiet Heart*. Oxford: Clarendon Press, 1980.

Mason, Michael. "Browning and the Dramatic Monologue." In *Writers and Their Background: Robert Browning*, edited by Isobel Armstrong, 231–66. Athens: Ohio University Press, 1975.

Maudsley, Henry. "Edgar Allan Poe." *The Journal of Mental Science* 6 (1859–60): 328–68.

———. "Recent Metaphysics." *The Journal of Mental Science* 11 (1865–66): 533–56.

Maury, L. F. Alfred. "The Ecstatic Mystics and the Stigmatics." *Asylum Journal of Mental Science* 2 (1855–66): 104–11.

———. "Des hallucinations hypnagogiques, ou des erreurs des sens dans l'état intermédiaire entre la veille et le sommeil." *Annales médico-psychologiques* 11 (1848): 26–40.

———. *La magie et l'astrologie dans l'antiquité et au moyen age. . . .* Paris: Librairie Académique, Didier et Cie., 1860.

———. "On Animal Magnetism and Somnambulism." *The Journal of Mental Science* 7 (1860–62): 76–96.

———. *Le sommeil et les rêves: Etudes psychologiques sur ces phénomènes. . . .* Paris: Librairie Académique, Didier et Cie., 1861.

Maynard, John. *Browning's Youth*. Cambridge, Mass.: Harvard University Press, 1977.

———. "Robert Browning's Evangelical Heritage." *Browning Institute Studies* 3 (1975): 1–16.

Mayo, Robert. "The Contemporaneity of the *Lyrical Ballads*." *Publications of the Modern Language Association of America* 69 (1954): 486–522.

Meredith, George. *The Poems*. 2 vols. Edited by Phyllis B. Bartlett. New Haven and London: Yale University Press, 1978.

Mermin, Dorothy M. *The Audience in the Poem: Five Victorian Poets*. New Brunswick, N.J.: Rutgers University Press, 1983.

———. "Speaker and Auditor in Browning's Dramatic Monologues." *University of Toronto Quarterly* 45 (1976): 139–57.

Miles, A. H., ed. *The Poets and the Poetry of the Century*. 9 vols. London: Hutchinson, 1899.

Miles, Josephine. *Pathetic Fallacy in the Nineteenth Century: A Study of a*

Changing Relation Between Object and Emotion. New York: Octagon Books, 1965.

Mill, James. *Analysis of the Phenomena of the Human Mind*. 2 vols. A New Edition with Notes by A. Bain, A. Findlater, and G. Grote. Edited with Additional Notes by J. S. Mill. London: Longmans, 1869.

Mill, John Stuart. *Autobiography and Literary Essays*. Vol. 1 of *Collected Works*. Edited by John M. Robson and Jack Stillinger. Toronto: University of Toronto Press, 1981.

————. *An Examination of Sir William Hamilton's Philosophy*. Vol. 9 of *Collected Works*. Editor of the text, John M. Robson. Introduction by Alan Ryan. Toronto: University of Toronto Press, 1979.

Miller, William. *Willie Winkie and Other Songs and Poems*. Edited by R. Ford. Paisley and London: Alexander Gardner, 1902.

Mineka, Francis Edward. *The Dissidence of Dissent: "The Monthly Repository," 1806–1838*. Chapel Hill: University of North Carolina Press, 1944.

Miyoshi, Masao. *The Divided Self: A Perspective on the Literature of the Victorians*. New York: New York University Press, 1969.

————. "Mill and 'Pauline': The Myth and Some Facts." *Victorian Studies* 9 (1965–66): 154–63.

Moorman, Mary. *William Wordsworth: The Early Years*. London: Oxford University Press, 1968.

Moreau (de Tours), Joseph. *Du hachisch et de l'aliénation mentale suivi de recherches sur les aliénés en Orient*. Yverdon: Kesselring, 1974.

————. *La psychologie morbide.* . . . Paris: Librairie Victor Masson, 1859.

Morgan, Thaïs E. "Swinburne's Dramatic Monologues: Sex and Ideology." *Victorian Poetry* 22 (1984): 175–95.

Morison, Sir Alexander. *The Physiognomy of Mental Diseases*. London: Longman & Co., 1843.

Moritz, Karl Philipp. *Magazin zur Erfahrungsseelenkunde.* . . . Berlin: August Mylius, 1783–93. Facsimile Reprint. Lindau: Antiqua-Verlag, 1979.

Morris, Harrison S. "Browning Versus Browning." *Poet-Lore* 1 (1889): 408–21.

Morris, Sir Lewis. *The Works*. London: Kegan Paul, 1907.

Morris, William. *The Letters of William Morris to His Family and Friends*. Edited by Philip Henderson. London: Longmans, Green, 1950.

————. *Prose and Poetry (1856–1870)*. London: Oxford University Press, 1920.

Morton, Edward P. "Ruskin's 'Pathetic Fallacy' and Keats' Treatment of Nature." *Poet-Lore* 12, n.s. 4 (1900): 58–70.

Motherwell, William. *Poems Narrative and Lyrical*. Boston: William D. Ticknor, 1844.

Mulock, Dinah M., later Craik. *Thirty Years: Being Poems, New and Old*. London: Macmillan, 1881.

Murray, Robert Fuller. *The Scarlet Gown.* . . . St. Andrews: A. M. Molden, 1891.

Myers, Frederic W. H. *Collected Poems*. With Autobiographical and Critical Fragments. Edited by E. Myers. London: Macmillan, 1921.

Nesbit, Edith (later Bland). *Ballads and Lyrics of Socialism, 1883–1908*. London: A. C. Fifield, 1908.

Newnham, W. *Essay on the Disorders Incident to Literary Men.* . . . London: Hatchard, 1836.

Nichol, J. *The Death of Themistocles, and Other Poems*. Glasgow: J. Maclehose, 1881.

Nisbet, J. F. *The Insanity of Genius and the General Inequality of Human Faculty Physiologically Considered*. London: Grant Richards, 1900.

Noel, Roden B. W. *The Collected Poems*. With a Notice by John Addington Symonds. Introduction by Lady Victoria Buxton. London: Kegan Paul, 1902.

Norton, Caroline E. S. *The Dream, and Other Poems*. London: Henry Colburn, 1840.

Ober, William B. "Swinburne's Masochism: Neuropathology and Psychopathology." *Bulletin of the Menninger Clinic* 39, No. 6 (1975): 501–55.

Ong, Walter J. "Psyche and the Geometers: Aspects of Associationist Critical Theory." *Modern Philology* 49 (1951–52): 16–27.

Orr, A. "Mr. Browning's Dramatic Idylls." *The Contemporary Review* 35 (April–August 1879): 289–302.

————. "Mr. Browning's Place in Literature." *The Contemporary Review* 23 (December 1873–May 1874): 934–65.

Orr, Sutherland. *A Handbook to the Works of Robert Browning*. London: G. Bell & Sons, 1937.

Palgrave, Francis T. *Idyls and Songs*. London: John W. Parker, 1854.

Palmer, D. J. "Tennyson's Romantic Heritage." In *Writers and Their Background: Tennyson*, edited by D. J. Palmer, 23–51. London: G. Bell & Sons, 1973.

Parker, Joseph. *Ecce Deus: Essays on the Life and Doctrine of Jesus Christ, With Controversial Notes on "Ecce Homo."* London: Hodder, 1868.

Parry-Jones, William Ll. *The Trade in Lunacy: A Study of Private Madhouses in England in the Eighteenth and Nineteenth Centuries*. London: Routledge & Kegan Paul, 1972.

Parssinen, Terry M. "Mesmeric Performers." *Victorian Studies* 21 (1977): 87–104.

Pater, Walter Horatio. *Selected Works*. Edited by Richard Aldington with an Introduction. London: William Heinemann, 1948.

———. *Studies in the History of the Renaissance*. London: Macmillan, 1873.

Paton, Sir Joseph N. *Spindrift*. Edinburgh: W. Blackwood & Sons, 1867.

Perceval, John. *A Narrative of the Treatment Experienced by a Gentleman, During a State of Mental Derangement*. . . . 2 vols. London: Effingham Wilson, 1838 and 1840. Reprinted as *Perceval's Narrative: A Patient's Account of His Psychosis 1830–1832*. Edited by Gregory Bateson. Stanford: Stanford University Press, 1961.

Pinel, Philippe. *A Treatise on Insanity*. Translated by D. D. Davis. Sheffield: Cadell & Davids, 1806. Facsimile Reprint. With an Introduction by Paul F. Cranefield. New York: Hafner, 1962.

Plumptre, Edward H. *Lazarus and Other Poems*. London: A. Strahan, 1864.

———. *Master and Scholar*. London and New York: A. Strahan, 1866.

———. *Things New and Old*. London: Griffith & Farran, 1884.

Porter, Roy. "A Rage for Mesmerism. . . ." *History Today* 35 (September 1985): 22–29.

———. "Was There a Moral Therapy in Eighteenth-Century Psychiatry?" *Lychnos* (1981–82): 12–26.

Preyer, Robert. "Robert Browning: A Reading of the Early Narratives." *English Literary History* 26 (1959): 531–48.

Prichard, James Cowles. "Insanity." In *The Cyclopaedia of Practical Medicine*, edited by John Forbes et al., 3: 26–76. Philadelphia: Lea & Blanchard, 1848.

———. "Somnambulism and Animal Magnetism." In *The Cyclopaedia of Practical Medicine*, edited by John Forbes et al., 4: 194–211. Philadelphia: Lea & Blanchard, 1848.

———. *A Treatise on Insanity*. . . . Philadelphia: Haswell, Barrington, and Haswell, 1837.

Procter, Adelaide A. *Legends and Lyrics, and Other Poems*. Everyman's Library. London: J. M. Dent, 1906 [1907].

Procter, Bryan W. ("Barry Cornwall"). *Dramatic Scenes: With Other Poems*. London: Chapman & Hall, 1857 [1856].

Quetel, Claude and Morel, Pierre. *Les fous et leurs médecins: De la Renaissance au XXe siècle*. [Paris]: Hachette, 1979.

Quiller-Couch, Sir Arthur, ed. *The Oxford Book of English Verse 1250–1918*. New Edition. Oxford: Clarendon Press, 1961.

Quiller-Couch, Sir Arthur T. ("Q"). *Poems*. London: Oxford University Press, 1929.

Rader, Ralph W. "The Dramatic Monologue and Related Lyric Forms." *Critical Inquiry* 3 (1976–77): 131–51.

———. "Notes on Some Structural Varieties and Variations in Dramatic 'I' Poems and Their Theoretical Implications." *Victorian Poetry* 22 (1984): 103–20.

Rae, M. J. "On the Uses and Influence of Mental Philosophy." *The Journal of Psychological Medicine and Mental Pathology* 8 (1855): 379–90.

Ray, Isaac. "Illustrations of Insanity by Distinguished English Writers." *American Journal of Insanity* 4 (1847–48): 97–112.

———. "Shakespeare's Delineations of Insanity." *American Journal of Insanity* 3 (1846–47): 289–332.

Raymond, William O. *The Infinite Moment and Other Essays in Robert Browning*. Toronto: University of Toronto Press, 1950.

Reed, John R. *Victorian Conventions*. Athens: Ohio University Press, 1975.

Reid, Thomas. *Philosophical Works*. 2 vols. With Notes and supplementary dissertations by Sir William Hamilton. 8th ed. Edinburgh, 1895. Facsimile Reprint. With an Introduction by Harry M. Bracken. Hildesheim: Georg Olms Verlagsbuchhandlung, 1967.

Reynolds, Arthur G. *Painters of the Victorian Scene*. London: B. T. Batsford, 1953.

Rhoades, James. *Collected Poems*. Edited by L. N. P[arker]. London: T. Fisher Unwin, 1925.

Ribot, Théodule Armand. *English Psychology. Translated from the French*

. . . *Hartley, James Mill, Herbert Spencer, A. Bain, G. H. Lewes, Samuel Bailey, J. S. Mill.* London: H. S. King & Co., 1873.

Riede, David G. *Swinburne: A Study of Romantic Mythmaking.* Charlottesville: University Press of Virginia, 1978.

Riese, Walther. *The Legacy of Philippe Pinel: An Inquiry into Thought on Mental Alienation.* New York: Springer, 1969.

Rimbaud, Arthur. *Oeuvres complètes.* Edition etablie, présentée et annotée par Antoine Adam. Bibliothèque de la Pléiade. Paris: Gallimard, 1972.

Robinson, A. Mary F. (Madame Duclaux). *The Collected Poems, Lyrical and Narrative.* With a Preface. London: T. Fisher Unwin, 1902.

Rodd, James Rennell, 1st Baron Rennell. *Feda With Other Poems, Chiefly Lyrical.* London: D. Stott, 1886.

———. *The Unknown Madonna and Other Poems.* London: D. Stott, 1888.

Ross, George. "Shakspere: The Mad Characters in His Works." In *Studies: Biographical and Literary*, n.p. London: Simpkin, Marshall & Co., [1867].

Rossetti, Christina G. *The Complete Poems.* 2 vols. Edited, with Textual Notes and Introductions, by R. W. Crump. Baton Rouge and London: Louisiana State University Press, 1979–86.

Rossetti, Dante Gabriel. *The Collected Works.* 2 vols. Edited with Preface and Notes by W. M. Rossetti. London: Ellis and Elvey, 1890.

———. "The Stealthy School of Criticism." *The Athenaeum* (December 16, 1871): 792–94.

Ruskin, John. *The Complete Works.* 39 vols. Edited by E. T. Cook and A.D.O. Wedderburn. London: George Allen, 1902–12.

———. *The Poems.* 2 vols. Edited by W. G. Collingwood. Orpington and London: G. Allen, 1891.

Russell, John A., ed. *Remains of the Late Rev. Charles Wolfe, with a Brief Memoir of His Life.* London: Hamilton, Adams, 1847.

Sadoff, Dianne F. "Erotic Murders: Structural and Rhetorical Irony in William Morris' Froissart Poems." *Victorian Poetry* 13 (1975): 11–26.

Sanders, Charles R. "Carlyle and Tennyson." *Publications of the Modern Language Association of America* 76 (1961): 82–97.

Sarrazin, Gabriel. *Poètes modernes de l'Angleterre.* . . . Paris: P. Ollendorff, 1885.

Scott, John. *Critical Essays on Some of the Poems of Several English Poets.*

With an Account of the Life and Writings of the Author, by Mr. Hoole. London: J. Phillips, 1785.

Scott, William Bell. *Poems: Ballads, Studies From Nature, Sonnets.* . . . London: Longmans, Green, 1875.

Scull, Andrew. "A Brilliant Career? John Conolly and Victorian Psychiatry." *Victorian Studies* 27 (1983–84): 203–35.

[Seeley, Sir John Robert]. *Ecce Homo: A Survey of the Life and Work of Jesus Christ.* London and Cambridge: Macmillan, 1866.

Selkirk, J. B. *Poems.* Edinburgh and London: Blackwood & Sons, 1896.

Shaffer, Elinor S. *"Kubla Khan" and the Fall of Jerusalem.* Cambridge: Cambridge University Press, 1975.

Shannon, Edgar F., Jr. "The Critical Reception of Tennyson's 'Maud.' " *Publications of the Modern Language Association of America* 68 (1953): 397–417.

Shaw, M. "Tennyson and His Public 1827–1859." In *Writers and Their Background: Tennyson,* edited by D. J. Palmer, 52–88. London: G. Bell & Sons, 1973.

Shaw, W. David. *The Dialectical Temper: The Rhetorical Art of Robert Browning.* Ithaca, N.Y.: Cornell University Press, 1968.

———. "Projection and Empathy in Victorian Poetry." *Victorian Poetry* 19 (1981): 315–36.

———. *Tennyson's Style.* Ithaca, N.Y.: Cornell University Press, 1976.

Shelley, Percy Bysshe. *Literary and Philosophical Criticism.* Edited by J. Shawcross. London: Henry Frowde, 1909.

Sheppard, John. *On Dreams, in their Mental and Moral Aspects.* . . . London: Jackson & Walford, 1847.

Shires, Linda M. Introduction to Special Issue devoted to the dramatic monologue. *Victorian Poetry* 22 (1984): 7–101.

Short, Clarice. "Tennyson and 'The Lover's Tale.' " *Publications of the Modern Language Association* 82 (1967): 78–84.

Showalter, Elaine. "Victorian Women and Insanity." *Victorian Studies* 23 (1980): 157–81.

Sitwell, Sacheverell. *Narrative Pictures: A Survey of English Genre and Its Painters.* London: B. T. Batsford, 1937.

Skipsey, Joseph. *Songs and Lyrics* . . . *Collected and Revised.* London: W. Scott, 1892.

Skultans, Vieda. *English Madness: Ideas on Insanity, 1580–1890.* London: Routledge & Kegan Paul, 1979.

Skultans, Vieda. *Madness and Morals: Ideas on Insanity in the Nineteenth Century*. London: Routledge & Kegan Paul, 1975.

Slinn, E. Warwick. *Browning and the Fictions of Identity*. Totowa, N.J.: Barnes & Noble, 1982.

Smidt, Kristian. "The Beaches of Calais and Dover: Arnold's Counterstatement to Wordsworth's Confession of Faith." *Victorian Poetry* 14 (1976): 256–57.

Smith, Roger. *Trial by Medicine: Insanity and Responsibility in Victorian Trials*. Edinburgh: Edinburgh University Press, 1981.

Smith, Walter Chalmers. *The Poetical Works*. London: J. M. Dent, 1902.

Southey, Robert. *The Poetical Works*. London: Longmans, 1873.

Spector, Jack J. *The Aesthetics of Freud: A Study in Psychoanalysis and Art*. New York: Praeger, 1972.

Stange, G. R. *Matthew Arnold: The Poet as Humanist*. Princeton, N.J.: Princeton University Press, 1967.

Stedman, Edmund Clarence. *Victorian Poets*. London, 1876.

Stephens, James Brunton. *The Poetical Works*. Sydney and Melbourne: Angus & Robertson, 1902.

Stevenson, Catherine Barnes. "Brief Articles and Notes: Swinburne and Tennyson's Tristram." *Victorian Poetry* 19 (1981): 185–95.

Stewart, Dugald. *The Collected Works*. 11 vols. Edited by Sir William Hamilton. Edinburgh: Thomas Constable and Co., 1854–60.

Stitelman, Alice N. "Lyrical Process in Three Poems by Matthew Arnold." *Victorian Poetry* 15 (1977): 133–46.

Story, William Wetmore. *Poems*. 2 vols. Edinburgh and London: W. Blackwood & Sons, 1885.

―――. "A Primitive Christian in Rome." *Fortnightly Review* 6 (August 15–December 1, 1866): 827–36.

―――. "A Roman Lawyer in Jerusalem—First Century." *Blackwood's Magazine* 104 (July–December 1868): 479–90.

Straumann, Heinrich. *Justinus Kerner und der Okkultismus in der Deutschen Romantik*. Wege zur Dichtung. Zürcher Schriften zur Literaturwissenschaft IV. Edited by Emil Ermatinger. Horgen-Zurich/Leipzig: Verlag der Münster-Presse, 1928.

Stuart-Wortley, Lady Emmeline Charlotte Elizabeth. *The Visionary: A Fragment, with Other Poems*. London, 1836–39.

Swain, Charles. *The Mind, and Other Poems*. London: Simpkin & Marshall, 1832.

Sweetser, William. *Mental Hygiene; or, An Examination of the Intellect and Passions*. New York: G. P. Putnam, 1850.

Swinburne, Algernon Charles. *The Complete Works*. 20 vols. Bonchurch Edition. Edited by Sir Edmund Gosse and Thomas J. Wise. New York: Russell & Russell, 1925–27.

———. "The Poems of Dante Gabriel Rossetti." *The Fortnightly Review* 13, n.s. 7 (January–June 1870): 551–79.

———. *Swinburne as Critic*. Edited by Clyde Kenneth Hyder. London: Routledge & Kegan Paul, 1972.

———. *The Swinburne Letters*. 6 vols. Edited by Cecil Y. Lang. New Haven: Yale University Press, 1959–62.

———. *Swinburne Replies*. Edited by Clyde Kenneth Hyder. Syracuse, N.Y.: Syracuse University Press, 1966.

Swisher, Walter Samuel. "A Psychoanalysis of Browning's 'Pauline.' " *The Psychoanalytic Review* 7, 2 (1920): 115–33.

Symonds, John Addington, Jr. *Letters and Papers*. Collected and Edited by Horatio F. Brown. London: J. Murray, 1923.

———. *Many Moods: a Volume of Verse*. London: Smith, Elder, 1878.

———. *New and Old: a Volume of Verse*. London: Smith, Elder, 1880.

Symonds, John Addington, Sr. *Miscellanies by John Addington Symonds, M. D.* Selected and Edited, with an Introductory Memoir, by His Son. London: Macmillan & Co., 1871.

Symons, Arthur. *An Introduction to the Study of Browning*. London: Cassell, 1886.

———. "Is Browning Dramatic." In *Browning Society's Papers*. 2: 1–12. London: Trübner, 1881–91.

Talfourd, T. N. "An Attempt to Estimate the Poetical Talent of the Present Age . . ." *The Pamphleteer* 5, 9 (February 1815): 413–71.

Tatar, Maria M. *Spellbound: Studies on Mesmerism and Literature*. Princeton, N.J.: Princeton University Press, 1978.

Tennyson, Alfred, 1st Baron Tennyson. *In Memoriam*. A Norton Critical Edition. Selected and edited by Robert H. Ross. New York: Norton, 1973.

———. *The Letters*. Volume 1. 1821–50. Edited by Cecil Y. Lang and Edgar F. Shannon, Jr. Cambridge, Mass.: Harvard University Press, 1981.

———. *The Poems*. Edited by Christopher Ricks. London: Longmans, 1969.

Tennyson, Hallam. *Alfred Lord Tennyson, A Memoir by His Son*. 2 vols. London: Macmillan, 1897.

Thelwall, John. *The Poetical Recreations of the Champion*. . . . London, 1822.

Thomson, James. *Biographical and Critical Studies*. London: Reeves & Turner, and Bertram Dobell, 1896.

———. *Essays and Phantasies*. London: Reeves & Turner, 1881.

Thornbury, George W. *Historical and Legendary Ballads and Songs*. London: Chatto and Windus, 1876 [1875].

———. *Songs of the Cavaliers and Roundheads, Jacobite Ballads*. . . . London: Hurst and Blackett, 1857.

Thornton, E. M. *Hypnotism, Hysteria and Epilepsy. An Historical Synthesis*. London: William Heinemann Medical Books, 1976.

Thorpe, Clarence DeWitt. *The Aesthetic Theory of Thomas Hobbes: With Special Reference to His Contribution to the Psychological Approach in English Literary Criticism*. Ann Arbor: University of Michigan Press, 1940.

Tilley, Arthur. "The Poetic Imagination." *Littell's Living Age* 53 (January–March 1886): 225–31.

Timrod, Henry. "A Theory of Poetry." *The Atlantic Review* 96 (July–December 1905): 313–26.

Todhunter, John. *Laurella and Other Poems*. London: Henry S. King & Co., 1876.

Trapp, Joseph. *Lectures on Poetry Read in the Schools of Natural Philosophy at Oxford*. Translated from the Latin with additional notes. London: C. Hitch and C. Davis, 1742.

Treves, Frederick. "The Physiology of Some Phases of the Poetic Mind." *The Journal of Mental Science* 24 (1878–79): 64–75, 233–43.

Tucker, Herbert F., Jr. "From Monomania to Monologue: 'St. Simeon Stylites' and the Rise of the Victorian Dramatic Monologue." *Victorian Poetry* 22 (1984): 121–37.

Vaughan, C. "Mr. Browning." *The British Quarterly Review* 80 (July–October 1884): 1–28.

Vickers, Brian, ed. *Shakespeare: The Critical Heritage*. 6 vols. London: Routledge & Kegan Paul, 1974–81.

Walker, Hugh. *The Greater Victorian Poets*. London: Swan Sonnenschein, 1895.

Ward. T. H., ed. *The English Poets: Selections with Critical Introductions*. 4 vols. London: Macmillan, 1880.

Warren, Alba H., Jr. *English Poetic Theory 1825–1865*. Princeton, N.J.: Princeton University Press, 1950.

Warren, John B. L., 3rd Baron de Tabley. *The Collected Poems*. London: Chapman & Hall, 1903.

Warton, Joseph. *An Essay on the Writings and Genius of Pope*. London: M. Cooper, 1756.

Wasserman, Earl R. "The English Romantics: The Grounds of Knowledge." In *Romanticism, Points of View*, edited by R. F. Gleckner and G. E. Enscoe, 331–46. Englewood Cliffs, N.J.: Prentice-Hall, 1970.

Watts, Alaric A. *Lyrics of the Heart: with Other Poems*. London: Longman, Brown, 1851.

Webster, Augusta, née Davies. *Dramatic Studies*. London and Cambridge: Macmillan, 1866.

————. *Portraits*. London: Macmillan, 1870.

————. *A Woman Sold and Other Poems*. London and Cambridge: Macmillan, 1867.

Weinstein, Mark A. *William Edmondstoune Aytoun and the Spasmodic Controversy*. New Haven and London: Yale University Press, 1968.

White, Richard G. Review of Swinburne's *Poems and Ballads*. *The Galaxy* 2 (September–December 1866): 655–70.

Wigan, A. L. *The Duality of the Mind: Proved by the Structure, Functions, and Diseases of the Brain, and by the Phenomena of Mental Derangement. . . .* London: Longman, Brown, 1844.

Wilkinson, Maude. "An Objection to Browning's Caliban Considered." *Poet-Lore* 5 (1893): 562–64.

Williams, Francis H. "Browning's Form." *Poet-Lore* 2 (1890): 300–305.

Williams, Ioan, ed. *Meredith: The Critical Heritage*. London: Routledge & Kegan Paul, 1971.

Willmott, Robert E. A. *The Poets of the Nineteenth Century*. London: G. Routledge & Co., 1857.

Wilson, John. *Essays Critical and Imaginative*. 4 vols. Edinburgh: W. Blackwood & Sons, 1866.

Winslow, Forbes. *The Anatomy of Suicide*. London: Henry Renshaw, 1840.

Winslow, Forbes. "The Legal Doctrine of Responsibility in Cases of Insanity, Connected with Alleged Criminal Acts." *The Journal of Psychological Medicine and Mental Pathology* 11 (1858): 214–46.

———. "The Mission of the Psychologist." *The Journal of Psychological Medicine and Mental Pathology* 10 (1857): 611–22.

———. *On Obscure Diseases of the Brain and Disorders of the Mind: Their Incipient Symptoms, Pathology, Diagnosis, Treatment, and Prophylaxis.* Philadelphia: Blanchard & Lea, 1860.

———. "The Psychological Vocation of the Physician." *The Journal of Psychological Medicine and Mental Pathology* 7 (1854): 106–50.

Wolfe, Charles. *Remains of the Late Rev. Charles Wolfe.* 2 vols. Edited by J. A. Russell. 4th ed. London, 1829.

Woods, Margaret Louise. *Poems.* London: John Lane, 1914.

Woodward, William R., and Mitchell G. Ash, eds. *The Problematic Science: Psychology in Nineteenth-Century Thought.* New York: Praeger, 1982.

Wordsworth, William. *The Early Letters of William and Dorothy Wordsworth (1787–1805).* Arranged and edited by E. de Sélincourt. Oxford: Clarendon Press, 1935.

———. *The Letters of William and Dorothy Wordsworth: The Middle Years.* 2 vols. Arranged and edited by E. de Sélincourt. Oxford: Clarendon Press, 1937.

———. *Literary Criticism.* Edited by W.J.B. Owen. London and Boston: Routledge & Kegan Paul, 1974.

———. *The Poems.* 2 vols. Edited by John O. Hayden. New Haven and London: Yale University Press, 1981.

———. *The Prose Works.* 3 vols. Edited, with Preface, Notes, and Illustrations by the Rev. Alexander B. Grosart. London: Edward Moxon, 1876.

———. *The Prose Works.* 3 vols. Edited by W.J.B. Owen and Jane W. Smyser. Oxford: At the Clarendon Press, 1974.

———. *Selected Poems and Prefaces.* Edited with an introduction and notes by J. Stillinger. Boston: Houghton Mifflin, 1965.

Worsfold, W. Basil. *The Principles of Criticism: An Introduction to the Study of Literature.* London: George Allen, 1902.

Wyrick, Deborah Baker. "The Hieros Gamos in William Morris' 'Rapunzel.' " *Victorian Poetry* 19 (1981): 367–81.

Young, Edward. *Conjectures on Original Composition*. Facsimile Reprint. Leeds: Scolar Press, 1966.

Zietlow, Paul. "Heard But Unheeded: The Songs of Callicles in Matthew Arnold's *Empedocles on Etna*." *Victorian Poetry* 21 (1983): 241–56.

Zilboorg, Gregory, in collaboration with Henry, George W. *A History of Medical Psychology*. New York: W. W. Norton, 1941.

Index

This index contains subject headings, names, and titles of poems and books cited in the text, as well as subjects and names of authors and editors cited in the endnotes and the appendix.